BRIEF HISTORY OF SOCIAL PROBLEMS

A Critical Thinking Approach

Frank J. McVeigh
Loreen Wolfer

University Press of America,® Inc.
Dallas · Lanham · Boulder · New York · Oxford

Copyright © 2004 by
University Press of America,® Inc.
4501 Forbes Boulevard
Suite 200
Lanham, Maryland 20706
UPA Acquisitions Department (301) 459-3366

PO Box 317
Oxford
OX2 9RU, UK

Library of Congress Control Number: 2004102475
ISBN 0-7618-2831-1 (paperback : alk. ppr.)

Dedicated to my beloved wife, Marie, and all our children and grandchildren, who have taught me much more than I knew about patience, love, marriage and the family.

Dedicated to my husband, Bill, and my parents who have always supported and encouraged me in all of my endeavors.

Contents

List of Figures and Tables

Preface

Challenged by the persistence of spirit-crushing poverty in the South (nations below the Equator) versus wasteful turbo-affluence in the North, we wonder how to reconcile a yawning and growing gap in well being and hope. Challenged by too frequent betrayals of trust by weak-willed mis-leaders, we wonder about our ability to soon earn a Civic Culture and a Public Commons that honors us all. And challenged by a *Jihad* inside the Muslim world between fanatical militants and peace-loving progressives, we worry about a yearly increase in the number of suicide bombers and the toll of deadly unrest in more and more parts of our pained planet

All the more valuable, therefore, is the synergy in this book that flows from the collaboration of two scholar-activists, Frank McVeigh and Loreen Wolfer. Our times cry out for a calm and cool-headed, but also quietly concerned and artfully passionate analysis of what is bothering us - and what we might do about it. We need a constructive explanation of the historic sources of our discontents. We need an account of what it is about our society that exacerbates our social and personal problems. And we need a cogent and engaging discussion of our options if we would improve matter - the pros and cons of our options.

Ironically, thanks in large part to the post-1990 Internet-based explosion of the Information Revolution we have more "stuff" (data and information) and arguable less knowledge and Wisdom than ever before. Using powerful search engines like Google we can ogle more cold numbers and words than our parents ever dreamed possible. Which is not to say we can make good sense of it: Quite the contrary, the times are so dizzying, and the pace and range of change so breathless that we may be more confused than ever before.

With close to 150,000 books published annually in English alone, to say nothing of articles in journals and magazines, we lost long ago, perhaps as far back as the 1950s, our individual ability to keep up with, to stay abreast of, to think ourselves on top of events. And thereby, to have an informed opinion, and to dare to take principled action. Computerized search engines may have compounded, rather than relieved the problem, as each puts a different menu of "Must read!" nominees under any heading we might enter.

What is one to do? I am leery of taking advice from "flavor-of-the-month" gurus, as their prattle enervates with its pieties and cliches. I am also leery of guidance from "arm chair" theorists who may not have left the Ivory Tower in years, and would be astonished by the changes in the off-campus world if ever they would venture again into it. Instead, I lean toward the counsel of the likes of McVeigh and Wolfer, as I recognize in their thoughtful musings two deeply concerned, and also hopeful lovers of humankind.

Employing a cordial unpretentious voice, the authors guide us through the contradictions, data gaps, disputes, and other ragged aspects of modern social problems. We learn to value the intricacies, the nuances, the shades of gray that make so many challenges appear intractable, too expensive to solve, and likely to leave more new vexations in the wake of any so-called "solution."

In on providing us with new tools, the authors teach us how to employ the Sociological Imagination, a brilliant perspective that traces and explicates links between our personal woes and societal forms (values, groups, institutions, etc.) We escape thereby from the crushing burden of inappropriate self-blame, and begin to look instead for ways to help correct wrongs embedded in the society itself. Above all, we learn to appreciate the centrality of conflicts over values and the urgent need we in the West have to reassess our crazed pursuit of material wealth.

As if this wasn't enough (and it is!), McVeigh and Wolfer strengthen the case for questioning by modeling it themselves, Valuable incisive questions follow every chapter, underlining the lessons therein. I especially like a representative question, #4 after the chapter on "Population and the Environment," (Chapter 10) that asks in a sensitizing "in-your-face" fashion - "What does your school cafeteria do with its extra food? Why? Is this feasible from a distributive perspective? What conflict does it address?"

By taking a historic approach, the authors, both sociologists, help us appreciate the soundness of keeping one foot solidly in an examined past, while the other carefully tests the ground ahead. They combine disciplines artfully, drawing the best from the "new" social history, and from economics, psychology, and sociology. In sociology they rely on Conflict Theory, a feisty and creative perspective that spotlights the role of unequal power in explaining reality, and whets our appetite to have power soon distributed in fairer ways. Honest about their own preferences, the authors pay us the high compliment of urging us to employ critical thinking skills to make up our own mind.

In sum, then, this book can be understood as a toolkit, an invaluable aid to tackling the many "repair jobs" that press for our creative, caring, and generous attention Š if we are all soon to live in One World as fine and ennobling as ever it might be.

Arthur Shostak, Ph.D.
Drexel University
Narberth, Pennsylvania
September 23, 2003

Acknowledgments

No book is really complete or completed without the sincere acknowledgments to all the people who made it possible.

First, my sincere thanks and gratitude goes to an outstanding sociologist, my professional colleague and friend of many years, Arthur Shostak. He graciously and astutely wrote a very meaningful and significant forward to this book. I am deeply grateful for his doing it so willingly and professionally.

Words are inadequate to express my heartfelt thanks to my co-authoress, Loreen Wolfer, who with enthusiasm and gusto joined forces with me to make this book a reality. Without her careful reading and suggested changes in some of the chapters I wrote, they would not have been as analytical and logical as they are now. For her hours of labor in formatting and setting up the layout of the book I am forever grateful and thankful. And please remember she did this "labor of love" while she was carrying and brought forth a beautiful baby girl Jessalyn Faith. In reality she has delivered two babies – Jessalyn and the book. Many thanks.

My special thanks and acknowledgments go to my colleagues and friends who read early drafts of particular chapters when the book was taking shape. Since appreciation is due to Richard M. Liberman, M.D., whose insightful ideas and input made the Medical and Health Care chapter a more meaningful and logical chapter.

Also my sincere thanks and kudos to Dr. Thomas Shey of the Social Science Division, Antelope Valley College, in Lancaster, Ca. A long-time friend and associate, Dr. Shey's review of the "Population and Environment" chapter made it more current and poignant.

Dr. Robert Moore, III of Frostburg State University deserves thanks for the historical insights into slavery and the race problem in America that I had overlooked. It made the chapter on "Race Problems" more accurate and informative.

We would also like to recognize Dr. Michelle Janning from Whitman College. Her thoughtful feedback regarding the "Family" chapter provided insightful suggestions that greatly improved the quality of that chapter.

The reference librarians at Muhlenberg College deserve a special note of thanks and appreciation for their diligence and computer-savvy to track down "fugitive material", as well as dates and publishing companies of a few books and articles that eluded my original citations. A sincere "thank-you" to Professor Joseph Elliott for giving us a plethora of his professional photos to publish in our book. Also my grateful thanks to Ms. Lauren Nicholas of Moravian College

Art Department, Bethlehem, Pa., for professionally designing and drawing most of the figures and graphs used in the book.

Also a grateful acknowledgment goes to Vice President Mike Brackner of the Muhlenberg Public Relations Department and Mr. Chris Sodl, Director of the Sacred Heart Hospital Public Relations and Marketing Department, Allentown, Pa., for providing us with photographs and permission to publish them.

All these acknowledgments would be incomplete (as well as the book itself) had it not been for the faithful, dedicated and committed work of Carol Hartz in typing into the computer, and retyping draft after draft of all the chapters I had written. For her persistence and perseverance, I am extremely grateful and thankful.

Last, but by no means least, to my steadfast and helpful wife, Marie, who endured temporary "widowhood" while I was writing and re-writing this book the last five years or so. I promise to spend more time with her now that this "special baby" has been delivered to the publisher.

Chapter 1

Introduction

As we enter with both feet into the 21st Century, to fully understand the social problems that lie before us, we must look back to see our footprints in the sands of time. We must look back to see where we as a society have been, the problems we have struggled with and the direction we are headed in today. Some social problems, like poverty, seem like they will never disappear and others, like discrimination, have been minimized, but not eradicated. For example, while some groups like minorities and women are still over-represented among the poor, relative to whites and to men, the African American middle class is larger now than its ever been and women have more employment, and therefore income, opportunities now than ever before as well (Mooney, Knox and Schacht, 2000). This is progress! But, even while we make strides with some social problems, other ones persist and new ones, such as global inequality and problems of technology, emerge.

But what can we possibly learn from social experiences hundreds of years ago? After all, we are constantly reminded by the media, our professors, and even our own friends or family, how quickly the world is changing. Surely society over two hundred years ago is irrelevant to our current way of life. Not so! While, on the surface, society is undeniably changing, many of the underlying values and beliefs that were present over two hundred years ago remain today – and in fact, these values frequently fuel the controversy over today's social problems! For example, the Puritans believed in the merit of hard work and independence. Those values are still present today and are reflected in issues such as American's hesitance to increase welfare payments and our desire to limit the amount of time someone can accept social assistance.   So, regardless of all the changes we are currently experiencing, some values and beliefs have persisted across time and are instrumental in understanding how we view and address social problems today.

To have a fuller grasp on the changes in social problems, we need to adopt a multi-disciplinary approach to their discussion. As we look back we notice four academic guides that have helped record, measure, understand and analyze our steps. The first, and oldest, of our faithful guides, is the historian.   Since the time of Herodotus and Josephus, historians have carefully noted both the social problems and progress that each society has made. They may have focused primarily on chronicling victories and defeats in wars or revolutions, but they also, consciously or unconsciously, recorded and commented on the positive or negative evolution of society during times of peace and tranquility. Historians refer to these latter times as "golden ages" in the life of any society. All saw each historical epoch of a society, and its social problems, in terms of either ascending or descending, rising or falling, waxing or waning.

Historian Edward Gibbon, of course, wrote about *The Rise and Fall of the Roman Empire* (1776-1788); Arnold Toynbee reviewed the ascent and decent of many societies historically in terms of "challenges" and "responses" in his *Study of Society* (1934); and Oswald Spengler wrote about *The Decline of the West* (1939). More modern historians see and report signs of rising or falling of the U.S. in terms of its power in the world (Kennedy, 1987; Nye, 1990) based on economic changes and military conflicts.

As with all else, however, even the discussion of history has changed and a new branch, "new social history", has emerged. This new branch of history is more analytical, sociological and theoretical than the "old" and began to emerge in the early 1960s when Harvard University established a Ph.D. field in social and economic history. Key professional journals emerged about the same time. *Comparative Studies in Society and History*, launched in 1958, dealt
primarily with non-American topics. Hence it was left to the *Journal of Social History* and *Historical Method Newsletter* in 1967 to herald the "new" American social history.

This "new" social history is where historians and sociologists linked arms and minds together to create a new kind of "academic history". Before the 1960s, older forms of social history were mostly simple descriptions of how people lived in the past. The new, more analytical and theoretical, social history emerged from varied interests of historian to wider the understanding of our history expressed in new theories and insights about the dynamics of society historically and the process of social change.

The new social historians argued, as we do in this book, the neglect of most people outside of the power elite and of most activities outside of those done by the power elite does not provide a complete picture of the past, or of social problems today. For example, the recent 2000 election reminded us all that the Electoral College, not the popular vote of the people, determines who becomes president of the United States. We were reminded too that this was not the only time in our history that this occurred. Newspapers and television reminded us that this also happened before in 1876 between Rutherford B. Hayes and Samuel J. Tilden. That election and the candidates involved, led directly to the withdraw of the Federal troops from the South. This, in turn, led, along with other changes, to the end of Reconstruction for Blacks (former slaves) and the beginning of the "Black Codes" and rise of the Klu Klux Klan.

This new history rests on three major points. The first is that the focus on groups, rather than individuals or personalities, outside the formal power structure, reveals much more about the past and about social change. This is true not only for the groups involved but also for society at large – including the State. The second point focuses serious, analytical attention to the history of activity such as family life and also reveals important characteristics about society. Finally, the new historians argue that history, in dealing with politics, or wars, or eating habits can be used to capture the past by focusing on patterns and processes of change in patterns rather than simply on a series of separate or discrete events (Stearns, 1993).

It was not accidental that the "new" social history appeared during the 1960s. The rise of the Civil Rights Movement, followed by a revival of feminism and the environmental social movements had obvious historical implications. This in itself shows how history is shaped by its own past! The ideological climate of the 1960s, challenging the American establishment on various fronts, encouraged a new radicalism among many young historians. It legitimized a search for non-establishment kinds of history (Stearns, 1993).

Of course, interpretations of history vary. For examples, a recent fundraising letter from the conservative Intercollegiate Studies Institute, Inc. asserts that most people are ignorant of history and how government at all levels has grown in size and power. It states:

> It's alarming that Americans are so ignorant of
> history and so comfortable with government intrusion

into all areas of their lives. It's frightening that many Americans are not concerned at all about the size and power of government.

The reason for this apathy is that the media, the schools, and other private organizations don't teach our youth the magnificent lessons of the American Revolution and the U.S. Constitution. And when they do teach American history they overlook the good and focus on the bad – real or imaged.

Students fail to learn important lessons from history about the dangers of powerful centralized governments. They are simply not taught that half the wealth produced each year in the U.S. is consumed by government. Forty percent is paid in taxes and 10 percent is paid by businesses and individuals to comply with government regulations. These students have no idea that the tax and regulatory burden is a peace time record for Americans in 224 years of existence. In fact, during most of that history, government at all levels consumed less than 10 percent of our nations' yearly production. (Cribb, May 2,2000:2)

Liberals, on the other hand, would view history differently when taxation was very low (since no Federal income tax existed before 1903) and government, especially the Federal Government, was limited in power. They would view that as a "repressive system" that benefited and "enriched only white males and exploited everyone else" who was relatively powerless (Cribb, May 2, 2000). These different views reinforce the need for the more objective, scientific and systematic approach to history that developed into the new form of social history. As James Lowen recently wrote: "History cannot be avoided. Understandings of the past seep into popular movies and television programs and help shape public policies."(May / June, 2000:8). So history cannot be avoided when critically analyzing today's life and social problems. Maybe that is why since the mid 1990s television has started the History Channel.

Our second academic guide along our journey in time is the sociologist. He / she met us about the middle of the 19th century as Europe and our nation moved inexorably from a predominately rural society, based on farming and small villages, to an industrial society built on manufacturing, large cities and urban areas. It was near the beginning of this historical shift in Europe in the 1840s and 1850s that French mathematician and philosopher August Comte (1798-1857), came to coin a new term for a new discipline: "Sociology". He envisioned a well-run, relatively stable society based on scientific facts and research. He was convinced that sociology and sociologists would discover the laws of social life and social structure that would determine how any industrial society could best be constructed and operate most effectively for the benefit of all. Society would not be perfect because some problems such as poverty and war were, thus far, unavoidable. Nevertheless, he believed that every society goes through progressive stages (theological, philosophical and scientific) and that a society guided by the scientific and systematic study of itself by social scientists, as well as other experts, could produce the best society possible, or even imaginable. Such knowledge could help social leaders, as well as the public, find remedies and solutions to our social problems (Kuper and Kuper, 1985: 800).

The purpose of sociology was to throw clear, factual scientific light on social problems and their interconnections to the complex, confusing and dynamic world in which we live. The first department of Sociology in the United States started in 1895 at the University of Chicago.

In 1907, three years after the formation of the American Sociological Society in 1904, its national meeting had "social conflict" as its main topic of discussion. So virtually from the beginning, sociologists came to know that social disorganization and social change were caused by conflict for the most part. They also knew that relative stability and social organization were part of every society. But perfect harmony in society eludes us and social problems, both old and new, persist in spite of the scientific efforts of sociologist and others. In attempting to control or resolve any social problem – crime, drugs, race relations or changing gender roles, -- there are winners and losers, costs (that some groups pay) and benefits (that other groups receive). Above all, are the persistent conflicts of power that produce social changes, major or minor. Other social processes, cooperation or competition, of course, can also contribute to social change.

A third academic guide along our path in time to address and analyze our social problems has been the political scientist – the youngest discipline to guide our steps. For thousands of years prior to the formal discipline, scholars and philosophers, such as Aristotle in his *Politics*, Plato in his *Republic* and Machiavelle in his *The Prince*, wrote about government and its policies. In the latter part of the 19th Century, more exact and precise data began to emerge so that more scientific and objective research could buttress and reinforce our understanding and theories about government and its social policies.

The Academy of Political Science was founded in 1880. It promotes objective, scholarly investigations of political, social and economic problems. It informs the public by presenting divergent views of the problems (Wessell, 1991: Inside front cover). Though it claims "it does not make policy recommendations", its studies, conferences and publications help policy-makers to decide upon the most rational reasonable, and politically-sound policies (Wessell, 1991). Its chief publication since 1886; Political Science Quarterly, "is a non-partisan journal devoted to the study and analysis of government, politics and international affairs" (Caraley, 2000: Inside front cover). Another periodical in political science is *Politics and Society*. It "publishes original analysis of politics, including its social roots and its consequences. In its broadest sense, politics encompasses conflicts over the shape of social life, whether on the shop floor, within the family, or in the realms of the state and world economy. The quest for a good society is also enduringly a part of political life." (Dec., 1998: inside front cover).

The story is essentially the same for our last guide: the field of economics. For centuries, philosophers and scholars wrote about the economy of a society or different societies. It wasn't until 1776 when Adam Smith wrote a book, *Wealth of Nations*, using new methods based on numbers and facts (as well as theory) that the discipline as we know it came into practice. Adam Smith was followed by David Ricardo (1772-1823) who in the 19th Century continued the new methods and developed a new method "model-building", which economists still use today (Kuper and Kuper, 1985: 707-708). Economists, like all the other social scientists, concerned themselves with social problems and policies. They also formed professional associations (*American Economic Association*) and periodicals (*American Economic Review*) starting in 1885 (Dec. 1998: inside front cover). So all four disciplines – History, Sociology, Political Science and Economics – have shed some light on the nature and magnitude of our social problems.

All of these guides have specific explanations for social problems, each with their own titles unique to their discipline. However, the underlying theoretical themes between and among the disciplines have common components. In this book, we will focus on the sociological theories because, as a discipline, sociology is the one that most concretely works to link the other three disciplines together. The main theories in sociology (called paradigms) are Conflict Theory, Functionalist Theory and Symbolic Interactionist Theory. The first two theories are *macro* theories and focus on broad social processes. These two theories are in direct opposition to each other. For example, Functionalists see elements in society as working together to create some type of balance. Social problems therefore are the result of disorganization that frequently stems from broader changing processes (like the Industrial Revolution or globalization). Functionalists argue that once a particular social component has a chance to adapt to the change, it will once again work smoothly with the other social components, thereby minimizing the social problem. Conflict theorists, however, do not view the components of society as striving for some balance, as functionalists do. Conflict theorists see each component of society as being in a struggle with each other over limited resources (e.g. money, power, status and prestige). According to conflict theorists, as each group tries to maximize its resources, it has to do so at the expense of others. This continual conflict, according to these theorists, is what threatens social order. Unlike Functionalist and Conflict theories, the third theory, Symbolic Interactionism, is a *micro* theory. This means it is most concerned with how people (verses social structures) react to their social environment and how it affects self-perception.

The authors of this book favor Conflict theory and have chosen to analyze social problems as a series of conflicts between those with power verses those who were at one time virtually powerless. There are many definitions of social conflict. We rely upon Lewis Coser's definition in his classic book *The Functions of Social Conflict* (1956). He wrote that conflict is "...a struggle over values and claims to scarce status, power and resources in which the aims of the opponents are to neutralize, injure or eliminate their rivals" (1956: 8). C. Wright Mills defines "power" (often involved in conflicts) as "...the capacity to make and carry out decisions even if others resist..." (Horowitz, 1963, 8).

With this approach we describe the various "ways and means" individuals, groups and social institutions change over time to lose or gain power. This was done either by changing social institutions bit by bit from within, as families often do, or over time from the outside, as the Civil Rights movement did. The social, political and economic mechanisms used varied. Sometimes mass social movements evolved through struggle and conflict with the power structure or violence was used (legal and illegal). Or the political power of the state was used.

Or gradually, via the mass media of the time, cultural norms, values, beliefs, and ideals were changed. All these social means changed major social institutions and social problems, from the outside. This has recently occurred in Serbia via revolution and the rise of the political process (election). Before that, major changes were made by trade unions in Poland and refusals of the Army in Russia to disperse revolutionary crowds in the streets in Moscow led to change. In 1989 the Berlin Wall was torn down by crowds and mobs of people in the streets of East Germany. As they say, "The rest is history!"

The primary goal of this book is to view social problems and changing social conditions in the United States as the result of conflicts over power, conflicts between groups, conflicts over norms, values and beliefs and conflicts between power elites and mass social movements (as described by Mills in Horowitz (1963) and by Domhoff (1998). All chapters have the same objective – to explain how social problems came about in the past and are maintained or changed over time. Another objective is to show how these problems have affected individuals, groups and social institutions and to examine what changes, if any, our society has made in attempts to resolve (if not solve) each social problem. Most social scientists – our four guides – believe that a society and government often address and control social problems, but never solve them completely. The goal is to reduce all social problems to an "irreducible minimum."

This book also weaves into it three major themes or directions our society has taken over time. The first theme that we will continually address is how our society moved from a Gemeinschaft to a Gesellschaft society over the past two hundred years. Coined by Tönnies (1887), a Gemeinschaft society is characterized by strong social bonds, intimate social interaction and a shared definition of the social order. These societies are usually small and a shared understanding of norms, values and beliefs connects people. A Gesellschaft society, on the other hand, is usually larger, more impersonal, and characterized by less agreement over basic social norms, values and beliefs.

These terms may seem abstract and, therefore, somewhat academic, but there is evidence of them even today. Think back to any picture by Norman Rockwell, a painter who is well known for capturing images of American life when life was simpler and purer, when people shared common values, and when communities were strong. Although Norman Rockwell presented an idealized view of society at the time (as you will see, during the time he was painting, life was not as simple and pure as he depicted). His paintings are a more modern attempt to represent a Gemeinschaft society (although Mr. Rockwell wouldn't have used those terms!). Now think of your typical, large urban environment today. People passing blindly on the street, disagreements over values of "right" and "wrong", and the relative anonymity of your neighbors. That's closer to a Gesellschaft society. Now, obviously both of these examples are somewhat extreme, but they do give you the general idea behind these two concepts. The move from small, closer-knit communities (Gemeinschaft) to larger, more impersonal communities (Gesellschaft) has had a profound impact on the definition and treatment of behaviors and social problems.

People lived very simply in a Gemeinschaft society. (Credit: Joseph Elliott)

The second direction, tied to the change from a Gemeinschaft to Gesellschaft society, has been a shift from relying upon community members addressing social problems to relying upon the state. Any social problem one can name has government – local, state, and / or federal – involved in it rather than the traditional institutions of society (i.e. families, religion, and local communities). This has been a long, gradual adjustment that will continue well into the future.

The last direction and trend has been the reality that most social problems today, compared with the past, have international dimensions. This trend is examined in detail in chapter 11, but some particular chapters briefly address it as well.

In structuring this book and ordering the problems, we have relied upon C. Wright Mill's distinction between "personal problems" and "social issues". Using that insight and analysis, we have organized this book into four parts:

1. Forming One's Biography: Personal Problems Leading to Social Issues
2. Groups, Immediate Social Environment and Social Issues
3. Institutions and Social Issues
4. International Dimensions of Social Problems

This division attempts to organize social problems from the most immediate life experiences of individuals to their participation in larger groups and social institutions. Part four recognizes that all social problems have an international dimension, as well as simply a societal base. The problems discussed in this book do not exhaust all the social problems that could have possibly been discussed. The ones discussed were based on empirical research centered on "Possible Criteria for Deciding on the Top Ten Social Problems" by the first author. His research paper was presented at the annual meeting of the Society for the Study of Social Problems and published in *Sociological Abstracts* (McVeigh, 2000).

As we discuss the evolution of social problems, we would like to encourage you, the reader, to think critically about them. If your knowledge and interpretations of history are going to continue to grow, you need to develop skills that will help you to critically assess the past, present and future. Critical thinking may also help you to use history to better understand social problems. C. Wright Mills referred to a "higher immorality" - - that while knowledge is available in abundance, there is a virtual absence of critical intellect. (Horowitz, 1963: 19) We hope the material in these chapters presents social problems in some new ways for you. Questions, which appear at the end of each chapter, are designed to review material and encourage you to think critically about what you have read.

Critical Thinking

But what is critical thinking? Critical thinking is a common phrase today and you may have heard your professors use it frequently without your really understanding what it entails. A full discussion of critical thinking is beyond the scope of this book, but we suggest you see Lauer (1998: 38-48) for an excellent discussion of critical thinking as it pertains to social problems. Critical thinking is evaluating the validity of material by first making sure you understand the information and then asking whether it is reasonable and logical. According to Lauer (1998) fallacies are often used to muddy the information presented, making it difficult to assess its validity and reliability. Lauer

(1998) mentions a number of fallacies in his book, but we will only highlight a few here which you want to keep in mind as you explore social problems.

First, Lauer (1998) discusses the "fallacy of dramatic instance" which is when information is over-generalized. This involves using a few exceptional, often sensational, examples to imply that those are the typical experiences. It's a "man- bites- dog" example. A classic example of this, prior to our current welfare reform, was the stories of people who stay on welfare for a lifetime and were comfortable with the government paying for them to be lazy. This obscures the fact that, even *prior* to the new welfare regulations, 34 percent of recipients were on welfare for less than a year and 27 percent were only on for one to three years (Mooney, Knox and Schacht, 2000).

A second technique is the "fallacy of personal attack", frequently known as "blaming the victim." This is used when there is an absence of "fact", but quite a lot of opinion. It entails drawing the discussion away from the issue by personally attacking either the victim or the opponent. It is frequently used to alleviate responsibility of those who are not directly involved in the situation. An example of this would be claiming that a battered woman is somehow at fault for her abuse because she doesn't leave the situation. This overlooks many factors such as that she may be afraid for her life if she leaves, she may have nowhere to go (nationally there are not enough women's shelter's to meet the need) or she may not be able to financially support herself and any children without her partner's income.

The last few fallacies involve tactics such as appealing to people's prejudices to convince other's of the correctness of a position, assuming that what works for one individual must then work for the group and omitting important information (Lauer, 1998). The last one frequently involves the interpretation of statistical data. For example, Daniel Bell (1960) showed that one year New York claimed assaults were up 200 percent and burglaries were up 1300 percent. A crime wave? No. Bell found that these figures reflected a new method in crime reporting which led to more effective ways of determining the amount of crime. So you see, when interpreting information there are some concrete considerations one can follow to determine whether information is valid. But that is an important skill that needs development and it doesn't occur over night. Using the "fallacies" we presented here, as a guide will help you develop these skills as you read through the chapters. Each chapter will contain a short article, or boxed item, about the history and need for critical thinking in our society today. It will include some of the skills and tools needed to learn how to think more critically.

To summarize, this book attempts to provide a historical understanding of how some currently defined social problems have come to be. The analysis involves consideration of historical, social, political and economic elements through the re-occurring theme of conflict. The shift from a Gemeinschaft to Gesellschaft society and the shift from community involvement to state (political) involvement in social problems are also common themes. Understanding the dynamics underlying social problems and their evolution is instrumental to tailoring remedies. Simply throwing money at a problem or passing legislation frequently only addressees the surface issue. Without considering the underlying evolution of the problem, the values and beliefs associated with that issue and the social, political and economic consequences or ramifications of that issue – any changes proposed will be ineffective in the long term.

Bibliography

American Economic Review. Nashville, TN: American Economic
    Association, 1998.

Aristotle. *The Politics*, with an English Translation by H. Rackham.
    New York: G.P. Putnum's Sons, 1932.

Bell, Daniel. *The End of Ideology*. New York: Free Press, 1960.

Caraley, Demetrios, ed. *Political Science Quarterly*. (Fall, 2000) .

Comte, Auguste. *Auguste Comte and Positivism: The Essential
    Writings* edited by Gertrud Lenzer. Chicago, Ill: University
    of Chicago Press, 1983.

Coser, Lewis. *The Functions of Social Conflict*. New York: The Free
    Press, 1956.

————. *Continuities in the Study of Social Conflict*, New York: The
    Free Press, 1967.

Cribb, T. Kenneth. Fund-Raising Letter (May 2, 2000) Wilmington,
    Del.: Intercollegiate Studies Institute, Inc.

Domhoff, G. William. *Who Rules America? Power and Politics in the
    Year 2000*. 3rd ed. Mt. View, CA.: Mayfield Publishing Co., 1998.

Gibbon, Edward. *The History of the Decline and Fall of the Roman
    Empire*, Vols. 1-6. London: Oxford University Press, 1776-1788.

Horowitz, Louis. *Power, Politics and People: The Collected Essays of
    C. Wright Mills*. Edited by Louis Horowitz. New York: Oxford
    University Press.

Kennedy, Paul. *The Rise and Fall of the Great Powers: Economic
    Change and Military Conflict 1500 to 2000*. New York: Random
    House, 1987.

————. *Preparing For the 21st Century*. New York: Random House,
    2000.

Kuper, Adam and Jessie Kuper, eds. *The Social Science Encyclopedia*.
    Boston, MA: Routledge & Kegan Paul, 1985.

Loewen, James W. "Who Controls the Past Controls the Future."
    Crisis. Pp. 8-10. (May/June, 2000).

Machiavelli, Niccolo. *The Prince*. Translated with an Introduction by
    George Bull. New York: Penguin Books. 1981.

McVeigh, Frank J. "Possible Criteria for Deciding on the Top Ten
    Social Problems." *Sociological Abstracts, Suppl. 188*. Pp. 87
    (August, 2000).

Mills, C. Wright. *The Power Elite*. New York: Oxford University
    Press, 1956.

Mooney, Linda A., Knox, David and Schacht, Caroline. *Understanding Social Problems*. 2nd. Ed. Belmont, CA.: Wadsworth, 2000.

Nye, Joseph S., Jr. "Still in the Game. Those Championship Years: The Changing Sources of World Power." *World Monitor: The Christian Science Monitor Monthly*. 3:3 (March, 1990). 42-47.

Plato. *Plato's Republic, Book I*, Gilbert P. Rose. Bryn Mawr, PA: Bryn Mawr Department of Greek. 1983.

Politics and Society. Thousand Oaks, CA. Sage Periodicals Press (December, 1998) Inside Front Page.

Smith, Adam. *An Inquiry Into the Nature and Causes of the Wealth of Nations*. 1776. London: Printed for W. Strahan and T. Cadell [New York: A.M. Kelley, 1966].

Spengler, Oswald. *The Decline of the West*. New York: A.A. Knopf., 1939.

Stearns, Peter N. "The Old Social History and the New." Pp. 237-250 in *Encyclopedia of American History, Vol. 1* edited by Mary K. Cayton, Elliott Gorn and Peter W. Williams. New York.: Charles Scribners' Sons, 1993.

Tonnies, Ferdinand. *Community and Society (Gemeinschaft und Gesellschaft)* 1887. Translated and edited by Charles Loomis. East Lansing: Michigan State University Press, 1963.

Toynbee, Arnold J. *A Study of History. Vol. 1-13*. London: Oxford University Press, 1934.

Wessell, Nils H. editor. *The New Europe. Revolution in East-West Relations*. Proceedings of the Academy of Political Science. Vol. 38, 1. New York: Capital City Press, 1990.

Chapter 2

Crime, Delinquency, and Administration of Justice

No society is without crime. As Durkheim (1951) pointed out, the very nature of crime makes it universal. Each society has norms that attempt to control behavior; nations and states pass laws against acts they consider harmful to their well being. The behavior already exists. Passing a law does not eliminate the behavior; it just makes it illegal. When laws (or norms) exist there will always be criminals. Thus, a society can never be exempt from crime. Although the whole society may agree that "stealing, kidnapping and rape are harmful and immoral, only law defines them as crimes" (Henslin, 2000: 169).

The principle that law "makes" crime has many effects. One is that crime is culturally relative; laws, and hence crimes, vary from one place and time to another. For example, in the early 1900's Margaret Sanger, the pioneer of the birth control movement, sent birth control information through the U.S. mail. Doing so *at that time* was illegal, since it was thought to be harmful to the family and the state. Sanger was found guilty for mailing "obscene, lewd and lascivious" materials. Today it is generally perceived differently – helpful rather than harmful to society (Henslin, 2000: 169-170). Contraceptives and abortion were once considered criminal acts; today they are not. Hence, determining what is or is not a crime is the result of a political process – a conflict among individuals, groups and institutions with different ideologies and interests. Such conflicts determine what individual behavior is criminal or non-criminal. A sociological analysis raises such questions as: Which groups in society have the power to get their views and opinions written into laws? Why do they pass laws against some acts and not against others? Why do some societies punish some behavior while others ignore, or even encourage such behavior? The history of crime, then, acts as ... "revealing windows on social structure and value systems. A critical analysis of crime enables us to see what past eras considered legitimate and illegitimate" (Papke, 1993: 2073).

The history of crime as a social problem means we also must look at the criminal justice system. This entails agencies that respond to crime - - police, courts, jails and prisons. Crime's character derives not only from legal definitions and arrests but also from perceptions of it's seriousness, growth or decline and meaning it has for people. Government and community leaders, powerful social groups and the increasingly important mass media all play crucial roles in conflicts that develop our society's perceptions and attitudes about crime. Rather than wringing our hands about the fuzziness of crime figures and unreported crime, we can critically assess the ways our society and ideology, values and norms, change the definitions of crime and thereby either challenge or reinforce the social order. This chapter will examine historically the conflicts and battles over:

1. What are "serious crimes" and how they have changed historically?
2. What is fair and just punishment (i.e. "cruel and unusual punishment" under the constitution)?
3. Treatment of children vs. adults who commit crimes
4. Use of violence in prisons
5. The death sentence vs. life imprisonment
6. Unequal justice for minorities, the poor, and the mentally disabled.
7. Rights of accused vs. rights of victims (and their families).

Serious Crimes and How They Have Changed

The history of serious crimes in the U.S. can be divided into three periods: the colonial period (Gemeinschaft), the modernizing 19th Century (transition from Gemeinschaft to Gesellschaft) and the era of Twentieth Century bureaucratization (Gesellschaft) and alienation (Papke, 1993: 2073).

Colonial Period – Gemeinschaft Society

The majority of North American colonists were of English birth or heritage. Therefore, most of their definitions of serious crimes came from English statute law and common law. While New England, "magistrates", like their counterparts in Great Britain, had leeway in interpreting and carrying out the law in the courtroom, Protestant ministers had control over the law outside the courtroom. Through law quotations from Biblical passages, Protestant ministers contributed to the definitions and interpretations of serious crimes. Consequently capital offenses included behaviors such as adultery, blasphemy and fornication. Robbery wasn't even mentioned as a "serious" offense.

But interpretations of the law were not uniform. Criminal law reflected the differences in what the various colonies viewed as important. While moral issues were the focus in New England colonies, protection of tobacco farms was the main focus in the Chesapeake colonies and regions in Maryland, Virginia and North Carolina. Maryland even passed a special law making the breaking into and stealing from a tobacco house a *capital* crime. Maryland and Virginia laws also helped to create slaves. They held that "African indentured servants could be sentenced to lifelong servitude for attempting to escape their masters" (Papke, 1993: 2075). These laws reflect the power of the large landowners, just as New England laws reflect the power of ministers.

Even in colonial times the definitions of serious crime affected most severely the colonial underclass – those outside the dominant religions- - indentured servants, unskilled laborers, and slaves. In New York State, far from the plantations of the South, African slaves were more likely to be found guilty than any other social group. On the other hand, ministers, city merchants and plantation owners in the South were rarely prosecuted or convicted; and if they were, their punishments were fines and restitution (like most white-collar crime today) rather than severe physical punishment or death. Defining crimes and punishing colonial criminals served, among other things, to reinforce the power and control of colonial elites.

19th Century Crime – Early Shift to Gesellschaft Society

As America began to develop from a small, personal, rural Gemeinschaft society, toward a larger, impersonal, urban society (Gesellschaft), the definitions of serious crime changed too. What offended the individual began to be defined as "criminal" more so than what offended the community. The arrest and prosecution of people who committed immoral acts such as bestiality, blasphemy and fornication declined. Instead, society (beyond the areas with tobacco farms) stressed crimes involving theft (especially stealing a horse) or destruction of private property (the foundation of capitalism and economic power) as much more serious. This shift is illustrated by data from seven counties in Massachusetts: "By 1800... more than 40 percent of all prosecutions were for theft, only 7 percent for conduct offensive to morality" (Nelson, 1975: 118).

However, during this middle stage, moral crimes didn't disappear, they simply shifted focus. In addition to property crime, vice, personal violence and disorderly conduct, could bring a person to the criminal courts and into prison. Vice involved illegal gambling and prostitution, since drugs and alcohol were for the most part not yet criminalized. Urban reformers in the 1820s, building upon the earlier Puritanical sacred beliefs, redefined gambling and prostitution as "a threat to civic virtues and social order" (Papke, 1993:2077).

The seed-beds of crime were usually in our cities. Davis and Haller recorded that crime was a never-ending problem in 19th Century Philadelphia (1973). The period from the 1830s through the 1850s was one of the most violent and crime-torn. One study by David Crimsted estimated about 1000 lives were lost from criminal rioting alone (Lane, 1976:9). Even frontier shoot-outs and violence came from people reared in crime-infested Eastern cities. Billy the Kid was born and raised in the slums of New York City.

Were the streets more dangerous than those later in the 19th Century? That is difficult to say because reliable counts of crime were not even started before 1850. The first statewide statistics on crime were in New York in 1829. And they were just from the courts – people prosecuted and convicted (Pepinsky, 1976:24). So "while no reliable index stretches back before mid-century, the figures begin to descend as soon as they appear. Contrary to both sociological theory and popular impression, population growth by itself does not generate criminal violence" (Lane, 1976:12).

For example, in the State of Massachusetts major crime was quite high in the 1830s as compared with the 1860s and around 1900. On the basis of 100,000 population there were nearly 17 imprisonments in 1834-62; and less than 6 in 1899-1901 (Ferdinand, 1967). However, this is related to the definition of "crime." If "crimes against public order," usually drunkenness, were counted, then crime in Massachusetts rose in the 19th Century. Like today, policing the public's morals in respect to drinking and drugging has added sharply to the total crime count in the United States.

Even with the drop in crime, during the 1870s, the growing specter of professional criminals made its appearance in a series of spectacular bank holdups. This led to a change in the existing detective methods in cities across the United States (Lane, 1969:481). About the same time, thousands of unemployed vagrants, victims of our sudden shift from rural to urban industrial life, became in the columns of sensational newspapers "wild-eyed" strangers, potentially violent and criminal. Police were augmented, and harsh action taken by them to keep the peace.

Furthermore, delinquency among the young thrived in 19th Century America. Charles Loring Brace, a pioneer in youth and child care in the 1800s, observed that delinquent gangs were endemic in New York City. They consisted of the children of Irish and German immigrants. He wrote: "The murder of an unoffending old man...is nothing to them. They are ready for any offense or crime, however degraded or bloody" (1880:27).

Others wrote about how broken homes, poverty and drunken parents led youngsters into a life of crime. Jacob Riis moralized in 1890:

> At the Elmira Reformatory, of more than five thousand prisoners...three-fourths possessed no culture or only the slightest. As to moral sense, 42.6 % has absolutely none, 35 % 'possibly some.' Only 7.5% came from good homes...38.4 % of the prisoners had drunken parents, and 13 % parents of doubtful sobriety. Of more than 22,000 inmates of juvenile Asylum in 39 years, one-fourth had either a drunken father or mother, or both. At the Protectory the percentage of drunkenness in parents was not quite one-fifth among over 3,000 children cared for in the institution last year (Cordasco, 1968:214-215).

In response to serious problems of delinquency in American cities, groups like the Children's Aid Society formed to lead them from the path of crime. The New York group, founded by Rev. Charles Loring Brace, was the result of a report by the Chief of Police in 1849 "calling attention to the thousands of children who were being arrested for vagrancy and other offenses" (Zietz, 1969:81). Horace Greeley, than editor of *The New York Times,* expressed his conviction that citizens "should not allow homelessness, want, and criminal behavior to befall the children of the city and would respond to the problem" (Zietz, 1969:82).

This was the age when most people thought crime and criminal behavior were biologically inherited from one's parents and grandparents. Charles Loring Brace believed a shift in environment, opportunity to learn a trade, and good religious training were the only things that could counteract the young criminal's biological background. For example:

> When a female child of nine or ten exhibited licentious
> habits and desires beyond control, as had her mother and
> grandmother before her, Brace believed that 'gem mules'
> were at work. The gem mules, or latent tendencies, or
> forces, or cells of her immediate ancestors were in her
> system, and working in her blood, producing irresistible
> effects on her brain, nerves, and mental emotions. If not
> controlled by moral or external physical influences, driven
> by her inherited tendencies, she would eventually succumb.
> (Zietz, 1969:82)

To give children and youngsters such new "external"
environments, they shipped trainloads of them from the city to farming
communities of the East and Middle West. Between 1853 and 1876,
the N.Y. Children's Aid Society placed some 35,000 children this way.
Eventually their work paid off. In New York City between 1860 and
1890, while its population doubled, the commitments of girls and
women for vagrancy fell off from nearly 6000 to under 2000. The
jailing of female thieves between 1865 and 1890 fell "from 1 in
743 to 1 in 7500. Stealing and vagrancy among boys has decreased
too; if not so fast, yet at a gratifying rate" (Riis, 1890:130).

Yet near the end of the 19th Century, crime and delinquency
still persisted (as it does today). For example, Chicago saloon keepers
expected to be robbed every three or four days. Even innocent gas-
meter readers were shot by nervous crime-conscious people.
Newspapers said too many six-year-old boys roamed the streets with
guns and knives. The mayor of Chicago suggested that the crime
problem could be solved quickly if people would "carry revolvers
strapped outside their clothing" ("The Crime Wave," 1975:14).

Most perpetrators of violence, not only in Chicago, were
young adult males who were frustrated and alienated in their work lives
and unable to build strong interpersonal relations. Many felt exploited
by the rich and were powerless whenever economic declines occurred.
Essentially, these individuals did not possess a feeling of "community"
or Gemeinschaft and, for them, it became an issue of "every man for
himself."

Although homicide was not the most frequent personal
violence crime, like today, it drew the most public attention.
According to one historian, Papke, the typical 19th Century homicides
resulted from a quarrel or brawl originating in a saloon and finished in
the street. Although occasional murders occurred within the upper
classes, most all murders involved members of the working class and
poor.

Social-disorder crimes occurred between individuals and between groups. Between 1830 and 1860, forty riots of significant size took place in Baltimore, Boston, Cincinnati, New York and Philadelphia.

In 1788, in New York City some 5,000 people rioted against doctors and student interns who were stealing bodies from graves and cemeteries for purpose of medical dissection (Heaps, 1970: 19-29). Anti-foreign feelings sparked the anti-catholic (Irish) riot in Philadelphia in 1844; the Astor Place Riot (followers of British vs. American Shakespearean actors); the Know-Nothings of the 1850s against Irish and other foreigners. Riots of these kinds reached a 19th Century peak in the Draft Riots of 1863 which ravaged cities from Boston to Detroit. They were most severe in New York City, lasting four days and nights and killing an estimated 500 people (Heaps, 1970). During the 1870s riots and social disorder grew out of strikes and labor rallies to organize workers and improve working conditions. In 1877 riots convulsed a dozen cities after railroad unions struck.

Exploitation, frustration, anger and powerlessness by working class "native" Americans and immigrants under-girded all these riots. Conflict essentially was over available jobs provided by newly industrialized factories. Mass unemployment fed most of these riots. Such social disorder was perceived by the power structure and rich as a threat to their power and thus had to be controlled by police and the military. And they were.

In the last third of the 19th Century, the criminal codes grew and grew as state legislators added new offenses. Many states criminalized vagrancy. Private prosecutions gave way to public ones by the district attorney. Criminologist Allen Steinberg maintains "the overall relationship of the average citizen to criminal justice shifted from one of participation to one of deference to elite judgments" (1989: 225).

20th Century Crimes – A Full Gesellschaft Society

During the 20th Century the legal definitions of property crime, vice, personal violence and social disorder, which emerged in the 19th Century, remained in place. During this period, definitions of crime changed less than in the past, except the definition of moral crimes became less restrictive. For example, the legal definition of prostitution narrowed to refer exclusively to the provision of a sex act for money.

However, largely due to the advances in technology, other traditional laws, such as theft, became more specific, making more crime appear on the books and crime rates increase. For example, the law of theft greatly extended beyond the mere physical taking of a victim's property such as an automobile (which replaced the horse's central role in American life). Embezzlement of employees, who had lawful possession of money or other property, became more common. Furthermore, in the mid and latter part of the 20th Century, laws were passed to cover fraudulent use of bank checks, financial records, credit cards and computers, as well as "identity theft".

Crime continued to grow as our nation grew in the 20th Century, as one would expect in a Gesellschaft society where individual concerns are more important than community concerns. Almost all of the available data suggests that the crime rate rose rapidly during the post-World War I period (after 1918) and the economic boom of the 1920s. For example, national murder figures (the only national ones collected before 1933) show that from 1918 to about 1929 the murder rate per 100,000 population almost doubled (from about 5 ½ to 10) (Graham, 1969). Delinquents committed to juvenile facilities increased from 14,147 in 1910 to 17,017 in 1933 (Cahalan, 1986:123).

Crime usually occurs in poor neighborhoods (Credit: Joseph Elliott)

With the Great Depression of the 1930s, crime declined. For many, community ties strengthened as people relied on neighbors to help survive. Figures from cities from 1930-1932 show that a downward trend began shortly after the stock market crash of 1929. For example, studies in Boston, Chicago, and New York and other cities, revealed crime rates higher in the World War I years (1914-1918) and the 1920s, than they were in the 1930s and 1940s.

But this relative tranquility did not spread to all areas. During 1930 in Chicago, gang warfare erupted over leadership of the Mafia. Guiseppi Masseria, leader of one group, put out a "contract" on leaders of other gangs. "In a period of two or three days, forty leaders of the older organization of the Mafia were killed, and later Masseria, who had started the war, was also killed. Eventually, Charles "Lucky" Luciano became the head of the organization..." (Stewart, 1976:308).

To clearly record trends for "serious" crimes, in 1933 the FBI began to collect nation-wide crime figures. Local police departments submitted their crime statistics to the FBI, the FBI issued quarterly reports, an annual review and an analysis in what are called *The Uniform Crime Reports.* As in the past, crimes against person and property are still considered the most serious. The main crimes the FBI tracks are called "Index Crimes" and specifically, they are murder and nonnegligent manslaughter, forcible rape, robbery, aggravated assault, burglary, larceny-theft, motor-vehicle theft, and arson. Notice, while crimes against morals are still enforced, they are not on the list of "major" crimes.

While changes in crime-reporting practices to the FBI across the years makes longitudinal comparisons prior to the 1960s difficult, a sharp increase in crime began in the 1960s, especially after 1965. Between 1960 and 1970, we were losing the battle against crime. During that decade, major crimes went up 176%, while the "clearance rate" (arrests for a crime) went down 34% (Mauss, 1975: 78-79).

By 1976, the two hundredth anniversary of our nation, the upward trend still persisted with some 11,349,700 total offenses (Major Crime Index of FBI, UCR Report) known to police (or 5287 crimes per 100,000 population) (Maguire and Pastore, 1998:261). From 1980 through 1988, Ronald Reagan served as President of the United States. He won each election on his strong stand against crime. However, the facts revealed that only the years 1982 through 1984 showed a drop in major crimes. Macguire and Pastore also note that with a new administration in Washington in 1992 (President Clinton), serious crime began to decline from 14,438,200 offenses to 13,476,600 in 1996 (1998). At the same time (since 1992) violent crime has dropped for seven consecutive years, with a 10% drop in 1999 alone. The murder rate was the lowest since 1966. In 2000, some 12,943 persons were murdered compared with 20,273 in 1990 (Statistical Abstract of U.S., 2002: 186). At the turn of the century, the crime rate was at its lowest in a quarter-century (Leary, 2000:A-10; Murray, 1999:A-22, Sniffen, 2000:A-3).

Various theories have developed to explain this decline. The strong economy, providing more employment for people, including the poor, as well as national welfare reform and more training in the last five years or so have been suggested as reasons. Other reasons include: the currently high incarceration rates in America (Mangino, 1999:A-7); the crackdown on the purchase of handguns from the Brady Bill which requires background checks and was passed in the early 1990's; and, litigation against gun makers, retailers and distributors, for millions of dollars for making "unreasonably dangerous products" (Hays, 1999:A-15; Witkin, 1998:28). However, as Richard Rosenfeld argues in his article in the book, *The Crime Drop in America* "...no single factor can be invoked as *the cause* of the crime decline of the 1990s" (Blumstein and Wallman, 2000: 188). Whatever the reasons, the historic battle against crime and delinquency is far from over. Criminal arrests of teens, ages 14-17, were up 150% between 1950 and 2000, as shown in Figure 2-1. The conventional wisdom is that increased arrests rates may explain some part of the dip in crime.

Figure 2-1 Criminal Arrests of Teens (14-17 year olds) Up 150%

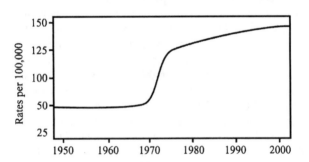

Source: U.S. Department Bureau of the Census, Historical Statistics of the United States.

Even though violent crime rates for juveniles decreased in 1996 and 1997, the gang population continues to grow. Gang members commit serious and violent offenses at a rate several times higher than non-gang members (Mangino, 1999). "The first national survey of gang activity by the United States Justice Department in 1996 showed an estimated 650,000 gang members and 25,000 gangs nationwide" (Tyson, 1998:70). What is alarming is that the population of young people (ages 12 to 20) will increase 21% by 2014. This will add almost 7 million new teenagers, the most violent segment of our society (Mangino, 1999).

Gangs form in all kinds of neighborhoods

Beyond criminal codes, the mass media influenced which crimes were serious. More so than in earlier periods of American history, "media managers" realized crime would sell. Whether in newspaper, or on radio or TV, "if it bleeds it leads". Crime reporting, with titillating details, and factual televised crime watching, with cops pursuing criminals by any means, fueled the country's perception of crime. Perceptions of "mobsters" or syndicate drug lords by TV and press "constitute a projection of criminality onto ethnic and racial groups" (Papke, 1993:2081). "Organized crime" has been neither as ethnic nor as organized as the media might suggest... the image of a bureaucratic, nationwide Italian Mafia is more fantasy than fact (Block, 1980). Such images were manifested and magnified by movies such as "The Godfather" and television shows like "The Sopranos".

Conflict Over a "Fair and Just Punishment"
Fundamental differences of opinions and norms have always existed (and still do) over: "What is a fair and just punishment for crime?" In constitutional language, there is historical conflict over: "What is cruel and unusual punishment?" Intertwined with such differences has been the question about the "death penalty" (i.e., "Capital Punishment") vs. Life Imprisonment (without chance for parole).
Let's look at these conflicts over time starting with colonial times, then the 19th, 20th and 21st Centuries.

Colonial Times

Criminal laws were essentially taken from English common or statute laws. The death penalty arrived in America with the English. Public hanging was required for a number of crimes and the first colonist executed, George Kendall, died in 1608 at Jamestown. As we mentioned in the last section, "capital" crimes in Massachusetts Bay were defined in language virtually identical to certain cited biblical passages. Therefore, the crimes of adultery and blasphemy, contrary to English approaches, were viewed in some colonies as capital offenses.

While, over the years the colonies built small jails and prisons, they used them less for punishment and more as "holding facilities" for those passing through the criminal justice system. Not surprisingly in a Gemeinschaft society where community opinion is very important, fines and various forms of public shame and humiliation were much more important than imprisonment as modes of punishment (Papke, 1993:2074). Convicted criminals were brought into the center of town to be dunked in water, placed in the stocks, or strung up on a pillory. Others were whipped, branded, forced to wear signifying letters and halters, or required to wear papers or emblems designating their offense. This punishment of wearing letters was described in Hawthorne's classic book *The Scarlet Letter* (1961). He wrote:

> ...Make way good people, make way in the Kings name [cried the jailer]... Open a passage and I promise ye, Mistress Prynn shall be set where man, woman and child may have a fair sight of her apparel, from this time til an hour past meridian. A blessing on the righteous Colony of Massachusetts, where iniquity is dragged out in the sunshine. Come along Madame Hester, and show your scarlet letter in the market place... On the breast of her gown, in fine red cloth,...appeared the letter "A" (1961:42-43). She had committed adultery.

In colonial times, punishments varied from region to region. Virginia courts were authorized to use castration as a punishment whenever a slave was convicted of rape. The Quakers of Pennsylvania pioneered the usage of prisons (i.e. "penitentiaries") believing "long incarcerations in the latter would allow the wayward to recognize their errors and reform their ways with the help of the Bible" (Papke, 1993:2075). In Massachusetts, the colonists turned increasingly to hard labor as a criminal punishment. In New York State, branding and hanging became more common as the colonists tried to stem the growth of crime.

Immediately following the Revolutionary War, reformers attempted to change the ways crimes were punished. In the 1760s and 1770s European intellectuals were rethinking punishments for crime that were more just and less severe. A significant influence on early American thinking was the writing of the Italian jurist, Cesare Beccaria. His treatise *On Crimes and Punishments* first appeared in 1764. It was quoted by John Adams in 1770 in defense of the British soldiers of the Boston Massacre. Beccaria argued that cruel physical punishment and capital punishment were an irrational approach to crime. They only made crime and criminals worse. He wrote: "The severity of punishment of itself emboldens man to commit the very wrongs it is supposed to prevent" (Rothman, 1971: 59). He was among the first to advocate education and rehabilitation as a means of lessening crime.

The feeling developed in society that imprisonment, with the goals of reform and rehabilitation, would be much better than cruel physical punishment and death. Such a plan was first set forth in 1787 at a meeting in the home of Benjamin Franklin. A paper was delivered there by Dr. Benjamin Rush. He urged a prison program that would: 1) establish various inmates "classification" system for housing assignments and treatment plans; 2) be self-supporting, based on inmate hard work and agriculture; and 3) impose indeterminate sentences so inmates would be released on evidence of their rehabilitation or reform. The Philadelphia Society for Alleviating the Miseries of Public Prisons, a Quaker group, was formed to implement Dr. Rush's program. It prevailed on the state to remodel the Walnut Street Jail in Philadelphia, in order to make a prison - - a "cellhouse" - - which would isolate the prisoner from evil worldly influences and each other. The Quakers believed if a prisoner was in "solitary confinement" together with a Bible, he would repent and change his life. About this time, legislators in various states reduced both the number of capital crimes and the severity of punishment generally. The Quakers and other death-penalty opponents in 1793 introduced the distinction between first-degree murder (premeditation to kill) and second-degree. These two types of murder are still used today in court.

19th Century Punishments

The development of the "penitentiary" continued into the 19th Century. Like the Quakers in Pennsylvania, reformers in other northern states, were not convinced that criminals were born bad (i.e. "bad seed") or that humans were essentially evil. They were more open to the ideas that one's family and environment led to criminal conduct. Jails and prisons had been used as "holding" areas prior to trial but the reformers and believers in rehabilitation felt they should be changed to emphasize hard labor, silence and penitent confinement. In such a setting, criminals could reflect on their wrongdoing and change their behavior.

The use of "penitentiaries" as punishment provoked some opposition as being too soft on crime. Nevertheless, the first decade of the 19th Century saw ambitious penitentiary construction. Two competing jail designs emerged - - the "Auburn Congregate" design and the "Cherry Hill" separate design. In the Auburn, New York, prison inmates ate, worked and exercised together, but slept in separate cells. The "Cherry Hill" design, at the Pennsylvania Eastern State Penitentiary in Philadelphia, separated prisoners from each other so they had little, if any, contact with one another. Sometimes they were forced to wear masks so they wouldn't communicate. They had not only individual cells but also individual exercise areas.

Both Charles Dickens (1812-1870) and Alexis de Tocqueville (1805-1859) made special visits to these innovative facilities for punishment. The use of penitentiaries by the states was one of the most significant historical developments in penal reform in the early 19th Century. Later it became clear that these facilities didn't always reform criminals but often led to repeat offenders and more imprisonment. Punishment in the 20th Century focused upon imprisonment and the death penalty vs. life imprisonment for capital offenses. This analysis appears in the section ahead.

Treatment of Children vs. Adults

About the mid 19th Century, youth "reformatories" were started. Reformers were naïve about the lasting impact an impoverished and dysfunctional family might have on juveniles. They believed that wayward children could be put on the right path simply by removing them from their poor families and subjecting them to strict discipline in their "reformatories", or "houses of refuge." Rich people financed youth reformatories in major cities, and eager judges used speedy sentencing to fill up the new facilities. Release came when a young person was believed to have changed for the better, or when an apprenticeship had been arranged. Their approach, though not always successful, at least kept young offenders out of the penitentiaries away from hardened adult criminals.

Historically, conflicts between the powerful and the powerless have always occurred to try to make justice more fair and impartial. For example, some gradual progress has been made by the courts in dealing differently with children and youth than with adults. In the latter part of the 19th Century, various social reformers were interested in "saving children" from exposure to poverty, privation and prison. The "child-saving" movement aimed to have the court system handle children differently than adults. Massachusetts in 1874 and New York in 1892 passed laws providing for separate trials of minors (under 18) from adults charged with crimes. In 1899, the first Juvenile Court in the U.S. was established in Illinois. This law set up a separate court in Cook County (i.e. Chicago) to hear only juvenile cases. Colorado, in the same year, through an educational law, set up a separate juvenile court. The purposes of these laws were "...to tear down primitive prejudice, hatred and hostility toward the law-breaker in that most hidebound of all human institutions, the court of law, and, as far as possible, to administer justice in the name of truth, love and understanding" (Allison, 1974:2).

The Illinois law was to serve as a model for other states: informal procedures, separate detention facilities, and a special recording system. Children and youth who broke the law were regarded as wards of the state, not criminals. By 1917, juvenile courts were established in all but three states and by 1932 there were over 600 independent juvenile courts throughout the United States. In 1967 in the famous *Gault* case, the Supreme Court ruled that constitutional rights of adults, such as right to a lawyer, should also apply to juveniles. Historically, juvenile courts are generally acknowledged to be one of the most significant steps (though far from perfect) toward justice for most young people (Platt, 1974).

Use of Violence in the Prisons

One way of obtaining power by either the powerful or the powerless is violence. One place in society where that has occurred historically is in prison. Brutality and violence by the guards grew as the state penitentiary became accepted by society as a way to deal with criminals. The religious ideas and ideals of reform through Bible-reading, understanding and love were quickly lost behind prison walls out of the sight of respectable society. At Sing-Sing Prison, N.Y., in the 1830s, guards relied freely upon the whip. As Robert Wiltse, assistant warden, told the state legislature in 1834: convicts "must be made to know that *here* they must...obey every command of their keepers... They must be *made to submit* to its rules. Corporal punishments for transgression, which to be effectual, must be certain and inflicted with as little delay as possible" (Rothman, 1971: 101-102). Later public investigations found their punishments "cruel and sadistic."

The whip also was used in Auburn, N.Y., Charlestown, Mass., Columbus, Ohio and Wethersfield, Conn. Pennsylvania resorted to the iron gag, Maine to the ball and chain, Connecticut to the cold shower. Ohio's warden considered the whip vital to any prison system. He declared "whenever the Penitentiary becomes a pleasant place of residence...then it loses all its influence for good upon the minds of men disposed to do evil" (Rothman, 1971: 102). This brutality and violence stemmed in part from fear: no one was yet sure that 40 men could control 800. But since criminals now were viewed as deviants, different from the rest of society, it was felt that only strict discipline, coercion and force could straighten them out.

In the 1830s, Auburn and "Sing-Sing" also faced a crisis of overcrowding. As a result, the State legislature added more cells so that inmates could be isolated at night. The "reformatory" system for juveniles, developed in the United States during the middle of the 19th Century, was designed to be different from the penitentiary but the "reform schools" suffered from the same problems as the adult prisons of the 19th Century. As one writer put it: "Although the reformatory system, as envisioned by urban reformers, suffered in practice from overcrowding, mis-management, inadequate financing and staff hiring problems, its basic ideology was still tough-minded and uncompromising" (Platt, 1974:381).

As our urban population and immigration grew and stricter courts and law enforcement agencies grew, so did our prison population. In State and Federal Prisons in 1880, 30,659 inmates were confined (61 per 100,000 population). By 1910 the number more than doubled to 68,735 (75 per 100,000). In 1950 about 178,000 were in prisons (118 per 100,000) (Cahalan, 1986:29-30).

By the 1950s, overcrowding and guard violence had become so unbearable that over 50 major riots occurred in prisons between 1950 and 1953. Until the prison riots of the 1970s, the early '50s were characterized as the worst period for American prison administration. These riots and strikes in the '50s were "spontaneous uprisings against intolerable living conditions." In April, 1952, at Jackson State Prison in Michigan, prisoners held guards as hostages for five days. The inmates refused to release them until officials heard their grievances and published them in the local newspaper. They were published.

Their demands were typical of other prison strikes and riots of the period:

- Adequate lighting and medical treatment facilities
- Counselors be given free access to all cells
- Only guards who would not be inhumane in their treatment of inmates be picked for duty in the cellblock for epileptic, semi-mentally disturbed, blind, handicapped and senile prisoners.
- The carrying of dangerous hand weapons and inhumane restraint equipment by guards be prohibited.
- Post-operative care be given under the direction of medical personnel
- Equal opportunities for dental care for all prisoners

(Palles and Barber, 1974:342)

Stemming from civil rights racial conflicts of the 1960s, opposition to the U.S. War in Vietnam and activities of groups like the Black Muslims and Black Panthers, black prisoners in jail became more militant in the early 1970s.

Revolts broke out in the California prison system at Soledad, Folsom, and San Luis
Obispo. The Folsom work stoppage in November 1970 was the longest and most non-violent prison strike in the history of our country. Nearly all 2,400 prisoners held out in their own cells for nineteen days in spite of constant hunger, discomfort and continued psychological and physical intimidation by guards and officials. They called for "an end to the injustice suffered by all prisoners, regardless of race, creed, or color." Their demands focused on the denial of political, religious, and legal rights and the economic exploitation involved in the in-prison work program. The latter was later declared unconstitutional as "involuntary servitude."

The demands at Folsom became the model of the striking prisoners at Attica State Prison in Attica, New York. In May, 1971, they formed a prisoners' rights group and negotiated with prison officials several times over 29 proposals for changes in the system. On September 9th, several hundred prisoners turned to violence, captured the prison yard and took several guards as hostages. Others joined immediately, so their numbers swelled to 1500. Leadership came from the Black Panthers, Young Lords, the Muslims, and other groups. Among other changes in the system, they demanded amnesty for those revolting, and the resignation of the warden. An observers' committee from the outside was set up to negotiate on behalf of the prisoners.

After four days, the authorities, with state police help, and approval of then Governor Rockefeller, launched an attack against the prisoners, killing 43 of them and several captive guards, and wounded 80. After they took over, systematic and brutal retaliation took place against the prisoners. Special investigations of the incident cleared guards and officials of any wrongdoing. Some of the top investigators disagreed or quit in disgust because they claimed there was a cover-up of violence and brutality by guards and state police ("Cover-Up in Attica" April 21, 1975: 58) ("Report Says Attica Probe Unfair", Dec 22, 1975: A1). It wasn't until July, 2000, that a Federal Court ordered that the survivors of the Attica "massacre" be compensated fairly (Chen, 2000:1- A).

Later after 1970s Prison Riots
        In 1980, over 320,000 people (133 per 100,000) were in State and Federal prisons. Hence, between 1880 and 1980 the rate of imprisonment more than doubled from 61 to 133 (per 100,000 population). Between the early 1980s and the early 1990s the number of inmates in prisons more than doubled again, in just one decade instead of 100 years. "On any given day 1.2 million Americans are behind bars" (Gest, 1992:28). As the accompanying Figure 2-2 from the U.S. Department of Justice shows: "As of 1997, more than 1.8 million people were in prisons, jails and juvenile facilities" (Murray, 1999:A-22). By the end of 2002, over 2 million people were behind bars (Butterfield, July 28, 2003: A-12).

Figure 2-2: Number of Persons in Prison (1960-2002)

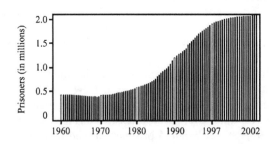

Source: U.S. Department of Justice.

        Although the U.S. has "only five percent of the world's population it has 25% of the world's prisoners" (Anonymous, July,/Aug., 2001:9). As a result, by 2003 over half the states had a serious problem of overcrowding in their State and Federal prisons. In 1997, some 31 states transferred state prisoners to local jails because of overcrowding (Maguire and Pastore, 1998: 486-487).

Death Sentence vs. Life Imprisonment

The northern states had fewer death penalty offenses than in the South. For example, South Carolina had a staggering 165 capital offenses on the books in 1813. But by 1838 the number of offenses were reduced to 51. In Michigan, Rhode Island and Wisconsin, the social movement to abolish the death penalty mobilized in the 1840's. In other states, such as New York, public executions were now conducted in enclosed yards only before official witnesses. Prior to that, rioting was not uncommon at public hangings, especially when the condemned was slowly strangled or was decapitated, rather than dying instantly of a broken neck. Kentucky and Missouri continued *public* hangings until the late 1930s (Cooper, 1999: 11).

Those who favor the death penalty argue:

1. A killer once executed is forever deterred from killing again.
2. The deterrent effect on others depends on how swiftly and surely the penalty is applied. Since states have not consistently applied it, it's impossible to evaluate its deterrent effect accurately and consistently. Too many other variables are involved in commission of a violent crime.
3. Deterrence should never be considered the primary reason for the death penalty. Rather it should be; is the punishment deserved and justice served by death?
4. It runs up costs to society when the death sentence is not swiftly enforced but is dragged out over decades.
5. Life imprisonment is not a substitute for the death penalty because so many "lifers" have escaped and kill again. Life sentences, especially with parole, do not adequately protect society, as does the death penalty.
6. Though some capital punishment cases may have involved discrimination (racial or class), all criminal laws throughout history have been administered imperfectly or unevenly by human beings. Why should this stop us from trying to attain perfection and justice in most cases?
7. It is society's way of showing its revulsion and justifiable anger against heinous crimes committed and ensures respect of the law. (Lee, 2003: 316-324)

Those who oppose the death penalty argue:

1. The death penalty does not deter violent crime (Bonner and Fessenden, Sept. 22, 2000: I-A & 23-A; Freedman, 2001: 307-308).
2. The death penalty is extremely expensive, three to six times the cost of life imprisonment without parole.
3. The death penalty actually reduces public safety by taking money that could be used to rehabilitate many other prisoners.
4. The death penalty discriminates against the poor, minority groups, males and breeds public cynicism on the whole system of administration of justice.
5. Capital punishment inevitably will be inflicted on the innocent. It produces an injustice that can never be corrected. (Freedman, 2001: 307-312).

In 1841, state courts in Alabama and Tennessee, bowing to populist sentiment against the death sentence, gave trial juries the right to make binding sentencing recommendations of either death or life in prison (Cooper, 1999:). Increased public grumbling against the death penalty also led to more humane capital punishment in the early 20th Century. First the electric chair was widely adopted to replace hanging. Later, the electric chair also came under attack as "cruel and barbaric" and was replaced in some states by the gas chamber and later still by lethal injection. Today all but four states give lethal injections as the most humane method.

However, after these changes, the movement to abolish the death penalty lost momentum in the late 1920s. Decreased support for capital punishment is believed to largely stem from the higher crime rates in the 1930s and 1940s. It wasn't until Delaware repealed the death sentence in 1958 that the movement was revived. The movement peaked in 1966, bringing the number of states without capital punishment to twelve. Two landmark court cases decided the fate of the death sentence in the U.S. In June, 1992 the U.S. Supreme Court ruled in *Furman vs. Georgia* that the death sentence, as administered by the states, was unconstitutional. The court later made three important changes to capital punishment:

1. It prohibited mandatory death penalties by the states.
2. It limited death sentences to criminal homicide only.
3. It required each death sentence to undergo review by a state appeals court.

Since the 1960s, the crimes punishable by death continued to decrease until murder and treason were the only two crimes punishable by death that the Supreme Court upheld as constitutional.

Those who want to abolish the death penalty have recently been helped by science. Improvements in DNA testing had proven that the death penalty could take innocent lives. Since 1976, when the Supreme Court supported the death penalty, more than 87 people had been freed from death row on the basis of new evidence. "... In 1997 the Death Penalty Information Center reported that twenty-one condemned inmates have been released since 1993... many of these cases were discovered not because of the normal appeals process but rather as a result of new scientific techniques..." (Lee, 2003: 320).

The influence of DNA testing is profound. For example, on January 13, 2000, Governor George Ryan of Illinois, imposed a moratorium on executions, commuted the death sentence to life imprisonment for all 156 inmates on death row in his state because thirteen death-row inmates were released when found through DNA testing that they were wrongly convicted (Howlett, 2003). Ryan was a pro death-penalty advocate but he is now deeply concerned about executing innocent people. By November, 2002, 115 prisoners nationwide, convicted of a serious crime, were found innocent due to DNA testing. (Bacon, 2002) Some state laws now mandate that *DNA testing* can be done for any convicted person facing the death penalty.

In spite of the ability of science to shed light on the truth, the public currently favors the death penalty and executions have increased. A *Newsweek* poll in 2000 found that 73% of Americans support capital punishment (a decline from 80% in 1994, but an increase from 42% in 1966). Furthermore, in the 1980s, 117 people were executed and 478 in the 1990s. In 2002 alone some 71 convicted murderers were executed (Howlett, 2003). This makes America a world leader in executions behind China with 1077, Iran with 165, Saudi Arabia with 103 and the Congo with 100. Most highly industrialized countries long ago abandoned the death penalty. Some 105 countries in all no longer use it (Hansen, June, 2000:41). In 2003, over 3,500 men and women were on death row. The U.S. Supreme Court in 2002 ruled that the death penalty could no longer be used against the mentally retarded with IQ's of 70 or lower. It held to do so was "cruel and unusual punishment" under the Eighth Amendment and, therefore, was unconstitutional (Talbot, 2003).

Unequal Justice for Minorities, the Poor, and the Mentally Disabled

"Equal justice under the law" is literally carved in stone on the front of the U.S. Supreme Court. Yet the longest ongoing conflict over "justice for all" has been the battle to ensure equal treatment by the law for the poor, racial minorities and mentally disabled. Ever since the debtors prisons of the early 19th Century and the "Black Codes" of the South, the poor and Blacks have not found true justice in a court system originally designed to protect the power structure of the white wealthy, and their property, from the poor. Sentencing was usually in the hands of white judges who were often prejudiced and had strong feelings against both the poor (especially immigrants) and Blacks. The law has always given magistrates and judges some discretion in choosing punishments for people (Rothman, 1971: 48). It often involves institutional discrimination though it's true that reported rates of crimes of minorities are generally higher than whites. Although African-Americans make up only 12% of our population, they account for 43% of local jail inmates, 47% of state prisons and 42% of death-row inmates (Henslin, 2000: 195).

Many studies have revealed that the criminal justice system is not colorblind. There are more unfounded arrests of blacks than whites due to "racial profiling" (See the Race Relations chapter). Blacks pay, on average, twice as much bail as whites. They also are more likely to be jailed before trial and get heavier sentences for the same crime as whites (Finsterbusch, 1999: 180). For example, researchers looked at detention decisions at three stages in the juvenile process: police detention, court intake detention and preliminary hearing detention (Wordes, Bynum and Corley, 1994). They found that, even given the *same seriousness of offense*, African-Americans and Hispanic youth were more likely than whites to be detained at *each* of the points. A later study in 1999 by the National Council on Crime and Delinquency concluded "...the results of the double standard of justice was that kids of color were much more likely to spend their formative years behind bars " (Jones, October 15, 1999: 6-7).

An earlier study, by Humphrey and Fogarty (1987) reported that the odds of imprisonment for adult offenders was greatly increased for minority offenders. Two more recent studies by Charles Crawford in *Criminology* (February, 2000: 263-280) and Spohn and Holleran (February, 2000: 281-306) revealed (after controlling for other variables) that both black female offenders in Florida and young black and Hispanic male offenders in Pennsylvania received "substantially harder sentences" than whites.

Many other studies, whose validity were confirmed in a major analysis for Congress by the General Accounting Office, have addressed those issues of racial inequality. "They uniformly have found that, even when all other factors are held constant, the *races* of the victim and defendant are critical variables in determining who is sentenced to death," Freedman notes (2001:311). Thus, black citizens are the victims of double discrimination. From initial charging, decisions to plea bargaining, to jury sentencing, they are treated more harshly when they are defendants but their lives are given less value when they are victims. Moreover, all white, or virtually all-white juries still are commonplace in many places (Mann, 1993: viii).

Not only jurors are implicated in unequal justice but also the legal profession itself. The Civil Rights struggle in the 1960s and the brief war on poverty "...exposed standards of professional behavior which preserved the glaring inadequacy of legal services for citizens who were black, poor or both...double standards of professional conduct protected the wealthy and powerful while destroying the promise and possibility of equal justice under law" (Auerbach, 1976: 263-264). As one attorney put it:

> Injustice for the poor is endemic in America law because the structure of the legal system is not designed for the indigent...A legal profession that remained divided along ethic and class lines could hardly serve the substantial segment of the American population that inhabited the underside of an identically divided society. Equal justice, like equal access, was incompatible with an elitist profession that remained distinguished by its 'scandalous failure...to serve those who need it most (Auerbach, 1976 :299).

Unequal justice persists among both the poor and racial minorities since anywhere from 28% to 31% of various minority group people are poor (Henslin, 2000:266). In order to examine the social structural effects of economic and racial composition on crime control, in a test of conflict theory, Liska and Chamin looked at arrest rates for personal and property crime in 76 cities. Consistent with the conflict thesis, property arrest rates were found to be strongly affected by income inequality (1984:394). Substantial effects on arrests were also due to segregation and proportion of a city's non-white population. Independent of police size and reported crime rates, Liska and Chamlin attribute variations in arrest rates in U.S. cities to their economic and racial makeup. It isn't a crime to be poor or a minority but it sure doesn't help when you're in trouble with the law (Henslin, 2000: 173).

Mentally Disabled

Not only is equal justice difficult to obtain for racial minorities and the poor, but also for people who are mentally disabled or mentally ill. Robert Perske, in his book, *Unequal Justice: What Can Happen When Persons with Retardation or Other Developmental Disabilities Encounter the Criminal Justice System?* (1991), documents some twenty-five cases of unequal justice for such people. It pinpoints how police and prosecutors alike are anxious to "clear" vicious crimes, especially murder, and extract a confession from innocent but mentally challenged persons.

Dolores Norley, a well-known educator and advocate for the mentally challenged, wrote:

> While working in a committee investigating Miami's Youth Hall, I had the soul-searching experience of finding dozens of inmates with mental retardation in a hellish environment. They had merely been picked up for loitering, having seizures, truancy and other non-crimes, with no hope of release or review for months or years. No lawyers. No advocates. No understanding of rights. (1972)

According to a report by the Correctional Association of New York, the New York City jail system has become, by default, New York's largest psychiatric institution. On any given day, nearly 8000 mentally ill people can be found in New York State's jails and prisons. Some 15% to 20% of New York City inmates are mentally ill. The report notes: "People with mental illness who have committed minor offenses, and desperately need treatment, are simply put in jail." New York City has no effective mechanisms, legal or informal, to divert offenders with mental illness into mental health treatment and out of the criminal justice system. Here is what happens to mentally ill people in prisons:

- They are victimized and segregated.
- They lose contact with their families and treatment providers.
- They lose their housing, income and insurance, the report said.

- Upon release, (if they are), they are discharged with usually no referral to community treatment, no income, no insurance or housing .
- None of the support they need to remain in treatment, maintain their psychiatric stability, and stay out of trouble is given to them (Barr, 1998).

For $33 per day, New York City could provide supportive housing and other social services to mentally ill people. By contrast, the city's jail system costs $175 per inmate a day Ms. Barr noted in her report: "By failing to divert mentally ill people out of the criminal justice system, New York maintains the "revolving door" of repeated incarcerations. It "squanders what may be a rare opportunity to intervene in the course of an individual's illness" (Barr, 1998). The report concludes that at every point in the criminal justice system, from arrest to release, "...alternatives to imprisonment for people with mental illness should be developed" (Barr, 1998: 6).

Michael A. Kroll, Director of the Death Penalty Information Center, best summarizes the continuing conflict for equal justice in America between the "haves" and the "have nots", the powerful and the powerless: "What distinguishes the overwhelming majority of those on death row from other homicide defendants sentenced to life is not their records or the circumstances of their crimes, but their race (and that of their victims), abject poverty, debilitating mental impairments, minimal intelligence - - and incompetent lawyers" (1990).

Rights of Accused vs. Rights of Victims

One notable historical conflict with the powerful system of justice was the Crime Victims Rights movement. It had its first stirrings in the early 1960s after Great Britain and other nations passed the first victim compensation laws. The movement started in California in 1965 with a "victim compensation program" as well as in St. Louis and Washington, D.C. (Clark, 1994: 634-635). By the 1970s, feminists and rape victims became the "victims rights" organizers. They lobbied states to pass victim compensation laws, shelters for abused women and children. It also produced professional journals such as *Victimology*.

In Fresno, California, in 1976 the National Organization for Victim Assistance (NOVA) was formed as an "umbrella" organization to coordinate victim advocates' work nationwide (Carrington and Nicholson, 1984: 2). California again led the way in 1978 with the first law in the U.S. letting crime victims deliver "personal impact" statements at sentencing of the offender. Today it is a movement that has spread to every part of the United States (Clark, 1994: 635).

However, it took a number of sensational cases to give momentum to the movement. One such case is that of Yale student Richard Herrin who, upset at the prospect of being jilted by his girlfriend, bludgeoned her with a hammer he found in her parents' house while he was a guest of theirs. Because Herrin was from a disadvantaged family, Yale and other community members offered Herrin sympathy, a defense fund and housing upon his release on bail. Herrin was found guilty and sentenced to 8-25 years in prison. Upset over the leniency of the sentence and the sympathy their daughter's killer received, the victim's parents sued Herrin for $3 million. Herrin was released from prison in 1997.

Another case is art student Stephanie Roper who dropped off a friend after an evening in a Washington, D.C., discotheque and drove toward her parents' suburban Maryland home. Her car stalled and went off the road. She accepted an offer of help from two men who were driving by. Once they got her in their car they raped her repeatedly. Then they drove her to an abandoned farmhouse, raped her again, and struck her with a logging chain. For fear that they would be recognized, one of them shot her and, perhaps while she was still alive, doused her with gasoline and set her on fire.

While the prime assailant was convicted of first-degree murder, rape and kidnapping, because of a wording technicality, he could be back on the street in less than 12 years.

The Ropers, however, took matters into their own hands. They, their friends and neighbors, formed the Stephanie Roper Committee and lobbied the Maryland legislature for tougher sentencing laws and victim protection bills. The Committee supports the rights of victims to speak out at the sentencing phase of trials. It also wants to require the state to tell victims when their assailants are being released from prison (Kiesel, 1984: 1).

The Victim Rights Movement continued to gain power in the 1980s. In 1982 a special Presidential Task Force on Victims of Crime was established. The chairperson of the Task Force called "the neglect of crime victims in the United States a national disgrace" (Office for Victims of Crime, 1998: 3). After that, significant progress was made, victim's rights laws now exist in every state. More than 10,000 victim assistance programs were developed around the country. Today every state has a crime-victim compensation program. A federal Crime Victim's Fund, first proposed by the task force in 1982, has provided more than $2-3 billion from fines paid by federal criminal offenders to support many life-long services for victims (Office for Victims of Crime, 1998). In addition, public opinion has backed most of the agenda of the Victims Rights Movement, overwhelmingly. In spite of progress made, even today, too many victims and their families are not active participants in the criminal or juvenile justice process. They are still "on the outside looking in." They are denied meaningful participation in the justice system and services that meet their most basic needs. For example, a 1994 poll by the *Los Angeles Times* showed that 84% of U.S. crime victims in the previous 12 months had not received assistance from a victim's rights group or social service agency (Clark, 1994: 633).

Though successful in getting state and Federal legislatures to pass victim rights laws, the movement has waged a continual battle against the power and control of judges. Judges have traditionally sought to keep their courtroom focused on facts rather than ruled by passion. Even the victims' rights laws have not stopped defense attorneys from trying to exclude murder victims' family members from trials.

The problem for the victims' rights movement is that many judges continue to resist the very idea that victims have any role to play in their courtrooms. They perceive a criminal trial legally as "...a battle between "the people", represented by the prosecutor, and the defendant, not the crime victim versus the defendant," a report of the Justice Department noted (1998: 4). The report continued:

> Many judges find it difficult to view victims as having a legitimate role in the justice process because they are not official parties to the proceedings. A focus group of judges and court administrators in 1997 saw other obstacles for victims. The judges control of the courtroom and rules of evidence are designed to control all participants, witnesses and spectators, and minimize emotional outbursts. Victims expressions of emotional trauma, fear, anger, confusion and psychological scarring in the courtroom can be an unsettling prospect and a threat to courtroom control (Office for Victims of Crime, June 15, 1998: 4).

Yet, victims in all 50 states now have a right to speak in court during the sentencing phase. For example, in December, 1993, Colin Ferguson murdered six riders and wounded 19 others on a Long Island Railroad commuter train. Two dozen people who lost relatives, or were wounded, had their say in court at Ferguson's sentencing. Robert Guigliano, who was shot in the chest, said: "The fear and pain I felt I will never forget." Then, glaring at Ferguson, he demanded: "Look at these eyes! You can't! You're nothing but a piece of garbage." Carolyn McCarthy, whose son was partially paralyzed and whose husband was killed by Ferguson's bullets said: "You are a evil person. You are not worthy of my time or thoughts or energy. You will be sentenced, and you will be gone from my thoughts forever." When Ferguson received six life terms, the survivors embraced in a bittersweet moment that seemed - - finally to close a terrible chapter of their lives (Thigpen and Mondi, 1995: 50-51).

The Federal crime bill passed in 1994 contained a provision known as a victim's "allocation" law. This "let-the-victims-speak" policy has led to some dramatic face-offs. Rose Falcone, the mother of an 18 year old who was murdered during the car-jacking of his Jeep, was permitted to address the killer, Edward Summers in court. "I just want to ask you," said Falcone, her voice taut with rage, "why didn't you just take the Jeep? Why? Why?" The prosecutor William Mooney, said "It seemed like a great weight had been lifted from her shoulders" (Thigpen and Mondi, 1995: 52).

Observers have noted that giving a victim a chance to speak to the attacker in court is very therapeutic and helps victims to finally come to closure on what had happened.

But the conflict and battle over victims' rights are still not over. For example, the 1982 report of the President's Task Force on Victims of Crime contained no recommendations at all for prisons, jails or probation. The early reform efforts were focused on the "front end" of the justice system: law enforcement, prosecution and the courts. Prisons are the last major part of the criminal justice system to deal with victims' rights. The 1998 report of the U.S. Office for Victims of Crime zeros in on correction facilities. For example, it recommends that:

- Prisons and jails should notify victims of any change in the status of offenders, including clemency or pardon, that would result in the prisoner's release.
- They should make information about offender's status available through toll-free numbers.
- They should designate staff members to provide assistance to crime victims.
- Correctional agencies also should collect and distribute restitution payments from offenders to victims.

- They should expand opportunities for inmates to earn wages that can be taken for restitution payments (Office for Victims of Crime, June 15, 1998: 4).

Summary and Conclusion

In conclusion, the report's *first recommendation* is to the court that: "the voices and concerns of crime victims should be recognized and institutionalized within the justice system. Judges should advise victims of their rights as routinely as they advise defendants of their rights (Ibid.). It remains to be seen if the courts will ever follow this recommendation.

This chapter started with crime, its nature and seriousness, and how definitions changed over time, especially as we evolved from a small, sacred society (Gemeinschaft) to a large, secular society (Gesellschaft). In this process, conflicts and controversy over what a community valued and who was in a position to decide what was a crime changed over time - - from emphasis on moral behavior to property-rights and protection.

Next we looked at the question: How fair and just are the punishments under our system of justice? We saw how some progress was made in the latter part of the 19th Century by setting up different jails ("reformatories") and separate courts (juvenile courts) for young offenders (under 18). We examined how power conflicts and violence often erupted in our prisons - - starting in 1950, and culminating in the 1970s with historic riots and massacre. Some thirty years passed before our court system compensated inmates for the grave injustice that occurred at Attica Prison, N.Y. Other steps have been taken to make prisons more humane yet keep inmates under control.

The "great debate" and conflict that have divided our country over what is "cruel and unusual punishment" was, and still is, "the death penalty vs. life imprisonment (without parole). New scientific evidence, DNA testing, has resolved cases of innocent men condemned to death and then released. What society finally decides to do about the death penalty remains to be seen. More critical thinking and debate are needed before this issue is resolved in America.

The longest and most persistent and insistent struggle for equal justice has been for the poor, racial minorities and mentally disabled. Historically, thanks to court decisions and public opinion, a more focused approach is being used in looking at such groups who have been discriminated against in the past. We as a society are much more sensitized to this issue today than ever before in the past. But the problem is still not resolved, though recently new approaches in handling the mentally retarded were ordered by the courts.

The last great conflict, still on going, in respect to crime and administration of justice is that between the rights of the accused and the rights of victims (and their families). Much progress has been made in the last 35 years, as compared with the distant past.

But much more still remains to be done by the courts to equally recognize rights of the victims as well as the rights of the accused. More conflict and controversy will occur in the future over these vital and critical issues.

Critical Thinking Questions

1. Is it humanly possible for any society to establish a truly just, fair and impartial administration of justice system?

2. Why does the "death sentence" still persist in the U.S. since most all the other "advanced democratic societies" in the world have abolished it?

3. Why do the rights of the accused in a crime take precedence over the rights of victims and their family? Do you think it should be this way? Why or why not?

4. Just because a person is poor, or a minority group person, or mentally disabled should they be given special consideration when they commit a crime?

5. Do you think "white-collar" crime is presently being handled in the correct way? After all, because of their status and position, publishing the fact they have committed a crime, or have lost their job, is punishment enough isn't it? Have the Enron and World Com cases, involving falsifying public financial statements, really led to a long-term change in how our society views "white-collar" crime?

Bibliography

Abrams, Jim. "U.S. Lawmakers Looking at Sentencing Guidelines. " The Associated Press (October 14, 2000): A-30.

Allison, Junius L. "Juvenile Court Comes of Age. " Public Affairs Pamphlet No 419. New York: Public Affairs Committee, 1974.

American Civil Liberties Union. "ACLU Says Court Case Exposes Dirty Little Secret: The Criminal Justice System is Racially Biased. " Freedom Network, Online (February 26, 1996).

Anonymous. "Of the 2 Million People in U.S. Jails." *Alive* (July/August 2001): 9.

Auerbach, Jerold S. *Unequal Justice: Lawyers and Social Change in Modern America.* New York: Oxford University Press, 1976.

Bacon, John. "After 20 Years, DNA Frees Innocent Man. " *USA Today.* (November 8, 2002): 3A.

Barr, Heather. "Prisons and Jails: Hospitals of Last Resort. " Criminal Justice Newsletter, 29, no. 22 (November 16, 1998): 6.

Bedau, Hugo A., ed. *Death Penalty in America: Current Controversies.* New York: Oxford University Press, 1998.

Block, Alan A. *East Side, West Side: Organizing Crime in New York, 1930-1950.* New Brunswick, New Jersey: Transaction Books, 1980.

Blumstein, Alfred and Joel Wallman, eds. *The Crime Drop in America.* New York: Cambridge University Press, 1999.

Bonner, Raymond and Ford Fessenden. "States With No Death Penalty Share Lower Homicide Rates. " *New York Times* (September 22, 2000): A1 & A-23.

Brace, Charles Loring. *The Dangerous Classes of New York,* 3d ed. New York: Wynkoop Hallenbeck, 1880.

Brewer, Thomas B., ed. *The Robber Barons: Saints or Sinners?* New York: Holt Rinehart and Winston. 1970.

Butterfield, Fox. "Effect of Prison Building on Crime is Weighed. " *New York Times.* (September 28, 2001): A-16.

Cahalan, Margaret W. *Historical Corrections Statistics in the United States: 1850-1984.* Department of Justice. Bureau of Justice Statistics. Rockville, Md: Westat Inc., 1986.

Carrington, Frank and George Nicholson. "The Victims' Movement: An Idea Whose Time Has Come. Victims' Rights Symposium. " *Pepperdine Law Review,* no. 2 (August 1984): 1-13.

Crayton, Mary K., Elliot Gorn & Peter Williams, eds. *Encyclopedia of American Social History*, no. 3. New York: Charles Scribners Sons, 1993.

Chen David W. "Compensation Set on Attica Uprising." *New York Times* (August 29, 2002): A-1.

Clark, Charles S. "Crime Victims' Rights: Do Victims Need New Laws and Protections?"*CQ Researcher*, 4, no. 27 (July 22, 1994): 625-48.

Coleman, James W. *Criminal Elite: The Sociology of White-Collar Crime,* New York: St. Martins, 1985.

Cooper, Mary. "Death Penalty Update: Is Capital Punishment Administered Fairly?"*CQ Researcher* 9, no. 1 (Jan. 8, 1999): 1-24.

Cordasco, Francesco, ed. *Jacob Riis Revisited: Poverty and the Slum in Another Era.*Garden City, New York: Anchor, 1968.

"Cover Up in Attica". *Time Magazine* (April 21, 1975): 58.

Crawford, Charles. "Gender, Race and Habitual Offender Sentencing in Florida." *Criminology*. 38, no. 1 (February 2000): 263-80.

"Crime Wave." *Time Magazine* (April 21, 1975): 14 & 58.

Davis, Allen F. and Mark H. Haller, eds. *The Peoples of Philadelphia: A History Of Ethnic Groups and Lower-Class Life: 1790-1940.* Philadelphia: Temple University Press, 1973.

Devlin, Frank. "Greenleaf to Present DNA Bill to Assist Death-Row Inmates." *Morning Call* (July 25, 2001): A-4.

Dulles, Foster Rhea. *Labor in America.* 2d rev. ed. New York: Thomas Y. Crowell Co., 1960.

Durkheim, Emile. *Suicide.* Trans. John A. Spaulding and George Simpson. Reprint. New York: Free Press, 1951 [1897].

Ferdinand, Theodore. "The Criminal Patterns of Boston Since 1849." *American Journal of Sociology* 73 (July 1967): 84-99.

Finsterbusch, Kurt, ed. "Crime in America: Violent and Irrational - - And That's Just The Policy." *Social Problems, Annual Edition.* 27th ed. Guilford, Conn.: McGraw- Hill/Dushkin, 1999-00.

Freedman, Eric M. "The Case Against the Death Penalty." Pp. 307-12 in *Taking Sides*, 11th ed., edited by Kurt Finsterbusch. Guilford, Conn.: McGraw Hill/Dushkin, 2001.

Gest, Ted. "The Prison Boom Bust." *U.S. News & World Report* (May 4, 1992): 28-31.

Graham, Hugh D. and Ted R. Garr, eds. *Violence in America: Historical and Comparative Perspectives.* New York: Bantam Books. 1968.

Hansen, Mark. "Death Knell for Death Row?" *ABA Journal* 86 (June 2000): 40-48.

Haskins, George L. *Law and Authority in Early Massachusetts.* New York: Macmillan, 1960.

Hawthorne, Nathaniel. *The Scarlet Letter.* New York: Classic Bantam Books, 1961.

Hays, Tom. "New York City Gun Verdict May Aid Other Cases." Associated Press (February 13, 1999): A-15.

Heaps, Willard. *Riots U.S.A.: 1765-1970.* rev. ed. New York: The Seabury Press, 1970.

Henslin, James W. *Social Problems.* 5th ed. Uppersaddle River, New Jersey: Prentice Hall, 2000.

Holland, Jesse J. "Rights Panel Urges Steps Against Abusive Police." Associated Press (November 4, 2000): A-31.

Holmes, Malcolm. "Minority Threat and Police Brutality: Determinants of Civil Rights Criminal Complaints in U.S. Municipalities." *Criminology* 38, no. 2 (May 2000): 343-67.

Howlett, Debbie. "Clamor Rises from Ill. Clemencies." *USA Today* (January 13, 2003): A-31.

Humphrey, John and Timothy J. Fogarty. "Race and Plea-Bargained Outcomes: A Research Note." *Social Forces.* 66 (September 1987): 176-82.

Jacobs, David. *"*Inequality and The Legal Order: An Ecological Test of the Conflict Model.*" Social Problems* 25 (June 1978): 515-25.

Jones, Michael. "And Justice For Some. Report of the National Council on Crime and Delinquency: Race Disparity Seen Throughout Juvenile Justice System." *Criminal Justice Newsletter* 30 no. 20 (October 15, 1999): 6-7.

Jones, Peter d'A, ed. *The Robber Barrons Revisited.* Boston: D.C. Heath & Co., 1968.

Josephson, Matthew. *The Money Lords: The Great Financial Capitalists, 1925-1950.* New York: Weybright and Talley, 1972.

———. *The Robber Barons: The Great American Capitalists*, 1861-1901. New York Harcourt, Brace & World, Inc. 1934-1962.

Kiesel, Diane. "Crime and Punishment: Victim's Rights Movement
     Presses Courts And Legislatures." *ABA Journal* 70, no. 25
     (January 1984): 1-10.
Kroll, Michael A. Press Kit. Washington, D.C.: National Death
     Penalty Information Center. (January, 1986).
Lane, Roger. "Criminal Violence in America: The First Hundred
     Years." *The Annals of the American Academy of Political and
     Social Science* 423 (January 1976): 1-13.
———. "Urbanization and Criminal Violence in the 19th Century:
     Massachusetts as a Test Case." Pp. 468-84 in *The History of
     Violence in America*, edited by Hugh D. Graham and Ted R.
     Gurr. New York: Bantam, 1969.
Leary, Warren E. "Violent Crime Continues to Decline, Survey
     Finds." *New York Times* (August 28, 2000): A-10.
Lee, Robert W. "Deserving to Die." Pp. 316-24 in *Taking Sides*, edited
     by Kurt Finsterbusch, 11th ed., Guilford, Conn.: McGraw Hill/
     Dushkin, 2003.
Liska, Allen F. and Mitchell B. Chamlin. "Social Structure and Crime
     Control Among Macrosocial Units." *American Journal of
     Sociology* 90, no. 2(1984): 383-95.
Lloyd, Henry Demarest. "Lords of Industry Destroy Free Enterprise"
     (1884) Pp. 1-9 in *The Robber Barons Revisited*, edited by
     Peter d'A Jones. Boston: D.C. Heath & Co., 1968.
Maguire, Kathleen and Ann Pastore, eds. *Sourcebook of Criminal
     Justice Statistics: 1997*. Washington, D.C.: Hindelang
     Criminal Justice Research Center, 1998.
Mangino, Matthew. "As Violent Crime Decreases, Focus Shifts to
     Homicides By Juveniles." *Morning Call* (February 1, 1999):
     A-7.
Mann, Coramae Richey. *Unequal Justice: A Question of Color.*
     Bloomington and Indianapolis, Ind.: Indiana University Press,
     1993.
Mauss, Armand. *Social Problems as Social Movements.* Philadelphia:
     Lippincott, 1975.
Murray, Charles. *"And Now for the Bad News" Wall Street Journal*
     (February 2, 2000): A-22,
Nelson, William. *Americanization of the Common Law: The Impact of
     Legal Change On Massachusetts Society, 1760-1830.*
     Cambridge, Mass.: Harvard University Press, 1975.
Niebuhr, Gustar. "U.S. Bishops Seek Changes in Criminal Justice
     System." *New York Times* (November 16, 2001): A-20.

Norley, Dolores. "Due Process is Overdue: Who is Protecting Whom
    From What?" Keynote Address at Seminar on Retarded
    Citizens and the Law Enforcement Process. St. Louis, Mo.,
    October 29, 1972.
Office for Victims of Crime. "New Directions From the Field:
    Victims Rights and Services For the 21st Century." (June 15)
    4. Rockville, Md.: U.S. Justice Department, 1998.
———. "Victims' Rights Compliance Efforts" Experience in
    Three States." (June 1): 3. Washington, D.C. National
    Criminal Justice Association, 1998.
Palles, John and Bob Barber. "From Riot to Revolution." Pp. 340-55 in
    Criminal Justice in America, edited by Richard Quinney.
    Boston: Little, Brown, 1974.
Papke, David Ray. *"Crime and Punishment."* Pp. 2073-87 in
    Encyclopedia of American Social History, 3, edited by Mary
    K. Cayton, et al., Charles Scribners Sons, 1994.
Pepinsky, Harold. "The Growth of Crime in the United States." *The
    Annals of the American Academy of Political and Social
    Science* 423 (January 1976): 23-30.
Perske, Robert. *Unequal Justice: What Can Happen When Persons
    with Retardation Or Other Developmental Disabilities
    Encounter the Criminal Justice System?* Nashville: Abington
    Press, 1987.
Platt, Anthony. "The Triumph of Benevolence: The Origins of the
    Juvenile Justice System in the United States." Pp. 356-89 in
    Criminal Justice in America, edited by Richard Quinney.
    Boston: Little, Brown, 1974.
Quinney, Richard, ed. *Criminal Justice in America.* Boston: Little,
    Brown, 1974.
Reiman, Jeffrey. "The Rich Get Richer and the Poor Get Prison:
    Ideology, Class and Criminal Justice." Pp. 288-96 in *Taking
    Sides*, edited by Kurt Finsterbusch, 12th ed., Guilford, Conn.:
    McGraw Hill/Dushkin, 2001.
"Report Says Attica Probe Was Unfair to Prisoners." *Allentown
    Morning Call* (December 22, 1975): A-1.
Riis, Jacob. "How the Other Half Lives: Studies Among the
    Tenements of New York." 1890. in *Jacob Riis Revisited*,
    edited by Franesco Cordasco. New York: Anchor, 1968.

Rosenfeld, Richard. "Patterns in Adult Homicide: 1980-1995." Pp. 188-235 in *The Crime Drop in America*. edited by Alfred Blumstein and Joel Wallman. New York: Cambridge University Press, 2000.

Rothman, David. *The Discovery of the Asylum*. Boston: Little, Brown, 1971.

Schmidt, Richard. "Some Towns Jail Indigents Illegally and Get Free Labor." *Wall Street Journal* (February 2, 1982): 1 & 16.

Sherrill, Robert. "A Year in Corporate Crime." Pp. 168-74 in *Annual Editions: Social Problems, '99/00*, edited by Kurt Finsterbusch Guilford, Conn.: McGraw-Hill / Dushkin, 1999.

Smith, B.L. and J.J. Sloan. "Public Support for the Victims' Rights Movement: Results Of a Statewide Survey." *Crime and Delinquency* 36, no. 4 (October 1988). 488-503.

Sniffen, Michael J. "Decline in Crime Longest on Record." Associated Press (October 16, 1999): A-3.

Sora, Joseph, ed. "Corporate Power." *The Reference Shelf* 70, no. 3. New York: H.W. Wilson Co., 1998.

Spitzer, Steven. "Toward a Marxian Theory of Deviance." *Social Problems* 22 (June 1976): 515-25.

Spohn, Cassia and David Holleran. "The Imprisonment Penalty Paid by Young Unemployed Black and Hispanic Male Offenders." *Criminology* 38, no. 1 (February 1999): 281-306.

Statistical Abstract of the U.S., U.S. Census Bureau, *"Murder Victims: 1999-2000."* Table 287, 186. Washington, D.C.: U.S. Government Printing Office, 2002.

Steinberg, Allen. *The Transformation of Criminal Justice: Philadelphia, 1800-1880*. Chapel Hill, N.C.: The University of North Carolina Press, 1989.

Sterngold, James. "3 of 4 Officers Convicted in Police Corruption Case." *New York Times* (November 15, 2000): A-20.

Stewart, Elbert W. *The Troubled Land*. 2d ed. New York: McGraw-Hill, 1976.

Sutherland, Edwin H. *White-Collar Crime*. New York: Dryden, 1949.

Talbot, Margaret. "The Executioners IQ Test." *New York Times Magazine* (June 29, 2003) Sec. 6, 30.

Tarbell, Ida. "The History of the Standard Oil Company." 1904. Pp. 20-27 in *The Robber Barons: Saints or Sinners?* edited by Thomas B. Brewer. New York: Holt, Rinehart & Winston, 1970.

Thigpen, David E. and Lawrence Mondi. "Confronting the Killer: Survivors of Violent Crime Find That Facing an Attacker in Court is Just the Medicine They Need." *Time Magazine*, 145, 14 (April 3, 1995): 50-55.

Tyson, Ann S. "How Nation's Largest Gang Runs Its Drug Enterprise." Pp.69-71 in *Annual Editions of Social Problems '98-'99*, edited by Harold Widdison. Guilford, Conn.: Dushkin Publishing Co., 1998.

Witkin, Gordon. "Making War on Handguns." *U.S. News and World Report* (November 23, 1998): 28.

Wordes, Madeline, Timothy S. Bynum and Charles Corley. "Locking Up Youth: The Impact of Race on Detention Decisions." *Journal of Research in Crime andDelinquency* 31 (May 1994): 149-165.

Zietz, Dorothy. *Child Welfare: Services and Perspectives*, 2d ed., New York: Wiley, 1969.

Chapter 3

Drugs and Alcohol

Ever since the Pilgrims came to America there has been a drug problem - sometimes grave, sometimes minor. When the Pilgrims sailed from England to America, they had on board 14 tons of water, 42 tons of beer and 10,000 gallons of wine (McKee and Robertson, 1975: 552). Within a few years after the Pilgrims landed, the Governor of Massachusetts commented in his diaries about the "excessive drunkenness" in the town of Plymouth. From the Indians they learned to grow and chew tobacco. For centuries American Indians in Mexico and the Southwest used peyote, a hallucinogenic type of cactus plant, in their religious ceremonies. It produced hallucinations and visions.

History recorded the use of opium poppy juice in 5000 B.C. in ancient Persia (now Iraq), referred to as "GIL", which means "joy". The Greek physician Hypocrites prescribed white poppy juice for a variety of ills in the eleventh century, B.C. (Raber and Ferguson, 1975: 38). But concern about opium use did not develop in the United States until about the middle of the nineteenth century (1850). Early in our history we attempted (unsuccessfully) to stop U.S. shippers from participating in the profitable international opium trade. The Treaty of Amity and Commerce of 1833 with Siam and in 1844 with China were early attempts to end U.S. involvement in shipping opium to China, started by the British East India Company in the 1600's (Susman, 1975: 17). Between 1805 and 1817, a German chemist was successful in separating morphine from opium. Morphine was welcomed as the drug to cure opium addiction. In 1853, the introduction of the hypodermic needle added to the use of morphine medically and in society. The myth then was that if the oral method of opium administration could be eliminated, the craving for the drug would disappear. Credit for the hypodermic needle went to Alexander Wood, whose wife was the first person known to have died from an overdose of morphine (Ferguson, 1975: 40).

During the 1850's, more immigrants and Chinese laborers were used on the West Coast to build the railroads. They brought with them opium, which was readily available in China. In the 1860's San Francisco blamed opium smoking for the poverty of the Chinese there and for their unwillingness to assimilate into our society. The city banned the drug and in this way it controlled activities of the Chinese. In the 1850's many states began to make it more difficult to get liquor, so heavy drinkers switched to opium. During the Civil War (1860-1865) morphine and opium were used to relieve the pain of wounded soldiers. So many became addicted to the drugs that it was called "the Army disease". Members of the soldiers' families also joined in the use of drugs. About this time, bottlers of popular patent medicines began to use opium and other drugs in their "cure-alls". They claimed to cure almost any ache or pain - - from stomach aches, to "female troubles", and to help teething infants. The major group of users of opium were professionals, businessmen and women, who could get the drugs at grocery stores, pharmacies or mail-order houses. Housewives and mothers, according to Ralph Susman, "comprised a sizable proportion of this group and outnumbered men by three to two" (1975: 17). In 1882, New York State passed a bill directed almost exclusively at Chinatown where opium dens flourished. Although a small number of deviants - - derelicts, criminals, prostitutes, etc. - - used drugs, they were quite small in the national picture of this period in our history.

In 1890, an act was passed to impose a tax on imports of morphine and opium and to control the smoking of opium (Ferguson, 1975: 41).

The discovery of heroin and its marketing in 1898 by the Bayer Company of Germany, contributed to a rising addiction rate. Heroin was heralded as a "wonder drug" and was quickly accepted as a cure for morphine (or "laudanum") addiction, free of addictive qualities. Heroin was some ten times stronger than morphine and easier to use than smoking opium; so many former morphine and opium addicts switched to heroin. It was not until 1903 that the addictive dangers of heroin were made clear by the medical profession. By that time, we had a serious social problem on our hands, though it was not fully recognized as such. By 1900 we had about one percent of our population addicted

(750,000 out of 75 million people).   Some state laws by 1900 had banned the import of foreign narcotics, but a Federal law was needed for national regulations.

Before the turn of the century, millions of Americans started smoking tobacco instead of chewing it and the use of tobacco was viewed by many people as a serious social problem.   For example, *The New York Times* editorialized in 1885 that:

> The decadence of Spain began when the Spaniards adopted cigarettes and if this pernicious habit obtains among adult Americans, the ruin of the Republic is close at hand...(First Report of the National Commission on Marijuana and Drug Abuse, 1972: 11)

It was considered immoral for women to smoke a cigarette. Charges were made that smoking tobacco led to "impotence, sexual deviance, and insanity", and was a stepping-stone to alcohol   (McKee & Robertson, 1975: 553).   In the early part of the Twentieth Century, 14 states outlawed the sale of tobacco but the laws proved ineffective. They were later repealed and only age restrictions were placed on their sale, though stricter enforcement exists today than in the past.

Marijuana was outlawed in the early 1900's by some states when its use became connected in the public's mind with unruly behavior among Blacks and Mexican-Americans. States in the South and the Southwest passed such laws to keep those minorities "in their place".

Cities as the Center of Illicit Drug Use
Cities have long had "underground" trades in sex, drink, gambling and sexually focused entertainment. Most large 19th Century cities had clearly defined vice districts, such as in New York City, New Orleans, San Francisco and Chicago.   These were all protected, formally or informally, by public policy that wanted to contain, control and isolate illegal activities. Drug selling was only marginally related to such enterprises until the 20th Century. The one exception was the opium dens in most vice districts in the 1880's and 1890's. Another link between drug use and vice was the high use of opium among female prostitutes (Butler, 1985).

In general, however, few or no formal legal sanctions controlled drug distributions. It was still defined as a private "personal problem" rather than a "social issue" (Mills, 1959).   Sensational newspaper stories emphasized the individual nature of the drug problem. Dr. Charles Bradley's story was typical: a compulsive cocaine user who started using it at the height of his very successful medical career. He ruined his marriage and lost his children, property and career and was finally arrested for trying to kill a drugstore clerk who refused to sell him cocaine. It was a sad story but not frightening enough to the public then (Spillane, 1998: 29). At that time of the 20th Century, retail drug stores were free to sell drugs usually with a prescription from a doctor, but over-the-counter medicines were widely available that might contain morphine or cocaine as a key ingredient. In some cases such drugs could be ordered by mail. Cocaine "was an active ingredient in Coca-Cola until 1906 when it was replaced with another drug - - caffeine" (Mooney, Knox and Schacht, 1997: 67).

After 1890, public awareness of the dangers of widespread drugs as recreation occurred. A powerful coalition of social forces attacking health, crime and safety concerns began in the first decade of the 20th Century to close off legal access to certain drugs. The old legal market was gradually replaced in large cities by an illegal underground market bearing most of the main features of today's drug trade in the cities (Spillane, 1998: 28). Three forces were at work to make Black ghettos the principal center of drug distribution in large cities. First, city officials and police both adopted a policy of vice containment. Studies in Chicago revealed that, since other economic opportunities were not available to Blacks, illegal vice would always exist and isolation of drugs and other vices was a more reasonable goal than elimination. The second force at work was the emergence of syndicate control of the high-level drug distribution system throughout the Black area of the city. A study by the sociologist Walter Reckless in the 1920's in Chicago, as well as Joseph Spillane's historical study in 1998, showed that to avoid police detection in part "the use of slum property - - more or less vacated building and houses [were] brought up by vice syndicates in large numbers" (Reckless, 1925; Spillane, 1998: 41). Today many "crack houses" are vacant houses used for selling drugs in the inner city.

The third social and historical force was the geographical concentration of drug selling that proved to be "one of the most enduring features of Chicago's underground enterprise going back to progressive-era, anti-drug crusades and ghetto containment of vice" (Spillane, 1998: 41). Though Spillane's social-economic historical study only covers the period 1900-1940, a 1996 study by a staff writer of *The Christian Science Monitor* revealed a very elaborate structure and hierarchy, known as the "Gangster Disciples" (GD), that controls the entire distribution system of illegal drugs in Chicago today. A detailed map of the city, and the metropolitan area, showed the number of GD members under each "Governor" and the turf it controls (Tyson, 1996: 1, 10-11).

As cities grew and drug use and abuse spread, a major conflict arose over an individual's right to pursue pleasure vs. controlling and containing the social harm attached to its use.

In 1906 a major step was taken nationally to control opiate and drug addiction by passage of the Federal Pure Food and Drug Act. It was passed over opposition from the patent-medicine industry. The Act required that medicines with opiates and certain other drugs must put that on their labels. Later, the law required the quantity of each drug be truly stated on the label and that it meet government standards of identity and purity. The Act set up the present U.S. Food and Drug Administration which tests, analyzes, and approves (or disapproves) most drugs marketed to the public. The efforts leading to passage of the Act included educational campaigns urging families not to use patent medicines that had opiates. Historical evidence seems to suggest that this education and the law served to modestly reduce opiate addiction.

In 1909, the first coordinated international attempt to control drug traffic was made by the International Opium Commission, spurred on by President Theodore Roosevelt's attempt to halt drug addiction in the Philippines. At Shanghai, China, the Commission met to discuss ways of controlling the manufacture and importation of narcotics. As a result, another law was passed forbidding the import of opium and derivatives into the United States, except for medical use. Another international conference in 1911, aimed at controlling the opium trade throughout the world, sensitized the United States Government to the dangers of narcotic drugs in our nation, especially since much was imported from foreign countries (Musto, 1973).

By 1914 our society had an estimated 200,000 to 500,000 drug addicts, about one out of 400 people. In 1914 the Harrison Narcotic Act was passed. It restricted the importing, manufacturing and distribution of narcotic drugs, but specifically excluded the medical profession from its restrictions. Physicians then retained the right to dispense drugs for medical purposes and even provide drugs to addicts. But the Narcotics Division of the Treasury Department, given power to enforce the Harrison Act, eroded this medical approach and succeeded by the 1930's in making drug abusers criminals. By vigorous prosecution of doctors, and favorable court decisions, the Bureau of Narcotics convinced most Americans that all drug addicts were criminals, not sick people to be helped. To achieve this, the bureau, from 1918 to 1938, charged and had arraigned some 25,000 physicians for criminal violation of federal laws. Dr. Henry Smith Williams in his book, *Drug Addicts Are Human Beings* (1938), called this federal government's prosecution of doctors "the American Inquisition" (Reasons, 1975: 26, fn. 2). Since 1926 the U.S. Supreme court has refused to hear the appeal of a convicted physician for dispensing drugs to addicts.

In 1930, a separate Bureau of Narcotics was set up, separate from the Bureau of Prohibition (which had been set up in 1920 to see that no alcohol was sold in the United States). Mr. Harry Anslinger, assistant commissioner of the Bureau of Prohibition, was named head of the new Narcotics Bureau. He, more than any other person, was to have tremendous power and influence over our national drug policy for 32 years, until he retired in 1962. It was he and his philosophy that scared the public and Congress into thinking that every drug user was a "dope fiend". He soon linked stories of murder, rape, robbery, insanity and moral degeneracy to the use of marijuana. This "dope fiend mythology", as sociologist Alfred Lindesmith called it, was accepted by the public (1940: 199-208). The idea was that once a person, especially a young person, took marijuana, he or she would graduate to heroin.

Taking drugs often distorts reality

His fear-tactics paid off. The Bureau of Narcotics budget had been cut 25 percent between 1933 and 1937. By finding, without scientific analysis or evidence, the Federal Government passed the Marijuana Tax Act to control traffic in marijuana and making it illegal to use. In 1935 the U.S. Public Health Service opened a hospital in Lexington,

Kentucky, to treat narcotic addicts convicted of federal crimes. A second hospital was set up in Ft. Worth, Texas, in 1938 to medically treat addicts (Brown, 1975: 111).   Nationally, the addiction rate declined from one in 400 in 1900 to one in 2000 by 1936. Figure 3-1 illustrates the historical decline and rise of drug addiction from 1900 to 1960 as computed by the Bureau of Narcotics. These figures are based only on federal narcotic violations; the problem is much more serious if state and local figures (and prosecutions) are taken into account.

Figure 3-1: History of Narcotic Addiction in the U.S. (1900-1965)

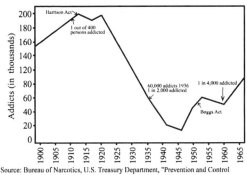

Source: Bureau of Narcotics, U.S. Treasury Department, "Prevention and Control of Narcotic Addiction" (Washington, D.C. : Government Printing Office, 1962).

Some figures suggest that narcotics use declined between the First and Second World Wars (1918-1941). One out of every 1,500 draftees in World War I was an addict of narcotics as compared with one out of every 10,000 draftees in World War II. As fear of marijuana spread, especially in the large cities, New York City's Mayor F. LaGuardia set up a special committee to study and investigate the matter. The committee's report in 1944 stated that most of the marijuana smoking occurred in Harlem, the Black ghetto in New York. It also found no visible signs of withdrawal symptoms when the users discontinued using marijuana. The committee thus concluded that "...the publicity concerning the catastrophic effects of marijuana smoking in New York City is unfounded and that marijuana is a minor nuisance rather than a major menace" (Ferguson, 1975: 81). This report caused consternation and concern in law enforcement. The December 15, 1945, issue of the *Journal of the American Medical Association (JAMA)* responded to the LaGuardia Committee's statement: "This statement has already done great damage to the cause of law enforcement. Public officials will do well to disregard this unscientific, uncritical study and continue to regard marijuana as a menace wherever it is purveyed" (Ferguson, 1975: 81).   Critical thinking tells us that New York City is one of the most liberal and permissive cities on the East Coast.

By the early 1950's, Blacks and Puerto Ricans in large cities turned to drugs to forget their ghetto-slum existence. Many minority group young people had easy access to illicit drugs. Prior to the 1960's, most of the drug addicts, according to the register of the U.S. Bureau of Narcotics, were Blacks, Puerto Ricans or Mexican-Americans. As long as the problem remained confined to lower-class minority groups in ghettos, the public outcry against drug abuse was muffled and the laws were quite severe (Sussman, 1975: 23). But with the coming of the tranquilizers and other drugs easily available, like amphetamines and barbiturates, both legal and illegal, drug use increased. In 1951, the Boggs Amendment, added to Federal drug laws, made it easier to prosecute users and pushers, and carried mandatory minimum jail sentences for anyone convicted.

Arresting the Drug Problem

In the 1960's there was a drug and chemical explosion of pills never experienced before in our history. Drug use and abuse diffused and spread to wealthy and middle-class suburban communities. College campus dormitories became permeated with the smell and aroma of marijuana smoke. Drugs were "in", even at some high schools. As drug use among the young spread, so did public and police concern. For the first time in the Twentieth Century the principal objects of the drug abuse laws were upper and middle-class whites seeking pleasure. Only then did Congress and state legislatures begin to rethink the "criminal approach" to the problem and question the strict and harsh enforcement of the law. Between 1950 and 2000, the percent of youth under 18 using illegal drugs increased from about 5% to over 75%. Figure 3-2 illustrates the sharp upward rise in illegal drugs used by youth in the U.S.

In 1965 there were 18, 815 state arrests for marijuana use but 420,000 in 1974.   Nevertheless, in 1965, 90 percent of federal marijuana arrestees were convicted; whereas in 1971 only 60 percent were convicted. Today laws and courts are much more flexible and lenient than in the past due to the social class, power and prestige of the parents of the young people using drugs for individual pleasure.

Figure 3-2: Percent of Youth Under 18 Who Have Used Illegal Drugs (1950- 2000)

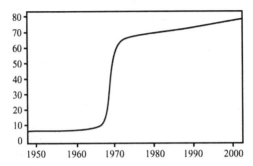

Source: National Institute on Drug Abuse.

During the 1960's arrests for drug violations increased and large seizures of heroin, cocaine or marijuana made newspaper headlines (as they do today). But all this effort failed to stem the growing tide of social acceptance by the young of illegal drugs. In September 1962, the First White House Conference on Narcotic and Drug Abuse was convened to reassess the drug situation in America. The Conference suggested that changes in public and professional attitudes were needed and released a statement that several misconceptions and stereotypes about drugs and their users had hindered solution of the drug problem (Mauss, 1975). In 1968, a new agency, the Federal Bureau of Narcotics and Dangerous Drugs, was created and placed within the U.S. Department of Justice. Social Scientists estimated that by 1969, the United States had 200,000 narcotic addicts. Also in 1969, the National Institute of Mental Health launched a mass-media public education campaign to confront and control drug abuse. One motto used in a poster listing various drugs asked: "Will they turn you on, or will they turn on you?"

In 1970, a new federal law was passed to deal with drug abuse. This was the Comprehensive Drug Abuse Prevention and Control Act of 1970. In 1971 the President of the United States set up a Special Advisory Board on Drugs to coordinate federal efforts to control drugs. The National Clearinghouse for Drug Abuse Information serves as a coordinator of all federal information on drug abuse. Drug abuse treatment centers and programs sprung up across the nation so that by 1971 there were over 2,000 centers. (Morland, et al., 1974) Early in 1972, the Ford, Carnegie, Commonwealth and

Kaiser Foundations formed a Drug Abuse Council to serve as an independent source of information on drugs and provide funds for research. In the same year the National Commission on Marijuana and Drug Abuse made its first report to Congress on marijuana with policy recommendations of how to deal with the problem.

In October, 1973, Oregon became the first state to eliminate jail penalties for possession of small amounts of marijuana. A citation-enforced fine system was adopted instead (Swift, 1975: 15). By 1976, six states (Alaska, Oregon, Ohio, Colorado, California and Maine) had reduced marijuana penalties for possession to a misdemeanor (minor offense) or a civil offense that does not produce a criminal record. Other states began considering such laws (Maugh, 1975). Many university-cities such as Ann Arbor (University of Michigan), East Lansing (Michigan State), Austin (University of Texas), and Oxford, Ohio (Miami University) adopted laws that imposed small fines ($5 in Oxford) for marijuana possession (Swift, 1975: 6). High social class, power and privilege trumped the efforts of local police (usually from the working class) to control the drug problem.

But in 1972 in California, a public proposition to decriminalize marijuana possession was voted down by a two to one majority. A 1974 vote in Washington State on the same issue also was soundly defeated. America's concern about drugs has varied over the years. When drugs reached their height in the 1970's, concern over drugs was relatively low. Public concern about drugs peaked in 1989 when 64 percent of Americans in a *Times/CBS* poll said that drugs were the number one social problem in the United States (Goode, 1994).

Illegal drug use is higher in the United States than in any other industrial nation. In 1988, more than one-half of American youth tried an illegal drug before they finished high school. "An estimated 14 ½ million Americans used a drug illicitly in the month prior to a national household survey in 1988" (Winick, 1992: 517). Overall illegal drug use in the United States started to decline a bit in the mid-1980's. In June, 1982, then-President Reagan's "War on Drugs" began and the conflict continues to the present day. In starting that war he said: "We're taking the surrender flag that has flown over so many drug efforts. We're running up the battle flag. We can fight the drug problem and we can win" (Finian, 1998: Inside Front Cover). The 1988 Anti-Drug Abuse Act declared that the policy of the Federal Government was to create a drug-free society by 1995,. Obviously, this did not happen, but some progress was made (Lauer, 1998). In 1989, the war became coordinated by a cabinet-level executive whom the mass media immediately called "The Drug Czar". By late 1990, the

National Institute on Drug Abuse reported in its survey that, "...use of an illicit drug dropped 44 percent during the last five years" (McShane, 1990: A-3). It also found a 72 percent drop in casual cocaine use since 1985. Between 1980 and 1990, the arrest rate for making, distributing of possessing illegal drugs almost doubled, from 256 to 435 per 100,000 population. By 2000, the arrest rate reached 587 (Statistical Abstract of U.S.: 2002, 2001). The arrest rate for possession of heroin or cocaine increased more than six-fold, from 22 to 144 per 100,000 population (Statistical Abstract of U.S.: 1998: 221). This might well explain some of the decline of such illegal drug use.

Another reason for any decline in drug use might be the effectiveness and spread of drug testing in the workplace. By 1998, nearly three-quarters of America's biggest corporations handed job applicants a plastic cup as part of the recruiting process. A decade before, only 21 percent of United States companies drug-tested recruits. Most companies only test job applicants. Others screen both applicants and "safety-sensitive employees" - - such as those who use machines or drive vehicles. Still other companies also test any employee who appears to be using drugs. Increasingly, more employers are doing random testing of all employees. Momentum for mass drug-screening in the workplace came from four major sources: The Federal Government, the courts, insurance companies, and testing labs themselves. The U.S. Transportation and Defense Department's rules require drug testing for certain "safety-sensitive jobs" (such as locomotive engineers) and the 1998 Drug Free Workplace Act requires all federal contractors or grant recipients to maintain drug-free workplaces (Koch, 1998: 1003). These social institutions have added strength to the battle against illegal drugs.

A series of court decisions recognizes private employers' right to test both employees and applicants without fear of being sued for "invasion of privacy". As a result of court decisions, drug tests are legally given to welfare recipients, prisoners, college-loan recipients and any one receiving public money of any sort. For years middle and high school athletes have undergone drug testing.

Insurance companies favor testing as a means of reducing accidents on the job and also controlling health-care costs. Testing labs that have a vested interest in drug testing, aggressively market their services to companies, schools and government agencies. In addition, employees know that 60 percent of companies fire any employee who tests positive for drugs; only 23 percent retain them and refer them for a treatment program (Koch, 1998: 1003). This is another weapon in the continuing conflict between personal, individual pleasure and the harmful effects of drugs on society.

Advocates for individual freedom on and off the job, as well as advocates for privacy, argue that such widespread drug testing erodes American's privacy and Constitutional right to "pursue happiness". Those in favor of drug testing say the nation's drug abuse problem and the harm and costs to society - - in lost productivity, workplace accidents, lateness, absenteeism, workplace theft, premature deaths, and increased health-care costs - - all justify testing, even if it infringes on individual privacy rights. (Worsnop, 1993). Society benefits in the long run. Drug testing advocates also argue that because 74 percent of illicit drug users are employed, the workplace is an excellent place to catch them. One advocate notes that: "If your job is contingent on your being drug-free, it creates a powerful incentive for you to get off and stay off drugs" (Koch, 1998: 1004).

Many abusers seek work in small companies because only three percent of small firms - - which employ half the nation's workforce - - have drug-testing programs. To close this small business "escape hatch", Congress released $10 million under the Drug-Free Workplace Act of 1998 to encourage small firms to set up testing programs.

In spite of the long-term over-all decline in reported drug use, due to increased arrests for possession or wide-spread drug-testing in the workplace, "national estimates across all socio-economic groups reveal that 10 to 20 percent of infants are exposed to cocaine prenatally" (Mayes & Granger, 1992: 407). In many inner-city populations nearly 50 percent of women giving birth, report or test positive for cocaine use at the time of delivery (Amaro, Fried, Cabral and Zuckerman, 1990).

In 1999, the Administration in Washington, announced a plan to cut the size of the nation's drug problem by 50 percent by the year 2007. The Drug Policy Director said, "Illegal drugs cost the country more than 14,000 lives annually" (Yost, 1999: A-3). Achieving the goal of cutting illegal drug use in half would mean that only three percent of the United States population (12 and older) would be using such drugs. The current figure is about six and a half percent. In 1979 it was 15 percent.

The historic battle over whether marijuana should be legalized is still being debated by groups in conflict with one another (Rosenbaum, 2002; Rusche, 2002). Medical researchers and doctors still differ over the helpful or harmful effects of marijuana (Kandel, 2003; Lynskey and Martin, 2003).

The International War Against Drugs

For almost 100 years, Americans have considered other countries the primary source of their drug problem. To some degree this is true because not all drugs are produced, by plants or by synthetic means, in the United States itself. Today this link between foreign countries and illicit drugs continues to influence United States international drug policy. America strongly supports government efforts to cut off foreign drug supplies. More than two-thirds of respondents in a 1997 poll by Pew Research Center for the People and the Press considered drug control to be a "top priority" goal of United States foreign policy (Falco, 1998: 145). A 1995 Chicago Council on Foreign Relations nationwide poll found that 86 percent of Americans consider "stopping the flow of drugs" one of our country's most important foreign policy goals.

America's drug habit has historically been fed from foreign sources: cocaine and marijuana from Latin America and the Caribbean; heroin from Southeast Asia's Golden Triangle (Burma, Laos and Thailand) and South Asia's Golden Crescent (Afghanistan, Pakistan and Iran). Much of the marijuana continues to be imported through Mexico and the Caribbean into the United States. Domestic production in the United States only supplies an estimated one-third to one-half of America's consumption.

In the beginning, the War on Drugs abroad focused on supplies and suppliers. Control at the source was the first thrust - - destruction of coca and marijuana plants in South America, crop substitution programs and aid to law enforcement agencies in Columbia, Peru, Bolivia and Mexico. A second strategy aimed to improve the efficiency of border searching and destroying drug shipments that escaped control at the production source. Record numbers of drub seizures - - up to 22 tons of cocaine in a single raid on a Los Angeles warehouse, for example, reflected a record amount of shipments to the United States. By 1991, cocaine seized by Federal authorities had risen to 134 metric tons. But an additional amount, estimated between 263 and 443 tons, escaped into the United States market each year (Wisotsky, 1993: 73).

Federal drug seizures reported from 1990 through 1996 reveal some minimal success in stopping the in-flow of drugs from abroad. In 1990, 737,318 pounds of illegal drugs were seized compared with 1,720,500 pounds in 1996. By 2001, almost 3 million pounds were seized (Statistical Abstract of U.S.: 2002; 2001). Of all the drugs seized (heroin, cocaine, marijuana and hashish) the most in all years was marijuana. Drug arrest rates (per 100,000 population) increased from 256 in 1980, to 435 in 1990 to 587 in 2000 (Statistical Abstract of U.S.: 2002; 2001: 193).

Though clearly action is being taken to control drugs both internationally and domestically, many critics of the War on Drugs argue all these efforts have failed to control drugs or cause the price of drugs to increase because of shortages. In an article "The Unwinnable Drug War", Eva Bertram and Kenneth Sharpe state: "There is no evidence of a decline in the amount of drugs crossing U.S. borders. Cocaine and heroin are still widely available – and in fact less expensive than in 1981. More important, problems of abuse and addiction are more serious today than 15 years ago" (1996/97: 42). The reported figures of "current users" are misleading and underestimate the actual numbers of users because the household survey data, and especially high school surveys, do not include high school dropouts, the homeless, persons in prisons or other institutions, groups that account for many "current users" (1996/97: 51).

"Despite impressive seizures at the border, on the high seas, and in other countries, foreign drugs are cheaper and more readily available today than two decades ago," according to Mathea Falco (1998: 149). Domestic production of illegal drugs such as marijuana and methamphetamines is increasing, further reducing the potential impact of seizure on United States drug use. The nation's battle strategy should shift from a primary focus on reducing drug supplies to reducing the demand for drugs through prevention, education, treatment and community anti-drug coalitions.

Peter Reuter of the Rand Drug Policy Research Center in Washington, D.C. notes that: "The effort to control drug production overseas has generally been viewed as ineffective and perhaps even counterproductive, both for the producing nations and for United States diplomacy" (1992: 153).

There is no question that diplomacy is involved in the Federal Government's war on drugs overseas. Congress in 1986 imposed on the Executive Branch the process of "Certification" or "Decertification" of foreign countries involved in the drug trade. This approach reflects a worldwide view that classifies countries into "producer", "consumer" or "truant" categories. The intent of Congress was to put teeth into U.S. efforts to compel cooperation of foreign countries, as well as to make the president accountable for enforcing a more vigorous international drug policy. This "certification" law requires the president to identify each year the countries that are "significant direct or indirect sources" of illicit drugs "significantly affecting the United States." Inclusion on this list, which comprised 30 foreign countries in 1998, automatically triggers certain economic and social sanctions unless the president decides to "certify" the country. Those which cooperated in drug control efforts are "certified", those that didn't are "decertified". This "decertification" results in the end of United States economic assistance (except for humanitarian and drug control funds), United States opposition to any development loans from any international agency and the stigma of being branded a drug-trafficking nation (Falco, 1998: 146). In August, 1997, the *Wall Street Journal* reported that Columbia's "decertification" had contributed to an atmosphere of uncertainty causing foreign investors to put off any new projects there. In 1988 and 1989, Panama was added to the "decertification" list, just before the United States sent in our military troops to remove President Noreiga because of his direct involvement in the drug trade. In 1994, Nigeria, a key trafficking country and a significant source of oil, was "decertified" for the first time.

By 1996, "decertification" had emerged as a major source of tension between the United States and its Latin American neighbors. Columbia was "decertified" for the first time because of alleged links between the president of Columbia and the drug cartels. Columbia was again "decertified" in 1997; Mexico, however, was "certified" despite revelations of extensive drug-related government corruption similar to Columbia. The United States State Department, for example, estimates that some 70 percent of South American cocaine enters through Mexico to the United States. Mexico also supplies 20 to 30 percent of heroin used in the United States, and up to 80 percent of imported marijuana (Andreas, 1998: 160). Revenues for Mexico of $7 billion to $30 billion come from the illegal drug trade. Anywhere from 200,000 to 300,000 Mexican workers earn a living by growing or distributing drugs for the United States market (Andreas, 1998: 160).

In February, 1999, then United States President Clinton visited President Ernesto Zedillo and stated that, "Mexico should not be penalized for its performance in the fight against illicit drugs" (Dillion, 1999: A-1). He said he was impressed with "the sincerity and valor of Mexican campaigns against drugs and drug-related corruption." Clinton then recommended that Mexico be "certified" in spite of the fact that it is a major producer of marijuana, heroin and amphetamines and "none of the biggest traffickers were arrested and none of those already jailed, whose extradition the United States has requested, were handed over" (Dillion, 1999: A-8).

In spite of "certification" or "decertification" of countries "...in the past ten years the production and supply of drugs has seen uninterrupted growth," according to the 1997 report of Geopolitical

Drug Watch in Paris who monitors the world drug trade. In addition, three new factors have become evident and have the potential to make the drug situation in the world worse, not better.

First, besides the large centralized cartels and criminal organizations in the drug trade, in the late 1990's "a massive number of small businesses have sprung up alongside of them" (Geopolitical Drug Watch, 1998: 150). The reason for this is when government action against the large cartels' production or supply of drugs shuts them down, their activity is "decentralized" to different geographic locations and involves new people, because illegal drugs are so profitable. Thus, the war on the supply of drugs creates a "hydra effect": growing fields, production labs and supply routes spring back to life and even expand despite repeated law enforcement efforts. "Like the mythical sea serpent that Hercules battled, the drug trade is an erosive enemy: each time one of the hydra's heads is cut off, two more grow in its place" (Bertram and Sharpe, 1996-97: 47). Besides the multi-ton shipments sometimes seized by the police, considerable quantities of drugs are transported in tiny batches. Placed end to end; they would stretch much further than the large shipments, as the monthly reports issued by the World Customs Organization demonstrated (Geopolitical Drug Watch, 1998).

A second new factor affecting the drug supply situation, in spite of the war on drugs, is chemically-produced drugs, rather than growing drug plants. This new development in the late 1990's allows organizations of any size, and even individuals, to obtain drug supplies of all kinds, anywhere.

A third striking development occurred in the early and mid-1990's. For the first time the countries of the former Soviet Union entered the drug trade. These producers' main market is Western Europe, as well as more distant markets in North America, South Africa and Australia.

These three new factors - decentralized and small batch production and distribution, synthetically produced drugs and new sources in the old Soviet Union - - taken together will only make the war on drugs difficult to win.

Clearly, some progress has been made in controlling and curbing illegal drug use in the United States since 1985. The fact still remains, however, that though we make up only six percent of the world's population the United States accounts for 60 percent of drug use and abuse in the world (Koch, 1998: 1004).

Alcohol: Brief History of the Problem

Before Columbus came to America in 1492, coffee, tea, and tobacco were unknown in Western Europe, and little or no opium or marijuana was used. Of course they did not have our modern medicine cabinet full of tranquilizers, sedatives, anesthetics or pain relievers. So they relied on alcohol.

The North American Indians were one of the few cultural groups in the world who had no history of alcohol use until it was brought in by the white explorers and settlers. It is said that Henry Hudson, upon spotting a small island around the northeast coast, brought some gin ashore in order to make friends with the "red savages". The Indians drank the alcohol and soon became exceedingly drunk. Afterwards, the Indians gave the island a name – "Manahachtanienk" – which meant "Place where we all got drunk", later shortened to "Manhattan" (Fort, 1973: 49). Today American Indians, as well as some residents of Manhattan, still suffer from acute alcoholism or heavy drinking.

In 1607, distilled alcohol (whiskey) arrived in America with the Jamestown, Virginia, settlers and within twelve years its use and abuse produced the first American drug law. In Colonial New England, people drank rum, wine, beer and hard cider containing alcohol. The Puritans, contrary to conventional wisdom, did not totally abstain from drink. They left England with 42 tons of beer and 10,000 gallons of wine on board their ships. The attitude of the Puritans was for temperance (moderate, light drinking), not total abstinence (no drinking). In the Massachusetts Bay Colony, brewing was the third most important industry. Rum was made from molasses of the West Indies, and made for a profitable "triangle trade", involving slaves. While early colonists did not prohibit drinking, they did punish excessive drinking or public drunkenness by whipping, fines, or the stocks. Drinking was originally confined to church or family functions and ceremonies. So our conflicting approach toward drinking and drinkers had early historical roots. Drinking is pleasurable for the individual but in excess it is often harmful to others and society.

In England the early Industrial Revolution led to excessive use of alcohol as former rural villagers experienced rapid social change and migrated to crowded cities in search of work. This abuse of alcohol led to a "temperance movement" which spread to America. The goal was moderation in drinking beer and wine, but total prohibition for the "hard stuff" (whiskey). "Demon Rum" was symbolic of the crusade to curb widespread use of this drink in early colonial America. But alcoholism was rare in the early United States, often due to regulated social use, the limited supply and the high price. As De Tocqueville wrote about the low incidence of alcohol abuse, "it was not virtue that was great but temptation that was small." High import duties imposed by England on molasses used for making rum was one of the factors leading to the American Revolution. Workers sometimes were paid in rum instead of money and the rations of Washington's soldiers included rum.

In 1785, Dr. Benjamin Rush, America's most famous doctor, wrote about alcohol in a pamphlet called: "An Inquiry Into the Effects of Ardent Spirits Upon the Human Body and Mind" (Butterfield, 1951: 270). He advocated total abstinence from "spirits" and called the excessive use of alcohol "addiction" (Fort, 1973: 30; Weisman, 1988: 282). Rush's essay was the first American medical paper to describe the effects of alcohol on humans and to define excessive drinking as a "disease". He called the disease "inebriety" (Butterfield, 1951: 270). The term "alcoholismus" was coined half a century later by Magnus Huss, a Swedish physician (Keller, 1943-44: 325-26).

After the revolution, Americans used their own grain and crops to produce their own whiskey and other brews. Whiskey making became a by-product of farming and in some areas whiskey became the medium of exchange instead of money (Miles, 1974: 20). The new Federal Government in 1791 imposed a tax on distilled liquor as a way of raising money and as a means of controlling the use of alcohol. Some farmers moved west into Ohio and Kentucky to avoid Daniel Shay, decided to fight against it. It took a large army to quell this "Whiskey Rebellion" and conflict to establish the right of the government to tax alcoholic beverages - - a practice that continues to this day.

With our westward expansion, alcohol moved West too. Frontier life was hard and dangerous and there was much time for social drinking in a relaxed social setting. In short, alcohol was regarded more as a necessity to ease the pain and discomfort of pioneer living, rather than as a social lubricant. Gradually back East, however, some people clamored not just for moderation (or temperance), but for total prohibition of all drink. Alcohol was attacked as unnecessary, harmful and poisonous. Many early Nineteenth Century religious and civic leaders made a distinction between the "hard" spirits - - rum and whiskey - - and those not as potent - - wine and beer. But soon this distinction broke down and all alcohol was condemned. Eventually, it was assumed that anyone who drank liquor was doomed to become a drunkard.

As a result of Dr. Benjamin Rush's famous essay, the first local Temperance Society was formed in Moreau, New York, in 1808 (Weisman, 1988). The first statewide society was started in Massachusetts in 1813. In 1851, total prohibition of alcohol was instituted in Maine. By 1855, 13 states had similar laws, though all remained in force only for a short number of years. With the Civil War (1861-1865) and the industrial revolution, drinking increased, as people experienced social disorganization produced by rapid social change. Because of this, "skid-row" alcoholism, as a phenomenon unique to the United States, began to appear. As a result of the War and movement from farms to factories in large cities, thousands of people became displaced from their homes and communities. Unable to find work or adapt to their new social environments, they became homeless, penniless, and destitute. The term "skid-row" is a corruption of the phrase "Skid Road", a road in Seattle, Washington, where logs from lumbering operations were slid on skids to the sawmills. The lumberjacks lived in squalid conditions and often drank heavily (Miles, 1974: 16).

As the use of alcohol increased, calls for its complete abolition or prohibition increased. The Women's Christian Temperance Union (WCTU) started in 1874, as an outgrowth of smaller groups throughout the country. A group called "the Washingtonians", made up of ex-alcoholics (and a forerunner of Alcoholics Anonymous) created local movements to ban all drinking. The drive toward national prohibition was spearheaded by the Anti-Saloon League. Founded in 1893, the League stressed that defective children and degeneracy followed the use of alcohol. It was sparked, too, by the direct social action of a woman named Carry Nation, a pioneer in civil disobedience and women's liberation, who went around, hatchet in hand, breaking up bars and saloons. Her efforts and the prohibition movement were strengthened by the appearance of two plays that ran for years - - *The Drunkard* and *Two Nights in a Bar Room and What I Saw There* (Fort, 1974: 51). The evils of alcohol were depicted as being destructive of good family life (and still is in many cases). Moral norms and beliefs reinforced opposition to drinking, as well as the injustices it produces against women and children.

In spite of the prohibition movement, alcohol use continued to grow and spread. A major cause was the brewing industry. Beer accounts for 80 percent of the business in saloons. Brewers financed them for the owners who promised to use only their brand. Hence, competition among saloons grew. If a competitor stayed open longer hours, he would, too. Sunday laws closed all bars, so owners established hotels and restaurants that served drinks. Everything was legal. In a symbiotic relation, prostitutes soon found their way into the hotels, conveniently located right above the gathering place for men. Hence it was fairly easy for the prohibitionists to show the connection between drinking and illegal sex. Soon the movement became a powerful political force. Their dedication and efforts culminated in a Constitutional Amendment (18th) on January 16, 1919, to take effect one year later, to prohibit alcohol. It actually prohibited just "the manufacture, sale, or transportation of intoxicating liquors", not the drinking of it. There were many reasons why our nation adopted Prohibition. Among these reasons were:

> -It was seen as a way of saving grain needed for food.
> -Many brewers and distillers were German and we
>   had just fought World War I (1914-1918) against
>   the Germans.
> -The prohibition movement had the commitment and
>   support in the South and rural areas of religious
>   fundamentalists who believed drinking of any kind
>   was morally wrong.
> -After World War I, a mood of "Spartan idealism"
>   was in vogue as a new world of peace seemed just
>   around the corner.

Prohibition helped to create a vast new network of organized crime that made millions by "bootlegging" and selling illegal alcohol. Joseph Kennedy, father of President John F. Kennedy (1960-63) made some of his millions by engaging in "bootlegging" operations during Prohibition. Within months it became clear that even though there was a Prohibition law, there was no Prohibition of drinking. People continued to drink liquor wherever and whenever they could get some. Some even took to building their own stills, and others brewed beer in their bathtubs. Though more money ($15 million) and manpower were given to the Federal Prohibition Department, the use and abuse of alcohol persisted. By police count there were some 32,000 "speakeasies" (illegal bars) in 1928 (Fort, 1974: 57).

By 1929 the Great Depression struck and Prohibition was not helping the economy or mood of the public. One bold step to end prohibition was taken by Mrs. Charles Sabin, the wife of a prominent banker. She resigned as the first woman member of the Republican National Committee and became the first president of the Woman's Organization for National Prohibition Reform. It was women's support that had gotten Prohibition; now they were pioneers to make alcohol legal again. In less than two years the "Sabine Women", as they were called, numbered one and a half million (Fort, 1973: 61). Prohibition was repealed on December 5, 1933, by another Constitutional Amendment (21st). But each state still had the right to have its own prohibition law. Today, every state permits the sale of alcoholic beverages, either statewide or by giving local communities the option to do so or not. Mississippi in 1966 was the last state to legalize alcohol, if approved by local option. The historical experience of prohibition ("the noble experiment") showed the limitations in using laws to try to solve social problems if social norms, values and beliefs are contrary to the law. Once again, the conflict between individual rights to pursue pleasure vs. the harm and injury to the family and society was resolved in favor of the individual rather than society.

Incidence and Prevalence of Drinking

Alcohol is the most widely used and abused drug in America. Yet over the century, there has been a decline in the amount of alcohol consumed by the average drinker in the United States (Borgatta and Borgatta, 1992: 44). Although most people who drink do so moderately and experience few negative effects, alcoholics are psychologically and physically addicted to alcohol and suffer various degrees of physical, economic, psychological and personal harm (Mooney,, et al., 1997).

Alcoholics in the United States number between nine and ten million but they affect many more millions of spouses, children, family members, friends, employers, and co-workers (Witters, Venturelli and Hanson, 1992) It is this ten percent of the adult population that consumes 50 percent of the alcohol produced in our nation (Weisman, 1988). Because the effects on people can be so dangerous and harmful, and because drinking is so prevalent in our country, many experts consider alcohol abuse much more serious than the abuse of harder drugs. Other drugs often receive more attention and are treated more dramatically by the mass media, but alcohol abuse is the major problem in the Unites States today, and has always been so (Lauer, 1998: 94).

The cost to families of alcoholics is staggering. When one or both parents abuse alcohol, needed family income may be spent on booze rather than food or other necessities of life. Children raised in alcoholic homes have a higher chance of neglect, behavioral disorders, absenteeism from school and lower self-concepts (Tubman, 1993; Easley and Epstein, 1991). Alcohol is also connected to family break-up. For example, alcoholics are seven times more likely to separate or divorce than non-alcoholics, and some 40 percent of family court problems are alcohol related (Sullivan and Thompson, 1994: 347).

Family violence is also linked to alcohol use. In a study of 320 men who were married or living with someone, twice as many reported hitting their partner only after they had been drinking as compared with those sober (Leonard and Blane, 1992). Alcohol use also was associated with higher levels of verbal abuse of spouses (Straus and Sweet, 1992). Though other countries and societies may drink more than the United States, violent behavior associated with heavy drinking in the United States is socially constructed. Behavior resulting from excessive drinking varies from culture to culture. For example, Levinson's research study of ninety small-scale societies reports that alcohol played little or no role in family violence in most countries around the world (1989).

Health is affected by excessive drinking too. Heavy drinking impairs major body organs including the heart, brain, and liver. Cirrhosis of the liver is often the result. A lesser-known effect is premature aging of the brain. Brain functioning of an alcoholic (as measured by eye-hand coordination and spatial ability) will be equivalent to someone about ten years older. Alcohol abuse can also lead to early death. In any year, there are more than 100,000 alcohol-related deaths, with an average twenty-six years of potential life lost per death (Center for Disease Control, 1990).

Other adverse social and personal effects of alcohol abuse that occur are:

- Alcohol intoxication is involved in 40-50 percent of traffic deaths.
- In 25 to 35 percent of motor vehicle injuries
- In 64 percent of fires and burns
- In 48 percent of frostbite and hypothermia cases
- In 20 percent of completed suicides and at least 40 percent of falls
- In nearly 50 percent of homicides
- In from 20-37 percent of emergency trauma cases (National Institute on Alcohol Abuse and Alcoholism, 1989).

More than 50,000 babies are born each year with alcohol-related defects, some 25 percent serious enough to be classified as "fetal alcohol syndrome".

In spite of all these adverse effects, the use, if not the abuse, of alcohol continues unabated in our society, except for a crackdown on drunk driving. When surveys were first started among teenagers in school in 1974-1975, it was reported that 54 percent of 12 to 17 year olds used alcohol and 90 percent of seniors in high school (under-age in most states). The peak years for drinking are ages 18-25 when about 8 out of 10 are drinkers; two-thirds are current drinkers and one in twenty are daily drinkers (Borgatta and Borgatta, 1992: 43). In 1979 more than two-thirds of American adolescents (12 to 17 years old) had experienced alcohol and nearly 40 percent were "current" drinkers (within the past month). In 1988, about a decade later, these proportions had dropped to one-half and 25 percent, respectively.

By 1994, 54 percent of Americans age 12 and older reported being "current users" of alcohol (U.S. Dept. of Health and Human Services, 1995). By 1998, several on-going national surveys, including "Monitoring the Future" by the National Institute on Drug Abuse, the National Household Survey on Drug Abuse and the Youth Risk Behavior Survey, all revealed that the majority of adolescents under 18 have used alcohol. Drinking rates may even have increased in recent years in some age groups (O'Malley, Johnston and Bachman, 1998). One place where drinking has increased in recent years has been on college and university campuses. According to a 1993 Harvard School of Public Health Study of more than 17,000 students nationwide, 44 percent had engaged in "binge-drinking" (or five drinks in a row within a short period for men and four drinks for women). Some 19 percent said they were frequent "binge drinkers" or had binged three or more times in the past two weeks (Scrivo, 1998). Henry Wechsler, Director of College Alcohol Studies at the Harvard University Department of Health and Social Behavior stated: "While there has been an overall decline in drinking in American society as a whole, recent studies have shown no proportionate decline among college students" (Scrivo, 1998: 244). Besides an increasing incidence of drinking, the prevalence rate is still a serious problem as it was in the 19th century.

Overall, about 64 percent of Americans identify themselves as "drinkers", 29 percent say they sometimes drink more than they should and 24 percent say that alcohol has been a source of trouble in their families (McAnemy, 1992). In absolute numbers, more than 14 million "problem" drinkers, and more than 6 to 10 million alcoholics (depending on definitions) exist in the United States (Lauer, 1998: 95). The U.S. Health and Human Services survey in 1995 reported about 13 million people (6.2 percent of persons 12 and older) were "heavy" drinkers (i.e. five or more drinks per occasion on five or more days in the last month). Persons ages 22-25 had the highest rate of "current drinking" and persons ages 18-21 had the highest rate of "heavy" drinking (Mooney, et al., 1997: 71).

The number one drug problem in the U.S. is alcohol

Alcoholics Anonymous and the Hughes Act

Two years after the repeal of Prohibition in 1933 an almost unnoticed event was to have a profound effect on the treatment of alcoholism.   On May 12, 1935, an alcoholic stockbroker, William Wilson and Dr. Robert Smith, met in Akron, Ohio. They were both alcoholics but they helped one another to remain sober and dry. As they talked, what was happening was the birth of a group called Alcoholics Anonymous (AA). AA does not regard itself as a treatment agency with professionals to help others. It is essentially a self-help group that follows twelve steps beginning with a recognition that: "I am powerless over alcohol" to eventual recovery from alcoholism. Health professionals generally regard AA as one of the most successful forms of treatment devised. In 1939, Dr. Bob and Bill W. published the Big Book (Alcoholics Anonymous), which was met with scorn and contempt by book reviews in the medical profession's journals (*Journal of the American Medical Association,* 1939: 1513; *Journal of Nervous and Mental Disorders,* 1940: 300). It wasn't until 1956 that the AMA endorsed the disease concept of alcoholism and recognized the value of AA.

In 1944, Marty Mann, the first woman member of AA, began her drive to change public attitudes about alcoholism - - from a public crime, freely chosen that should be punished, to a disease over which the individual had little if any control and that treatment was needed. She founded the National Committee for Education on Alcoholism (later the National Council on Alcoholism). She had the support and backing of Doctors Howard Haggard and E.M. Jellinek of Yale University (Lewis, 1988: 241). Today the prevailing concept about alcoholism revolves around the one developed by Dr. Jellinek from 1940 to 1960. He defined alcoholism as "...a disease entity that is diagnosed by the 'loss of control' over one's drinking that progresses through a series of clear cut 'phases'. The final phase means that the disease renders a person powerless to drink in a controlled, moderate, nonproblematic way" (Borgatta & Borgatta, 1992: 45)

As early as 1945 in Connecticut and in the 1950's and early 1960's in Georgia, Florida, Minnesota, Massachusetts and West Virginia, alcoholism was decriminalized and attempts were made to start medical treatment for alcoholism. Until the late 1960's, however, no state had passed laws designed to steer alcoholics into the mainstream health care system. At that time historically, "close to 10 million men and women in the United States were alcoholics, but fewer than one percent were getting any direct help for their disease" (Weisman, 1988: 283).

During the 1960's momentum began to develop to involve Federal agencies and laws to treat alcoholics rather than imprison them. In 1967, a five year study by the Cooperative Commission on the Study of Alcoholics issued *A Report to the Nation* (Plaut, 1967). Created by Thomas Plaut, an official of the National Institute of Mental Health (NIMH), it highlighted problems of alcoholism. It reported that more than 20 percent of men admitted to state mental hospitals and men discharged from general hospitals were diagnosed as alcoholics (Lewis, 1988: 241). Also in 1967 the Task Force on Drunkenness of the U.S. President's Commission on Law Enforcement recommended that public drunkenness be decriminalized and that public detoxification centers be established (1967).

Congressional action in the mid and late 1960's became evident. The Highway Safety Act of 1966 required a report on alcohol and traffic accidents. The Economic Opportunity Act amendments in 1968 and 1969 resulted in the first federally funded alcoholism treatment programs. Not to be overlooked was the District of Columbia's Alcoholic Rehabilitation Act of 1967 that mandated a treatment system for alcoholics in place of "the revolving door of arrest, incarceration, release and rearrest" (Lewis, 1988: 242).

The major change in attitude and federal law came December 31, 1970, when President Nixon signed into law the Comprehensive Alcohol Abuse and Alcoholism Prevention Treatment and Rehabilitation Act. This new law created the National Institute on

Alcohol Abuse and Alcoholism. It authorized $300 million over the first three years for grants to the states and local-based programs for prevention and treatment of alcoholism. It also set up the National Advisory Council on Alcohol Abuse and Alcoholism and discouraged private and public hospitals from refusing to admit alcoholics.

The 1970 Law is popularly known as the Hughes Act, named for U.S. Senator Harold Hughes, who was a recovering alcoholic when he introduced the legislation. It was truly a "Bill of Rights" for alcoholics and attacked the social stigma that for so long surrounded the disease. Through federal government intervention and laws, most believe it is a disease but others reject that belief and instead emphasize the role that individual choice and responsibility play in drinking and getting drunk. Many sociologists and behavioral scientists remain highly skeptical and critical of the disease concept of alcoholism which they say is a myth and "socially constructed" (Borgatta & Borgatta, 1992: 46).

In recent years, starting in the 1980's, citizens groups have begun to hold individuals responsible for what they do when they drink and drive. Campaigns against alcohol-impaired drivers began when a California woman founded Mothers Against Drunk Drivers (MADD). She took action after her teenage daughter was killed by a man who was not only drunk but out on bail for drunk-driving just two days prior to the accident (Lauer, 1998: 107). Within two years, the group had chapters in more than 20 states and today in most states, with over three and a half million members (Mooney, Knox, and Schacht, 1997: 86). Other similar groups sprung up as well, such as Students Against Drunk Drivers (SADD) and Remove Intoxicated Drivers (RID). As a result of such groups, most states have passed laws raising the drinking age (from 18 to 21) using roadside sobriety tests by police, and suspending drivers' licenses of offenders (Ayres, 1994: 4). In most states, any driver with a blood-alcohol content of more than 0.10 automatically loses his license for 90 days. Organizations in some states have pushed for laws to hold bartenders personally liable if a patron is later involved in an alcohol-related accident. Also to reduce the number of teens driving after drinking, local groups of parents have organized parties at bowling alleys or school gyms, with designated sober drivers as alternatives to high school graduation parties (Lauer, 1998: 107-108; Mooney, Knox and Schadt, 1997: 86).

More than 16,000 lives have been saved since states began setting the drinking age at 21 in 1975, according to the National Highway Traffic Safety Administration. Now in force across the country, minimum age laws have reduced traffic deaths of drivers ages 18-20 by an estimated 13 percent (Scrivo, 1989).

Under the Federal Transportation Equity Act of 1989, $500 million in incentive grants were offered states if they would adopt an 0.08%+ blood-alcohol level as the standard for drunk-driving (instead of 0.10%+). It also will penalize states that don't ban open containers of alcohol in vehicles or do not adopt tougher penalties for repeat drunk-drivers (Facts on File, 1998).

Treatment Programs for Alcoholism

It wasn't until the passage of the Hughes Act in 1970 that America began to think and act about treatment of alcoholics. Prior to then, they were either treated as mentally ill or as a criminal. In both cases they were put away into an institution. Since 1970 a wide variety of treatment programs have emerged. "Special Reports to the U.S. Congress on Alcohol and Health", required since 1970, shed light on some of the approaches used in treating alcoholics. The 1974 report noted that:

> New developments in caregiving are seen in the areas of detoxification, family therapy, behavior modification and transactional-analysis techniques and activities associated with Alcoholics Anonymous...It has become increasingly evident that no one treatment modality can be successful with all persons who exhibit drinking problems. Because individual problems, needs and resources vary greatly, a variety of treatment strategies should be available in each community and they should be utilized discriminately by caregiving personnel (1974: 121-22).

In the 1978 report: "Pharmacological agents [i.e. drugs] are advocated and used during various stages of treatment including detoxification, [de]sensitization against alcohol, and post-detoxification long-term treatment" (1978: xvi). In treatment there was a continuing controversy over complete abstinence vs. controlled drinking as a legitimate treatment goal. AA and NIAAA-sponsored research have supported abstinence as the most appropriate treatment outcome (Weisman, 1988). Nevertheless, persons who are interested in overcoming their alcohol addiction and dependency have numerous treatments from which to choose. Their options today include: in-patient treatment at a hospital or residential treatment center, family therapy, alcohol and drug counseling, private or state treatment facilities, community care programs and employer-employee assistance

plans (EAP's).   One of the most successful programs is that of
Alcoholics Anonymous (and companion 12-step programs of Al-Anon
and Al-Ateen for relatives of alcoholics).   They are self-help groups
with a fellowship of caring individuals, all in the same situation, who
meet daily or weekly to renew their commitment to deal with alcohol,
relying on "a higher power" and bonding with the group.

Therapeutic communities for alcohol (or other drugs) house
between 35 to 500 people from 30 days to over a year. They abstain
totally from alcohol and receive counseling and even vocational
training in some cases.

In   1958   Synanon   was   the   first   therapeutic   treatment
community for alcoholics. It was later expanded to include other drug
addicts.   More than 400 residential treatment centers are now in
existence, including Phoenix House and Daytop Village. New York's
Phoenix House, the nation's largest residential treatment program, uses
what *Rolling Stone* magazine described as a "military-style, in-your-
face, group encounter approach" (Glazer, 1995: 5).

Yet the effectiveness of treatment programs are questioned.
Do treatment programs really work? It all depends on how well the
right person is matched with the right program.   For example,
Alcoholics Anonymous finds impressively high success rates among its
voluntary members. In a 1992 survey conducted by AA, 35 percent
said they had been sober for more than five years and 34 percent more
for one to five years. Yet the drop-out rate from AA is high - - 68
percent- - suggesting that AA works for a minority of those who try it;
those who are really committed to change (Glazer, 1995; Mooney, et
al., 1997).

A study by the Institute of Medicine in Washington, D.C.,
reported that anywhere from 45 to 75 percent of alcoholics are known
to recover without any treatment at all (1990). On top of that, treatment
programs for alcoholics (as for drug addicts) face very discouraging
relapse results.   "About 50 percent of alcoholics relapse within three
months of entering hospital or residential programs" (Glazer, 1995:4).
Anywhere from an estimated 50-90 percent of alcoholics will drink
again after completing treatment. For this reason, both alcohol and
drug treatment experts refer to addiction as a "chronic relapse disorder"
(Glazer, 1995:4).

But studies are underway in drug addiction treatment
programs at Columbia University to review 200 treatment programs,
looking at age, gender, employment, ethnic and racial backgrounds of
2,000 patients. It aims to answer the basic question: "Which programs
do better for which kinds of patients?" (Kleber, 1994: 361). A similar

study has been underway at the National Institute on Alcohol Abuse
and Alcoholism for five years known as Project Match. It placed 1,700
patients into one of three different types of therapy: treatment using
AA-type methods, a cognitive behavioral approach to teach new coping
skills, and a therapeutic approach that tries to affect the patient's
underlying motivation to change (Woody, 1995). The Institute found a
combination of methods worked best rather than one alone.

Success rates in treatment programs vary according to one's
social status. Among impaired physicians, treatment success rates
range from 70 to 90 percent. For blue-collar workers with family
support, 40-50 percent success rates are attainable. But for people who
started alcohol or drug use in their teens, dropped out of school, never
worked and never learned to cope with life's problems in an alcohol or
drug-free way, "you'd do well to get 20-40 percent success", Dr.
Herbert Kleber reports (1991: 361). There are people for whom any
kind of treatment has always worked - - best-educated, white-collar
professionals with strong social support from employer, family and
friends. What we are left with is a population less likely to give up
frequent drug use or drinking - - those who are poorer, less educated
and more prone to support their habits through crime or panhandling
(Reuter, 1994).

Whether a treatment program is successful or not depends on
two factors: What is meant by "success" and how and by whom
"success" is measured. Many treatment experts argue that life-time
abstinence from alcohol on the first try should not be what is meant by
"success". Margaret Mattson, a biologist from the NFAAA says: "You
have to look at the nature of this illness. It's not like a bacterial
infection where when it's cured, it's cured. It is a cyclic kind of
disorder, like quitting smoking. Often many tries have to be made
before it's successful" (Glazer, 1995: 9).

Recognizing this cycle, some experts advocate "harm
education" as the goal of treatment rather than total abstinence. The
goal of treatment and "success" should be to return alcoholics to lead a
normal, productive life. The goal should not just be tied to no use of
alcohol because many productive and successful members of society
use alcohol. This disagreement over what is meant by "success"
explains why experts and researchers looking at the same results might
come away with either pessimistic or optimistic conclusions.

Another factor in success or failure of a treatment program is
how, and by whom, is "success" measured. Harvard Medical School
psychiatrist Robert Apsler writes that: "We do not know that drug [or
alcohol] abuse treatment is effective...With few exceptions, drug abuse

treatment has not been subjected to rigorous tests for effectiveness". It "is based largely on reports from clinicians and recovered drug addicts" (1994: 48).   So the debate goes on about how successful or unsuccessful any alcohol treatment program really is today.

Both drug and alcohol use and abuse illustrate an important point about the history of this problem.   Social problems have consequences not only at the individual, personal level but also at the community and societal level. In a real sense, a community and society can become victim of a problem like illegal drugs and legal alcohol. For these social problems strain the community's resources and deprive the community and society of the positive contributions that could have been made by people caught up in these problems (Lauer, 1998).

As we know, all drugs and their use and abuse are socially defined.   Legal drugs, sometimes referred to as "the other drug problem", is for the most part ignored by society, though its impact on people may be nearly as devastating as illegal drugs. Legal drugs such as paxil, prozac, xanax and zoloft are prescribed to millions of Americans (including children and teens) for anxiety, depression and insomnia creating "the largest group of prescription drug-dependent people in the United States" (Witters, Venturelli and Hanson, 1992: 160).   Yet this fact is often ignored when we talk about "the drug problem" in the United States (McVeigh, 1990).

There is also little doubt that rapid change, anomie, alienation and inequality encourage illegal drug use and abuse of alcohol. Both effect whites and minorities alike. The meaning of the drug problem for the quality of life is seen in its social consequences. It affects our physical health, psychological health, interpersonal relations and economic costs in out entire society. We often forget that abusers besides suffering serious side effects also inflict suffering on others.

In treating the problem, conflicts arise over whether to help the individual abuser, or reduce the supply available in the War on Drugs, or increase the age of drinking, have far exceeded our efforts to get at the underlying social roots and causes of the problem - - such as hopelessness in the ghettos of U.S. cities. If the problem of illegal drugs and alcohol are to be dealt with more effectively, many approaches are needed - - we must attack the social structural causes, as well as provide help and treatment to individual abusers.

Critical Thinking Questions

1. What explains the essential public perceptions of the drug problem from 1900 to the 1960s? What significant changes began to take place in the mid-1960s about the perceptions and spread of drug usage?

2. What major conflicts have been involved in the definition and solutions of the drug problem in America?

3. What explains the successes and failures of the international war against stopping the flow of drugs into the U.S.? How successful or unsuccessful has the process of "certification" or "decertification" of foreign countries been? What new policy could the U.S. Government use to control the international drug flow?

4. How specially did your socialization as a teen affect your use or non- use of alcohol. How do you personally handle the problem of drinking at your college or university?

5. What approach to solve the social problem of alcoholism seems most effective from your perspective? Why do you think that approach is best?

Bibliography: Drug Addiction

Andreas, Peter. "The Political Economy of Narco – Corruption in
    Mexico." *Current History:* 97, no. 618 (April 1998): 160-65.

Amaro, Hortensia, Lise E. Fried, Howard Cabral and Barry Zuckerman.
    "Violence During Pregnancy and Substance Use". *American
    Journal of Public Health* 80, no. 5 (May 1990): 575-79.

Bertram, Eva and Kenneth Sharpe. "The Unwinnable Drug War: What
    Clausewitz Would Tell Us." *World Policy Journal.* (Winter)
    41-51. Pp. 78-85 in *Annual Editions: Social Problems, 98/99.*
    edited by Harold A. Widdison. Sluice Dock, Guilford, Conn.
    Dushkin/McGraw Hill, 1999.

Borgatta, Edgar and Borgatta, Mamie, eds. "Drug Abuse."
    Encyclopedia of Sociology, (A-D). New York: MacMillan,
    (1992): 516-19.

Brown, Bertram S. "Drugs and Public Health: Issues and Answers".
    Annals American Academy Of Political and Social Science.
    417 (January 1975): 110-19.

Butler, Anne M. *Daughters of Joy, Sisters of Misery: Prostitutes in
    the American West,* Urbana, Ill: University of Illinois Press,
    1985.

Dillion, Sam. "Clinton Indicates Support to Mexico in Battling
    Drugs". *New York Times,* (February 16, 1999): A-1 & A-8.

Falco, Mathea. "America's Drug Problem and Its Policy of
    Denial." *Current History,* 97, no. 618 (April 1998): 145-49.

Ferguson, Robert. *Drug Abuse Control.* Boston: Holbrook, 1975.

Finian, William W., Jr., ed. Editor's Note. *Current History,* 97, no.
    618 (April 1998): Inside Front Cover.

First Report of the National Commission on Marijuana and Drug
    Abuse. Marijuana: A Signal of Misunderstanding.
    Washington, D.C.: U.S. Government Printing Office, 1972.

Geopolitical Drug Watch. A Drug Trade Primer for the Late 1990's.
    Current History, 97, no. 618 (April 1998): 53.

Goode, Erick. *Deviant Behavior.* Englewood Cliffs, New Jersey:
    Prentice-Hall, 1994. Kandel, Denise B. "Does Marijuana Use
    Cause the Use of Other Drugs?" *Journal of American Medical
    Association* 289, no.4 (January 22/29, 2003): 482-83.

Koch, Kathy. "Drug Testing." *CQ Researcher,* 8, 43 (November 20,
    1998): 1003-20.

Lauer, Robert H. *Social Problems and the Quality of Life,* 7th ed. New
    York: McGraw-Hill, 1998.

Lindesmith, Alfred A. "Dope Fiend Mythology." *Journal of Criminal Law, Criminology And Police Science,* 31 (1940): 199-208.

Lynskey, Michael T. and Nicholas Martin. "Escalation of Drug Use in Early-Onset Canabis Users vs. Co-Twin Controls." *Journal of American Medical Association*: 289, no. 4(January 22/29,2003) 427-33.

Masci, David. "Preventing Teen Drug Use." *CQ Researcher.* 12, no. 10 (March 15, 2002): 217-40.

Maugh, Thomas. "Marijuana: New Support for Immune and Reproductive Hazards." *Science 4217* (November 28, 1975): 865-67.

Mauss, Armand L. *Social Problems as Social Movements.* Philadelphia, Pa.: Lippincott, 1975.

Mayers, L.C. and R..H. Granger. "The Problem of Prenatal Cocaine Exposure." *Journal of American Medical Association*: 267, no. 3 (January 15, 1992): 406-08.

McKee, Michael, and Ian Robertson. *Social Problems.* New York: Random House, 1975.

McShane, Larry. "Drug Treatment Experts Score Claim That Abuse is Down." Associated Press (December 21, 1990): A-3.

McVeigh, Frank. "The Other Drug Problem Among Women and Elderly" *Sociological Viewpoints,* 5 (1990): 48-69.

Mills, C. Wright. *The Sociological Imagination.* New York: Oxford University Press, 1959.

Mooney, Linda A., David Knox and Caroline Schacht. *Understanding Social Problems.* New York: West Publishing Company, 1997.

Morland, J. Kenneth, Jack O. Balswick and Rubin J. Belcher. *Social Problems in the United States.* New York: Rand McNally, 1975.

Musto, David F. and Robert Fergerson. *The American Disease.* Cambridge, Mass:* Yale University Press, 1973.

Reasons, Charles. "The Addict as a Criminal: Perpetuation of a Legend." *Crime And Delinquency* 21, no. 1 (January 1, 1975): 19-27.

Reuter, Peter. "The Limits and Consequences of United States Foreign Drug Control Efforts". *The Annals of the American Academy of Political and Social Science.* 521 (May 1992): 151-62.

Rosenbaum, Marsha. "Do Efforts to Legalize Marijuana for Medical Use Encourage Teen Drug Use? No!" *CQ Researcher* 12, no. 10 (March 15, 2002): 233.

Rusche, Sue. "Do Efforts to Legalize Marijuana for Medical Use Encourage Teen Drug Use? Yes!" *CQ Researcher.* 12, no. 10 (March 15, 2003): 233.

Spillane, Joseph. "The Making of an Underground Market: Drug Selling in Chicago, 1900-1940." *Journal Of Social History.* (1998): 27-47.

Statistical Abstract of the U.S.: 1997. "Law Enforcement, Courts and Prisons." U.S. Census Bureau. U.S. Commerce Dept., Washington, D.C.: U.S. Government Printing Office, 219-21. 1998.

Susman, Ralph. "Drug Abuse. Congress and the Fact-Finding Press." *American Academy of Political and Social Science* 417 (January 1975): 16-26.

Swift, Pamela. "Marijuana's Future: Keeping Up…With Youth." *Parade Magazine.* (November 2, 1975): 15.

Tyson, Ann Scott. "How Nation's Largest Gang Runs Its Drug Enterprise" *Christian Science Monitor* (July 15, 1996): 1, 10 & 11.

Widdison, Harold A., ed. *Annual Editions: Social Problems, 98/99.* Sluice Dick, Guilford, Conn.: Dushkin/McGraw-Hill, 1998.

Williams, Henry Smith. *Drug Addicts Are Human Beings.* Washington D.C.: Shaw Publishing Company, 1938.

Winick, Charles. "Drug Abuse." *Encyclopedia of Sociology,* (A-D) 516-19. New York: Macmillan, 1992.

Wisotsky, Steven. "The War on Drugs and Civil Liberties." *USA Today Magazine.* (July 1993): 17-21.

Worsnop, Richard L. "Privacy in the Workplace" *The CQ Researcher.* (November 19, 1993): 1021-41.

Yost, Pete. "Drug Abuse Plan's Aim: Reduce It 50%". New York: *Associated Press.* (1999): A-3.

Bibliography: Alcohol Addiction

Apsler, Robert. Is Drug Abuse Treatment Effective? *The American Enterprise* (March-April 1994): 48-52.

Ayres, B. Drummond, Jr. "Big Gains Are Seen in Battle to Stem Drunk Driving." *NewYork Times,(* May 22, 1994): 7.

Besharov, Douglas J., ed. *When Drug Addicts Have Children.* Washington, D.C.: Child Welfare League of America and American Enterprise Institute, 1994.

Borgatta, Edgar and Mamie Borgatta, eds. *Encyclopedia of Sociology, 1 (A-D), 41-8.* New York: Macmillan, 1992.

Butterfield, L.H. ed. *Letters of Benjamin Rush (1761-1792):* Princeton, New Jersey: Princeton University Press, 1951.

Centers for Disease Control. "Alcohol-related Mortality and Years of Potential Life Lost: United States, 1987." *Morbidity and Mortality Weekly Report 39(March 23, 1990): 3.*

Easley, Margaret and Norman Epstein. "Coping with Stress in a Family with an Alcoholic Parent." *Family Relations,* 40, (1991): 218-24.

Facts on File. Congress Approves Massive Transportation Bill. 58,3000 (June 4, 1998): 372.

————. *Highway Bill Corrections.* 58,3006 (July 16, 1998): 483.

Fingarette, Herbert. *Heavy Drinking: The Myth of Alcoholism as a Disease.* Berkeley: University of California Press, 1988.

Fort, Joel. *Alcohol: Our Biggest Drug Problem.* New York: McGraw-Hill, 1988.

Fort, Joel and Christopher Cory. *American Drugstore: A(Alcohol) to V(Valium).* Boston: Little Brown Company, 1975.

Glazer, Sarah. "Treating Addiction." *The CQ Researcher.* 5, no. 1 (January 6, 1995): 1-20.

Institute of Medicine. *Broadening the Base of Treatment for Alcohol Problems.* Washington, D.C.: Institute of Medicine, 1990.

Keller, M. "Classics of the Alcohol Literature." *Quarterly Journal of Studies on Alcohol.* 4 (1943-44): 325-41.

Kleber, Herbert D. "Our Current Approach to Drug Abuse—Progress, Problems, Proposals." *The New England Journal of Medicine. (*February *3, 1994): 361-65.*

Lauer, Robert H. *Social Problems and the Quality of Life.* 7th *Ed.* Chapter 4. New York: McGraw-Hill, 1998.

Leonard, K.E. and H.T. Blane. "Alcohol and Marital Aggression in a National Sampling of Gang Men." *Journal of Interpersonal Violence.* 7 (1992): 19-30.

Levinson, D. *Family Violence in Cross-Cultural Perspective.* Newbury Park, Calif.: Sage Publications, 1989.

Lewis, Jay S. "Congressional Rites of Passage for the Rights of Alcoholics." *Alcohol Health & Research World.* 12, no. 4 (1998) 240-51.

McAnemy, Leslie. "Number of Drinkers on the Rise Again." *Gallop Poll Monthly.* 317 (1992): 43-9.

McVeigh, Frank. "The Other Drug Problem Among Women and Elderly". *Sociological Viewpoints.* 5 (1990): 48-69.

Miles, Samuel A., ed. *Learning About Alcohol: A Resource Book for Teachers.* Washington, D.C. Association for Health, Physical Education and Recreation, 1974.

Mooney, Linda A., David Knox and Caroline Schacht. *Understanding Social Problems,* Chapter 3. St. Paul, Minn.: West Publishing Company, 1997.

National Institute on Alcohol Use and Alcoholism. "Alcohol and Trauma." Alcohol Alert, (January 1989): 1-4.

O'Malley, Patrick, Lloyd Johnston and Jerald G. Bachman. "Alcohol Use Among Adolescents." *Alcohol Health and Research World.* 22, no. 2 (1998): 85-93.

Plaut, Thomas F.A. *Cooperative Commission on the Study of Alcoholism. A Report to the Nation.* New York: Oxford University Press, 1967.

Reuter, Peter. "Patterns of Drug Use" Pp. 3-11 in *When Drug Addicts Have Children,* edited by Douglas J. Besharov. Washington, D.C.: Child Welfare League of America and American Enterprise Institute, 1994.

Scrivo, Karen Lee. "Drinking on Campus." *The CQ Researcher.* 8, no. 11 (1998): 243-60.

Special Reports to the U.S. Congress on Alcohol and Health. Second Special Report. U.S. Dept. of Health and Human Services. No. 75-9099. Washington, D.C.: U.S. Government Printing Office, 1974.

———. *Third Special Report.* U.S. Dept. of Health and Human Services. No. 79-9099. Washington, D.C. U.S. Government Printing Office, 1978.

Straus, Murray and S. Sweet. "Verbal Symbolic Aggression in Couples: Incidence Rates and Relationships to Personal Characteristics." *Journal of Marriage and the Family.* 54 (1992): 346-57.

Sullivan, Thomas and Kendrick S. Thompson. *Social Problems.* New York: Macmillan, 1994.

Tubman, J. "Family Risk Factors, Parental Alcohol Use and Problem Behavior Among School-Aged Children." *Family Relations.* 42 (1993): 81-6.

U.S. Department of Health and Human Services. *National Household Survey on Drug Abuse: Services Publication ADM-1995.* Washington, D.C.: U.S. Government Printing Office, 1995.

U.S. President's Commission on Law Enforcement and Adminstration of Justice. *Task Force on Drunkenness.* Washington, D.C.: U.S. Government Printing Office, 1967.

Weisman, Maxwell N. "Musings on the Art of Treatment." *Alcohol Health Research.* 12, no. 4 (1988): 282-87.

Witters, Weldon, Peter Venurelli, and Glenn Hanson. *Drugs and Society.* 3d ed. Boston: Jones & Bartlett, 1992.

Chapter 4

Changing Gender Roles

One of the first things children learn is whether they are girls or boys. Furthermore, at very young ages children can identify the socially expected roles that correspond to these statuses. However, as we have alluded to before, the social expectations surrounding these statuses have changed over time; and in this chapter we will discuss some of the social forces and normative conflicts relevant to the changing gender roles. To do so, let's look at the historical record more closely. As we mentioned, up to nearly the end of the Eighteenth Century, American women were subordinate to men –socially, economically, educationally, and politically. This subordination stems from, among other sources, cultural and religious beliefs. The Judeo-Christian religion, for example, depicts man as being made in God's image and women coming from men – therefore being secondary to men (Hutter, 1998). According to Hutter (1998), in medieval times women had a dual depiction – either as the temptress Eve, responsible for the fall of mankind, or the pure Virgin Mother Mary. Only nuns could really be the latter; hence, ordinary women were treated with suspicion. In order to prevent women from deceiving men a second time, religious based laws (remember, during the Medieval times there was little distinction between church and state) supported the control or subjugation of women by men. Furthermore, also keep in mind, that most of America during the 18th Century was Christian; therefore, its cultural values were also influenced by this religious tradition and practices. Consequently, both religion and law justified the subordination of women by men.

Today, we describe women as a "minority" – even though they are frequently the numerical majority in the population. This in itself reflects historical change as the term "minority" was not applied to women until the mid-Twentieth Century. During the mid-1900s sociologists began to note the similarities between the plight of women and African Americans. In 1944 Gunnar Myrdal, a Swedish sociologist, noted in his work *An American Dilemma* that the legal status of slaves stemmed from the legal status of women in the 17th Century in which women, children and slaves were all controlled by male heads of the family (Myrdal, 1944). Around the same time, in 1951, in recognition of women's subordinate social status, Helen Hacker first used the term "minority" to describe the social position of women.

These cultural beliefs about men and women, supported by a long-standing legal tradition, serve as the foundation behind many of the gender conflicts we will discuss in this chapter. These conflicts are:

1. The conflict over biological differences and gender roles
2. Conflict reflected in language
3. The conflict surrounding women in the workplace
4. Conflict regarding sexual behavior
5. The conflict over access to education
6. The conflict resulting from women's fight for change

The Conflict Over Biological Differences and Gender Roles

In the introductory paragraph to this chapter, we said that the subordination of women partially stems from religious and cultural beliefs. The key word here is "partially". Obviously, one can make the argument that the differences in gender roles stems from undeniable biological differences between men and women. For example, many men (although not all) are physically stronger than women and only women can (without the aid of advanced science) give birth to children. According to sociologist Stephen Goldberg, (1989), there is cultural evidence that the differences between men and women have to do more with nature (biology) than nurture (the environment in which one lives). He argues that since all known societies are patriarchal and that male roles in all societies have higher status (regardless of what those roles are – a point we will re-encounter shortly), then this must exist because males adjust their behavior to whatever is necessary to obtain dominance in any society. According to Goldberg, this universal behavior is explained by the innate biological differences between males and females. You may ask, what about the examples of women, such as Golda Mier in Israel and Margaret Thacher in England, who have obtained status and socially recognized high achievement? According to Goldberg, these are exceptions; and, given that we are discussing human behavior, exceptions are to be expected. However, Goldberg argues that exceptions are not enough to disprove his hypothesis (Goldberg, 1989). Hence, according to this perspective, social institutions and relations reflect inborn differences; they do not create these differences.

Even so, many sociologists generally maintain that our concept of gender roles is socially constructed. Why? Because the roles we associated with the biological sex of male and female vary cross-culturally, as do the relative importance of those roles. For example, George Murdock, who studied 324 different societies, found that what a group considered "men and women's work" varied for almost all occupations. While making weapons and hunting were frequently men's work, for example, there were exceptions. Likewise, sometimes care for cattle was men's work; sometimes it was women's. Sometimes women's roles focused on establishing physical beauty; sometimes, men's roles focused on this. The only role that was exclusively for men was metal working (Murdock, 1937). Furthermore, these social scientists argue that women are increasingly exhibiting other behaviors typically associated with men. For example, Epstein (1988) argues that the crime rate, a stereotypically aggressive behavior associated with men, is increasing among women. Furthermore, like men, women in power, such as Mier and Thatcher who we have recently mentioned, resorted to violence and force to deal with enemies. The notion that female leaders would find more peaceful solutions to conflict does not seem to be the case. Consequently, sociologists favoring this view argue that when social forces allow, women, like men, exhibit aggressive or competitive behavior. Therefore, there is not something inherently biological about the social order of gender roles. These theorists argue that while there are biological distinctions between men and women, they are only physically relevant in a few instances that involve issues of physical strength and child birth. Hence gender roles and behaviors emerge from *perceptions* of sex differences. In response to the claim that "exceptions" like female world leaders do not in and of themselves make a rule, the proponents of the cultural perspective would argue that as more social opportunities for female power and control appear, these "exceptions" will become less unique and more obvious.

The traditional mother's role

The debate of nature vs. nurture continues. So how does this relate to our historical look at gender roles? As we mentioned at the beginning of the chapter, subordination of women by men was historically supported by the Judeo-Christian religion. During the industrial revolution, with the advent of the doctrine of separate spheres that we will discussed in Chapter 7, women's subordination became less based on religious doctrine, and more so on their association with the emotional work of raising children and running a home. This separated women from economic production. With the industrial revolution, women became stereotyped as emotional, dependent and weak; whereas, men were logical, independent and strong. Consequently, men believed that women did not have the temperament for more male pursuits like paid employment or higher education.

Given the long history that associated women with child care and men with economic production, it is no wonder that even today elements of these traditional concepts remain in our Gesellschaft, specialized society. Studies suggest that parents are still more tolerant of aggressive, dirty and defiant play among boys than among girls

(Henslin, 1999). These behaviors are consistent with the aggression and competitiveness stereotypically associated with being a man. Likewise, mothers touch, speak to and keep physically closer to their girls – behavior that is consistent with the more emotional dependence stereotypically associated with femininity.

**In spite of changing gender roles, little girls are
usually socialized to marry**

When we discuss changes in gender roles, we generally are really recognizing the move of women into traditional male roles more so than males into traditionally female roles. We talk about women becoming more involved in the labor force, women entering nontraditional occupations like being a doctor, or women getting advanced degrees. Parents tell young girls that they can be anything they want. Yet, we hear very little about men becoming househusbands, or men entering nontraditional occupations like nursing. The message is that it is okay for girls to pursue male interests; but, not for boys to pursue female interests.

This rather one-sided change reflects conflict over power. Moving into traditionally male- dominated areas is associated with increased wealth, status and power; and, therefore, is considered "improvements" in status. On the other hand, moving into traditionally female roles illustrate greater dependence, less status and less prestige. Furthermore, when men do try to break gender roles, their behavior is frequently viewed with skepticism or disapproval by others. Househusbands featured in an issue of *Fortune* magazine report that other adults frequently treat them with suspicion for their decision to remain at home (Morris, 2002). Other mothers reject these fathers under the premise that they are not successful "mothers" because of the assumption that these fathers cannot nurture children like women can; other fathers reject them for being willing to let their wives support the family, thereby forgoing their traditional male status as "breadwinners". In similar articles appearing in *Time* and *People* magazines, other househusbands report similar reactions to their role reversal.

However, the fact that these magazines had enough information for three different articles, does illustrate that change is occurring, albeit slowly. Consequently the fact remains that traditional concepts of gender roles continue to fuel the discrimination and institutional conflict we will discuss in the rest of this chapter. But before we do that, let's briefly examine how gender inequality is reflected in such a daily experience as language.

Conflict Reflected in Language

Language even reflects the subordinate status of women relative to men. Everyday language serves to show women as possessions and can be used to demean individuals (most notably boys and men). However, men are not the only culprits. The way women and men *both* interact when speaking also subtly reinforces the concept of women's inferiority.

Let's first discuss how language is used to show possession. A young unmarried woman has her father's last name; when this same woman marries, she will traditionally take the name of her husband. In both instances, a woman is either the possession of her father or her husband and her name reflects this. For boys, one can argue that their last name is also the name of their father and, therefore shows possession; but, when the boys marry, they don't change their name. Their father's name becomes "theirs" as a representative of a family name.

Second, think about what boys call other boys when they want to tease, pick on or diminish them. Expressions such as "You throw like a girl" or "Sissy" or "Mamma's boy" are all references to women meant to demean others. This behavior isn't restricted to children, however. Sam Stouffer argues in *American Soldier* that during World War II officers used feminized terms to insult, and therefore, motivate soldiers. Other research found that similar behavior occurred among soldiers during the Vietnam war as well (Eisenhart, 1975; Gilham, 1989).

However, as we said, these gender differences, and the corresponding messages about power, are reproduced in daily language patterns by *both* men and women. For example, in conversation, men are more likely to interrupt others – a subtle symbol that they are trying to control the direction of the conversation (Tannen, 1990). Likewise, in conversation, women are more likely to use disclaimers such as "It's only my opinion, but..." or "That play was good, *wasn't it*?" (Sapiro, 1994). Such behaviors give the impression that women are looking for agreement or approval from their conversation partner – a symbolic sign of subservience. Lastly, women are more polite in conversation and tend to talk less while men are less polite and talk more (Tannen, 1990).

So what you may ask? Language, you may argue, is not going to deny a woman job opportunities or be the sole culprit in creating low self-esteem among women. You're probably right. However, our speech patterns are subtle symbolic indicators that men and women still occupy different social positions. Why care? Because these subtle messages are perhaps the hardest to change *because* they are so subtle and are, therefore, the hardest to detect. Subtle messages over a long span of time *can* affect behavior in that these messages become so ingrained as to be thought of as normative.

The Conflict Between Women and The Workplace

In the family chapter we discussed that women and men worked side by side. However, not all women worked with their husbands. Women who were not involved in the agrarian economy were frequently involved in the domestic or business economy. For example, during the Colonial era, many women paid for their passage from England by indenturing themselves as domestic servants. Wages were low during the years of indentured servitude and once completed, the women only received a limited amount of clothes and money as a start for their new life. Consequently, domestic service during the Colonial era was relatively low status (Weiner, 1985). However, as the nation entered the 19th Century and more families acquired wealth, the demand for domestic labor increased. This increased demand, coupled with a strong moral code at the time in which workers (including single women) avoid the "sin" of idleness, slowly improved the status of domestic servants (Weiner, 1985). It wasn't until the mid-1800s when *other* immigrants began to compete for domestic work in earnest that the resulting conflicts led back to a decrease in the professions' prestige, which we will discuss in a moment.

In the "new world," domestic work was not the only professional outlet for respectable women. While women were still generally thought of as inferior to men, pressing labor shortages made it necessary for women to participate in the marketplace as economic helpmates for their husbands. The high mortality rates, cultural ambiguity over roles in a new frontier environment, and the shortage of skilled workers in a new world created opportunities for women, at least widows, to become involved independently in the marketplace. Consequently, while it is unclear as to the actual number of women who owned independent businesses during the Colonial era, according to Brownlee and Brownlee (1976), these numbers (as a proportion of the urban labor force) are likely to be higher than previously thought and higher than the proportion during the next century.

A key point to keep in mind regarding early women's employment is that, in the Colonial era, *independent* women's employment was restricted to widows and lower income single women. Otherwise, women worked in business side by side with their husbands. By the mid-1800s this had not changed. However, the nature of women's work did. As factory work expanded, more workers were needed to run the machines – and factories expanded quickly. In 1820 only about 12,000 people worked in factories; as little as 30 years later this number grew to 100,000 people (Kava, 1994). However, there was still a reluctance to hire married women – especially since the separate spheres phenomena we discussed in Chapter 4 was beginning to take root – so, once again, unmarried women were the employees of choice – especially since they could be paid wages that were one third what male workers would expect to make (Kava, 1994).

However, just because there was factory work available to single women, didn't mean that single women flocked to these positions. In the early 19th Century, the popular writings of Catherine Beecher, such as her book *The Evils Suffered by American Women and Children: The Causes and the Remedy*, reinforced the doctrine of separate spheres for married women by not only providing practical household advice, but explaining it in a context of the political and economic changes of the time. This made caring for children and the home instead of participation in the paid labor force seem like a natural extension of social forces and therefore *right* (Edwards, 2001). Beecher especially wove the political and economic nature of the times into the argument that domestic jobs were in line with women's innate nature, further reinforcing the fit between women, children and the home. Beecher argued that both the home and public spheres were of equal importance because both were mutually dependent upon the other. Men could not successfully compete in the paid economy if they had to worry about running their households and raising their children; conversely, women wouldn't be able to focus their attention on children and the home if they had to worry about the economic survival of their family (Edwards, 2001). This belief is still accepted by some people today, since many women only work part time. Unfortunately, as we will see, even though Beecher argued that these two spheres should be treated equally, they were in fact, not.

Furthermore, a vocal minority of women disagreed with Beecher's ideas and the doctrine of separate spheres. Elizabeth Cady Stanton and Susan B. Anthony are two examples. These women focused on the similarities between men and women in an attempt to bring women into the paid labor force, thereby, giving them some economic power (Edwards, 2001). Furthermore, male academics like Karl Marx also disagreed. Marx argued that capitalism weakened the home economy as people no longer produced their own goods and instead worked for wages. By not producing goods, the home became less important to the economic survival of the family and those associated with the home, namely women, lost power and status as a result. According to Marx, the home became a separate realm of reproduction and consumption – frivolous pursuits compared to economic survival (Edwards, 2001). Yet in a mass, Gesellschaft, society such as the one today, consumption has become a crucial and critical function for economic prosperity. On the other hand, Hewitt (1985) argues that the separate spheres, instead of alienating, worked to make men and women mutually dependent upon each other.

Furthermore, even if some women did reject the doctrine of separate spheres, remember, America was largely rural at this time and cities were just beginning to grow in size and number. Consequently, working in factories frequently involved being away from home; and, parents were uncomfortable with their unmarried daughters living away from the family homestead. To address this cultural concern, Francis Lowell from Massachusetts was the first factory owner to try to make mill work (which is what factory work was called) acceptable by creating a boardinghouse plan in which the young women would live in boardinghouses owned by the company and run by older women (Kava, 1994).

Even though employers like Lowell tried to make the idea of mill work more palatable to the parents of these young ladies, it would be irresponsible to glorify the work that these women did. Mill work was harsh. These women would frequently work 12-13 hours a day for six days a week only earning $1.25 for room and board and $.55 for salary (Kava, 1994). These low wages were not a mistake. Women's wages were lower than men's because the only way women could compete with men for jobs was to work for less pay, otherwise cultural biases would have continued to make men more attractive employees (Brownlee and Brownlee, 1976). In addition to being lowly paid, mill work was also dangerous as the buildings were poorly lit (making it hard to see the machinery clearly), they had low ceilings that impeded ventilation and had no means of temperature control so rooms were hot in the summer and extremely cold in the winter.

Consequently, it is not surprising lower income women were the ones willing to work in factories (or even in domestic work for that matter). Thanks to the development of the separate spheres and the inhospitable conditions of the factories, women's work was beyond the respectability of the middle class (Weiner, 1985). Even so, as we mentioned a few paragraphs ago, this type of work was less stigmatized and was considered more respectable at this time in history than it was later. During the early 1800s, the women who were working in mills and in domestic services were "American" girls – women who had families entrenched in rural communities, who were from similar backgrounds (at least based on country of origin) as their employers, and who participated in the communities in which their employers lived. As more immigrant women began working in these industries, conflicts between the "old" and "new" Americans arose. New immigrant women were willing to work for less money than were the more established "old" immigrants and this served to decrease the respectability of these occupations. As the wages and respectability decreased, so did the proportion of non-immigrant women participating in these industries, leading domestics and mill work to be less desirable occupations overall (Rutz, 1994; Weiner, 1985).

By the time of the Civil War, in the 1860s, working women were more stigmatized than in the 18th Century. With the growing middle class and increased labor force participation of "new" immigrants the idea that "respectable women" did not work continued to grow. However, just like we will see later with World War I and World War II, the conflict of war – here the American Civil War - temporarily opened the doors of employment to women – even the middle class – as women worked as nurses, spies, cooks, and office help (Kava, 1994).

Women still select mostly female roles and occupations

However, as with World War II, women's employment was not necessarily by choice. These women were working to support their families while their husbands were away fighting; and, they were not earning much. According to Kava (1994), a New York City commission found that in the 1860's, women were trying to support families on as little as 12.5 cents (not dollars, but *cents!)* a day.

The numbers of wage-earning women continued to climb in the postbellum years (Weiner, 1985). While the majority of female workers at this time were still young, unmarried and lived at home, an increasing proportion *did* live alone in the cities. Why this change? According to Weiner (1985), the continual influx of immigrants, delayed marital patterns and changing age structures interacted with changing economic and cultural factors to create a large supply of young single women who were attracted to work away from rural homes and domestic occupations. During the late 1800s women were still marrying later (about age 25) than they did in the early 20th Century (Weiner, 1985). Second, young single women migrated at earlier ages and faster rates to the cities than did their male counterparts. Third by the turn of the Century, agricultural technology minimized the need for female labor on farms, whereas factory work provided new opportunities – making factories and city living attractive alternatives to young, single, rural women (Weiner, 1985). However, it is important to remember that these opportunities opened to *single* women; married women received much more prestige and respect by taking care of their family and home even though they received no money.

After the Civil War, the nation suffered a Depression much like the one we hear about from the 1930s where there was high unemployment. During this time there was a persistent tendency to downplay the need for women's labor force participation because the cultural attitude was that working women took jobs away from men who had to feed their families. Now, before you ask why a woman wouldn't be seen as "feeding her family", remember that during this time, the doctrine of separate spheres was still alive. Many employers felt that women were working for luxuries, while men were working to provide food and shelter for their families (Weiner, 1994). Consequently, women earned less than men and in periods of economic conflict were the first to lose their jobs to men. What employers overlooked, however, was that many working women were *not* working for luxuries, but instead were working to support children or supplement their husband's earnings in order to provide food and shelter – much like today. However, as a result of this Depression and the cultural ideology that treated women's employment as frivolous, women's employment became even more marginalized. The few instances of occupations still open to women – mill work and the food industry – were related to the "traditional" roles of women in the home (thereby subtly reinforcing the idea that this is where women "belonged"), were paid very little, were considered unskilled and did not generally offer benefits. Even in the food industry – a role primarily thought to involve "women's work" of cooking, the men did the cooking and the women were relegated to the low skilled jobs of preparing the fruit or vegetables for cooking and waitressing (Kava, 1994).

By the time the 19th Century Depression ended, women who wanted to work, but who wanted more respectability than was offered in domestic and factory work looked to other opportunities for employment. By the 1900s, these new types of jobs were in the service economy. The emerging service economy did not involve outright manual labor, but instead involved clerical skills (especially typing), work in stores, teaching and nursing (Kava, 1994). Because these jobs required a certain level of interpersonal skills or training, they were considered to be more genteel and, therefore, acceptable, than the more traditional avenues of service work. This shift in occupational focus was facilitated by the increasing educational attainment of women at this time. By the late 1800s not only were women increasingly finishing high school, but they were increasingly going on to college, as we will discuss in the next section. This increased educational training served to open the doors to new occupational opportunities. Consequently, as time went on, the menial and marginalized jobs of domestics and mill work became overpopulated by minority and poor women. Middle-class women were in a better position to improve their occupational opportunities due to changes in women's education and the economic move to more service-oriented, white collar work (Edwards, 2001)

However women still had to compete with men for these positions, which led to conflict. Conflict here involved conflict over the image of respectable women, but more concretely it involved conflict over money and power. As with factory work, women only managed to compete in the service economy because they were willing to work for less money (Brownlee and Brownlee, 1976). But women's economic "bargain" was not enough; they had to prove themselves competent in a man's world because for most of the 19th Century, prior to the typewriter, men served as private secretaries in industry. The *Business Women's Journal* was an influential magazine catering to this new group of women. It published job opportunities for women and encouraged women to compete with men for these clerical positions by obtaining office skills and by teaching women how to present oneself in business. The goal of this journal was to help women elevate their employment positions from the lower paid, less respected traditionally female occupations of the time to the higher paid, more respectable positions available in the new emerging service economy (Brownlee and Brownlee, 1976).

The real change in women's labor force participation in the 20th Century was the addition of married women, and around the 1960's married women with children, to the labor force. In 1900 only 15% of female workers were married while 67% were unmarried (Weiner, 1985); by 2002 over half of all employed women were married (U.S. Bureau of Labor Statistics, 2002). The reason behind married women's employment also changed. Prior to the early 1900s, married women worked primarily out of economic necessity; their wages were necessary for the survival of their families. As we mentioned numerous times, women were also generally reluctant to work outside the home for pay because the doctrine of separate spheres and employer attitudes led to a loss of social status for working wives. These cultural attitudes also led women to participate only in the most menial of jobs that also provided flexibility for their family chores.

However, even in the early 20th Century, a noticeable minority of wives were working not for absolute need, as described above, but for relative need instead. In other words, in the beginning of the 1900s we see the first stirrings of women who worked not because of dire necessity, but instead to increase the resources available to their families so they could move up the social class ladder. A 1918 survey in Philadelphia found that 18% of mothers who worked in industry reported working to build family savings or afford a vacation (Hughes, 1925). This trend is supported by Census data of the time (U.S. Census Bureau, 1929). These reasons aren't very different than why many mothers work today!

One cannot ignore the influence of World Wars I and II on shaping women's work experiences for the latter half of the 20th Century. For example, between 1940 and 1945 over 6 million women, three quarters of them married, entered the labor force for the first time (Chafe, 1972). This was much higher than the proportion of women who entered the labor force during World War I (Chafe, 1972). Many of these women were forced to leave the labor force after the war, when men returned and wanted to claim their original jobs; many others stayed and took advantage of the expanding economy to obtain economic freedom and independence. Consequently, World War II gave many married women a taste of the independence, stimulation and social interaction of paid employment – and many women found that they *liked* these opportunities. It gave them a new alternative to staying in an unhappy marriage – as we discussed in the family chapter.

Consequently, each decade from 1940 to 1970 saw an increase in the labor force participation rate of 28% for married women (Weiner, 1985). According to Weiner (1985), this change is due less to economic issues than it is to a shift in cultural values. Weiner argues that during this period, wage work began to be valued as highly as work within the home. Furthermore, other social changes such as a decrease in single women, a decrease in fertility and an increase in women's educational attainment led to a greater societal acceptance of the employment of married women. During this time, technological changes and decreased fertility meant that women spent less time caring for children or the home in the mid-20th Century than they did in the past. Their higher levels of education meant that they were more skilled to compete with men in the labor force and were less willing to devote their entire time to a home economy that, overall, required less time to begin with. Furthermore, during this time, the weekly hours of work decreased for both men and women, making work even *more* attractive to married women. Lastly, during this time, the demand for white collar, service work began to increase and this type of work was especially attractive to women.

Women's labor force participation rate continued to increase past the 1960s. In fact, this rate has increased over 20 percentage points from 37.7% in 1960 to 60.2% in 2001 (SAUS 1998; U.S. Department of Labor, 2003), even though it has leveled off a bit since the late 1990s. During the same time the male-participation rate has dropped 11.5 percentage points, from 89.2 in 1960 to 77.7 in 1997. This was due to early retirement options before age 65 or pursuit of higher education in earlier ages.

The last large shift in the experience of working women during that 20th Century was the increase in working mothers, especially those with young children. In 1976 only 31% of women with infants under age one were in the labor force; by 1998 this percentage jumped to 59% (United States Bureau of the Census, 2000). Only 3.3% of such women worked in 1975; by 1985 over 50% worked and by 1997 some 61% of women with children under 3 held jobs. About one in four (25%) working women work part time (Heslop, 1997:162). This trend clearly shows how the sole role of motherhood for most women has been diversified to include the role of employee as well.

Furthermore, occupational segregation has decreased as more women enter traditionally male jobs such as doctor, accountant and lawyer (Statistical Abstracts, 1998). The changing role of women will become even more pronounced in the future as younger, career-oriented women replace older homemakers in society. For example, women make up 50.4% of all managerial / professional specialties, 42.7% of all college / university teachers and 29.2% of all attorneys and judges (Bureau of Labor Statistics, 2002). However, occupational segregation is still present in some fields. The majority of secretaries / stenographers / typists are still women (97%) as are the majority of elementary/secondary teachers (75.1%) (Bureau of Labor Statistics, 2002). Consequently, while women have come a long way over the past 200 years, there is still room for improvement. Even within medicine and law, women disproportionately chose to specialize in family medicine and domestic civil law.

Now more than any time in the past, women seek fulfillment and identity from work, and not family roles alone. However, as with the other changes in women's labor force participation, this one was fraught with conflict. The concept of separate spheres has not entirely gone and many feel that mothers, especially of young children, belong in the home and not in the workplace. Consequently, much like in the past, women still earn less than men, regardless of the level of education, are still less likely to be in professional or managerial occupations than men, contribute more hours to the home economy and child care even if they have a full time job, and often experience a glass ceiling in employment (Statistical Abstracts, 1998; Hochschild, 1989, Klein, 1998).

For example, as Figure 4-1 shows the gap in median earnings

**Figure 4-1: Median Income by Sex for all Races
1947-2001 in 2001 Dollars**

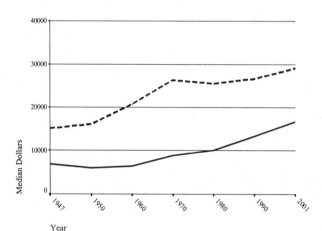

----- Men   _____ Women

U.S. Bureau of the Census, 2002. Table P-2. Race and Hispanic Origin of People by Median Income and Sex: 1947-2001. Historical Income Tables. (People 15 years and over beginning with March 1980, and people 14 years and over as of March of the following year for previous years. Data is presented for all races.

between men and women has closed little over the past 50 years. In 1947 the median earnings for all women (in 2001 dollars) was $6,845 compared to $15,010 for men, meaning that women earned 45.6% of what men earned. By 2001 women earned 57.1% of what men earned. The median income of all women in 2001 was $16,614 and for men it was $29,101.

So what does this all mean? Optimists can argue that changing over 200 years of gender role ideology takes time and that any change is good news. Pessimists, on the other hand, could argue that the rate of change is too slow and labor inequality reflects that we are still a patriarchal society that is organized by men for the benefit of men. Sociologists who agree with this view argue that making women's labor force experience unrewarding, discourages women from working which will increase their dependence on men – which, in turn, would increase men's power in the family and society. With more mothers working, child care and changing family roles have become even more important issues.

Women's Employment and Child Care

Since we are discussing women's work and family roles here, it is appropriate to examine the conflicts of working mothers in more detail since the tension around working mothers reflects both the conflict between women and employment and the conflict in gender roles that have been present over the past 200 years.

The need for affordable and available child care has become apparent. A new Council of Economic Advisers Report found that "the average time parents and children spend together has decreased by 22 hours a week in the past 30 years" (Cummings, 1999: a-32). Consequently, about 13 million children under 6 whose mothers work-- including 6 million infants and toddlers--are cared for by someone other than their parents (Scrivo, 1998). According to the U.S. Census Bureau, 51% of those children are cared for by day-care centers, preschool or other providers. The rest are cared for by the father or relatives. Some 16% are cared for by their grandparents. About 4 million children under 18 (52%) live in the household of their grandparents (Lugaila, 1998).

Working mothers' dependence on child care has become problematic due to the low availability of affordable, high quality non-maternal care. Many child care experts say the supply of licensed care givers has not kept up with society's demand, especially for infants, toddlers and school-age children. Parents, especially single working women, who work nights and/or weekends, those whose regular care giver is unavailable or whose child is sick or live in rural and inner-city areas, often have trouble finding care givers. In California, for example, a recent study found that just 4% of the child care centers are licensed to serve toddlers or infants under age 2. Only 2% of that state's centers were open on weekends, evenings or overnight. (Scrivo, 1998).

While child care is a major expense costing up to $10,000 a year per child, more than the cost of tuition at many public universities, about half of all American families with children earn less than $35,000 a year (Children's Defense Fund, 1998). Even so, "child-care workers are in the lowest tenth of all wage earners and they have a turnover rate of 41% per year at an average day care center" (Etzioni, 1993: 57).

Furthermore, the quality of care for children with others is also questionable. Some 60 percent of parents' out-of home care, and 50 percent of parents using an in-home provider, reported having had a bad experience with the kind of care their child received that they discontinued that particular arrangement (Children's Defense Fund, 1998:1-2). Yet as David Elkind observes, "Child care by paid professionals is rapidly becoming the national norm as large numbers of women with children enter the full-time work force" (1994:3). Children require a commitment of time, energy, and attention. Quality child rearing takes time.

The plight of working mothers illustrates the clash between historical and modern ideals. The family values supporters, as James Q. Wilson points out, argue that what is needed is to "...stress the overriding importance of two-parent families that make child care their central responsibility" (1993:31). This also implies that working parents should give the vocation of parenthood priority over careers (Fillingin, 1995:80). Yet, there is consumerism. How much more do we value material goods rather than valuing children? We even calculate the economic costs of having and rearing a child, rather than the psychic income children might mean to us. As Fillingin writes: "Western consumerism promotes self-indulgence rather than self-mastery. The ideal person is assumed to be responsible only for and to himself. This is particularly damaging to the family, where responsibility for and to others is required" (1995:78). Consumerism dominates our values and overshadows whatever value we place on children in our society. One group that questions changing gender roles in the family states that "...bringing children into the world entails a moral responsibility to provide not only material necessities but also moral education and character formation." It adds that such education "...is not a task that can be delegated to baby-sitters or even professional child care centers" (Etzioni, 1993:256-57).

Conflict Regarding Sexual Behavior

Using sex as a means of exhibiting power is not new. What *is* new is defining such behavior as a social problem instead of a personal problem. For much of history, any sexually violent actions against women were seen as either men's "right" or "due", and therefore, not problematic, or were thought to be brought on by women's actions, and therefore, women's "fault". In this section we will examine two conflicts involving sexual behavior: sexual harassment and rape.

<u>Sexual Harassment</u>

While women can (and increasingly are) holding power positions, women are still more likely to be the victims, instead of perpetrators, of sexual harassment. In 2002, U.S. Equal Employment Opportunity Commission received 14,396 charges of sexual harassment and 85.1% of them were filed by women (U.S. Equal Employment Opportunity Commission, 2002). There are two types of sexual harassment. The form most commonly known is *quid pro quo* which implies one behavior in exchange for another – here sexual favors in return for a promotion, keeping one's job, a raise, etc. Because this form implies the granting of a favor, it assumes that one person is in a position of authority to grant a favor (the employer), provided the subordinate person (here an employee) provides a favor in return (here sexual). The second form of harassment, which has been recognized as such only relatively recently by the Equal Employment Opportunity Commission, is the existence of a hostile work environment which causes discomfort in the workplace. This second form does not necessarily involve a power differential and, therefore, any employee is a potential culprit. Furthermore, this second form of sexual harassment is vague; *any* behavior deemed unwanted can fit the criteria as creating a "hostile work environment". In fact, Hayes (1991) presents an example of where a woman who was *not* asked for sexual favors was ruled to be a victim of sexual harassment.

Sexual harassment as a social issue gained greater attention in 1991 when Anita Hill testified against Clarence Thomas in his Senate Judiciary Committee confirmation hearings. During the hearings, Hill claimed that Thomas repeatedly committed sexual harassment against her; and, even though he was still elected to the U.S. Supreme Court, Hill's testimony brought public awareness to the problem of sexual harassment. According to Gross (1992), the number of workplace harassment claims increased by more than 50% in the six months following the hearing. However, some sociologists argue that the majority of cases still go unreported. Giuffre and Williams (1994) argue that women are still reluctant to report instances of sexual harassment because they fear that they will not be believed or because, especially when discussing a "hostile work environment", they are unsure when a co-worker's behavior is joking (albeit perhaps inappropriately) or purposely harassing.

Tied to the last point, it is difficult to prove sexual harassment claims. Cases frequently come to a "He said; she said" scenario and whether an environment is "hostile" is very subjective. Nonetheless, some landmark cases have led companies to take note; but as expected in a Gesellschaft society, it took the involvement of the Courts to get companies to address this issue. For example, in 1998, 300 women from the Mitsubishi Motors plant in Illinois claimed that male co-workers continually groped them and that they had no support from management when they tried to complain. As a group, the women were awarded $34 million and other companies took note. Now companies frequently have seminars and information sessions educating workers about example of sexually harassing behaviors.

So sexual harassment is a source of conflict between men and women that does not need to involve a direct power differential. However, proving the existence of this type of conflict remains challenging. It is easier for companies to try to educate their employees to prevent conflict such as this than it is to deal with a law suit stemming from this conflict. Furthermore, as more women gain power positions, men are increasingly becoming victims of sexual harassment (Carton, 1994). In 1992, only 9.1% of all sexual harassment charges were filed by men; ten years later this increased to 14.9% (U.S. Equal Employment Opportunity Commission, 2002). This observation supports the cultural explanation for gender differences that we discussed earlier in this chapter. Given the same social opportunities, the behavior of women – both good and bad - is not necessarily all that different than the behavior of men.

Rape
        In 2001, 62.2 per 100,000 women in the United States were victims of forcible rape; and preliminary data for 2002 suggests that this figure increased by 4% the following year (U.S. Department of Justice, 2002; 2003). Traditionally, the female victim would be blamed for the rape. Under this ideology, women are raped because they "asked for it" by dressing provocatively or acting flirtatious, triggering men's overwhelming sex drives. If women restricted their behavior

and acted "chaste" then men would not have to deal with their overwhelming sexual urges and women would not be raped. This argument weakens when one realizes that rape victims are not just young, attractive or flirtatious individuals. Elderly women and young children are also raped.

Shifting the focus of rape from women's fault, an individual issue, to a consequence of men and women's unequal social position, hence a social issue, began in the 1960s and 1970s as part of the Women's Movement. During the Women's Movement, feminists argued that rape was a means for men to establish dominance over women. The observation that many rapes involve beatings, even if women submit, serves as tangential evidence for this view. Other evidence includes the instances of when soldiers rape women after conquering the enemy during war. One would be hard pressed to provide a convincing argument that these soldiers' behavior stems from men's sexual urges. Furthermore, rape is frequently planned rather than spur of the moment in response to an overwhelming sexual desire.

Feminists also argue that the power struggles that lead to rape can be subtle and stem from the messages of gender socialization. For example, from childhood men are taught that aggression, power and dominance are associated with masculinity and passivity, inferiority and submissiveness are associated with femininity (Scully and Marolla, 1999). Hence to be "manly" is to exert control over one's environment –which includes one's interactions with others, especially women. Furthermore, despite the slogan "No means No", many components of popular culture like movies, television and songs suggest that this is not the case and that women really *do* want sex, but are socialized to say "no" because "good girls" do not willingly have sex or they need to be coaxed into it (Finkelhor and Yllo, 1989). Taken together, these messages create a "rape culture" which leads some men to believe that sex is their "right", that women exist for their pleasure or that the women they are having sex with "really want it" regardless of what they say, so the sex isn't rape…even though many laws now recognize that it is.

The Conflict Over Access To Education

During Colonial times, as we would expect in a Gemeinschaft society, most children received their education from their parents – fathers primarily taught sons and mothers taught daughters. This was possible because, as also mentioned previously, the home was the center of economic production and both parents were physically

available to educate children.   However even though women were
involved in the economy during Colonial times, as we discussed, and
enjoyed a certain level of independence as a result, that does not imply
that men and women were treated or thought to be equal.   During this
time, women were thought to be intellectually inferior to men and to
physically lack the stamina necessary for higher mental thinking.
Therefore, sons learned reading, writing, arithmetic and how to run the
family farm.   Daughters learned only the most rudimentary reading,
writing and arithmetic skills and instead focused on learning cooking,
needlework and child care.   Given the somewhat practical nature of
education and the availability of both parents for teaching, there was
little need for formal education as we know it.   Consequently, only the
very wealthy families bothered with any level of education (usually in
the form of private tutors) for their daughters (Tiball, Smith, Tiball and
Wolf-Wendel, 1999; Faragher and Howe, 1988; Newcomer, 1959).

      One exception to this cultural rule was the Moravians.   The
Moravians established schools that tried to enrich the mental, spiritual
and social development of their children in family-like settings.   In
these schools, children lived away from their parents in sex-segregated
housing; however, the academic experiences were divided by academic
ability, not sex.   Consequently, both Moravian boys and girls learned
English, German, geography, gardening and household chores in
addition to the standard topics of education (e.g. reading, writing and
arithmetic).   In response to wide social support and recognition for the
level of education they provided to women, in 1785 Moravian schools
began accepting women of any faith, not just Moravian (Haller, 1953).
Other avenues for women's education, such as Quaker schools and
New England summer schools for girls, followed (Faragher and Howe,
1988).

      However, schools like the Moravian program were rare; and,
it was not until 50 years later the next educational step for women was
made when Mary Lyon began Mount Holyoke school in New England.
Mount Holyoke, however, did not receive the same support as the
Moravian schools and Lyon had a much harder time trying to
encourage others, most notably men, to devote funds to an all women's
school.   Eventually, Lyons was able to start the school with 80 women
in its first class.   The three-year curriculum focused on college-level
courses and the attending women were responsible for contributing to
the daily functioning of the school.   This latter component served to
sooth the impression that women didn't have the stamina for academic
work.   By incorporating physical endeavors and physical education,

Mount Holyoke was able to give the impression that its curriculum was working to overcome the innate frailty of women. Such physical endeavors, however, were not required at all male schools like Yale and Harvard (Tidbell, et.al., 1999).

According to Tidbell and colleagues (1999) the women's colleges that originated during this time and persevered to the present day shared six characteristics. These characteristics are:

1. Involving the total collegiate environment in the education of women
2. Making study in all fields, including those traditionally only available to men, available to women
3. Providing ample female role models
4. Involving networking
5. Creating an atmosphere that fostered deep and lasting friendships among women
6. Encouraging the generosity of women on behalf of others   (Tidbell, et.al., 1999: 10)

However, not all avenues of higher education for women were limited to exclusively female colleges. Frontier expansion and the usefulness women exhibited during this time served to, at least temporarily, break down the stereotypes of women as fragile and incapable of higher thinking. This paved the way for their admission into institutions of higher learning which was still, at least for women, primarily reserved for the wealthy only.

However, as in the economic institution, as the involvement of men in education decreased (largely due to increased work opportunities in a newly industrializing society), acceptance of women into these institutions increased. In search of tuition dollars, schools began accepting women when, for various reasons, men were not as vigorously applying (Tidbell, et.al., 1999). Consequently, by 1869, 41% of all collegiate institutions were open to women even if women were not frequently enrolled and even if women were primarily in curriculums that focused on fostering feminine values and characteristics (Tidbell, et. al, 1999). For example, women's curricula frequently included topics such as needlework, cooking, and women's history. In fact, the reasons for educating women focused on religious self-appraisal (fundamental in the Calvinist teachings of the day), preparation for teaching one's children (thereby fulfilling traditional family expectations) and self-indulgence. The first two were socially acceptable; the third was generally not (Faragher and Howe, 1988).

By today's standards the curricula of higher education would be considered somewhat simplistic in their scope (Faragher and Howe, 1988). Nonetheless, this approach served to pave the way for future possibilities and opportunities for women because the curricula did not deviate from the prevailing cultural values which would have discouraged and alienated women (and, more realistically their paying parents) from obtaining a college degree. In fact, according to Faragher and Howe (1988), having some educational background served as a means of distinguishing woman eligible for an upwardly mobile marriage.

By the end of the 19th Century, collegiate education became so popular for women that between 1875-1900 women's enrollment increased six fold – much faster than that of the overall student population (Dexter, 1906). More women, however, also meant more potential conflict as men became concerned that college curriculums would be dominated by females. Consequently, during this time, some colleges established majors that would more certainly cater to male interests over female interests (like engineering) and others established quotas that limited the number of women admitted (Tidbell, et.al., 1999). Therefore, even though women were increasingly entering college, men and women's curriculum was very sex segregated. This sex segregation influenced the economic institution to such a degree that the conflict resulting from this practice is still evident over 100 years later, as we discussed in the previous section. On the other hand, Oberlin College was the first college to grant degrees in *any* major to both men and women – even though the majority of women continued to pursue the traditionally female curricula (Tidbell, et.al., 1999). Even here, however, men and women had clearly different experiences. At Oberlin, female coeds were expected to do the men's laundry and to clean their room; the men, however, did not have similar responsibilities towards their female coeds (Flexner, 1972). During the 1950s, women's education took a few steps backwards as the growth of science and technology (symbolized by our competition with Russia over space exploration and Sputnik) tipped the scales of social payoffs to men – those who traditionally enrolled in the science and technology curricula. Therefore, while education for women continued to gain social acceptance, the social rewards were geared to men and male endeavors (Tidbell, et.al., 1999). For example, in 1960 women received only 6% of medical degrees, 4% of MBA and 2% of law degrees – degrees that generally lead to higher paid occupations (Bianci and Spain, 1996) By 2000, women received approximately 45% of medical degrees, 38% of all MBA degrees and 41% of legal degrees (Digest of Educational Statistics, 2001).

Conflict theorists wouldn't be surprised. They content that the real purpose of our education system is to reinforce the status quo – not challenge it; and, they also would argue that even given the changes in conferred degrees noted above, education *still* serves to reinforce traditional gender roles.

Their evidence? First, while improvements have been made, there *still* are differences in the types of majors boys and girls select. Second, conflict theorists argue that school activities are still sex typed. For example, while women's sports have definitely emerged as a result of Title IX, which requires that all schools receiving public funds devote the same amount of money and resources to girls' teams as they do boys' teams, differences persist. For example, there are few girls football or wrestling teams. Likewise, there are few, if any all boys cheering squads whose primary goal is to cheer for a girls' sporting event. Sociologists favoring the nature argument for sex differences would claim that this is because women biologically do not have the inherent aggressiveness that is associated with these types of male sports. Furthermore, men are *too* competitive and aggressive to be content in support roles such as cheerleading. On the other hand, sociologists who favor the nurture argument would argue that these differences stem from different opportunities that exist because of *perceptions* of roles and interests based on sex. In other words, these sociologists would argue that there are few female football teams and few all- male cheering squads because people do not associate football with girls and cheering with boys and, therefore, do not create opportunities for these activities for the opposite sexes. Regardless of which view you support, these activities reinforce the idea that boys perform the most aggressive activities and girls are in the supportive roles. Gender stereotypes such as these are enduring because they are based on partial truths. There *are* differences between boys and girls; however, how those differences translate into social behavior is still debated.

The Conflict Resulting from Women's Fight for Change
Women's Rights Movement

Women always had an active role in shaping social history, even if it was downplayed. Women worked hard to help America win its freedom from England in 1776. Molly Pitcher, who fired a cannon at the Battle of Monmouth, is an example of one woman who fought in the American Revolution. Furthermore, many poor wives traveled and fought beside their husbands because they had nowhere else to go (*Call Chronicle*, July 28, 1975:11).

Therefore, contrary to the cultural stereotypes of women mentioned in the first section, women were not always passive, nor did they necessarily accept their social position. Abigail Adams, whose lively letters of social comment were to earn her a part in history, wrote to her husband John Adams while he was at Philadelphia forging the Declaration of Independence. She wrote: "In the new code of laws which I suppose it will be necessary for you to make, I desire you would remember the ladies, and be more generous and favorable to them than your ancestors. If particular care and attention is not paid to us, we are determined to foment a rebellion, and will not hold ourselves bound by any laws in which we have no choice" (Meyerson, 1975:71). John Adams responded to his wife's pleas in the spirit of other "Founding Fathers" throughout the colonies. He wrote: "As to your extraordinary code of laws I cannot but laugh." He warned her that men who would stand and fight the tyranny of a powerful king would never give in to the "despotism of the petticoat" (Meyerson, 1975:71).

Abagail Adams was not alone. In 1790, a woman writing under the pen name "Constantia" argued that if men were superior "may we not trace its source in the difference of education and continued advantages?" She pleaded for equality of education for girls and women so they would be less likely to fill up their time with "useless trifles" and would make better wives (Scanzoni and Scanzoni, 1976:19). Picking up on this theme, in 1792, Mary Wollstonecraft called for a reform of marriage in her book, *A Vindication of the Rights of Women*. She argued that women should have greater social and economic rights as well as a greater education so they would not have to be submissive to men.

Change was slow because these women were voices crying in the wilderness until thousands of other women joined in chorus together to form a Women's Equal Rights Movement. The Women's Equal Rights Movement began in 1848 when several hundred women and men, headed by Elizabeth Cady Stanton (a daughter of a judge, who became well versed on the legal standing of women) and Lucretia Mott (a Quaker schoolteacher) came together at Seneca Falls, N.Y., to launch a program of gender role reform. Most of the leaders were interested in abolishing slavery, or "were without marital or family ties, ex-wives, non-wives, childless wives, whose need to support themselves triggered concern for equal rights to vote, to work and to advance in their work" (Rossi, 1972:349).

Elizabeth Cady Stanton read a "Declaration of Sentiments" modeled after the Declaration of Independence. It started:

> The history of mankind is a history of repeated injuries and usurpations on the part of man toward woman, having in direct object the establishment of an absolute tyranny over her. To prove this, let facts be submitted to a candid world.... (Flexner, 1973:6).

The Declaration went on to document the many forms of discrimination, subordination and powerlessness suffered by women at the hands of men. They were barred from education, except for basic reading, writing and arithmetic courses in primary schools. They could not vote. They could not own property, retain their own earnings, be guardians to their children, testify in court, or sue a person. So, they called for revolution and reform. Women used their socially recognized expertise in children and domestic issues to further their causes. For example, the women's suffrage movement argued that neglect of domestic issues was hurting the nation and that men, because of their innate tendencies, were not equipped to look at issues from a more collective nurturing stance. Hence these women argued that women's vote was important because women focused on different concerns than men and would, therefore, provide a balance in shaping political culture (Edwards, 2001).

The formation of a social movement like this is consistent with a Gesellschaft society. During this time people's roles became so divided and specialized individual community members did not necessarily look out for the well being of each other. As a result, small groups of interested people re-organized into a formal organization to engage in social conflict and to enact change.

The changes did not come easily. Many men objected to ideas such as equal rights for women. For example, the same year the women held their first convention in Seneca Falls, the "Philadelphia Public Ledger" was writing:

> A woman is nobody. A wife is everything. A pretty girl is equal to ten thousand men, and a mother is, next to God, all powerful.... We trust that the ladies of Philadelphia will resolve to maintain their rights as Wives, Belles, Virgins and Mothers, and not as Women ("View of Women Through the Ages," N.D.).

Considering the re-organization that the Women's Rights group advocated, it is unsurprising that men were generally unsupportive – they would potentially lose much of their social position if women gained rights that elevated them to the same power levels as men. Consequently, these men saw women's rights as a conflict that threatened their own self-interests. But women like Fanny Wright, Ernestine Rose, and Lucy Stone spoke out for their rights. They were called names: Fanny Wright was called "the red harlot of infidelity" and Ernestine Rose "a woman a thousand times below a prostitute" (Betty Friedan, 1963:86). But they and others continued to fight for change throughout the Nineteenth Century. When the Black slaves were freed and women were not, more women joined the ranks for women's rights. Women did not limit the charge for change to topics that only benefited themselves. They also fought against alcohol, child labor, and development of slums. They also were in the vanguard for public schools, libraries, playgrounds, and laws to protect children and women. Historically, consistent with traditional gender roles, women have been the "social conscience" of America.

In 1869 the women's equal rights movement split into the liberal and conservative factions. Under Elizabeth Cady Stanton and Susan B. Anthony a group of women formed the National Woman's Suffrage Association (NWSA). a group that went far beyond women's suffrage or the vote. It pressed for easier divorce laws, greater economic participation, and social freedom (including "free" sex). A more conservative faction led by Lucy Stone and Julia Ward Howe, formed the American Woman Suffrage Association (AWSA), and worked only for the vote, avoiding other social issues that might alienate other women and the public. By 1890 the legitimacy of the NWSA was destroyed by its advocacy of free love and licensed prostitution; so it merged with the AWSA to form a new group--the National American Women's Suffrage Association (NAWSA) (Mauss,

1975:428-29). It fought to get the vote for women in the states, and was most successful out West.

By 1912 the NAWSA had succeeded in getting the women's right to vote in federal elections into the platform of the Progressive Party. After pressure, demonstrations, letters to Congressmen and other direct action, by August, 1920, the Nineteenth Amendment was ratified by the states to grant women the right to vote in Federal elections. Shortly thereafter, most states passed laws enabling women to vote in all elections.

But women's fight for equal rights was not over. It was not until the 1950s and 1960s that a serious attempt was made to extend equal rights to women and minorities. Protests and demonstrations by the Black Civil Rights Movement, led by Dr. Martin Luther King, led to passage of the Civil Rights Act in 1964. This was the first such legislation in over 100 years. The 1950s helped to produce what Betty Friedan in the mid-1960s called "the feminine mystique". This, according to Friedan, was a false ideology that maintained a woman's highest fulfillment, identity and satisfaction were to be found as a wife and mother within the home (1963:32). As we discussed earlier in the family, this ideology ensures men's social dominance because it discourages women from competing for men's' positions and, therefore, power. However, this ideology and belief were soon challenged in the 1960s when the Women's Liberation Movement came on the scene once more, as it had in the mid-19th Century. The formation of the National Organization for Woman (NOW) in 1966 spearheaded the drive for women's new rights and roles.

In 1972 Congress passed the Equal Rights Amendment (ERA) (originally proposed in 1923) to be added to the Constitution. The ERA needed approval by three-fourths of the states within seven years. By 1979, only 35 states approved of it so it never passed (Blair, 1997:6-11). Nevertheless, by a series of Supreme Court decisions women, in effect, got new rights and protection, including Affirmative Action programs and protection from sexual harassment at work.

International Woman's Year in 1975 was marked by the United Nations World Conference on Women in Mexico City. It adopted a "world Plan of Action for Woman". It pointed out that "the necessity of a change in the traditional roles of men as well as women must be recognized." (*New York Times*, July 3, 1975:8). In addition, the 45-page plan spelled out guidelines for action to provide equality for women in education and employment. In June, 1975, representatives proclaimed the U.S. National Women's Agenda. It was an 11-point agenda for action that demanded changes in women's roles in government, business, the professions, education and the community. They all aimed to bring about equal rights and equality for women. The blending of gender roles and conflict over family issues is best seen with working mothers and the concern over child care.

Child care is also the responsibility of fathers

Rights of Working Women

Women were also active in trying to improve their own working conditions.   By the mid-1800s women, like their male counterparts, began forming unions to protest mill work conditions. The first female labor union, called the Female Labor Reform Association, was founded by Sarah Bagley in Lennox, Massachusetts, in 1845 to protest wage cuts and production speed ups. These women threatened to publish the name of any weaver who did not support the union's cause and, instead, agreed to work with higher production quotas and lower pay. Surprisingly, the women won this conflict and the mill owners lost (Kava, 1994).

However, the plight of women's unionization was not always so successful. Unions like the American Federation of Labor, formed in 1886, consisted of trade unions and, therefore, did not really involve women (who were generally more likely to work in non-trade fields). According to Hewitt (1985), this was in response to conflict over the breaking down of the sexual division of labor which threatened skilled male wages (remember, women worked for less money). To the degree that men and women's jobs remained separate, men and women joined forces to fight for better working conditions.

However, the fact remains that women were trying to break into the better paying male jobs and, in some instances, this alienated male support. To further discourage women, the AFL would charge them higher dues and discouraged them from taking part in meetings. As a result, Elizabeth Morgan, a former mill worker, was the motivating force behind a women's branch of the AFL called the Ladies' Federal Union Number 2703. This women's union eventually included 23 different trades before it joined with other groups to expand its focus to issues like child labor, suffrage and temperance and become the Illinois Women's Alliance. Even so, according to Brownlee and Brownlee (1976), aside from the garment and textile industries, women were generally uninvolved in unions. Brownlee and Brownleee (1976) argue that only 10% of women in manufacturing were in any unions.

But not all unions excluded or discouraged female membership. Lenora Barry, a widowed mother by her 30s, had to work in a factory in central New York to support her children. She earned 11 cents the first day and only 65 cents total by the end of her first week. To fight these conditions, in the 1880's she joined a union called the Knights of Labor and, a couple of years later, rose in its ranks and used her position to investigate unsafe working conditions as well as fight for fair wages. In 1888, a member of the local clergy in Pennsylvania called her a "Lady Tramp" for her efforts to which she responded that as " 'an Irishwoman, a Catholic and an honest woman' she had every right to do what she could to help workingwomen" (Kava, 1994: 46). The Knights of Labor were somewhat unique in that they included all workers (except lawyers and prostitutes), regardless of race, background, gender or level of skill; and, consequently, also fought for rights such as equal pay for women, which also was unusual at the time (Kava, 1994). However, according to Brownlee and Brownlee (1976), this acceptance of women stemmed from declining union membership that the union hoped to curb. Barry originally favored a separate woman's section of the union, but later claimed:

> I believe now we should, instead of supporting a Woman's Department, put more women in the field as Lecturers to tell women why they should organize as a part of the industrial hive, rather than because they are women. There can be no separate or distinction of wage-workers on account of sex, and separate departments for their interests is a direct contradiction of this, and also of that part of our declaration which say 'we know no sex in the laws of

> Knighthood.' Therefore, I recommend the abolition of the
> Woman's Department, believe, as I now do, that women
> should be Knights of Labor without distinction, and should
> have all the benefits that can be given to men – no more, no
> less – thereby making it incumbent upon all to work more
> earnestly for the general good, rather than for sex,
> Assembly, or trade. (Barry, 1889)

In the early 20th Century a gendered division of labor was still generally thought to be integral to the overall social good. However, during this time social science was developing as a field and saw some of the differences between men and women to be more due to socialization than biology. Even so, the doctrine of separate spheres was so deeply entrenched during this time that this research was not treated as a means to equalize men and women's roles, but instead as a means to socialize women to be better wives and homemakers (Edwards, 2001).

Women's unions did achieve some success. They led to a restriction in the hours of work women could do, so that by 1933 all but 6 states restricted the number of hours women could be forced to work (Brownlee and Brownlee, 1976). Furthermore, by 1923 states began to institute minimum wages for women's employment as well (Brownlee and Brownlee, 1976).

Furthermore, thanks to the efforts of organized labor (AFL-CIO) and the National Organization for Women, among other interest groups, legislation such as the Family Medical Leave Act (FMLA) have been passed. Until 1996, the United States was one of the few industrial countries which did not have federally protected extended family leave (which is different than maternity leave). However, thanks to the FMLA *both* men and women can have up to three months of job protected, albeit unpaid, leave to care for a newborn, an immediate family member who is sick, or a newly adopted child if they work for a company with at least 50 employees and employed there for at least one year. This law was a noticeable improvement for families because not only does it apply to *both* men and women (which is important when trying to establish gender *equality*), but also because, unlike the traditional maternity leave, this law guarantees the individual the same level of employment upon his or her return. Maternity leave only guaranteed employment where a mother could feasibly be demoted upon her return. This is no longer the case. On the other hand, this too was not a complete victory for women because by being unpaid, only middle class women or men can afford to utilize this right.

Summary and Conclusions

  Few would argue today that women are too emotionally fragile for work or should be subordinate to men. When you stop to think critically about how long this ideology *was* present, the strides women have made in the past two hundred years are impressive. …And the fact that they are still not completely treated as equal to men is also less surprising. After all, change takes time; and, in the past 200 years, women have earned the right to choose whether they want to work or stay home with children (versus having the choice made for them by default due to few occupational opportunities). They also have earned the right to higher education, they can even take any classes in any college that they want, and the gap in men and women's earning are smaller now than at the turn of the Century.

  Perhaps even more importantly, women were not passive in enacting this social change. They actively organized and mobilized through social movements like the Civil Rights movement and the National Organization of Women. Women successfully argued their case so that new Civil Rights laws were passed to strengthen the power and positions of women.

  Yet, the conflicts have not been obliterated. What many women viewed as liberation and freedom for themselves in the 20th Century has become a double-burden in the 21st Century--pursuing work while tending to a home and children--at least trying to. One can even view women's liberation as a liberation for men as well – liberation from traditional masculine responsibilities towards women. While very significant changes have taken place in the family and to women's roles, not much has changed in the roles or responsibilities of men. For most men, work and career comes first; the family is perceived as the reason *why* they work so hard and long to succeed. Work is the only socially acceptable addiction in our society.

  Often in desperation, because of the built-in conflict between home and workplace, both women and men have turned to the Federal Government for help. For example, they sought help in funding and financing decent child care, through the income tax system or advocating more government funds for child care centers. They also sought help from the federal government to guarantee them similar work conditions should employees need to take time off to care for new or ailing members of the family. Even Presidents in the White

House have called Conferences on the Family and Child Care with proposals and promises to help working couples in America and to strengthen the American family and its children. But at the same time Administration and Congress passed Welfare Reform Laws that forced single mothers with children out to work, without providing adequate, reasonable day care.

Women themselves seek in vain for happiness at home and success in the workplace. Danielle Crittenden in her book *What Our Mothers Didn't Tell Us: Why Happiness Eludes the Modern Woman* (1999) points out the dilemma of the working woman. She writes: "While we are freer and more equal than any woman in history, you still see a lot of unhappiness. Woman want work, children and family, but have no idea as how to make it fit together" (Hill, 1999:5)

This indeed is the challenge to our society, economy and government alike -- to help the family and working women to put it all together in a way that will be functional and beneficial to everyone involved.

Critical Thinking Questions

1. Why do you think World War II was instrumental in changing gender roles? Do you think that gender roles would have changed to the extent that they have without the occurrence of World War II? Why / why not?

2. What are the pros / cons of being in a dual career family? A single career family? What are the social problems associated with each family form? Why?

3. How has the workplace changed to accommodate family roles? Who makes more use of these changes? Why? How can this be changed?

4. Why do you think that women still earn less than men for every level of education? How can this be changed?

Bibliography

Barry, Leonora. "Record of the Proceedings of the General Assembly of the Knights of Labor." Philadelphia, Pp. 1-6. 1889 in Brownlee, W. Elliot and Mary M. Brownlee. 1976. *Women in the American Economy: A Documentary History 1675 to 1929.* New Haven, Yale University Press, 1976

Beecher, Catherine. *The Evils Suffered by American Women and Children: The Causes and the Remedy.* New York: Harper and Brothers, 1846

Bianchi, Suzanne M. and Daphne Spain. "Women, Work and Family in America". *Population Bulletin,* 51 (December 1996): 21.

Brownlee, W. Elliot and Mary M. Brownlee. *Women in the American Economy: A Documentary History 1675 to 1929.* New Haven, Yale University Press, 1976.

Bureau of Labor Statistics. "Families with own Children: Employment Status of Parent Child Family Types, 2000-2001 Annual Averages." Table 4. United States Department of Labor, Washington, D.C., 2002.

Carton, Barbara. "At Jenny Craig, Men Are Ones Who Claim Sexual Discrimination." *Wall Street Journal.* (November 29 1994): A1 & A7.

Chafe, William H. *The American Woman: Her Changing Social, Economic and Political Roles 1920-1970.* New York: Oxford University Press. 1972

Children's Defense Fund. *Common Myths About Child Care.* Washington, D.C.: Children's Defense Fund, (January 26), 1998.

Digest of Educational Statistics. "Table 258. – Bachelor's, Masters and Doctor's Degrees Conferred by Degree-Granting Institutions, by Sex of Student and Field of Study: 1999-2000." 2001: 304-11. <http://nces.ed.gov//pubs2002/digest2001/tables/PDF/table258.pdf>

Eisenhart, Wayne. "You Can't Hack It, Little Girl: A Discussion of the Covert Psychological Agenda of Modern Combat Training." *Journal of Social Issues.* 31, (Fall 1975): 13-23.

Epstein, Cynthia Fuchs. *Deceptive Distinctions: Sex, Gender and Social Order.* New Haven, Conn: Yale University Press. 1988.

Etzioni, Amitai. *The Spirit of Community: Rights, Responsibilities, and the Communitarian Agenda*. New York: Crown Publisher, Inc., 1993.

Faragher, John M. and F. Howek, eds. *Women and Higher Education in American History: Essays from the Mount Holyoke College Sesquicentennial Symposia*. New York: W.W. Norton and Company, 1988

Finkelhor, David and Kersti Yllo. "Marital Rape: The Myth Verses the Reality." Pp. 382-391 in *Marriage and Family in a Changing Society*, edited by James Henslin. New York: Free Press, 1989.

Flexner, Eleanor. *Century of Struggle: The Women's Rights Movement in the United States*. New York: Atheneum. 1972

Fraundorf, Martha Norby. "The Labor Force Participation of Turn-of-the-Century Married Women." *Journal of Economic History*. 34 (1979): 401-418.

Gilham, Steven. "The Marines Build Men: Resocialization in Recruit Training." Pp. 232-244 in *The Sociological Outlook: A Text with Readings*. 2ᵈ ed. Edited by Reid Luhman. San Diego, CA: Collegiate Press, 1989.

Giuffre, Patti and Christine Williams. "Boundary Lines: Labeling Sexual Harassment in Restaurants." *Gender and Society*. 8:3 (1994): 378-401.

Gross, Jane. "Suffering in Silence No More: Fighting Sexual Harassment." *New York Times*. (July 13, 1992): A-1.

Hacker, Helen. "Women as a Minority Group." *Social Forces*. 30, (October 1951): 60-69.

Haller, M. *Early Moravian Education in Pennsylvania*. Nazareth, PA. Moravian Historical Society, 1953.

Hayes, Arthur. "How Courts Define Harassment" *Wall Street Journal* (October 11, 1991: B1 & B3

Hewitt, Nancy A. "Beyond the Search for Sisterhood: American Women's History in the 1980s". Pp.1-19 in *Unequal Sisters: A Multicultural Reader in U.S. Women's History*. 2ᵈ ed., edited by Vicki L. Ruiz and Ellen C. DuBois. New York: Routledge, 1985.

Hochschild, Arlie. *The Second Shift: Working Patterns and the Revolution at Home*. New York: Viking Penguin, 1989.

Hughes, Gwendolyn Salisbury. *Mothers in Industry: Wage-Earning Mothers in Philadelphia*. New York: New Republic. 1925.

Hutter, Mark. *The Changing Family.* 3^d ed. Boston, Mass.: Allyn
    and Bacon, 1998.

Kava, Beth Millstein. *Women in the U.S. Work Force 1876-1914.*
    Paramus, New Jersey: Globe Book Company. 1994.

Klein, Matthew. "Women's Trip to the Top." *American
    Demographics,* (February 1998): 22.

Montagu, Ashley. *The Natural Superiority of Women.* 5th ed.,
    Altamire, Thousand Oaks, CA, 1999.

Morris, Betsy. "Trophy Husbands". *Fortune Magazine.* (October 14,
    2002): Pp. 78-98.

Murdock, George. "Comparative Data on the Division of Labor by
    Sex." *Social Forces.* 15 (1937): 551-53.

Myrdal, Gunner. *An American Dilemma.* New York: Harper, 1944.

Newcomer, M. *A Century of Higher Education for American Women.*
    New York: Harper and Brothers, 1959.

Sapiro, Virginia. *Women in American Society.* Mountain View, CA:
    Mayfield, 1994.

Scully, Diana and Joseph Marolla. "Riding the Bull at Gilley's'
    Convicted Rapists Describe the Rewards of Rape." Pp. 45-60
    in *Down-to-Earth Sociology: Introductory Readings,* 10th
    ed., edited by James M. Henslin. New York: Free Press,
    1999.

Statistical Abstract of the United States: 1998, 118th ed. U.S. Bureau
    of the Census. Washington, D.C.: U.S. Government Printing
    Office. 1999.

Stouffer, Samuel, Arthur Lumsdiane, Marion Harper, Robin Williams,
    Jr., M. Brewster Smith, Irving Janis, Shirley Star and
    Leonard Cottrell, Jr. *The American Soldier: Combat and Its
    Aftermath.* 2, New York: Wiley, 1949.

Tannen, Deborah. *You Just Don't Understand: Women and Men in
    Conversation.* New York: Ballantine Books, 1990.

Tidball, M. Elizabeth, Daryl G. Smith, Charles S. Tidball, Lisa E.
    Wolf-Wendel. *Taking Women Seriously: Lessons and
    Legacies for Educating the Majority.* American Council
    on Education: Oryx Press, 1999.

United States Bureau of the Census. *Women in Gainful Occupations,
    1870-1920* by Joseph Hill. Washington, D.C.: GPO, 1929.

United States Bureau of the Census. "Record Share of New Mothers
    in the Labor Force". *Census Bureau Reports.* U.S.
    Department of Commerce News. (October 24, 2000).

United States Bureau of Labor Statistics. "Table A-8 Employed
        Persons by Age, Sex and Marital Status, Seasonally Adjusted
        (in Thousands)". 2002.
        <ftp://ftp.bls.gov/pub/suppl/empsit.cpseea8.txt
United States Department of Justice. Federal Bureau of Investigation
        Press Release October 28, 2002.
        <http://www.fbi.gov/pressrel/pressrel02/cius2001.htm. 2002.
United States Department of Justice. Federal Bureau of Investigation
        Press Release June 16, 2003.
        <http://www.fbi.gov/pressrel/pressrel03/12month2002.htm.20
        03.
United States Department of Labor. Women's Bureau. 2003.
        http://www.dol.gov/wb.
United. States Equal Employment Opportunity Commission. "Sexual
        Harassment Charges: EEOC and FEPAs Combined: FY
        1992 – FY 2002". February 6, 2003.
        http://www.eeoc.gov/stats/harass.html. 2003.
Weiner, Lynn Y. *From Working Girl to Working Mother: The
        Female Labor Force in the United States, 1820-1980*.
        Chapel Hill: University of North Carolina Press, 1985.

Chapter 5

The Racial Problem in America

> -- What white Americans have never fully understood --
> but what the Negro can never forget -- is that white society
> is deeply implicated in the ghetto. White institutions
> created it, white institutions maintain it and white society
> condones it. (Kerner Commission Report, 1968:2.)

> -- The issue of equal rights for American Negroes is...an
> important issue. And should we defeat every enemy, and
> should we double our wealth and conquer
> the stars and still be unequal to this issue, then we will have
> failed as a people and as a nation. (President Lyndon
> Johnson, March 15, 1965.)

One of the greatest conflicts and struggles in American history for freedom, equality and power, has been fought by African-Americans, with help from liberal or radical whites. Though today African-Americans account for only 12% of our population, white society's social structures and attitudes have changed significantly toward them. Nevertheless, the conflict still goes on, as it has for almost 400 years.
Other racial minority groups - - Hispanics, Native Americans and Asians - - have endured similar inequalities as the African-Americans. We could have summarized a very, very brief history of each racial or ethnic minority group. Instead, we have chosen to focus in greater depth and with greater analysis on the leading racial group in America that has defined our racial social problem for nearly 400 years - - African-Americans. They are, as a group, more politically organized and active than other minority groups.

Though each racial group has had a distinct and different history than African-Americans, all racial minorities share the same fate: segregation, institutional racism, discrimination, prejudice, lower life expectancy and "life chances" than whites. (Moore, 2001) They all suffered from a lack of equal opportunities in the work force and in education.

Who is African-American? Since "race" is socially-constructed by white society, it is difficult to know exactly who is or is not. For example, many people have multi-racial backgrounds (such as Tiger Woods). In the 2000 Census, for the first time, 6.8 million persons defined themselves as being from more than one race. The U.S. Census Bureau defines Hispanics as an ethnic group, not a race. Even the word to designate racial groups changed in the U.S. historically from one period to another. During slavery days whites called the group "colored" or "darkies" (or the derogatory "n" word) or "nigra". Then, starting about the 1900's, and thanks to the *New York Times* "Negro" came into wide use. In the 1950's and 1960's the word "Black" was used. Lastly, the term "African-American" emerged thanks to Malcolm X and "Roots", a book and television show in the late 1960's. Some in the 20th Century dropped their slave name and adopted an African name - - like Cassius Clay became Muhammad Ali. African-Americans were the only racial group to be slaves for about 300 years. The other racial groups were never formally enslaved as were the African-Americans. Both American Indians and Hispanics were a conquered people due to prolonged wars instigated by the whites for territorial expansion from ocean to ocean. Not until the Civil War were some Blacks involved in a war to finally gain their freedom from slavery.

In 16th Century England, prior to slavery in the United States, there is historical evidence that "...a negative, stereotyped view of blackness and black people was widely held." (Shapiro, 1992:2089). In contrast, Jerome Bennett in his book, *Before the Mayflower* (1966) argues that racial designations were unknown until 1660. As Europe continued to exploit and explore the New World, existing ideas about white superiority were reinforced.

The first boatload of slaves (originally indentured servants) came to America in 1619 at Jamestown, Va. Ever since then the "problem of the color line" (as W.E.B. Du Bois called it) has been a social problem, sometimes recognized, sometimes not. Our nation was born with a "congenital defect" - - slavery. Our Constitution originally did not abolish it, though it did allow Congress to abolish the slave trade after 1808, about the time England outlawed it. (Hamilton, 1974:3) But it never did until after the bloody Civil War ended in 1865.

Between 1790 and 1808, over 100,000 slaves were brought into the U.S. and at least 250,000 were smuggled in illegally (Raab and Selznick, 1964). With the invention of the cotton gin in 1773, slavery as an institution spread, particularly in the South. In 1790 there were less than 700,000 slaves in the U.S.; by 1830 there were over 2 million (Vander Zanden, 1966). As Booker T. Washington in his autobiography put it:

> "Having once got its tentacles fastened onto the economic
> and social life of the Republic it was no easy matter for the
> country to relieve itself of the institution." (1959:11)

Slavery was rationalized on religious, economic, and social grounds. But no rationalization could justify the inhuman and inhumane treatment the slave trade inflicted on some 40 million Africans throughout the world. (Liszkowski, 1969)

As an Englishman, named Walsh, described it, the slaves on the ship

> ....were all enclosed under grated hatchways, between
> decks. The space was so low that they sat between each
> other's legs, and stowed so close together that there was no
> possibility of lying down, or at all changing their position,
> by night or by day...They were all branded like
> sheep...burnt with a red hot iron. (Davidson, 1961:xvi)

They were chained by the neck and legs, jammed like sardines into cramped quarters during their trip to America. The filth and stench caused by such quarters brought on diseases and epidemics. If the men did not die of disease on the ship they jumped overboard to end their misery.

This was the dreaded "Middle Passage" between Africa and the Americas. Millions died before they reached the U.S. or Caribbean. Many who survived were disabled or maimed by the treatment they received. Once on land, their treatment was often no better. The slave in the United States lost his status and identity as a human being. Because of the English legal system, he was viewed as a cow or horse, "chattel" or property, not as a human person. This idea was to serve as "...the whole tenor of legislation regarding the Negro in the days before and after the Emancipation Proclamation." (Barbour, 1967:100). Even freed "colored" in the United States, almost half a million *before* the Civil war, were not viewed as fully human. They were denied many legal and social rights, not only in the South but in the North where over half lived.

19ᵗʰ Century Slavery Conflicts

From time to time the conflict with whites over freedom flared up as slaves rebelled and rioted against their "masters". Gabriel Prosser in 1800 planned one of the first recorded slave uprisings in the United States.   Denmark Vesey died in an unsuccessful revolt in Charleston, S.C. The famous Nat Turner led a rebellion in 1831 in Virginia, killing more than 60 white people. These were the more publicized of the some 250 riots or attempted revolts against slavery. But the system had so demoralized, dominated, and depersonalized the slaves, for the most part, they were conditioned and socialized to accept white authority and power over them. (McVeigh, 1970)

The extension of slavery to new areas in the western states became a conflict between the North and the South. It was temporarily settled by the Missouri Compromise of 1850.   In the Dred Scott decision (1857) the Supreme Court declared that Compromise unconstitutional and denied Congress the right to control slavery in the new territories in the West. It also ruled that slaves had "no rights or privileges but such as those who held the power and the government might choose to grant them". (Zinn, 1980: 186)

This, among other reasons, led to a Civil War (1861-1865). During that war, thousands of black "freemen" fought in the Union Army. In 1863 the Emancipation Proclamation was issued by Lincoln. On paper, it freed the slaves in the South. The hope was that the slaves would rise up against their southern masters and the South would be fighting on two fronts. The revolt never occurred, but for enslaved people the Emancipation became a powerful symbol of black freedom and liberty

Post – Civil War Developments

The birth of our *modern* race relations problem dates from the emancipation of almost four million slaves *after* the Civil War. During the "Reconstruction Period" (1865-1884) an attempt was made to set up a new political, economic and social structure in the South to benefit the majority of whites and "colored" alike. In South Carolina, the new legislature, made up of both black and white legislators, introduced free public schools for the first time. Not only were 70,000 "colored" children going to school by 1876 (where none had gone before) but 50,000 white children were going to school where only 20,000 had attended in 1860 (Zinn, 1980:195). Between 1865 and 1870, three new amendments were added to our constitution to protect former slaves. The Thirteenth Amendment abolished slavery. The Fourteenth Amendment granted citizenship to "all persons" and guaranteed everyone "due process of law" and "equal protection of the laws". The Fifteenth Amendment granted all citizens the right to vote (except women). In 1866, a Civil Rights Act declared that "…all citizens of the United States shall have the same right to inherit, purchase, lease, sell, hold and convey real and personal property as is enjoyed by white persons." (Clark, 1995:178) In 1875, another act prohibited exclusion of Negroes from hotels, theaters, railroads and other public accommodations. (Raab & Selznick, 1964)

For a time, black people held political office and made some gains because of help from the Federal government, particularly through the Freedmen's Bureau. In 1871, due to opposition in both the North and South, the Bureau was discontinued.

Also the new Federal laws and amendments were enforced only when Federal troops were present. Secret white groups, such as the Ku Klux Klan, sprang up as "an instrument of terror" and violence against blacks in their attempt, and the North's, to change the traditional social system of the South. (Shapiro, 1992)

When Federal troops withdrew from the South in 1884, it left the South in economic and political chaos. A new era in race relations – Jim Crowism – began. "Black codes" and state laws gave power to whites to keep the "colored in their place" in the South. The Civil Rights and black political power of the Reconstruction was savagely reversed. "White supremacy" became the rallying cry of the South. With it came a deliberate, conservative emphasis on racism, discrimination and segregation.

In 1896 the case of *Plessy vs. Ferguson* reached the U.S. Supreme Court. It legally established the principles of "separate but equal" in transportation such as railroad cars for "Whites only" and "Colored only". This practice was not overturned by law until 1954 in the famous case of *Brown vs. Board of Education of Topeka, Kansas*. That 1896 decision "enforced almost 60 years of legal (de jure) segregation and discrimination between the races, especially in the South in housing, employment, schools and transportation". (Clark, 1995:178)

20th Century Race Relations

By the 20th Century, the social and economic basis and bias of our present social system of race relations had been firmly established both in society and by Government, Federal, state and local. It was to last another 65 to 100 years. By 1900, most of the state constitutions in the South had been changed or repealed. State laws in the South reflected the "separate but equal" doctrine. Societal prejudice, discrimination, segregation and white racism impeded any steps toward equality for blacks, in both the South and the North. Segregation became firmly established all over America and other ways of how to relate to free black people were gradually pushed aside or ignored. (Woodward, 1966)

Racist Ideology
          The embrace of imperialism, the triumph of segregation and the heightening of class tensions all worked together to generate a powerful surge of racist ideology in America. The historian I.A. Newby writes that from 1900 to 1930 "...anti-Negro thought reached its zenith, the years which produced the greatest proliferation of anti-Negro literature, and the years in which that literature enjoyed its broadest appeal". (1965:xi) In the field of history, the writings of U.B. Phillips applauded the resolve of white Southerners that the region "...shall be and remain white man's country" (Newby, 1965:3). In 1914 the University of Mississippi professor Thomas Pearce Bailey, summarized the white southern racial creed as consisting of such notions as "blood will tell" and "the Negro is inferior and will remain so". (Newby, 1965:4) Bailey strongly doubted that any future changes would enable Negroes to catch up with whites. These racist assumptions, according to Bailey, formed "...a core of ideas to which non-southerners also generally subscribed" (1914:93). These ideas and beliefs of whites prevented any serious conflict or revolt from the Negro community.
          Not only historians spread the racist ideology but also certain segments of religious and fiction writers early in the century spread the same negative ideas about Negroes. Possibly the most extreme statement of white racism came from Charles Carroll, author of *The Negro a Beast* or, *In the Image of God* (1900). Carroll declared that as the white man was the last act of creation, Negroes were therefore "pre-Adam" inhuman animals.
          In the world of fiction Thomas Dixon, Jr. wrote two novels: *The Leopard's Spots* (1902) and *The Clansman* (1905). He reached millions through his novels and through D.W. Griffith's silent movie, *The Birth of a Nation* (1915), based on *The Clansman*. Joel Williamson observed that Dixon "...probably did more to shape the lives of Americans than have some Presidents". (1984: 150) Dixon's central message was that white women had to be saved from black

bestiality; he interpreted Reconstruction policies as a plot by black Republican legislators to force white women into the arms of black men.   Dixon had one of his characters declare, in the course of opposing black education, that "…the Ethiopian can not change his skin, or the leopard his spots" (1902:459).   In writing about Dixon, Williamson notes that "…racism is essentially a mental condition, a disorder of the mind in which internal problems are projected upon external persons". (1984: 151)   However, "…this psychological perception must also take into account the reality that Dixon would have had little impact had there not been the impulse to preserve the status quo in the distribution of political and economic power by white Americans." (Shapiro, 1992:2092)

Among the well-known publicists of the period Rebecca Latimer Felton lashed out against blacks. Felton, the first woman U.S. senator, ardently justified lynching and argued for the existence of a "racial antipathy natural to the Caucasian in every age and country" (Shapiro, 1992:2092). The use of violence and barbaric lynchings went hand in hand with the spread of such racist ideology. In the single year of 1892, according to the *Chicago Tribune,* white mobs murdered 241 black persons. Between 1886 and 1914, 3,380 black people were hung in the South. This violence continued as a way of life in the South until the 1950's. (Howard, 1974)

To try to combat and oppose such violence and racial ideology, in 1909 the National Association for the Advancement of Colored People (NAACP) was founded and in 1911 the Urban League was formed. Both were designed to help blacks get jobs and obtain their rights and justice. When the First World War (1914-1918) started, some blacks began to leave the South (where 90% lived). By 1920, the southern states had a net loss of 122,000 blacks. By 1929 they had lost over half a million (Steinberg, 1981). The historical trend was clear – leave the South for a more tolerant and industrial setting in the North and other parts of the country. This out-migration made race-relations a large-scale national social problem, which in some aspects had been confined to the South. America could no longer afford to ignore the problem – but for the most part it did.

As the black population spread throughout the nation, white racists ran amok in repeated pogrom-like violence against Negro communities in: Atlanta, Chicago, Detroit, New York City, Springfield, Ill., Tulsa, Okla., Washington, D.C. and Wilmington, N.C. (Howard, 1974:18; Shapiro, 1992:2092). Many working class whites felt threatened that their housing and jobs were being encroached upon by blacks. In every corner of white America, due to the spread of the racist ideology, prejudice, discrimination, racism and segregation reigned supreme.

One of the most powerful writings of racist ideology was that of wealthy and aristocratic Madison Grant (1865-1937). He was author of *The Passing of the Great Race* (1916), a book read by thousands of Americans. According to Grant, "The lesson is always the same, namely, that race is everything." Grant, for twenty-five years a vice president of the Immigration Restriction League, contended that the superior white race in the United States was threatened by constitutionally inferior immigrants. America, according to Grant, was in danger of losing its essentially "Nordic" character; such a loss would inevitably lead to the collapse of its civilization.

A publicist who reached a considerable audience with his advocacy of racism was Lothrop Stoddard (1883-1950). In an early work, *The French Revolution in San Domingo*, Stoddard wrote: "The world-wide struggle between the primary races of mankind—the 'conflict of color' as it has been happily termed-will be the fundamental problem of the Twentieth Century." (Shapiro, 1992: 2094) How prophetic. In his major work, *The Rising Tide of Color* (1922: 3), Stoddard proceeded from the premise that "the basic factor in human affairs is not politics but race...." He saw "superabundant animal vitality" as the outstanding characteristic of blacks and therefore believed they would multiply prodigiously, but he also asserted that they had no historical past and in that respect were quite distinct from other nonwhites. Stoddard's racism served as the rationale for the spread of American imperial domination over the Western Hemisphere, as well as segregation and racism at home.

Challenge to Racist Ideology

At about the time that the writings of Grant and Stoddard appeared, a serious scholarly challenge to racism emerged in the United States. Foremost in mounting this counterthrust was Franz Boas, the great anthropologist. In his book *The Mind of Primitive Man* (1911 & 1938) he wrote that various authors assume characteristic mental differences between the races of man. This viewpoint was reinforced by modern nationalism, with its exaggerated self-admiration of the Teutonic and Nordic race. These ideas, Boas wrote, "are not supported by the results of unbiased research." (1938:144). He found that the prevalence of belief in the existence of gifted races "was based essentially on the assumption that higher achievement is necessarily associated with higher mental faculty, and that therefore the features of those races, that in our judgment, have accomplished most are characteristics of mental superiority." (1938:16). Boas subjected these assumptions to critical study and discovered little evidence to support them. He contended that "achievements of races do not warrant us assuming that one race is more highly gifted than the other." (1938:17). Anatomical and physiological evidence also did not support the notion that the white race represents physically the highest type of man (Shapiro, 1992:2096).

Another towering opponent of racism was the sociologist-historian-poet W.E.B. Du Bois. His article "The Study of the Negro Problems" was first published in the January 1898 issue of *The Annals* and reprinted in that journal in March, 2000 (W.E.B. Du Bois, 2000:13-27). His *Souls of Black Folk* (1903), a prose-poem called for the creation of a world in which the "color line" would no longer exist. It became a classic affirmation of the African-American's humanity. In 1935, Du Bois's *Black Reconstruction* gave the world a ringing scholarly defense of Reconstruction as a noble experiment in creating an interracial democracy. In it he provided a devastating critique of the white racist American histories that for decades had defamed the Reconstruction state governments in the South. Powerful opposition to racism also was offered by scores of other African-American intellectuals and activists. These included such figures as: A. Philip Randolph, Langston Hughes, Paul Robeson, Mary McLeod Bethune, Ralph Bunche, Walter White, Richard Wright, and Maya Angela. Racism was further opposed by innumerable unsung heroes within the black and liberal white communities who challenged segregation, participated in the organization of new industrial unions, worked for civil rights legislation, and risked membership in unions of black sharecroppers and tenant farmers.

The Civil Rights Struggle
During World War II (1941-1945), a threatened Black protest march on Washington, D.C. got a Presidential order for Fair Employment Practices and Fair Housing. But black soldiers during the war were kept in segregated units, usually cooking, digging latrines, or doing other menial labor. It was not until 1948 that President Truman ordered the Armed Forces to desegregate. Today the Armed Forces are fully integrated.

In 1944, a historical, sociological study on race relations in the United States was published. It was *An American Dilemma* by the Swedish sociologist Gunnar Myrdal (1944). In it he concluded that a gap existed between the "American Creed" and "the American deed"; between what we preached and what we practiced in our race relations.

The "American Creed" emphasized dignity of all persons as human beings, equality of opportunity, and justice for all. But the long history of slavery, prejudice, discrimination and segregation of blacks (which he documented in great detail) did not conform to the "American Creed." This was the great "American Dilemma."

Many critics of Myrdal's classic work disagreed. They pointed out that most whites had no dilemma or sense of guilt as to how they had treated or ignored Blacks (Campbell and Pettigrew, 1959; Campbell, 1971; Silberman, 1964; Westie, 1965). Charles Silberman summed it up this way:

> The tragedy of race relations in the United States is that there is no American Dilemma. White Americans are not torn and tortured by the conflict between their devotion to the American Creed and their actual behavior. They are upset by the current state of race relations to be sure. But what troubles them is not that justice is being denied but their peace is being shattered and their business interrupted. (1964:10)

Myrdal's study received little public attention, but in 1954 a Supreme Court decision (*Brown vs. Board of Education of Topeka, Kans.*) it did. It outlawed "separate but equal" facilities, ruling that "*separate* educational facilities are inherently unequal." Legally, and societally, that was a turning point in American race relations.

The winds of change were starting to blow strongly in society. In 1955, a Black woman, Rosa Parks, was arrested on a segregated bus in Montgomery, Alabama, for refusing to give up her front seat to a white person. Reverend Martin Luther King successfully led a bus boycott there over this incident. This was the beginning of the modern Civil Rights social movement for blacks (and liberal whites) in America. Under Dr. King the Southern Christian Leadership Conference, and other non-violent civil rights groups, made strides in civil rights thru "sit-ins", "freedom rides" and other direct actions in the South during the early 1960's. It was through non-violent conflict by Blacks that social changes began to emerge.

Outside the South, white America had begun to awaken to the brutality of racism in the South. Television networks regularly broadcast the indignities and injustices suffered by Black people. They were jailed, beaten and had dogs sicked on them by the police. Such dramatic media coverage helped effect a swift shift in public opinion in favor of civil rights. By 1963, 83 percent of all whites said they favored equality in the workplace, almost double the number who responded to the same question 19 years earlier (Masci, 1998:62). Also in 1963 Dr. King gave his stirring "I Have a Dream Speech" to a large protest march in Washington, D.C., calling for civil rights and racial equality.

This campaign for equality resulted in the Civil Rights Act of 1964. It prohibited discrimination based on race, national origin or sex. The following year, Congress passed the Voting Rights Act. It put an end to literacy tests and other tactics used by Southern states to stop Blacks from registering to vote. These two laws, and others that followed, did not end institutional discrimination or racism overnight. They did reflect, however, the Federal government's commitment to rooting out the race-based policies that had long been a part of American society. Society itself at its depths was very slow to change.

During the early civil rights battles of the 1950's and 1960's, many white Americans came to believe in the injustice of racial prejudice and discrimination by whites. In the post-civil rights era of the late 1960's, however, white consensus began to break down. This was due, in some respects, to the violence and conflicts that happened in 1967 and 1968. Also white prejudice, discrimination and racism were deeply buried in our social institutions and in our minds and hearts.

In 1967, urban riots occurred in Newark, Detroit, Tampa, and 163 other communities, between blacks and police (resulting in 84 deaths, mostly blacks). Black Power groups and Black Muslim groups began to appear. Malcolm X became an outspoken black leader during the 1960's. Many white Americans got very uncomfortable and began to see the depth and fear of the racial problem all over America.

As a result of these riots, in July, 1967, President Johnson (who supported Civil Rights laws) appointed an 11-member Commission headed by Otto Kerner, Governor of Illinois. The Kerner Commission had three basic questions to answer: What Happened? Why did it happen? and What can be done to prevent it from happening again?

Many white people were upset and disturbed to hear from the lips of this Presidential Commission in 1968 that "white racism was responsible for racial unrest and riots in our cities".(1968: 1) The Kerner report didn't stop there. It stated: "Race prejudice has shaped our history decisively; it now threatens to affect our future.... Our nation is moving toward two societies - one black, one white - separate and unequal". (National Advisory Commission, 1968: 1) It gave a detailed explanation of "Why did it happen?".

Box 5 - 1
Why Did It Happen?
Can It Happen Again?
(Summary Report of the National Advisory
Commission on
Civil Disorders, 1968, pp. 9-11)

In addressing the question "Why did it happen?" we
shift our focus from the local to the national scene,
from the particular events of the summer of 1967 to
the factors within the society at large that created a
mood of violence among many urban Negroes.

These factors are complex and interacting; Despite
these complexities, certain fundamental matters are
clear. Of these, the most fundamental is the racial
attitude and behavior of white Americans toward '
       black Americans.

Race prejudice has shaped our history decisively; it
now threatens to affect our future. White racism is
essentially responsible for the explosive mixture
'which has been 'a cumulating in our cities since the
end of World War II.

Among the ingredients of this mixture are:

--Pervasive discrimination and segregation in
employment, education and housing, which have
resulted in the continuing exclusion of great numbers
of Negroes from the benefits of economic progress.

--Black in-migration and white exodus, which have
produced the massive and growing concentrations of
impoverished Negroes in our major cities, creating a
growing crisis of deteriorating facilities and services
and unmet human needs.

Box 5 – 1 con.

--The black ghettos where segregation and poverty converge on the young to destroy opportunity and enforce failure. Crime, drug addiction, dependency on welfare, and bitterness and resentment against society in general, and white society in particular, are the result.

At the same time, most whites and some Negroes outside the ghetto have prospered to a degree unparalleled in the history of civilization. Through television and other media, this affluence has been flaunted before the eyes of the Negro poor and the jobless ghetto youth.

Though the principal cause of racial disturbances, the Commission found, was white racism, in the latter part of the report (where it offered various solutions to the problem) virtually no mention was made for the need to educate and to communicate to the white community about the spread of white racism. Indeed a follow-up report of the Commission's Report 20 years later (in 1988) revealed that the positive recommendations that were made to cope with the racial situation had been ignored. (Kotlowitz, 1988)

Whatever hopes and expectations Black Americans had for equality, desegregation and the end of white racism, they were all shattered in April, 1968. Dr. Martin Luther King was assassinated. Two months later, Robert Kennedy, a liberal candidate for President of the United States, also was killed. It was clear that white racism still dominated and controlled American society, in spite of the Civil Rights movement, as well as the Federal and state civil rights laws passed.

Another reason for the breakdown of white consensus over civil rights for blacks was new laws to fight poverty and foster black economic advancement. These new measures had proven much more controversial than the Civil Rights Act and Voting Rights Act. The "Great Society" programs to help the poor failed and were later cut by Congress, and eliminated in the 1970's. Millions of whites turned their attention to the war in Vietnam and the environment and put the racial problem on the back burner of social issues.

Affirmative Action Conflict

Another policy developed during the 1960's and 1970's was "affirmative action". An executive order by President Johnson in 1965 required Federal contractors not only to not discriminate against blacks but to actively recruit them. Certain goals or quotas were imposed by the Federal Government on employers and other sectors of society. Colleges and universities all over America were using it in admissions and the Federal Government "set aside" a certain percentage of contracts for minority-owned businesses.

Even as affirmative action was becoming more commonplace, it was coming under attack from white conservatives. During the 1970's, the Supreme Court heard several challenges to the policy, including the landmark 1978 case *University of California Regents vs. Bakke*. The case involved a white law student applicant (Bakke) who claimed he was rejected in favor of less-qualified black applicants under the university's affirmative action program. The justices agreed and outlawed the use of racial quotas or goals in university admissions. The court ruled, however, that while quotas were unconstitutional, race could still be *a factor* in making admission decisions.

Attacks against affirmative action programs and plans intensified during the 1980's. President Ronald Reagan and his successor, George Bush, Sr., were both opposed to race-based preferences. The U.S. Justice Department in their administrations worked to eliminate quotas and other race-based hiring programs. During the 1980's, six new justices were chosen for the Supreme Court. They either opposed or had serious reservations about affirmative action programs. Hence, in the 1990's, the justices handed down decisions ending affirmative action in particular cases. Besides government putting the brakes on affirmative action, such policies and programs were attacked at white society's grass-roots level, starting in California. Citizens voted to approve Proposition 209. That repealed most state-wide, affirmative-action programs. By 1998, four other states cracked down on affirmative-action programs.

In 2003, the U.S. Supreme Court "revisited the constitutionality of affirmative action admissions [programs] since its landmark 1978 Bakke ruling". (Steinberg, Feb 23, 2003: 32) Three white students filed suit against the University of Michigan because they were not admitted while lesser-qualified minority students were. The Bush Administration filed a brief in support of the three students while a coalition of universities and some Fortune 500 corporations supported the university's affirmative action program. In June, 2003, by a vote of 5 to 4, the Supremes upheld the use of race as a factor in admission to the University of Michigan, and other universities and colleges. (Greenhouse, June 24, 2003)   Thus, it upheld existing affirmative action programs. Today, according to recent public-opinion polls about 60% of whites and 40% of Blacks oppose such programs. (Masci, 1998) William Julius Wilson, ,a Black sociologist, in his book *The Declining Significance of Race* suggested that "affirmative action programs might have been created from a critical thinking perspective, and contributed to...the growing economic class divisions within the black community". (1967: 19) It is a national conflict based on deep-felt feelings of both races. (Terkel, 1992) Also, one must remember it is not just a black-white issue since many *white females* have benefited immensely from such programs.

Problems, Progress, Promises and Pitfalls

Four social and economic conflicts and struggles reveal historically that the U.S. has had, and continues to have, serious racial problems. Yet it has made *some* progress in resolving them. Society itself, as well as government policies, programs and procedures have either helped or hindered the process of resolving the conflicts between the races over the years. These four historical conflicts involve:

1. Housing Segregation
2. Employment, Unemployment and Income
3. Political Power
4. Police Violence and Racial Profiling.

Other conflicts that affect African-Americans, such as Education and Health, are covered in those chapters in this book.

Housing Segregation

Karl Taeuber in his article "Residence and Race: 1619 to 2019" points out the key role that housing segregation has played historically in "...maintaining the subordinate status of blacks." (1989: 22)   More than any other factor today it affects employment, unemployment, income, health care, education, as well as political power, police violence and racial profiling. Though some corporations and organizations are integrated, to a greater or lesser degree, recent cases involving racial discrimination by Texaco, Coca Cola and various Federal Government agencies point out the historical persistence of racial prejudice, discrimination and segregation. (Bachman, 2000) Even when racial harmony prevails at the workplace, at the end of the day "blacks go home to black neighborhoods and whites go home to white neighborhoods". (Taeuber, 1989:121)   As we enter the 21st Century, racial separation prevails in family life, playgrounds, churches and local community activities.

It is now easy to assume that U.S. cities have always been segregated by race. Yet, in fact, it wasn't always so historically. There was a time, before 1900, when blacks and whites lived side by side in American cities—both South and North.

In the North, a small native Black population was widely scattered throughout white neighborhoods.   Even Chicago, Detroit, Cleveland, and Philadelphia were not segregated before 1900.   In southern cities, such as Charleston, New Orleans and Savannah, black servants and laborers lived in alleys and side streets near the homes of their wealthy white employers. In this urban world of immigrants from abroad, blacks were more likely to share a neighborhood with whites than with other blacks. In 1870, 80% of black Americans still lived in the *rural* South.   Fully 89% of the nation's 10 million blacks still resided in the *southern states* in 1910, a mere 3 points lower than the Census figures of 1860. (Thernstrom & Thernstrom, 1997) Before World War I (1914) the residential patterns of blacks were like "those of various European immigration groups, and historians refer to this as the period 'before the ghetto'" (Thernstrom & Thernstrom, 1997: 59). In Cleveland in 1910, for example, blacks were less strongly segregated from native whites than were both Italian and Romanian immigrants and not much more segregated than Russians and Hungarian newcomers from abroad. The urban ghetto, as we know it today in America, was constructed by whites starting in about 1914 until the 1950's. It was successively reinforced thereafter. It represents the key institutional arrangement ensuring the continued subordination of blacks in the United States today and in the future.

Before and in the early 1900's blacks occupied a place in cities little different from that of other minority groups. They were not particularly segregated from whites.   Although they were over-represented in the poorest housing and the most crowded streets, "their housing status did not differ markedly from that of others in the same economic circumstances" (Massey and Denton, 1993:19).

Historically, the emergence of the "black ghetto" did not happen as a chance by-product of other socioeconomic process. Rather *white* Americans made a series of deliberate decisions to deny blacks access to urban housing markets to reinforce their spatial segregation. Through its actions, individual and collective, both white society and governments maintained the housing segregation that built and structured "the black ghetto" (Massey and Denton, 1993:19). These actions will be described as they developed historically.

Large sections of the African-American ghetto are abandoned and become slums (Credit: Joseph Elliott)

The Great Migration

The "Great Migration" of blacks from the South to northern cities began about 1914. Like most major social changes, this movement had many causes. The boll weevil insect repeatedly destroyed the cotton crops in the South. Many black tenant farmers lost their jobs due to that, as well as continuing "push and pull" mechanization and had to seek other ways to survive. (Steinberg, 1981) Continued repression of civil rights of blacks was a constant feature of life for southern blacks. Both these factors, spurred more blacks to seek out the better economic and social conditions rumored to be found in northern cities. (Taeuber, 1989)

Events in the North also were causes for the Great Migration. The greatest causal event was the start of World War I (1914-1918). That war changed the picture for thousands of blacks. The outbreak of fighting in Europe cut off the flow of immigrant laborers. This created an acute labor shortage. This shortage became even greater when the U.S. entered in the war in early 1917. Young white men who had worked in industry left for the battlefields at the same time wartime orders created a booming economy. Thus plenty of work was available. Needing laborers, for the first time in history northern industrial employees opened up jobs to black workers (and women) who heard the call and came in from the South—the Great Migration. Prior to this time, blacks were used only as "strike-breakers" when white workers struck (Heaps, 1970:110). After the war, in 1920, restrictive immigration laws cut down the supply of immigrants and more employers retained or hired more black workers. Of course, they always paid blacks less than white workers.

By 1920, close to half a million blacks had left the South; they were joined by another three-quarters of a million more by the end of the 1920's. (Steinberg, 1981; Thernstrom & Thernstrom, 1997) From 1910 to 1930, the black population soared from 92,000 in the North to over a third of a million. In 1930, Chicago had over 200,000 black residents, almost six times as many as twenty years before. Detroit had a stunning twenty-four times as many. (Thernstrom & Thernstrom, 1997) This Great Migration acquired a dynamic of its own. Black newspapers in the north kept urging southern blacks to escape their oppression and move north. As a result, black out-migration from the South continued as a substantial rate even during the Great Depression. As the Great Migration started in the early 1900's, the use of violence by whites to keep blacks out began. In city after city, a series of community riots broke out to prevent blacks from moving into formerly all-white neighborhoods. Race riots struck New York City in 1900; Evansville, Indiana in 1903, Springfield, Illinois in 1908; East St. Louis, Illinois in 1917 and Chicago in 1919 (Heaps, 1970; Massey and Denton, 1993). In each case, individual blacks were attacked because of the color of their skin. Those living away from recognized "black" neighborhoods had their houses ransacked or burned. The progressive segregation of blacks by violence and the use of the racially restrictive "covenant" recorded in deeds by the real estate industry, continued in subsequent decades. These were enforced by all-white neighborhood associations. These covenants kept blacks out of all-white neighborhoods. (Taeuber, 1989) Even the Federal Government agreed with white society that blacks should not live in all-white neighborhoods.

Home Owners Loan Corporation
          During the Great Depression, in 1933, the Federal Government launched many programs to make home ownership widely available to the American public. The Home Owners Loan Corporation (HOLC) was the first of such programs. It provided loans for refinancing urban mortgages in danger of default and granted low-interest loans to owners whose mortgage had been foreclosed. Unfortunately for blacks, the HOLC had started and institutionalized the practice of what came to be called "redlining". Their rating procedures (four grades) were based on the price or rent of a house and

Black areas were seen as containing an "undesirable element". Hence, a red-line was drawn on a map around such areas and no funds or loans would be given in that area. It is a bank procedure that exists in many large cities even today though it is now against the law. The HOLC claimed it did not want these standards of racial worth in real estate—they were already well established by the 1920's; it just applied them as a matter of course. (Massey and Denton, 1993) This practice lent the power, prestige and support (or lack of it) of the federal government to the systematic, institutional racism, discrimination and segregation in housing in the 1930's. During 1937, as part of Roosevelt's New Deal legislation, the Federal Housing Administration (FHA) began programs to increase the supply of working and middle-class housing and reduce the cost of such housing. It insured and guaranteed bank mortgages. The FHA manual in 1938 made clear in one section ("Protection form Adverse Influence") that restrictive covenants work best if they cover a broad area and prohibit "the occupancy of properties except by the race for which they are intended." Appraisers of property were advised in the FHA manual to consider the existence of physical or artificial barriers that would help prevent "infiltration of inharmonious racial groups". (Sec. 935, in Taeuber, 1989) Surrounding areas were to be examined, and if "incompatible racial groups" were present, the appraiser was to include in his report a prediction of the probability of "being invaded". Together with the code of Ethics of the National Association of Real Estate Boards to never introduce other races into all-white areas, and the real estate practice of "steering" people of different races into their "own areas", insured all-white areas would remain that and all-black areas would remain a ghetto.

Hence by World War II (1939-1945) firm foundations for the large urban racial ghettos had been laid in every northern city. But during the Second World War, and the 1950's, a second Great Migration (larger than the first) hit both northern and southern cities. Just as during World War I, there was a need for labor in war plants that sprung up in or near the large cities of America. Blacks left rural areas to either serve in the armed forces or obtain war-time jobs. In addition, though the First World War was to "make the world free for democracy", Blacks after that war found that their status as second or third-class citizens hadn't changed any. During 1941 a black labor leader, A. Philip Randolph, organized a major protest march in Washington, D.C. He called for both integration of the armed forces (which were segregated until 1948) and for equal opportunity to get war-time jobs, just like whites had always enjoyed. As a result of Randolph's threat to demonstrate in D.C., President Roosevelt created a

Fair Employment Practices Committee (FEPC) to hear complaints of blacks of discrimination and take "appropriate steps to redress grievances" (Thernstrom and Thernstrom, 1997:72). Historically, the federal government had been forced to make its first major concession toward ensuring black rights since the Reconstruction of the 1860's. Yet the FEPC was ineffective and not much changed.

All this set the stage for a civil rights movement that would eventually awaken the nation's conscience about the racial situation and destroy the southern caste system. With the huge influx of blacks into the cities during World War II, huge gains by black Americans occurred in a time of great economic growth and spreading affluence. This felt all the more remarkable because it followed within a decade the worse economic catastrophe in American history—the Great Depression. (Thernstrom and Thernstrom, 1997)   Blacks not only shared in the rising prosperity of the war and the immediate post-war years of the 1950's; they advanced more rapidly than whites. In the 1940's and 1950's, the economic gap between the races narrowed with greater speed than in any comparable short span of years. Since then the number of African-Americans living in poverty plunged significantly. In perspective, it is not an overstatement to say that no group in American history has ever improved its position so dramatically in so short a period, though it must be said in the same breath that no other group had, and still has, so far to go.

The nation's mobilization for and involvement in World War II transformed American race relations and problems from a regional to a national one. This second "Great Migration" to the cities was a result not only of wartime expansion of jobs but also mechanization of farms in the South, as well as the cutting off of immigrants from Europe. On top of that, some 11 million men were being drafted or enlisted in the Armed Forces, taking them out of the work force. Blacks came from the rural South to a much greater extent than in the first Great Migration. Between 1940 and 1950 "nearly over half of Mississippi's young blacks aged 15 to 34 left the state and moved north". (Taeuber, 1989:133).

The new migration continued twice as long as the first one. During the 30 years from 1940 to 1970 the net migration of blacks from the South to the North and West averaged over 100,000 persons a year. The northern and western share of the total black population jumped from 23% in 1940 to 47% in 1970. (Taeuber, 1989) At the same time that millions were leaving the South, the social and economic position of the South was changing more toward manufacturing and services rather than farm jobs. The percentage of southern blacks living in cities, rather than in rural areas, reached 67% in 1970, nearly double the pre-World War II ratio.

In spite of their increasing numbers, blacks moving into the cities still faced a variety of discriminatory actions by employers and unions to maintain occupational segregation and keep blacks out of the better-paying jobs. In housing, landlords, speculators, financial and insurance agencies, as well as Federal government programs, continued to conspire to keep blacks contained in traditionally all-black areas. As during the first Great Migration, whites turned to violence and riots to keep blacks out of their neighborhoods. Black organizations, such as the NAACP, vigorously publicized the irony of fighting for democracy abroad while racism flourished on the home front. In 1944, this was the overarching theme in Gunnar Mrydal's *An American Dilemma*. It carried the subtitle "The Negro Problem and Modern Democracy". Mrydal saw the situation as a continuing value conflict throughout American history between "the American creed (of equality and freedom) and the American deed (in respect to prejudice, discrimination, segregation and racism) against black Americans by whites. In 1942 the Office of War Information financed a study of white Americans attitudes toward blacks. Conducted by the National Opinion Research Center, it found "only 46% of whites opposed having separate Jim Crow sections for blacks on buses and trolley cars". Most revealing was that 86% said that blacks should live in separate sections in cities and towns. A clear majority thought that whites should get "the first chance" at jobs and were not ashamed to say so. (Thernstrom & Thernstrom, 1997:73).

During World War II, a chief advisor on black affairs to the Secretary of War called for "the integration of the Negro soldier into the Army". Chief of Staff General George Marshall dismissed it as an effort to solve "a social problem which (had) perplexed the American people throughout the history of this nation" (Thernstrom & Thernstrom, 1997:73-74). How true that was—and still is in 21st Century America. Sociologist Kenneth Clark, who worked with Gunnar Myrdal as a student in the 1940's, later in 1965 wrote a book *Dark Ghetto*. He argued that "...the dark ghetto's invisible walls have been erected by the white society, by those who have power, both to confine those who have *no* power and to perpetuate their powerlessness" (1965:11).

In the 1960's, thanks to a mobilized Civil Rights movement, passage of a Civil Rights Act in 1964, followed by riots and the Kerner Commission report, many people began to question the white power structure that created, maintained and retained the black ghettos throughout the U.S. Depending upon one's beliefs in the insistence and persistence of racial segregation, leads to a different set of expectations about recent and future trends in housing segregation. Actions such as the 1968 fair housing law was looked upon as symbolic rather than any substantive change in housing patterns. It took 20 years, before the 1988 amendments to the Civil Rights Act, added "meaningful enforcement powers and accessible remedies" (Taeuber 1989:138). Rapid white departure from central cities to suburbs continued while blacks remained concentrated in the central cities.

In 1970 less than 16 2/3% of the total black population (33 million between 1950 & 1970) lived in suburbia as compared with 40% of whites. (Thernstrom &Thernstrom 1997) Trends between 1970 and 1980 in black and white suburbanization, in 30 metropolitan areas (with the largest black populations), showed an average in 1980 of 71% white in northern suburbs and 23.1% of blacks there. In southern suburbs the average was 65% for whites and 33.8% for blacks. In almost every metropolitan area there was an increase in suburbanization (both white and black) from 1970. (Massey & Denton, 1993) Another measurement of desegregation occurring in these same 30 metropolitan areas is the percentage of blacks living in the suburbs in 1980. In northern suburbs the average was 5.2% blacks whereas in southern metropolitan areas the average living in the suburbs was 15 ½ %. (Massey & Denton, 1993) Figures for 1995 *Current Population Report* _(U.S. Census Bureau, 1996) show blacks now represent 8.1% of the U.S. suburban population.

The decline in metropolitan segregation indices and the surge of black suburbanization seem consistent with the view that our nation, as we enter the 21st Century, is on a path of residential desegregation. But not all the evidence points in this direction. The persistence of many cases of extreme (or hyper-) racial segregation is an indicator of an inertia in the housing segregation system. A decade or two of desegregative trends in some major metropolitan areas has not been enough to transform or reform the "essentially segregated character of housing" in America. For example, at the time of the 1980 Census, the suburbs surrounding Gary-Hammond-East Chicago were more than 99.75% white. The suburbs surrounding Milwaukee, Wisconsin were more than 95% white. In the 31 metropolitan areas with a population over one million, the proportion of blacks moving to the suburbs nearly doubled from 21% to 38% between 1970 and 1990. (Thernstrom and Thernstrom, 1997) Nevertheless, the opening up of formerly all-white suburbs was accompanied by growth in nearly all-black suburbs and rapid racial succession by blacks in other suburbs. It's possible that declines in the metropolitan index (of segregation) result from a temporary process that is still essentially segregative. Data for a single decade or two may be insufficient to predict whether increased integration is only a passing or permanent situation in the future. Many racially-mixed suburbs today may be on their way from nearly all-white to nearly all-black. Only time will tell.

Wilson's Three Major Stages of Race Relations

William Julius Wilson describes, as we have in this brief history of housing segregation and migration from the South, three major stages of black-white relations. He simplifies these stages as: pre-industrial; industrial; and, modern industrial. "Each stage embodies a different form of racial stratification" and control by whites "...structured by the particular arrangement of both the economy and the polity". (1967: 2-3) In each stage, a different group of whites has benefited from racism. Whites always won. Blacks always lost. The first stage of the "plantation-economy and racial-caste oppression" begins with slavery until about 1875. The big white winners were the large land owners - - with slave or oppressed cheap labor. The second stage, as described earlier, ends at roughly the mid-1930's - - the industrial period with class and racial conflict. The major winners during this stage were the eastern and southern European immigrants, your grandparents. They could work in unskilled and factory jobs long before Blacks were ever hired. The third stage, modern (or post-modern), involves middle class whites during World War II and post-war prosperity - -"the period of progressive transition from racial inequalities to class inequalities". (1967: 3) As pointed out earlier, (and in the Education Chapter), white middle class people generally fight affirmative action (as in the recent court action of three white middle class persons against the University of Michigan). They also vote against local tax increases to fund poor Black school systems. The point here throughout this whole chapter is that during every stage of race relations, and even today, whites benefit from racism and Blacks consistently lose.

Hacker's View of Segregation

Andrew Hacker in his article (and book) "Two Nations: Black and White, Separate, Hostile and Unequal" (1992) offers a logical reason why neighborhoods, areas and cities in America remain segregated. Hacker calls our segregated housing "residential apartheid" (as in the Union of South Africa). He observes that: "Black segregation differs markedly from that imposed on any other group.

American blacks are one of the oldest immigrant minority groups in America" (Horton et al., 1997:299). Even newly-arrived immigrants of both the past and present, were more readily accepted into white neighborhoods and are now integrated. In none of the "ghettos" reported by Burgess in the 1920's and 1930's did the ghettoized group constitute even a bare majority of the population. However, "in areas that Burgess identified as the black ghetto, blacks comprised 82% of the population (Park, Burgess and McKenzie, 1925:47-62; Burgess, 1928:1-11; Massey and Denton, 1993:32).

Most black residents do *not* prefer the racial ratios in areas where they live. Many surveys, Hacker points out, have shown, on average, only about one in eight (12 ½%) say they prefer a neighborhood that is all or mostly black. Yet this is the condition most blacks presently live in. "The vast majority surveyed, usually about 85% of blacks, state they would like an equal mixture of black and white neighbors" (Hacker, 1999:96). Unfortunately, this degree of racial balance (50-50) has no chance of being realized in the future. Again, we have no shortage of scientific studies or research about the willingness of whites to live in neighborhoods or areas with blacks as long as blacks do not make up more than 8% of the total residents. Other studies have shown a "tipping point" anywhere from 5% to 20% (Taueber, 1989:143). But once the black numbers pass the "tipping point" whites begin to flee and leave the neighborhood. No new whites will move in. The vacant houses or apartments will be bought or rented by blacks; the whole area will be on its way to becoming all-black. What makes real integration so difficult, if not impossible, is that so few whites will accept even a racial proportion that reflects the *overall* national proportion of 12% or 13% black. As Hacker, concludes: "No matter what your talents or attainments, you are seen as infecting a neighborhood simply because of your race. This is the ultimate insult of segregation" (1999:96).

Hence, today as we enter the 21st Century, two conflicting interpretations of housing segregation of the races are possible: Discrimination is lessening or discrimination persists? The cup is half full or half empty? In housing segregation, as in every domain of race relations, the historian, sociologist, economist or political scientist may emphasize progress or problems, a promising outlook or pitfalls in the future. The scholar or student who gathers objective evidence is not freed from this choice. Evidence does not speak for itself. It must be interpreted by using critical thinking.

Persistent housing segregation in America over the past 100 years has had a direct impact on the employment-unemployment and income of African-Americans. As Kenneth Clark stated in 1965: "The dark ghettos are social, political, educational and—above all—economic colonies. Their inhabitants are subject people, victims of the greed, cruelty, insensitivity, guilt, and fear of their masters". (1965: 11)

Massey and Denton also show the connection between the segregated black community and the lack of equal opportunity for jobs and income. They note:

> Segregation concentrates poverty to build a set of mutually reinforcing and self-feeding spirals of decline into black neighborhoods. When economic dislocations deprive a segregated group of employment and increase its rate of poverty, socio-economic deprivation becomes more concentrated in neighborhoods where that group lives. The damaging social consequences that follow from increased poverty are spatially concentrated as well, creating uniquely disadvantaged environments that become progressively isolated—geographically, socially and economically—from the rest of society (1993:2)

So historically whatever data is presented about employment-unemployment and income of African-Americans must be seen and interpreted in the light of a highly segregated society, even today.

Employment Discrimination

Historically, blacks have had unequal access to employment in four ways: First, blacks have been discriminated against at the job candidate, job entry and job promotion stages (Braddock and McParland, 1987); Second, blacks have been clustered at the lowest levels of occupational categories; Third, a greater portion of blacks than whites are unemployed or underemployed, and may eventually become disillusioned and drop out of the work force; Fourth, as a result of these experiences, and white discrimination, both earnings and family income for blacks have been traditionally much less than for whites, even with education comparable to whites.

At the job candidate stage many of the better jobs are still discovered through personal contacts and word of mouth from friends, as much as formal recruitment or newspaper ads. In Chicago, a survey of 185 firms found that employers focus their efforts on white neighborhoods and avoid recruiting from the inner-city, black labor force (Neckerman and Kirscherman, 1991). Also many new jobs today are being created in the suburbs (mostly all-white) not in the center cities where the majority of blacks live (Mooney et al; 2000). In high residentially segregated areas the predicted probability that a young black male will be jobless ranges from 39.9% to 53.3% (Massey, Gross and Eggers, 1991:415). Consequently, "only half of African-American men, aged 18 to 64, have full-time, year-round jobs, compared with two-thirds of white males" (Thernstrom and Thernstrom, 1997:245).

<u>Blacks Clustered at Lower-Level Occupations</u>
          Though blacks made some progress in being hired during WW I, WW II, and the 1950's, they were generally clustered at the lower-level occupations. By the 1960's, they still had a long way to go to advance to higher-level job levels that most whites had already attained. For example, in 1965, 43 ½% of non-whites were employed in the three lowest job classifications (i.e. industrial laborers, farm laborers and "service" jobs) but only 15% of whites worked in these three lowest occupations. By 1989, (about 25 years later) this situation had changed somewhat so about 29% of blacks held these jobs as compared with 18% whites (McVeigh, 1990:10-11).
          If the bottom rungs of the job ladder were historically "reserved" for blacks, the top rungs were always (and still are) "reserved" for whites. In 1965, the top three job classifications (professional and managerial, technical, sales and administration, and precision production, craft and repair) were held by 60% of the white workforce but only 27% of the black work force. By 1989 blacks had made some progress in moving into the top three occupational slots. Though 71% of the white workforce held the top three positions over half (53%) of the black workforce was there too. Hence, though an 18 percentage-point gap existed between whites and blacks, it was a 26 percentage-point gain for blacks since 1965, as compared with only an 11 point gain for whites (McVeigh, 1990:13).
          Table 5-1 shows the three highest and the three lowest job classifications in 199 according to the U.S. Bureau of the Census. African-Americans are still disproportionately represented in various occupational categories. If there were perfect equality in obtaining jobs, the proportions in the table would be exactly the same as the group's proportion in the labor force. For African-Americans that would be 12.6%. Looking of African-Americans in each classification:

Table 5-1: Employed Civilians by Occupation and Race: 1998

Occupation	Percent Blacks
Managerial and professional	7.6%
Technician, sales and administration	11.1%
Service workers	17.6%
Precision production, craft and repair	8.0%
Operators, fabricators and laborers	15.7%
Farming, forestry, fishing	5.1%

Source: Statistical Abstract of the United States: 1999. U.S Bureau of the Census, (1999: Adapted from Table 675, 424-428)

This means they are over represented in "service workers" and "operators, fabricators and laborers" and under-represented in all the other categories. "Clearly we have not yet resolved the problem of discrimination in job opportunities" (Lauer, 1998:329).

Today in the 21st Century, blacks remain underrepresented in the professions of engineering, law and medicine, as well as architecture and dentistry. Even more so than white women. "While virtually all professions are saying they would like to have more minorities on their payrolls, it still remains to be seen whether they simply want a few faces for showcase purposes or if they mean jobs with real responsibilities:" (Hacker, 1999:97).

Because of private employer discrimination or prejudice or unwillingness to hire many blacks into professional positions, public and non-private organizations have become havens for much of the black professional workforce. Over one-third of all black lawyers work for government departments, as do almost 30% of black scientists. In addition, blacks account for over 20 percent of our nation's armed forces, twice their proportion in the civilian economy. They also hold almost a fifth of all Postal Service positions and have similar ratios in many county and city agencies. Unfortunately this makes middle-class blacks vulnerable to public budget cuts (Hacker, 1999:97).

Unemployment and Underemployment

Among the most convincing data about inequality in employment and occupational distribution are unemployment rates. For the past 50 years, unemployment rates of African-Americans have been double or more than those of whites (Horton et al., 1997; Kornblum and Julian; 1998: Lauer, 1998: Statistical Abstract of U.S.,

1999). In 2001 it was 4.2% for whites and 8.7% for blacks. (Statistical Abstract of U.S., 2002)

If blacks lose a job, they may suffer more than whites in the process of job or career change. A study among workers displaced from some high-technology industries found that African-Americans (and other minorities) suffered greater earning losses than whites whether their new jobs were within or outside the high-tech sector (Ong, 1991) and when they have a job minorities may be more vulnerable to loss. They are often "the last to be hired and the first to be fired or laid off" during hard times. Zuerling and Silvers (1992) found that African-Americans were more than twice as likely as whites to be fired from jobs in the Federal government, even after controlling for such factors as tenure, union protection, absenteeism and disciplinary actions. (Lauer, 1998)

Underemployment is also more common among minorities. In 1993, Zhou looked at employment data on six different minority groups. In general, 40% or more of each group was "underemployed" even when controlling for education and age difference. (Lauer, 1998)

Unemployment among African-Americans is double the rate of unemployment among Whites (Credit: Joseph Elliott)

Many unemployed today are young and/or non-white. For example, in 1995, 35.7 percent of black teenagers were unemployed; in 1954 the figure was 16.5 percent. (Kornblum and Julian, 1998) Many of them today are high school dropouts. Their low education equips them only for low-skilled, temporary or seasonal jobs. The long-established definition of "unemployment" grossly understates the size of the labor force and the extent of unemployment among blacks and others. First, it excludes unemployed people who "...did not actively seek work during the survey week." A second factor is that the official data doesn't reflect "underemployment" of people with part-time jobs. In 1968, R. A. Nixon estimated that a more accurate measure of unemployment would be about double the official rate. The problem of "invisible" unemployment among blacks becomes more serious during economic recessions, when the duration of unemployment increases; eventually millions of people stop looking for jobs. They think it is virtually impossible to find one. They are known as "discouraged workers" and they know industries and manufacturers have cut back production and eliminated a large number of jobs. "The Bureau of Labor Statistics estimated that the recession of the early 1990's caused about one million people to drop out of the labor force in a single year". (Rackham, 1991) Blacks are a large part of such "discouraged workers" and have always been historically. Today, of course, most new job opportunities are found in outlying white suburban areas while opportunities in center-city areas are shrinking. (Kornblum and Julian, 1998)

Some Progress Made in Earnings and Income
        Ever since blacks started receiving wages, they were usually paid less than whites, even in the Civil War Army. For years, employers only used blacks as strike breakers, which accounted for some white workers hatred of blacks (Heaps, 1970:110). Historically, starting during World War II (1941-1945), some progress has been made by blacks in their earnings and income. In 1940, 87% of black families were in poverty. By 1960, this figure was down to 47%; in 1997 it was down to 26 ½% (Statistical Abstract of U.S., 1999) and 19% by 2000. (Statistical Abstract of U.S., 2002) Today, well over three-quarters of black families are *above* the poverty level, though over 30% of black children live in poverty, compared with about 12 % of white children. (U.S. Census Bureau, 2002)   In 1940, 60% of all employed black women were domestic servants, cleaning white people's houses; today very few are. In fact, a majority of black women hold white-collar jobs. (Thernstrom and Thernstrom, 1997) Historically it was not usually the case. Quite the contrary.
        During the past 50 years (1942-1992) the relative earnings of black males have increased from 45% of white males in 1940 to 72% in 1992. (Hacker, 1999) Some of the most significant economic gains for blacks came during World War II (1941-45) and the post-war years of the late 1940's and the decade of the 1950's. These gains occurred in a time of buoyant economic expansion and spreading affluence. They

felt all the more remarkable following so close on the heels of the worse economic catastrophe in American history (i.e. the Great Depression of the 1930's).   Blacks not only shared in the rising prosperity of the war and post-war years but they advanced more rapidly then whites. In the 1940's and '50's, as new jobs opened up to blacks for the first time, the economic gap between the races narrowed with greater speed then in any comparable short span of years since then. (Thernstrom and Thernstrom, 1997) The importance of these two decades (the '40's and '50's) must be underscored because it is too often *assumed* that the significant economic advances blacks have made all occurred in the 1960's and after, due to civil rights protests and federal laws provoked by those protests. This common-sense view is wrong, both about the timing and causes of changes.   The Urban League's Annual Report on the state of black America in July, 2000 noted that the strong economy of the 1990's "…is proving a powerful magnet for growth" for blacks. (Report on Black America, 2000: A-16)

Even though the high school and college educational gap between blacks and whites is closing, the great paradox is that the normal connection between "more education means more money" does not apply to blacks as often as it does for whites. In spite of record economic progress for blacks during the 1940's and '50's, by 1965 a significant gap between black and white income still persisted, in spite of comparable education.

According to the *Monthly Labor Review* (Johnston, May, 1965:525) the following income gaps existed between blacks and whites of the same educational achievement:

Education	Gap (1965)
8 years schooling	$1,000 gap
High school diploma	$1,800 gap
Some college	$2,800 gap

Even in 1988, the median income for all households produced a black income-gap compared with whites of the same educational level as follows:

Education	Gap (1988)
4 years of high school	$5,813
4 years of high school or some college	$ 9,248
4 years or more of college	$13,395

The paradox by 1988 was that the higher the black educational level the greater the median income gap. Thus, education, so often viewed as "the answer" by whites to the blacks' employment, unemployment and income problems may not, in fact, be the panacea and "magic bullet" that white society envisions. A report in the *New York Times*, revealed that of nearly 20 million non-white Americans living in families had family incomes (in 1965) under $3,000 a year (less than $60 a week); only 16% of white families had such low family income (Lissner, 1967:40). The percentage of black and white families with incomes from $3,000 to $6,999 had less of a gap (41% vs. 48% of whites). The families with incomes of $7,000 or more was 11% of black families and 36% of white families. So nearly 40 years ago (1965) a wide gap existed between poor and rich black families and whites.

By 1988, long after the civil rights movement of the 1960's, differences in family income *by race* still persisted. For annual family income of "under $10,000", 30% were black but only 9% were white. For those with incomes of $50,000+, 24 ½% were white families but only 9 ½% were black". (U.S. Census Bureau, 1989)

In 1967, white median family income was $7,450 compared with $4,325 for blacks, 59% of white family income. By 1988, the white median family income was $33,920 compared with only $19,330 for black families. This represented 57% of the white income, two percentage points *less* than in 1967. (Kotlowitz, 1988) In 2000, the latest figures available, white median family income rose to $53,256; the black family income was only $34,192, 64% of whites. (Statistical Abstract of U.S., 2002)

Recent research has shown that focusing on income differences between blacks and whites can be deceptive. Melvin Oliver and Thomas Shapiro (1995) in their research on "Asset Inequality" found that about a third of all Americans own almost no assets, other than a car or a home. The asset gap is much greater than that for African-Americans. Though there is today a growing black middle-class who owns property and have investments and pensions, "...it is far outnumbered by those who own almost nothing and have no assets to fall back on during hard times" (Kornblum and Julian, 1998:277). For example, in 1993 the median net worth of the average white household was $45,740; the average black household was worth only $4,418" (Masci, 1998:64). This means the typical white household had *ten times* the material assets of the typical black household. In addition, in 2001 some 73.2% of whites owned their homes while only 47.5% of blacks owned theirs. (Statistical Abstract of U.S., 2002)

Asset inequality has a profound impact on intergenerational inequality. People with property and investments can pass on their wealth and estates to their children or grandchildren. Hence, their heirs will have a distinct material advantage over others. This is not possible for those with very low or no assets, whatever their racial background. The asset gap, even among high-earners, largely is determined by inherited wealth. Thermstrom and Thermstrom note that "...only within the past few decades have any but a handful of black people had the opportunity to acquire substantial property; few of their parents *and* grandparents, living under slavery and then Jim Crow, bequeathed significant estates to their descendants" (1997:198).

So though some progress has been made over the years for African-Americans in the areas of employment, better job categories, unemployment and income, much more remains to be changed before true equality and equity are reached. (Report on Black America, 2000)

**African-Americans and Whites are increasingly interacting together
(Credit: Jay Kainz)**

Conflict Over Voting and Political Power

Of all the struggles and conflicts between whites and blacks over integrated housing, employment, better income, none have proven so successful for blacks as obtaining the vote and political power. After 100 years, the vote opened up real access to political power for blacks. Within the last 35 years or so, significant progress has been made, though the conflict for more power continues to this day.

Historically, it wasn't until five years after the Civil War ended (1870) that blacks (but not women) received the right to vote from the Federal Government (15th Amendment). For about 15 years or so, black people voted and held political office, as long as Federal troops were in the South. Under Jim Crow laws and violence by the Ku Klux Klan in the 1880's and afterwards, voting and holding office was no longer a possibility in the South for most all blacks. Poll taxes, literacy tests, threats of violence or economic reprisals insured that blacks would not vote or hold political positions at all in the South, and sometimes even in the North.

Between 1870 and 1901, 20 blacks served in the U.S. House, three in the U.S. Senate and numerous others at the state and local levels in the South, because of their right to vote.   (Barker and McCorry, 1980) By 1901 few blacks remained in those positions. This picture didn't start to change until 1928 when the election of Oscar DePriest from Illinois' First District began the return to Congress by blacks.   (Walters, 1989)   By 1936, blacks had begun to vote overwhelmingly for Democratic candidates at the presidential and local levels. Roosevelt's recovery programs had given them some access to greater employment and social opportunities. Under the Democrats, blacks began to obtain valued appointments within the urban political machines of the North and in the Roosevelt Administration. By the election of 1944, there was a consensus that blacks held the balance of power in the Democratic party, with the potential to eclipse white southern votes. (Moon, 1948)

The period from 1944 to 1964 saw expanding voting rights for blacks. The Supreme Court decision outlawing the "white primary" in 1944 caused what Henry Lee Moon called a "revival of Negro participation in politics" that resulted in thousands registering and voting. Though blacks had nearly been eliminated from the electoral process, with the election of 1948 they returned to the polls in increasing numbers. (Walters, 1989)

But it wasn't until the Voting Rights Act of 1965 (exactly 100 years after the end of the Civil War), and mobilization of black voters by the civil rights movement that gave blacks the balance of power in some key elections. Due to mobilization of black voters by 1968, registration for blacks was 66.2% and voter turnout was 57.6%, compared with 75.4% and 69.1%, respectively, for whites. (Walters, 1989)

Tremendous strides have been made since the Voting Rights Act. In the South alone registered black voters rose from about 1 ½ million in 1960 to about 5 ½ million by 1988, a gain of 283% (Horton et al. 1997:289). This pattern is altering the political structure of the whole nation. Within the past 10 years numerous cities and towns have elected black officials and several states have elected black governors.

As the accompanying table reveals, black elected officials have grown a lot since 1970.

Table 5-2:   Local Elected Officials by Race and Government

	1970	1994	2000
Total elected black officials	1,479	7,984	9,001
U.S. & state legislators	179	561	621
City & county officials	719	4,819	5,420
Law enforcement officials	213	922	1,037
(Judges, magistrates & sheriffs)			
Education	368	1,682	1,923
(College boards, school boards)			

Source: Statistical Abstract of U.S.: 1982; U.S. Bureau of the Census. Table 799 in Horton et al., 1997: 290. Statistical Abstract of U.S.: 1995, Tables 455, 459; Statistical Abstract of U.S.: 2002. Tables 396; 252: 2001.

Since 1985, blacks have won mayoral elections in Atlanta, Boulder, Cincinnati, Cleveland, Dallas, Dayton, Detroit, Grand Rapids, Hartford, Little Rock, Los Angeles, New York City, Philadelphia and Pontiac, MI. (Thernstrom and Thernstrom, 1997:)   The conventional wisdom is that most black mayors are elected in cities that are already over 50% black. The major changes that occurred in respect to political power by blacks was that whites voted for a black candidate. As Thernstrom and Thernstrom point out: "Between 1967 and 1993, African Americans won the mayor's seat in eighty-seven cities with a population of 50,000 or more. A remarkable two-thirds of those mayors were elected in cities in which blacks were a minority of the population. Half of them in fact, were in municipalities less than 40 percent black and over a third in cities in which no more than three out of ten residents were African-American" (1997:286). For example, in 1967, when Carl Stokes first became the mayor of Cleveland, the city was only 38.3 percent black. He picked up 20 percent of the white vote. The city of Los Angeles was never more than 18 percent black in the twenty years Tom Bradley was mayor. In fact, when he was first elected in 1973, he didn't even need his black support; with white voters alone, he would have won. All this is truly a remarkable change in the attitudes and actions of white voters in major U.S. cities. The same incredible change took place over time in the state legislatures of southern states. As late as 1970, no African Americans held elective office in state governments in Alabama, Arkansas or South Carolina, though Florida, Louisiana, Mississippi, and North Carolina each had *a single black* in its state legislature. The total for the eleven ex-confederate states was just 32. By 1993 those states had almost ten times that many black state legislators -- a total of 321 -- and 16 African Americans represented them in the U.S. Congress. In fact, 69 percent of all black elected officials in the U.S. in 1993 were southerners. The largest numbers were in Alabama and Mississippi, the most hard-core of the segregationist states prior to 1965. (Thernstrom and Thernstrom, 1997:) Change often comes about through conflict in our Gesellschaft society.

Nor is all of this past history now. From time to time the news media reports efforts by whites to keep minorities from voting. Rather than intimidation or illegal laws, a tactic more likely to be used is drawing voting district lines in such a way that it neutralizes the power of minority votes. This is called "gerrymandering" and has been used for centuries by both political parties. Fortunately, the 1965 Voting Rights Act contained a Section 5 that gave the U.S. Department of Justice the right to "preclear" any redistricting. The point of Section 5's "preclearance provision" had been to stop southern states from devising clever new ways to keep blacks from the polls. Hence, no change in voting procedures could be made without Federal Government approval. Southern white resistance to black voting and political power thus began a process that strengthened the Voting Rights Act. For example, in 1969 the Court suddenly applied Section 5 to all changes that might have a "disparate racial impact", whether intended or not. A re-districting or annexation plan that was racially neutral in intent could be found discriminatory in effects if it left black voters worse off than the prior districting. In 1982 the law was amended again, this time to give minority voters more leverage in challenging districting or annexation plans all across the nation, not just in the South, as the original law covered. A Supreme Court case in 1995 *(Miller vs. Johnson)* made it clear that in the pre-clearance process the U.S. Justice Department enforced a standard of "proportional representation" that fairly reflected minority voting strength and population. This would guarantee (to the extent possible) proportional black office holding.

In no other area of race relations in the U.S. had government intervention by a law, as well as Supreme Court enforcement of that law, so clearly helped to overcome societal resistance to and conflict over blacks obtaining political power -- particularly in the South. In 1996 a suit was brought against Hempstead, L.I. which had elected only one black council member since its start in 1784. The problem, as in certain areas of the South and North, was the "at-large electoral system". This system elects all candidates town-wise or city-wise rather than by political districts. The court decision required districting so that a minority candidate could represent a smaller minority district. But the conflict over blacks voting still goes on, as suggested by the blacks denied voting in the 2000 Presidential election in certain counties in Florida.

So though much black progress has been made in obtaining political power, the struggle and conflict for equality in this most fundamental of rights still goes on today. (Lauer, 1998:324)   For example, in July 2000, the Congressional Black Caucus charged the U.S. Senate of holding up the President's minority judicial appointments. As of November, 1999, it reported the Senate confirmed 42% of the white nominees but less than 18% of the black nominees. Also in the 1999 session, senators considering black nominees took two months longer than for whites.   The white chairman of the Senate Judiciary Committee had rejected the charge that race plays a role in the confirmation of court nominees. (Dewar, July 20, 2000: A-10) Yet in 2003, Senate Democrats delayed and tried to stop the approval of a well-qualified Hispanic, Judge Estrada, merely because of his political and social beliefs. Racism is far from dead in America.

Police Violence and Racial Profiling
In spite of the growing political power of blacks in major cities, police violence and racial profiling are serious conflicts between "law and order" and rights of citizens. Historically, use of "excessive force", or what is popularly called "police brutality" is nothing new in our Gesselschaft society. In the past small communities would know police who used violence.   Even whites have experienced it but disproportionately blacks have been those most often seriously injured or killed by police.   Major cities in the U.S., particularly New York City, Los Angeles and Philadelphia have had long histories of such violence against blacks. Recent figures reveal in New York City, 34% of the 40,000 officers are minorities; in Los Angeles it has 50%. (C.J. Chivers, April 6, 2000: B-3)   Geoffrey Alpert, a professor at the University of South Carolina College of Criminal Justice in Columbia notes: "Whenever police abuse their authority, it's a social problem that needs to be controlled". (Jost, 2000: 216)

Historian Samuel Walker noted that "...Urban police departments in the United States were beset by continuing scandals throughout the 19th century".   Police departments were guilty of "pervasive brutality and corruption". (1980: 61) Very little external control was imposed. In 1931, a federal Crime Commission - - the famous Wickersham Commission - - again reported that physical brutality was "extensively practiced" by city police departments around the country. (1931: 103) Many abused by police were minority group members.

The Supreme Court first stepped in to question the police interrogation process in 1936. This involved a flagrant case in which three black tenant farmers "confessed" to the murder of a white farmer after being brutally tortured by local sheriff's deputies in Mississippi (*Brown vs. Mississippi*). The court said an involuntary confession was unreliable and its use in court would violate the 14th amendment, depriving one of life or liberty without due process of law. In a second confession case in 1941 (*Lisenba vs. California*) the court, under the due process clause, prohibited the use of any evidence, true or false - - that police obtained (as it had) through techniques that "shocked the conscience" of the community or violated fundamental standards of fairness. (Jost, 2000: 220) The high court ruled on more than 30 "confession" cases between 1936 and 1964, looking at the "totality of the circumstances" in each case. Most involved blacks. The court ruled certain police methods were coercive and therefore, unconstitutional. These methods included: "physical force, threats of harm or punishment, lengthy or incommunicado questioning, solitary confinement, denial of food or sleep and promises of leniency". (Jost, 2000: 223)

Back in the 1940's racial disturbances in Detroit and New York City's Harlem both produced accusations of "discriminatory enforcement of the law against the cities' African-American populations", by police while the "Zoot Suit" riots in Los Angeles "exposed tensions between blacks, Hispanics and the city's overwhelmingly white police force". (Jost, 2000: 223)

The efforts to control police conduct from outside (rather than inside the department through "internal review") began in earnest in the 1960's. In 1961, the Supreme Court ruled that "illegally obtained evidence" could not be used in state courts. Two years later it ruled the states had to provide lawyers for poor criminal defendants if they could not afford one. In 1964, the court held in *Escobedo vs. Illinois* that a suspect has a Sixth Amendment right to consult with his lawyer during police questioning once an investigation moved from a general inquiry to focus on a specific suspect. The best known of the 1960's rulings to protect minorities (and whites) from police forcing a confession out of them was the Miranda decision in 1966. This is now an ingrained police practice - - widely known through three decades of police stories on television or in movies to protect people from self-incrimination or police using excessive force.

All these decisions at the highest level of Government eased the conflict between blacks and whites over questioning and interrogation practices of police in America. But a more violent and volatile conflict between white people and black civilians emerged - - police brutality, use of excessive force. During the 1960's police shootings of blacks had touched off several racial riots that erupted in some of the nation's big cities. The 1968 Kerner Commission Report to study the causes of the riots found "...deep hostility between police and ghetto communities" to have been a 'primary cause' of the disorders. (Jost, 2000: 226)

Shortly afterwards some local police departments began adopting rules to guide officers in the use of force. For example, under N.Y.C. Police Commissioner Patrick Murphy, a rule was instituted in 1972 allowing police to shoot "only in the defense of life" and requiring reports and reviews of any weapons fired. Officer-involved shootings declined 30% over the next three years, according to Professor James Fyfe at Temple University. (Walker, 1998: 232) Historian Walker, however, points out that unlike this 1972 rule "even the best departments had no meaningful rules on deadly force, offering their officers many hours of training on how to shoot but not when to use their weapons". (1998: 197)

Since the early 1970's, Walker maintains that over the next 25 years much progress was made, especially cities establishing civilian review boards. By the early 1990's, Walker reports, "more than three-fourths of the police departments in the nation's biggest cities had some form of external or civilian review of complaints". (Jost, 2000: 226) Just how effective they were in curbing police violence was unknown.

Police Brutality in the 1990's

During the 1990's the conflict over police brutality was put back on the national agenda because of *four* well-publicized cases by the mass media. The *first case* was the beating of Rodney King by four white Los Angeles policemen after a high-speed chase on March 3, 1991. An 81-second video tape by a resident of a nearby apartment, showed the officers repeatedly kicking King and hitting him 56 times with their clubs as he lay on the ground. This video film was broadcast on television all over the world the next two years. This episode of police brutality produced a national outcry against such behavior. Nevertheless, a predominantly white jury acquitted all four officers of state charges in 1992. A year later, two of the four were convicted in a

Federal court of violating King's civil rights. They were given relatively light jail sentences of 30 months each.

In 1997 police brutality once again became a national issue from a *second case* this time in New York City. It involved the sodomizing of a Haitian immigrant, Abner Louima, by a white policeman, Justin Volpe.

Volpe later also admitted he struck Louima while taking him to the police car. Once at the police station, Volpe took the prisoner into a restroom, (and with the help of another white policeman) plunged a broken broomstick handle into the Haitian's rectum. Volpe later pleaded guilty to six federal charges of civil rights violations (after other officers testified against him). He was sentenced to 30 years in jail. The second policeman, Charles Schwarz, was convicted of beating Louima and holding him down during the sodomizing. He faces up to a life sentence but has appealed. Two other policemen were convicted in federal court of conspiracy to obstruct justice for attempting to cover up the incident but they have appealed also.

The Louima case caused universal revulsion, even among normally supportive policemen and the public. Historian Walker said the King and Louima cases represented a real setback for public perceptions of the police - - usually very positive perceptions by most whites according to public opinion polls. (Gallop Poll Topics: A-Z, Dec. 12, 1999); (Yost, June 1999: A-9) These two cases "make it appear to the average citizen that nothing has changed (since the 1960's) and maybe things have gotten worse". (Jost, 2000: 227)

Indeed things did get worse for the blacks and New York City police. The third case, in 1999, involved not physical brutality per se, but shooting to death an unarmed black man. He was shot 41 times by four white policemen, who later were acquitted of criminal charges in his death. Protests and demonstrations by blacks followed. (Foreno, 2000) The man killed by the police was Amadou Diallo, a street vendor and immigrant from Guinea. The U.S. Justice Department is considering whether or not to prosecute the four white officers on civil rights charges. The parents of the dead man have filed a civil suit against the police. Their lawsuit hopes to show that the police approached him "for no other reason but that he was black". (Waldman, April 19, 2000: B-4) A week before they filed their suit, a judge ruled that New York City is liable for the actions of a white off-duty cop who mistakenly shot a black undercover officer. The prosecuting lawyer said; "It demonstrated the need for more racial sensitivity training of city police". (Ronde, April 11, 2000: B4)

The fourth case, caught on videotape by a news helicopter, took place in Philadelphia in July, 2000. This was the case of Tom Jones who stole a police car, and shot a policeman. The videotape showed him being kicked and beaten by 10 policemen after he had surrendered. "A frame-by-frame analysis of the tape by *The Philadelphia Inquirer* newspaper "...showed that the victim was punched and kicked 59 times in 28 seconds before a supervisor rushed in and backed the officers away", the *New York Times* reported. (Lewin, July 15, 2000: A-l) The local NAACP President in Philadelphia said such police behavior "...comes out of a history of violence and brutality in this department for over 30 years". (Brown, July 16, 2000: A-6) The Philadelphia Police Department first earned a reputation as one of the most brutal police forces in the nation in the 1960's and 1970's under the late Frank Rizzo, police commissioner and later mayor.

In 1985, a police standoff and 90-minute gun battle with the all black MOVE group led police to drop explosives on the group's rowhouse. When the house caught fire the mayor and police let it burn. It destroyed two city blocks and killed 11 people, including two children. In 1995, a tow truck driver, whose wife called police to take him to the hospital for an epileptic fit, was beaten by the police. He died three days later. In summer, 1998, police clashed with black fraternity members. Videotape showed one policeman kicking a young man and another one beating a person with his club. (Brown, July 16, 2000: A-6)

In fall, 1998, police shot and killed Donta Dawson who was unarmed and sitting alone in his car blocking traffic. Charges have been dropped twice against the cop who shot Dawson, claiming Dawson made a sudden movement with his left arm. So the July, 2000 incident was just another case in a long history of police abuse in Philadelphia.

One must put all these four recent well-published cases in perspective. Internal police statistics show that police rarely use excessive force in the more than two million incidents that Philadelphia police are called to each year. In 1998, 662 incidences involving "excessive force" were reported by police officers and less than one-quarter were investigated by Internal Affairs. (Brown, 2000) Rutgers University and Arizona State University did a scientific study of the use of force by and against the Phoenix Police Department in June, 1994. It was sponsored by the National Institute of Justice. "In 349 of the 1,585 arrests surveyed (22%), the police reported using some form of physical force. In nearly four out of five adult arrests, police used no physical force at all." (Garner et al., 1996:5) The survey also revealed that suspects arrested used physical force in 228 (14%) of the 1,585 incidents.

Police organizations nationwide also are trying to reassure the public about how rarely "excessive force" is used. A study released this year by the International Assn. of Chief of Police showed that police used force fewer than 3.5 times per 10,000 calls for service and suspects were injured in fewer than 3% of the instances where force was used. (Jost, 2000)

So the issue of "excessive force" by police against blacks has been made public (more than once), and steps taken to control it. The reality, however, is how does society and the state control the behavior of thousands of police officers when they must each use their own discretion to protect themselves and fight crime to protect the public. So the conflict and controversy goes on.

Racial Profiling

Closely connected to "police brutality" in the 1990's was the practice of "racial profiling" by police departments. This became a new flashpoint of police – black relations. African-Americans from all social classes have experienced being stopped and questioned by police, seemingly for no reason other than their race.

A 1999 Gallop public opinion poll revealed that while 38% of whites felt the practice of "racial profiling" by the police was "not widespread" only 16% of blacks felt that way. (Gallop Poll Topics: A-Z, 1999:3) By the year 2000, conservative law enforcement groups were joining liberal civil-rights and civil-liberties groups in saying that race *alone* should never be the basis for a traffic stop or police investigation. But police also continued to defend the use of race *as one factor* in criminal profiling, especially anti-drug enforcement and "street crimes". The courts in the past okayed such practices. In 1975, the Supreme Court upheld a policeman's decision to question a minority male because he was sitting in a parked car in a white neighborhood. The use of race, the court said, was "a practical aspect of good law enforcement". (Jost, 2000: 228) In 1996 the Supreme Court gave police a blank check to use traffic violations as a pretext for stopping motorists for suspected drug violations. That ruling (*Whren vs. U.S.*) turned aside the plea by two black defendants that they had been stopped because of their race.

In spite of these court cases, two states, Maryland and New Jersey, have signed federal court consent degrees agreeing to end "racial profiling" in highway stops by the state police. As part of settling a "racial profiling" suit, the ACLU monitored stops from Jan. 1995 through June 1999 on I 95 in Maryland. It found that more than two-thirds of the cars stopped by state police were driven by blacks. Their offense was a DWB - - "driving while black". (Schneider, 1998: A-3)

A draft report of the United States Commission on Civil Rights said that "evidence suggested the Police Department (of New York City) engaged in racial profiling". (Flynn, 2000: B-1) After reviewing records filed in 1998 by officers, the staff found evidence that racial profiling played a role in the department's "stop-and-frisk" practice. For example, the data from 1998 showed that "...51 percent of the people stopped and searched by police on Staten Island were black, even though the Island's population in only 9 percent black. Everywhere, African-Americans were stopped far out of proportion in any of the communities policed". (Barnes, 2000: B-4)

On the same day the U.S. Commission on Civil Rights issued its draft report showing evidence of "racial profiling" by N.Y.C. Police Department, investigators for the Civilian Complaint Review Board determined that police routinely failed to file required paperwork after "frisking or searching people on New York City's streets". (Rashbaum, 2000: B-1)

The review board's study cases found that while African-Americans "...make up 25.2% of New York City's population, they accounted for 63.8% of the people who complained about being stopped and frisked or searched on the street by police. Whites account for 43.2% of the population but just 10.6% of the complaints". (Rashbaum, 2000: B-4) The Diallo law suit also accuses the police department of "making a policy of racial profiling by targeting black males for 'stop and frisk' searches on the street". (Waldman, 2000: B-4)

Many other civil suits are pending in other states across the nation accusing police departments of such "racial profiling". In 2003, New Jersey passed the first state law against "racial profiling" by the police. The battle between "law and order" vs. social justice and equality for minorities continues as we enter the 21st Century.

Summary

So in the four major conflicts historically between blacks and whites over the last 100 years - -

segregated housing; employment-unemployment and income; political power; and, police violence and racial profiling - - some institutional changes have occurred as blacks have mobilized themselves and used the power of Congress and the courts to demand change. Attitudes and behavior of some whites have changed somewhat in society at a personal level but much more needs to be done at a social structural level before equality and parity are obtained. (Martinez, 2000) Institution of Black Studies in college and universities have helped young African-Americans to better understand their heritage in America. White Studies are needed to educate and sensitize millions of young white Americans as to how white institutional racism, discrimination and segregation have made life for blacks almost unbearable in America.

Critical Thinking Questions

1. Since African-Americans have made economic progress since the 1940's, (where now only about 25% of Black families are poor), in another 50 years do you think economic equality will be obtained by Blacks? If so, why so? If not, why not?

2. What explains the fact that the U.S. is one of the most racially-segregated societies in the world, especially if we believe (if we do) that White and Black people are equal?

3. If African-Americans and Whites are treated fairly and equally, why is it that so few couples marry inter-racially? Do you think this situation will change significantly in the next 25 years in the U.S.? If so, why? If not, why not?

4. After the Civil Rights Act of 1964, reported attitudes of Whites toward Blacks in the U.S. changed. Why do you think that happened? Is it possible for national laws to "legislate morality"?

5. Kenneth R. Adamson in his article "Critical Thinking and the Nature of Prejudice" points out that human motives and actions arise from our desires to enhance our prestige, wealth, power and peace of mind. We are favorably disposed to all our own ideas and interests. How then can we ever overcome our racial prejudice in favor of the white race (of which we are a part) over all other races?

172 Brief History of Social Problems

Bibliography

Anderson, Elijah and Tukufu Zubei. "The Study of African American Problems: W.E.B. Dubois's Agenda, Then and Now." *The Annals of the American Academy of Political and Social Science.* 568 (March 2000): 7-313.

Bachman, Justin. "Coca-Cola Agrees to Settle Discrimination Lawsuit". Associated Press. (June 15, 2000): A-7.

Bailey, Thomas Pearce. *Race Orthodoxy in the South and Other Aspects of the Negro Question.* N.Y.: Neale Publishing Co., 1914.

Barbour, Russell B. *Black and White Together: Plain Talk for White Christians.* Philadelphia: United Church Press, 1967.

Barker, Lucius J. and Jesse McCorry, Jr. *Black Americans and the Political System*, 2d. ed. Cambridge, Ma.: Winthrop Publishers, 1980.

Barnes, Julian. "Mayor Denounces Panel's Report on Police." *New York Times.* (April 28, 2000): B-4.

Bennett, Lerone. *Before the Mayflower: A History of the Negro in America: 1619-1964.* Rev. ed. N.Y.: Penguin Books, 1966.

Boas, Franz. *The Mind of Primitive Man.* N.Y.: MacMillan, 1938 [1911].

Braddock, Jomills Henry II and James M. McPartland. "How Minorities Continue to Be Excluded from Equal Employment Opportunities: Research on Labor Market And Institutional Barriers." *Journal of Social Issues*, 43, no. 1 (1987): 5-39.

Brown, Jennifer. "Police Beating Stirs Memories." Associated Press. (July 16, 2000): A-6.

Burgess, Ernest W. "Residential Segregation in American Cities." *The Annals Of the American Academy of Political and Social Science* 2180 (November 1928): 1-11.

Campbell, Angus. *White Attitudes Toward Black People.* Ann Arbor, Mich. Institute For Social Research, 1971.

Campbell, Angus and Thomas F. Pettigrew. "Racial and Moral Crisis: The Role of Little Rock Ministers." *American Journal of Sociology* (March 1959): 509-16.

Carroll, Charles. *The Negro A Beast or in the Image of God?* St. Louis: American Book and Bible House, 1900.

Cayton, Mary Kupiec, Elliot J. Gorn and Peter W. Williams, eds. *Encyclopedia of American Social History.* I-III. N.Y.: Charles Scribners, 1992.

Chivers, C.J. "Poachers Add New Hurdle to Police Recruiting
    Efforts." New *York Times.* (April 6, 2000): A-1 and A-3.

Clark, Charles. "Housing Discrimination: Are Minorities Still Treated
    Unfairly?" *CQ Researcher.* 5, no. 8 (February 24, 1995):
    169-92.

Clark, Kenneth. *Dark Ghetto: Dilemmas of Social Power.* N.Y.:
    Harper & Row, 1965.

Cooper, Kenneth. "Emotions in Check in Job Bias Settlement." *The
    Washington Post.*(July 20, 2000): A-23.

Davidson, Basil. *A Decade of Equal Employment Opportunity, 1965-
    1975.* Tenth Annual Report, United States Equal Employment
    Opportunity Commission. Washington, D.C.: U.S.
    Government Printing Office, 1977.

Dewar, Helen. "Racist, Sexist Patterns Seen in Senate Record." *The
    Washington Post.* (July 20, 2000): A-10.

Dixon, Thomas, Jr. *The Leopard's Spots: A Romance of the White
    Man's Burden – 1865-1900.* N.Y.: Doubleday Pages & Co.,
    1902.

--------- *The Clansman: An Historical Romance of the Ku Klux Klan.*
    N.Y.: Grosset & Dunlap, 1905.

DuBois, W.E.B. *The Souls of Black Folk.* Chicago: A.C. McClurg,
    1903.

———. *Black Reconstruction in America.* N.Y.: Atheneum, 1935
    (1983).

———. "The Study of the Negro Problems." *The Annals of the
    American Academy of Political and Social Science.* 568
    (March 2000): 13-27.

Flynn, Kevin. "Rights Panel Scolds Police on Race Issues." *New York
    Times.* (April 27, 2000): B-1 and B-8.

Foreno, Juan. "18 Are Arrested As Students Hold Police Brutality
    Protest." *New York Times.* (April 6, 2000): B-3.

Gallup Poll. *Topics: A-Z – Race Relations. Social Audit on
    Black/White Relations in U.S.* (December 12, 1999)
    http://www.gallup.com (June 10, 2000).

Garner, Joel, John Buchanon, Tom Schade and John Hepburn.
    "Understanding the Use Of Force By and Against the Police."
    National Institute of Justice: Research in Brief. 1996.

Grant, Madison. *Passing of the Great Race.* N.Y.: Charles Scribner,
    1916.

Greenhouse, Linda. "Justices Back Affirmative Action by 5 to 4."
    New York Times (June 24, 2003): A-1 & A-23.

Hacker, Andrew. *Two Nations: Black and White, Separate, Hostile Unequal*. New York: Charles Scribner's & Sons, 1992.
————. Two Nations: Black and White, Separate, Hostile, Unequal." Pp. 95-8 in *Annual Editions: Social Problems*, 27th ed., edited by Kurt Finsterbusch. Guilford, Conn.: Dushkin/McGraw-Hill, 1999-2000.

Hamilton, Charles V. *The Fight for Racial Justice: From Court to Street to Politics*. Public Affairs Pamphlet 516. New York: Public Affairs Committee, 1974.

Heaps, Willard A. *Riots, U.S.A.: 1765-1970*. rev. ed. New York: The Seabury Press, 1970.

Henslin, James, M. *Social Problems*. 5th ed. Upper Saddle River, N.J.: Prentice Hall, 2000.

Horton, Paul B., Gerald R. Leslie, Richard F. Larson and Robert L. Horton. *The Sociology of Social Problems*. 12th ed. Upper Saddle River, New Jersey: Prentice Hall, 1997.

Howard, John R. *The Cutting Edge: Social Movements and Social Change in America*. Philadelphia: Lippincott, 1974.

Johnston, David. "Black Secret Service Agents Say Agency Tried to Intimidate Them." *New York Times* (June 2, 2000): A-14.

Johnston, Denis F. "Educational Attainment of Workers." *Monthly Labor Review*. 88, no. 5 (May 1965): 517-27.

Jost, Kenneth. "Policing the Police: How Can Abuses Be Prevented?" *CQ Researcher*. 10, no. 10. (March 17, 2000): 209-40.

Kornblum, William and Joseph Julian. *Social Problems*. 9th ed. Upper Saddle River, New Jersey: Prentice Hall, 1998.

Kotlowitz, Alex. "Racial Gulf: Black's Hopes Raised by 1968 Kerner Report are Mainly Unfulfilled." *Wall Street Journal*. 39 (February 26, 1988): 1 and 9.

Lauer, Robert H. *Social Problems and the Quality of Life*. 7th ed. New York: McGraw-Hill, 1998.

Lewin, Tamar. "Images of Police Beatings are Subject to Blurring." *New York Times*. (July 15, 2000): A-1 and A-11.

Lissner, Will. "Migration of Rural Poor to Nation's Cities Expected to Continue for Decade." *New York Times*. (August 13, 1967): 40.

Liszkowski, R.J. *Let's Talk Sense About Black Americans*. Chicago: Claretian, 1969.

Martinez, Ruben. "The Next Chapter: Talking About Race." *New York Times Magazine*. (July 16, 2000): 11 and 12.

Masci, David. "The Black Middle Class: Is Its Cup Half Full or Half Empty?" *CQ Researcher* 8, no. 3. (January 23, 1998): 49-72.

Massey, Douglas S. and Nancy A. Denton. *American Apartheid: Segregation and the Making of the Underclass.* Cambridge, Mass.: Harvard University Press, 1993.

Massey, Douglas S., Andrew B. Gross and Mitchell L. Eggers. "Segregation, The Concentration of Poverty, and the Life Chances of Individuals." *Social Science Research* 20 (1991): 415-25.

McVeigh, Frank J. "The Life Conditions of Afro-Americans." *Afro-American Studies* (1) 45-9. 1970.

———. "A New Old Way of Measuring Progress in Race Relations." Paper presented at annual meeting of Pennsylvania Sociological Society, Scranton, Pa., October, 1990.

Moon, Henry Lee. *Balance of Power: The Negro Vote.* Garden City, New York: Doubleday, 1948.

Mooney, Linda A., David Knox and Caroline Schacht. *Understanding Social Problems.* 2d ed. N.Y.: Wadsworth, 2000.

Moore, Robert. *The Hidden America: Social Problems in Rural America for the 21st Century.* Selinsgrove, Pa.: Susquehanna University Press, 2001.

Myrdal, Gunnar. *An American Dilemma: The Negro Problem and Modern Democracy.* New York: Harper and Row, 1944.

National Advisory Commission on Civil Disorders. Washington, D.C.: U.S. Government Printing Office. 1968.

Neckerman, Kathryn and Joleen Kirscherman. "Hiring Strategies, Racial Bias, and Inner-City Workers." *Social Problems* 38 (November 1991): 433-47.

Newby, I.A. *Jim Crow's Defense: Anti-Negro Thought in America: 1900-1965.* Baton Rouge, La.: Louisiana State University Press, 1965.

Oliver, M.L. and T.M. Shapiro. *Black Wealth/ White Wealth: A New Perspective on Racial Inequality.* New York: Routledge, 1995.

Ong, Paul M. "Race and Post-Displacement Earnings Among High-Tech Workers." *Industrial Relations* 30 (Fall 1991): 456-68.

Orlans, Harold and June O'Neill, eds. "1992 Affirmative Action Revisited." *The Annals of the American Academy of Political and Social Science.* 523 (September 1992): 5-220.

Park, Robert E., Ernest Burgess and Roderick D. McKenzie. *The City.* Chicago: University of Chicago Press, 1925.

Phillips, V.B. *The Central Theme of Southern History.* Lancaster, Pa.: Lancaster Press, Inc., 1928.

Raab, Earl and Gertrude Jaeger Zelnick. *Major Social Problems.* 2d
    ed. New York: Harper & Row, 1964.

Rackman, A. "Economic Downturn Creates Growth in Ranks of
    Overqualified or Discouraged Job Seekers." *Los Angeles
    Business Journal* (January 7, 1991): 27.

Rashbaum, William K. "Review Board Staff Faults Police on Stop-
    and-Frisk Report." *New York Times* (April 28, 2000): B-1
    and B-4.

———. "Report on Black America Finds a College Gender Gap."
    New York Times (July 26, 2000): A-16.

Ronde, David. "Judge Holds City Liable for White Officer's Shooting
    of a Black Officer." *New York Times* (April 11, 2000): A-2.

Schneider, Mike. "Officers Trial to Spotlight Profiling of Motorists."
    Associated Press (January 12, 1998): A-3.

Schroeder, Michael. "Summers Calls for Legislation to Curb Predatory
    Lending in Mortgage Markets." *Wall Street Journal.* (April
    13, 2000): A-2.

Shapiro, Herbert. "Racism." Pp. 2089-99 in *Encyclopedia of
    American Social History* 3, edited by Mary K. Cayton, Elliot
    Gorn and Peter Williams. New York: Charles Scribners,
    1992.

Silberman, Charles. *Crisis in Black and White.* New York: Random
    House, 1964.

Statistical Abstract of the United States. 116th ed. 405-07. 1996.

———. 119th ed. "Black Elected Officials by Office, 1970-1996, and
    State 1997." Table 483:298. 1999.

———. 119th ed. "Employed Civilians by Occupation and Race:
    Table 695": 424-28. 1999.

———. 119th ed. "General Purpose Law Enforcement Agencies –
    Number and Employment: 1996." Table 367: 195. 1999.

———. 119th ed. "Local Elected Officials by Sex, Race, Hispanic
    Origin, and Type of Government: 1992." Table 481: 297.
    1999.

———. 119th ed. "Money Income of Households - Median Income
    and Income Level, by Household type: 1997." Table 747:
    430. 1999.

———. 121st ed. "Occupied Housing Units – Tenure by Race of
    Households: 1991-2001." Table 938: 599: 2001.

Steinberg, Stephen. *The Ethnic Myth: Race Ethnicity and Class in
    America.* New York: Atheneum, 1981.

Stoddard, Lothrop. *The Rising Tide of Color.* New York: Charles
    Scribner's & Sons, 1922.

Taeuber, Karl E.   "Residence and Race: 1619-2019." Pp. 121-53 in
    *Race: Twentieth Century Dilemmas - - Twenty-First Century
    Prognoses*, edited by Winston A. Van Horne and Thomas V.
    Tonnesen. Madison, Wis.: The University Press of
    Wisconsin System, 1989.

Terkel, Studs. *Race: How Blacks & Whites Think & Feel About the
    American Obsession.* New York: Anchor Books, Doubleday,
    1992.

Thernstrom, Stephan and Abigail Thernstrom. *America In Black and
    White: One Nation Indivisible.* New York: Simon &
    Schuster, 1997.

U.S. Census Bureau. Current Population Reports, Series P-20. "The
    Black Population in the United States." (March 1989): 438.

Vander Zanden, James W. *American Minority Relations: The
    Sociology of Race and Ethnic Groups.* 2d ed. New York:
    Ronald Press, 1966.

Van Horne, Winston A. and Thomas V. Tonnesen, eds. *Race:
    Twentieth Century Dilemmas – Twenty-First Century
    Prognoses.* Madison, Wis.: The University of
    Wisconsin System, 1989.

Waldman, Amy. "Diallo Parents Sue City and Officers Over Son's
    Death." *New York Times.* (April 19, 2000): B-4.

Walker, Samuel. *Popular Justice: A History of American Criminal
    Justice.* New York: Oxford University Press, 1980.

———. Popular Justice: A History of American Criminal Justice, 2d
    ed. New York: Oxford University Press, 1998.

Walters, Ronald W. "Black Politics: Mobilization for Empowerment."
    Pp. 255-88 in *Race: Twentieth Century Dilemmas – Twenty-
    First Century Prognoses*, edited by Winston A. Van Horne
    and Thomas Tonnesen. Madison, Wis.: The University of
    Wisconsin System, 1989.

Washington, Booker T. *Up From Slavery: An Autobiography.* N.Y.:
    Bantam Books, 1959.

Westie, Frank. "The American Dilemma: An Empirical Test."
    American Sociological Review (August 1965): 308-15

Whites, Lee Ann. "Rebecca Latimer Felton and the Wife's Farm: The
    Class and Racial Politics of Gender Reform." *Georgia
    Historical Quarterly.* 76 no. 2 (1992): 354-72.

Wickersham Commission, United States. "National Commission on
    Law Observance and Enforcement: Report." Washington,
    D.C.: U.S. Government Printing Office. *1931.*

Williamson, Joel. *The Crucible of Race: Black-White Relations in the American South Since Emancipation.* N.Y.: Oxford Press, 1984.

Wilson, William Julius. *The Declining Significance of Race.* Chicago: University of Chicago Press, 1967.

Woodward, C. Vann. *The Strange Career of Jim Crow.* N.Y.: Oxford University Press, 1966.

Yost, Pete. "Blacks Dislike of Police is High, Survey Finds." Associated Press. (June 4, 1999): A-9.

Zhou, Min. "Underemployment and Economic Disparities Among Minority Groups." *Population Research and Policy Review* 12, no. 2: 139-57.

Zinn, Howard. *A People's History of the United States.* N.Y.: Harper & Row. 1980.

Zuerling, Craig and Hilary Silvers. "Race and Job Dismissals in a Federal Bureaucracy." *American Sociological Review* 57 (October 1992): 651-60.

Chapter 6

Social Problems Related to the Family

The family is the basic social unit of every society. The groups we belong to, the town or city we live in, and the social milieu we find ourselves in are linked to our families. It is the group and social institution we know the best, and our deepest emotions and memories--positive or negative--are linked to it. Yet we know that within our lifetime, many changes have taken place that affect our relationships and feelings toward our families. What do these changes mean for the family? What will the family look like fifty years from now?

The family is the oldest social institution; and, it is a cultural universal – meaning that it is found everywhere in the world even though it varies in form and functions. It almost seems that any time you turn on the news, you hear some new controversy regarding the family. Sociologists and other social scientists had debated for years whether the American family had declined or "withered away;" to what degree urbanization had separated the nuclear family from kin; whether the extended family had declined in importance and whether changes in the family's structure and functions were due to, or came before, industrialization and urbanization. On these and many other family issues social scientists were and remain divided. Nevertheless, the basic questions for most scholars and Americans remain. What effects have social change had on the families in the United States and what social problems have emerged from societal change? Optimists argue that the family is merely reorganizing, adapting or adjusting to a new society and becoming more individualistic and free (Coontz, 1992; Skolnick, 1991). Pessimists argue that the family is decaying, disintegrating, dying and losing its social solidarity and unity (Furstenberg, 1990; Popenoe, 1996).

An extended family where three generations live in the same house

Armand Mauss calls the pessimists the "defenders" of the traditional family who want to "conserve and preserve" the structure, norms and values of the past. He calls the optimists the "challengers" who want to "liberalize or radicalize" the traditional family structure, norms and values (1975:475). Since these two conflicting perspectives--the "defenders" and the "challengers"--exist, various demographic and social indicators agreed upon by both sides measure the social problems of the family. What is not agreed upon is what the indicators mean, how they should be interpreted, and in what direction the indicators should be pointing. These questions are intertwined with core values associated with the family. Consequently, interpretation of these issues involves critical thinking skills to disentangle the rhetoric from the fact. The major family conflicts and issues covered in this chapter are:

1. Conflict in marital roles
2. Changes in marriage and divorce rates
3. Changes in family size and birth rates
4. Conflicts involving births to single mothers
5. Conflicts in pre-marital sex, extra-marital sex, and cohabitation
6. Family violence conflict
7. Conflict from alternate family forms

Conflict in Marital Roles

Family life in America, a direct descendant of European families, customs and traditions, has historically involved a patriarchal family with children. In fact, the Seventeenth Century New England Puritan family formed the basis of today's norms and values about marriage, family, sex, and roles of men and women. Religion was the foundation of beliefs about this family. According to one story of creation in the Judeo-Christian religion, man was created first in the image of God and woman was created second in order to serve man (I Corinthians, The Bible).   Seventeenth and Eighteenth Century law formalized this position by decreeing that women and children were the legal property of their husbands and fathers (Schechter, 1982).

However, as people moved West, rigid status symbols and customs gave way to "initiative, originality, independence, and particularly the contribution each could make to the family" (Burgess et al., 1971: 260).   In Colonial and frontier America, families had to cooperate to form a unit, care for livestock, make clothes, build sheters, etc.   Hence, both the husband and wife contributed to the economic survival of the family.   Recent historical reinterpretation (Coontz, 1992) of family life in early America shows that women in colonial and pioneer America worked and were somewhat independent. However, this was usually reserved for widowed women or unmarried older women. Betsy Ross, famous for her flags, was typical of a widow who successfully kept up her former husband's upholstery business.

In the 1830s and 1840s household production gave way to wage work outside the home as families increasingly moved to cities. A new division of labor by age and sex emerged among the middle class. Women's roles once again became primarily focused on the home. Men became the "breadwinners." This separation led to the doctrine of "separate spheres" where women's work became associated solely with the home and men's work became solely associated with labor for wages outside the home.   Under the "separate spheres", women and their roles focused on concrete family care, emotional care and domestic issues. Men and men's roles focused on competition, danger and economic care. Consequently, the home became both an escape from the harsher realities of urban economic competition and a symbol of purity. As a result, women's roles, now linked with the home, assumed a moral superiority and the "Cult of True Womanhood", evolved. According to Barbara Welter, under the "Cult of True Womanhood", feminine roles were idealized by the virtues of piety, purity, submissiveness and domesticity (Welter, 1966).

However, to fulfill these ideals, the middle-class family depended on other poor and powerless families for its existence. The spread of textile mills, especially in New England, freed middle-class women from the most time-consuming of their domestic chores-- spinning and making cloth – but were fueled by child laborers at slave wages. Rhode Island investigators found children in sparse clothing making their way to the textile mills before dawn. Furthermore, in 1845 shoemaking families and makers of artificial flowers worked 15 to 18 hours a day (Coontz, 1992).

Furthermore, even though middle class women were freed from the time-consuming tasks of making fabric and clothing, prior to the invention of modern home conveniences, food preparation and house cleaning were also very time-consuming tasks. Middle-class women were able to shift more time for childbearing and rearing to leisure only by hiring domestic help. Between 1800 and 1850, the proportion of servants to middle class households doubled. Some servants were poverty-stricken mothers who had to board or bind out their own children as servants. In his study of Buffalo, New York, in the 1850s, historian Laurence Glasco (1979) found that Irish and German girls often became servants at age eleven or twelve. So the leisure associated with being middle class came at the expense of working class women and children.

As Stephanie Coontz notes:

> For every Nineteenth-Century middle-class family that protected its wife and child within the family circle, then, there was an Irish or German girl scrubbing floors in that middle-class home, a Welsh boy mining coal to keep the home-baked goodies warm, a black girl doing the family laundry, a black mother and child picking cotton to be made into clothes for the family and a Jewish or an Italian a daughter in a sweatshop making "ladies" dresses or artificial flowers for the family to purchase (1992: 11-12).

Summary

Between the 1700s and the early to mid-1900s, family roles have become more divided along gender lines and the family has become more isolated from the community, paving the way for a more Gesellschaft form of society. Traditional gender roles suggest that men, as the heads of households, had almost undisputed social control over women and children. Or so it would seem; be leery of the "fallacy of over-generalization". Prior to the Industrial Revolution, women were an important part of the home economy. Remember that the home was an area of economic production. While women had few formal rights and many were mistreated, women still had some power in that it was not economically advantageous for men, given the importance of family production, to antagonize their wives by beating them severely, beating them frequently or otherwise grossly mistreating them (Young and Willmott, 1973). Furthermore, during this time, the family was still a community entity, meaning that most of their behaviors occurred under the scrutiny of the wider community (Aries, 1962). Community scrutiny was a very strong form of social control. Consistent with the Gemeinschaft ideology, any deviation from the group's norms was dealt with swiftly. While husbands had ultimate power in the family, it paid husbands to use this power wisely and it was not unusual for the members of the community to intervene if they thought that these men were abusing their privileged position (Young and Willmott, 1973). Consequently, prior to the Industrial Revolution, while men had more power in the family than women, their power was not absolute.

However, by the mid-1800s when the Industrial Revolution was clearly underway, families were becoming more private and focused on the emotional relationship between family members. This served to essentially remove the family from the outside community. At the same time, for middle class families, as the doctrine of "separate spheres" evolved, gender roles became increasingly divided where men assumed the "breadwinner role" and women took care of the home. The divided gender roles and increased separation from the community served to make women increasingly isolated and dependent on their husbands. This weakened women's position in both the family and society, thereby strengthening male dominance and strengthening the belief that families were ruled by men.

While some women undeniably had influence on their husbands, the virtues of "The Cult of True Womanhood" associated with women's new role focus limited women's exposure to the outside world and made their views and concerns more frivolous in the eyes of men (Shorter, 1975). True, it is believed that women's family position made them morally superior to men; however, this new position did not serve to provide women with much practical power in deciding family issues. Conflict theorists would see this token granting of moral superiority as a placating gesture by men that gave women some status while simultaneously ensuring that men's economic and political superiority were unchallenged. Remnants of this ideology are still evident today, as we saw in Chapter 4 on gender roles.

Changes in Marriage and Divorce Rates

During Colonial times marriage was considered an obligation as well as a privilege. People were expected to marry, and the unmarried were generally looked down upon. Taxes and irksome controls over behavior were applied to bachelors to get them to marry. Consequently, most people married and they normally did so at an early age due to one's life expectancy. Girls married in their early teens and boys usually before age 20. When life expectancy was about 30 years, one could not afford to wait to marry and have children. "'Til death due us part" was not that long. High mortality rates meant that the average length of marriage was less than a dozen years.

For most of American history, marriage was (and continues to be) the norm. However, by the mid-1900s a shift in marriage rates became evident. While the number of marriages has steadily increased since the 1950s as the population increased, the marriage rate per 1,000 population has declined from 10.6 in 1970, to 9.8 in 1990 and to 8.5 in 1998 (Statistical Abstracts of the United States, 1998). Some argue that these rates reflect a more significant change, which is the delay of marriage for many women and men. In 1960, the median age at marriage for women was 20.3 (Cherlin, 1988) but by 2000 it was 25.1 (Current Population Survey, 2000a). To put this another way, in 1970 only 36 percent of women between ages 20-24 had never been married, but by 2000 this percentage rose to 73 percent, double that of 1970 (Current Population Survey, 2000a). Many sociologists believe the delay of marriage reflects contemporary women's longer pursuit of higher education and / or careers before they get married now than in the 1950s. cite necessary?

Moreover, a growing number of adults will never marry: almost 60 million in 2000 – up from 46 million in 1997 (Statistical Abstracts of the United States, 1998; United States Bureau of the Census, 2000b). Still, while the rate of marriages may be declining, marriage is still the norm. In 2000, 63.1 percent of women were married (at least once) by age 54 (United States Bureau of the Census, 2000a).

Furthermore, marriages "until death do us part" are becoming less likely. Divorce rates have been steadily increasing since the Civil War (Jacobsen, 1959) and experienced an artificially high peak in 1946 following World War II. This peak (which would not be exceeded until the 1970s) was due to hasty wartime marriages and married women gaining economic independence by working in industry during the war. However, by the end of the 1950s divorce rates dropped sharply and were no higher than in 1947. The rates did not pick up again until between 1965 and 1975 when the divorce rate doubled (Kellogg and Mintz, 1993) and peaked at 22.8 divorces per 1,000 married couples in 1979. Since then, divorce rates have slowly begun to decrease, but the number of divorces in 1998 were still twice as high as in 1966 and three times higher than in 1950 (BacaZinn and Eitzen, 2002).

**Figure 6-1: Divorce Rates per 1,000 in Population
1920-2001**

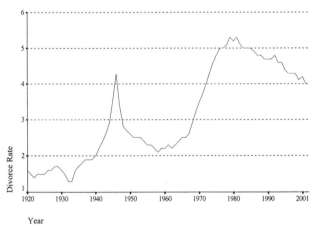

Source: Years 1920-1970 are from "Series B 216-220 of the Vital Statistics and Health and Medical Care Report" from the *Historical Abstracts of the United States: Colonial Times to 1970*, U.S. Department of Commerce, Bureau of the Census. Years 1971-2001 are from No. 66, "Life Births, Deaths, Marriages and Divorces: 1950-2001" found in the *Statistical Abstract of the United States 2002*, 122nd Edition, U.S. Census Bureau.

Currently, the most widely used and quoted figures about divorce and marriage is that "50 percent (or half) of all marriages end in divorce" every year (Gallagher, 1996). Pollster Louis Harris has written: "The idea that half of American marriages are doomed is one of the most specious pieces of statistical nonsense ever perpetuated in modern times...It all began when the Census Bureau noted that during one year, there were 2.4 million marriages and 1.2 million divorces.

Someone did the math without calculating the 54 million marriages already in existence, and presto, a ridiculous but quotable statistic was born." Harris concludes: "Only one out of eight marriages will end in divorce. In any single year, only about two percent of existing marriages will break up," not 50 percent (Fastats, A to Z, 1996: 60).

There are a number of reasons why the divorce rates have increased and stabilized at these high rates. Goode (1963) argues that as love became the focus of marriage, it strengthened the husband-wife (conjugal) bond at the expense of the bond between extended family members. Spouses became mutually dependent on each other for support and emotional ties became intense...an inherently unstable situation. In other words, the functions of the family changed from providing education, economic production and job training to providing love, affection and emotional support. This change was accompanied by a change in cultural views from familialism to individualism. The pursuit of individual happiness is now paramount (Mindel, Habenstein and Wright, 1998). When family members feel that the marriage is no longer fulfilling their individual emotional needs, conflict results and they are likely to seek personal happiness elsewhere.

Indirect support for the instability of marrying for love is the example of "starter marriages" which are increasingly common among young people. Paul (2002) defines "starter marriages" as marriages which end in divorce usually within five years of the wedding date and do not involve any children. Paul finds that most of the people she studied who experienced starter marriages married for love, thought that their marriages would be for life, and still believed in love even after their divorce. Many reported that they just "drifted apart" from their partner or just wanted "different things" – in less than five years. However, the point is that all of these marriages did end for one reason or another – love was not enough to hold the couple together. Pamela Paul's study notes that with our increasing life span, marriages can feasibly last at least 50 years (verses the 12 years typical in Colonial life) so proponents of the family like Popenoe argue that they are not surprised the divorce rates are high.

Second, with the increasing urbanization and geographic mobility, community and religious institutions lost control over family members. In the past, collective religious rituals reinforced the sanctity of marriage and the responsibility of parents to children. The community embodied these beliefs and reinforced them. But as people moved away from the community, the community lost the ability to control and sanction wayward individuals, making it easier to break norms. This is what one would expect in a Gesellschaft society.

Lastly, an undeniably important influence on divorce rates is women working for wages. As women's' wages increase, so does their likelihood of divorce (Greenstein, 1990). The economic security women experience with employment gives them more freedom to leave an unhappy marriage. Remember, traditionally in industrial society, women's powerlessness is tied to their economic dependence on their husbands. Women who work for pay, even if at lower wages than men, perceive more opportunities for self-sufficiency than women who do not earn a wage and are still completely reliant on their husbands for economic support. These perceived opportunities give women power in the event of conflict. We will explore this point further in the section on gender roles. When you look at these reasons more closely, one way or another, they all illustrate the individualism that is characteristic of a Gesellschaft society.

There are both positive and negative effects of divorce. One of the reasons for lifting the prohibition on divorce in 19th Century Europe (and later in America) was to reduce violence by providing greater freedom to adults (and children) to escape dangerous situations. It may have worked too as research suggests that reported rates of serious domestic violence decreased in the 19th Century as marital dissolution became more common (Davidovitch, 1961). However, whether this association was causal or the coincidental product of either improving economic circumstances or a widespread increase in civility is unclear. Also, some studies suggest that divorce benefits children more so than staying in a conflict-ridden intact home (Jekielek, 1998).

For much of American history, when divorces were granted, the father retained custody of the children unless there was proof that he was clearly an unfit parent (Polikoff, 1983). Some believe that this is tied both to the legal and economical power of men who "owned" their children; but also because in early American history children were economic assets due to their labor potential. At the 1848 Seneca Falls, New York Convention, feminists argued that since the home and family were the domain of women, in the event of a divorce, mothers should have custody of children. With the rise of the Industrial Revolution children became less of an economic asset, and the increased social belief in the "Cult of True Womanhood" that we previously discussed took hold. Consequently, public sentiment and the laws shifted towards support for maternal custody. Now Courts still overwhelmingly give mothers primary custody of children during divorces.

However, financially and emotionally women are hurt more by divorce than men, especially when children are involved. When divorce occurs, 40% of women lose half of their income, however, only 17% of men have the same experience (Arendell, 1995). This is largely linked to maternal custody, the low level of child support and women's generally low wages relative to men. For example, mothers often have trouble collecting child support from the non-custodial fathers. In 1999 60% of single mothers were awarded or agreed to receive child support, yet only 60% of *these* women received *any* of the support to which they were entitled. Likewise, the amount of this support is not large. The average annual amount of support that women received in 1999 was $3,800 (Current Population Survey, 2000b). When one links this to the low wages for women, the result is that women frequently support more people in their household (the children and themselves) on less money than men. All of these factors combine to make women more susceptible to poverty than men – hence the coining of the phrase "feminization of poverty". In addition to the economic strain, women now experience role overload and role strain as they try to juggle the responsibilities of two parents by themselves.

These tensions will obviously affect children. David Popenoe in his 1996 book, *Life Without Father*, reported that in just three decades, 1960 to 1990, the percentage of children living away from their father more than doubled, from 17 percent to 36 percent. To put this another way, between 1970 and the year 2000 the number of female headed households increased from 3 million to 10 million (U.S. Census Bureau, 2001).

A child living with one parent is not historically new to late Twentieth Century. In Colonial America –and throughout much of history – children frequently lived in single parent households. The difference is that in the past, the single parent household formed due to the death of a parent whereas now it is most likely the result of a divorce. Unlike death, divorce is a conscious choice to alter a relationship; therefore, it is feasible to assume that children's sense of abandonment (which leads to behavioral and emotional issues) is stronger after a divorce than it is after a death.

Some argue that children of divorced parents have lower scores on aptitude tests, have lower levels of self confidence, and have more behavioral problems than do children whose parents are married (Amato and Keith, 1991; Amato and Booth, 1997). Likewise, according to some this gap persists well into adulthood as studies based on large national data sets consistently show that parental divorce also increases the risk that offspring will see their own marriages end in divorce, be unemployed in late adolescence, and be parents outside of marriage (Faust and McKibben, 1999; McLanahan and Sandefur, 1996). McLanahan and Sandefur (1996) find evidence suggesting that these potential issues are not just because of the economic challenges of single parent families, but also because, according to the high school sophomores they studied, divorced parents provide less supervision and academic help than do their married counterparts. More recently, Wallerstein, Lewis and Blakeslee (2000) who followed 131 people twenty-five years after their parents' divorce found that even after almost a quarter of a century, their parents' divorce still affects these young adults. Wallerstein and colleagues find that adult children of divorced parents have more difficulty forming lasting intimate adult relationships, are more likely to avoid intimate relationships and have general troubles dealing with conflict.

But once again, one cannot fall prey to the fallacy of over-generalization. Other researchers take issue with findings such as Wallerstein's and frequently fault the data collection methods (e.g. Wallerstein's research is based on individuals who came to her for counseling and who were already having trouble coping with divorce) or the manner of data interpretation. These researchers argue that while the data does seem to suggest that divorced children have more behavioral problems than children whose parents are married, the majority of children of divorce do not and the majority of these problems are not long lasting (Coontz, 1997). In other words, the majority of children of divorce do not experience any more behavioral problems than children whose parents have not divorced; but, more children have, at least short term problems, if their parents are divorced as opposed to not divorced. Hence, unquestioningly accepting the divorce statistics runs the risk of the fallacy of dramatization. Sure, some children suffer long term negative consequences of their parents' divorce; but, the research suggests that that majority do not.

Regardless of the debate over the potential long term negative effects of parental divorce, most people do agree that children are frequently hurt by their parents' divorce in the *short term*. So why does divorce have at least short term negative effects on children? Children's behavioral problems after divorce may be tied to the decrease in their economic resources and the emotional stress of the changing family relationships. Children often feel powerless in the face of divorce. They have no control over their parents' marriage and little control in how they fit into the family after the divorce. Conflict theorists argue that this powerlessness is the root of the behavioral problems (Widdison and Delaney, 1993). Furthermore, with the weakening of Gemeinschaft community relations, family, friends and peers are in a weakened position to encourage non-custodial parents to help support their children. Consequently, in our Gesellschaft society, people now rely on the government to dictate the financial responsibility of non-custodial parents and to force them to pay. However, as the high rate of deadbeat dads suggests, the government is not very successful.

Even remarriages of a biological parent doesn't help children too much. Though 15 percent of all children of divorce were living with their biological mother and step-father, second marriages with children break up more frequently and earlier than do first marriages (Furstenberg, 1990; Cherlin, 1992). Furthermore, there is a race effect. African-American children are much more likely to live with one parent (about 60%) than are White children (23.5%) and Hispanic children (33.0%) (U.S. Bureau of the Census, 1999). Therefore, it is likely that children in stepfamilies will experience multiple family divorces. Hence, these children deal with adjusting to the breakup of their parents' marriage, remarriage by one or both parents – which comes with new roles and relationships – and the breakup of these "new" marriages as well. Obviously that's a lot of transition, potential conflict, and instability.

Historically the legal process of divorce was conflict-oriented where spouses had to show fault in their partner in order to distribute the couple's assets – even if both people wanted to part amicably. Consistent with the individualistic ideology in our culture today, in 1970 "No Fault" divorce was introduced in California and by 1985 adopted by all states (in some version). Now spouses just have to cite "irreconcilable differences" as the reason for wanting to end a marriage. While differences across states do exist, No Fault legislation generally has the following six major components: 1) No grounds are needed to obtain a divorce; 2) Neither spouse has to prove fault to obtain a divorce; 3) One spouse can decided unilaterally to obtain a divorce; 4) financial awards are not linked to fault; 5) new standards for alimony and property awards seek to treat women and men equally; 6) new procedures aim at undermining the conflict process and creating a social-psychological climate that fosters amicable divorce (Weitzman, 1985; 15-16).

Initially people thought that "No Fault" divorce would benefit women and children because it avoided the nasty court experience and was supposed to illustrate the "equality" between sexes that women sought. However, "No Fault" divorce has had the unintended consequence of worsening the economic position of women and children and contributing to the "feminization of poverty" we mentioned previously. Unfortunately, men and women's experiences are not yet equal. "No Fault" divorce assumes they are and distributes assets equally, even though women do not earn as much as men and usually have the additional responsibility of childcare.

Is the family coming full circle? In 1998, "for the first time in 25 years, the number of American divorces has fallen below one million, dropping from 1,153,000 in 1997 to only 974,000 in 1998" (McManus, 1998. B-25). One has to go back to 1974 for below one million divorces. Whether this is a one-year blip or a new trend is difficult to say. Since fewer marriages are occurring in the 20-24 age category, later ages of marriage usually means fewer divorces. Furthermore, newer research specifically documents the benefits of marriage. According to Waite and Gallagher (2000) individuals who are married are in better health, are more satisfied and happy with life, report more frequent and satisfying sex and have more money than are individuals who have never married, who are divorced or who are cohabiting. In fact, Waite and Gallagher discuss unhappy couples and find that those who "stick with" the marriage are happier and more content five years later than those who divorced.

Changes in Family Size and Birth Rates

In Colonial America, couples were expected to have children. Favorable attitudes toward reproduction dominated society since children, as in any underdeveloped nation, had economic value. Women produced many children (about seven on the average in 1800) to insure that some would survive. The increase in wage work among husbands and changing laws regarding children's wages made children increasingly less viable as economic assets. Consequently, at least for the middle class, childhood was extended and required more emotional and economic (as education became more important and children contributed less economically) investment that led families to have fewer children. Families apparently began to feel that they could offer more opportunities to their children if they had fewer of them. With industrialization, families also moved to the cities, thereby weakening the extended family and community ties. As a result, not only did families become smaller, but they increasingly focused on the nuclear relationships (mother – father – child) and become more privatized as well. Therefore, as industrialization progressed, the family grew smaller, more "nuclear," and more isolated from kin and neighbors.

As cities grew, they became fearful places characterized by illegal behavior and physical danger. As a result, people moved to the suburbs which, with their green lawns and large trees, were marketed as a place where women could provide the appropriate atmosphere to raise their children (Palen, 1995). The move to the suburbs reinforced the private nature of families and further weakened ties to the wider society.

As we mentioned previously, however, the 1950s experienced an unusual increase in the number of babies born. In fact, the 1950s was the only period in the previous 150 years when the birthrate increased. The long-term trend had clearly been a decline in both birth rates and number of children born per woman. Furthermore, in addition to the unusually high number of births in the 1950s, during this time young adults married at earlier ages than they did in any 20th-Century decade before or since (Cherlin, 1988). Consequently, it is ironic that while most people think of the 1950s as "traditional" and many opinions about the family and family values stem from this era, historically, the 1950s were probably the most unusual decade for family life in the 20th Century. People's persistence on using this era as the traditional reference point for the American family is based on the "fallacy of omission". Here the omission is the fact that the 1950s were *not* a typical era; and, instead, the 1960s and 1970s were more congruent with long-term historical and social trends – even though these decades are treated as the beginning of the unraveling of the family.

Now approximately 30% of married women by age 30 have no children at all. To put this another way, in 2001, 67.2 babies were born for every 1000 women in their reproductive years (ages 15 to 44) compared with 125 babies in 1960, a decline of almost half. (Kurian, 1994; National Vital Statistics Report, 2001). In spite of the decline in the birth rate, the *absolute number* of births in the in the early 21st Century are comparable to the 1950's--3.9 million births to over 4 million per year (Kurian, 1994; National Vital Statistics Report, 2001). Since married women are having fewer children today (and expect to have few) the size of the family is decreasing. The Census Bureau has also noted that people are occupying more and more separate living quarters with fewer occupants per unit. Those who defend the traditional family structure might argue that this separate living is a sign of the deteriorating family and the division and "apartness" that tears at the American family. However, a rebuttal may be that this is evidence of the liberation, individualism, and freedom from traditional forms of the family.

No matter what this smaller family size and "household separation" means, for the first time in our history the average household consists of less than 3 people (from 3.14 in 1970 to 2.84 in 1997) (Statistical Abstract of the United States, 1998). As we will see in our discussion of the elderly, family size may have profound effects on other social relations.

Conflicts Involving Births to Single Mothers

With harsh punishments for adultery (especially by women), taboos regarding premaritcal sex and a strong emphasis on marriage, unwed parenthood was stigmatized for most of American history. Even as late as the mid-Twentieth Century, women who became pregnant without benefit of marriage were described as "getting themselves in trouble". These women were expected to either marry the fathers quickly (hence the concept of "shotgun weddings") or to subtly disappear to have the baby in quiet (and then generally put the baby up for adoption).. By the late Twentieth Century, this began to change.

The rate of single mother births per 1000 unmarried women (15 to 44) rose from about 7 in 1940 to 29 in 1980 to 45.2 in 2000 (Center for Disease Control, 2000a). As a percent of all births, unwed ones accounted for 18 percent in 1980, 28 percent by 1990 and 33 percent in 2000 (Statistical Abstract of the United States, 1998; Center for Disease Control, 2000a). If just 15-19 year old unmarried girls are counted, the births per 1,000 rose from about 15 from 1950 to 1967 to 60 by 1990 and 90 in 2000 as graph 4-2 shows. These figures do not take into account the some 1.2 million abortions that have occurred every year since 1990. (Statistical Abstract of the United States, 1998).

Why the increase? One reason is that people are becoming increasingly sexually active at younger ages – relative to Twentieth Century norms (Forrest and Singh, 1990). A second reason is the decreased emphasis on marriage – at least for people in the teenage years. As mentioned previously, pregnant women were frequently expected to marry the father. Now with the delay in marriage in general, the pressure to marry when young and pregnant has also diminished. Furthermore, the unmarried birth rate, especially among teenagers, is higher among certain groups, like African Americans.

Some boys grow up without a father

The rate of unmarried births for 15-19 year old African Americans is 78.4 / 1,000 unmarried women, compared to the rate of 33.7 / 1,000 unmarried white women aged 15-19 (Center for Disease Control, 2000b). African Americans, as we discussed in Chapter 5 on race relations, frequently experience social discrimination and blocked opportunities. Under these conditions, having children is a potential path to adulthood when others, like gainful employment or the completion of higher education, are blocked.

As the previous paragraph suggests, unwed pregnancy is frequently associated with teen pregnancy. However, contrary to popular beliefs, births to teen mothers have been declining for the past 40 years (Aulette, 2002); even though, most of the discussion of unwed births continues to focus on the births to teen mothers. So why the concern if the rates are decreasing? There are a number of reasons. First, fertility for non-teens has decreased more rapidly than the fertility rate for teens – which means that a greater proportion of babies born are born to teen mothers (Aulette, 2002); and, as we discussed, these teens are less likely to get married now than in the past. Second, some suggest that young mothers and their children have greater health problems (independent of the problems associated with single parenthood) and that these babies are more likely to have low birth weights (Luker, 1992). Third, today unmarried teen mothers are more socially visible (Phoenix, 1991).

Obviously the conflicts of role overload and economic support in these families are the same as with single parent families formed by divorce. Children from both types of families are more likely to drop out of school, get in trouble with police, and live in poverty (Henslin, 2002). There is one exception. While children from divorced families and unwed mothers are both less likely to see their fathers than children in intact families, children from unwed mothers are *the least* likely to see their fathers or receive emotional or economic support from them.

Conflicts in Pre-Marital Sex, Cohabitation, and Extra-Marital Sex

The so-called "sexual revolution" is no longer new. The beginning of the Twentieth Century exhibited increased rates of pre-martital sex (although the majority of it was thought to be between engaged couples) and changes in behavior among young women who cut their hair short, went out alone at night with men and participated in the paid economy. Again, this behavior in itself is not new; but, traditionally behaviors such as pre-marital sex, independence and working were distinctly masculine behaviors. This does not imply that women did not partake in such behaviors – just that they did not partake in them as frequently and that these behaviors were more tolerated by men than by women. This is no longer the case.

Pre-Marital Sex

In Colonial America, courtship was limited, privacy for unmarried couples was generally looked upon as an evil temptation to be avoided, and pre-marital sex was strictly forbidden. Yet people deviated, even then. Records of the Groton, Connecticut, Church show that of 200 baptized Puritans, between 1760 and 1775, 66 (a third) confessed to having sex before marriage (Bell, 1967). Furthermore, some couples who were about to be betrothed would be allowed to practice "bundling" whereby they would be allowed to share the same bed – albeit fully clothed – in order to get to know each other better. Nevertheless, for much of American history, pre-marital sex was taboo.

Some scholars trace an increase in premarital sex in the U.S. to the First World War (1914-1918). Prior to that time, as best we know, only about 7% of women engaged in sex before marriage (Packard, 1970), but a study done using the National Health and Social Life Survey asked people to provide their age and their sexual history and shed some light on a topic previously not discussed (Laumann and Gagnon, 1994). This survey showed that 50% of men who had graduated high school between 1925 and 1930 had had intercourse by the time they graduated high school; this percentage rose to 78% for those who graduated high school in 1991. The changes for women were even more startling. Only 8% of women who graduated high school between 1925-1930 had intercourse by the time they graduated, whereas by 1991 this number increased to 67% (Laumann and Gagnon, 1994)

The real changes in pre-marital sex took place, especially among women, in the 1960s (the decade of the Pill). In 1958, most believed that a girl had to be engaged before sexual intercourse took place. By 1968, 23% to 28% of the "dating" or "steady" college females had engaged in sex, compared with only 10% and 15% in 1958. (Scanzoni and Scanzoni, 1976). A similar 10-year follow-up study by Christensen and Gregg showed that pre-marital sex had more than tripled. Not only that, but the age at which people experienced it was decreasing (Scanzoni and Scanzoni, 1976).

Darling, Kallen and VanDusen (1992) argue that American's attitudes about sexuality have progressed through three stages. The first is the "era of the double standard" which lasted from the 1900s to the 1950s. During this time, premarital sex was acceptable for men (but not widely discussed in wider social circles), but not for women. Men who engaged in premarital sex were "sowing their wild oats" while women were "sluts". The high percentage of men in high school between 1925-1930 who admitted to having intercourse relative to the percentage of women indirectly supports this notion. The second era, dubbed the "era of permissiveness with affection" was the brief period between 1960 and 1970 where the proportion of women having premarital sex began to catch up to the men. During this era, cohabitation, which we will discuss in a moment, increased as did divorce rates. The last era (beginning in the 1980s) according to Darling, Kallen and VanDusen is the "era of permissiveness" where premarital sex is now the expectation for men and women and that sex without love (e.g. for fun between friends) is more tolerated. Other researches have noticed this increased focus on the actual act of intercourse between young people. Schwartz and Rutter (1998) allude to the "lost art of petting" – meaning the kissing, fondling and touching- that for much of the 20th Century was the staple of teen romance. They argue that this more innocent form of sexual expression has essentially been lost as young people quickly move from light touching in a given encounter straight to intercourse.

Consequently pre-marital sex is related to the conflicts discussed in other parts of this chapter (like births of unwed mothers) as well as other issues like welfare recipients, gender issues and economic stratification we discuss in other chapters. Furthermore, the greater acceptance of premarital sex further illustrates the individualism associated with a Gesellschaft form of society.

Cohabitation

Unsurprisingly, as the frequency of premarital sex increased, so did cohabitation. Once considered "living in sin", as mentioned previously, cohabitation in the U.S. has increased ten-fold since 1960. According to the U.S. Census Bureau, it increased from 430,000 in 1960 to over five million couples in 2000 (United States Bureau of the Census, 2000a). In fact, this noticeable increase over the past 40 years has led Gwartney-Gibbs (1986) to speculate that cohabitation is becoming a newly institutionally recognized stage of mate selection.

So how did cohabitation move from "living in sin" to becoming a socially acceptable step in mate selection? According to Bumpass (1990) one of the biggest reasons is the loosening of sexual restrictions. Initially, the main criticism of cohabitation was that people were sharing a bed without the benefit of marriage. Now that marriage is no longer a socially held prerequisite for sex, one of the main obstacles to cohabitation has disappeared. Other researchers cite reasons like the greater tendency of young single people to live away from their parents (either in dormitories or apartments in or out of college), later age people are marrying, young people's concerns over the divorce rates and increasing individualism among people (Goldscheider and Waite, 1991; Bianchi and Casper, 2000; Bumpass and Lu, 2000).

One of the points mentioned above involved young people's concern over divorce. As a result of divorce rates, more young people want to "test" a relationship prior to committing to marriage because they feel that leaving a cohabiting relationship is easier than leaving a marriage if two people find themselves incompatible. However, contrary to conventional wisdom that living together is good preparation for marriage, data in recent studies show quite the opposite for a number of reasons. First, those who cohabit are the least likely to marry each other. A Columbia University study found that only 26 percent of cohabiting women surveyed and 19 percent of cohabiting men married the person with whom they lived (McManus, 1998; Weston, 1998). Non-cohabiting engaged couples have a much higher likelihood of marrying each other. Another study by Bennet, Blanc and Bloom (1998), from the 1981 Women in Sweden Survey, reported "women who cohabit premaritally have almost 80 percent higher dissolution rates than those who do not. Women who cohabit for over three years prior to marriage have over 50 percent higher dissolution rates than women who cohabit for shorter durations" (127).

Second, those who live together before marriages have higher separation and divorce rates (Krishnen, 1998). The National Survey of Families and Households in 1994, based on interviews with 13,000 people, concludes: "Unions begun by cohabitation are almost twice as likely to dissolve within ten years compared to all first marriages: 57 percent to 30 percent" (Weston, 1998:25).

Third, those who live together before marriage report unhappier marriages overall than those who did not cohabit. A study by the National Council on Family Relations of 309 newlyweds found that those who cohabited first were less happy in marriage (Weston, 1998). In addition, cohabitors do not experience fulfilling sex. The best sex is found in marriage. Couples who abstain from sex before marriage are 29 to 47 percent more likely to enjoy sex in marriage (Weston, 1998).

Fourth, cohabiters are more likely to experience depression and alcohol problems. Howitz, McLaughlin and White (1998) compared 1220 cohabitors and married couples aged 25-31 in 1985-1987 and 1992-1994 found that both depression and alcohol problems were greater for cohabitors than for married couples. These results remained even after controlling for pre-cohabiting and pre-marital levels of mental health.

Finally, violence and abuse were more likely to occur among cohabiting couples than married ones. Magdol and colleagues (1998) studying a representative sample (N=941) of young adults age 21 found that, on average, physical abuse for cohabitors was one and a half times greater than for married couples and over two times greater than for daters.

Such changes as these strike at the very foundation of family life and to some unknown degree explain fewer marriages, delay of marriages, increased unwed pregnancy and use of abortion, as well as childless marriages. Today people associate sex with having fun not children. This "fun" attitude reflects the current value of individualism in Gesellschaft societies and clearly does not contribute to stable families. When family relations experience conflict by no longer being fun or personally fulfilling, people today are more likely to seek satisfaction outside the family – whether on their own (as in divorce) or with others (as in extra-marital affairs).

Extra-Marital Sex

The community in Colonial America was also very involved in the family. Most social functions and interactions took place in family units as communities – which comprised of families linked together economically, politically, religiously and socially for survival. So deviant behaviors like extra-marital affairs were difficult to keep quiet. When community members broke social rules – even if it occurred in the context of the family – the community would enact *charivari*. The charivari were demonstrations by community members (frequently masked) who would surround an offender's house at night and beat on pans, blow horns and, generally, create havoc (Shorter, 1975). However, charivari can take other forms. For example, in the novel *The Scarlet Letter*, a woman guilty of adultery had to wear a scarlet "A" sewn into her clothing so her transgression would be evident to the entire community.

While the majority of couples do not experience an extra-marital affair, 16% of people researchers studied who were married or had been married reported that they had committed adultery at some point in the past, and men were still more likely to do so than were women (Morin, 1994). However, contrary to the tabloids and talk shows, attitudes about adultery are becoming more conservative. While a study by Hunt (1969) found that many men did not consider sex with a call girl to be infidelity because it did not involve love, 20 years later a *People* magazine survey found that 70% of their respondents felt that lust alone was enough to warrant infidelity – sex didn't even have to occur. (Frenkeil, 1990).

Family Violence

Perhaps the conflict between gender, power, and isolation is clearest with domestic violence. As mentioned in the history section, Christian beliefs supported a social system in which men dominated all spheres of social life, including the family. This sentiment was codified into law where a man was allowed to beat his wife as long as the switch was "no thicker than his thumb", hence the phrase today, "rule of thumb". The saying "spare the rod, spoil the child", on the other hand, is cultural evidence of the tolerance of violence against children. Furthermore child infanticide and abandonment have been practiced by most societies to varying degrees throughout history (Solomon, 1973).

However, this does not imply that husbands/fathers were free to practice family violence to any degree they wished. Remember, as we mentioned before, the community in Colonial America was also very involved in the family. When community members broke social rules – like beating a wife too severely – the community would enact *charivari* to sanction the offending individual. So the family as the private unit we associate it as being today was not usually present in Colonial America.

With the privatization of the family community control over its members lessened. The home became a man's "castle" and what went on behind closed doors was supposed to remain private. In order to regulate behavior, people increasingly looked to formal organizations or the government for help, as expected in a Gesellschaft society. Consequently, it was not until the latter half of the 19th Century that protective child agencies emerged; and, as late as 1978 only 3 states had made it illegal for a husband to force marital relations with his wife against her will, although now all 50 states have such laws (Mooney, Knox and Schacht, 2000).

Perhaps, the largest change is actually in defining family violence as a social problem. Family violence did not receive much attention until 1971 when John O'Brien published an article in the *Journal of Marriage and the Family* indicating that from the journal's inception in 1939, not one article mentioned the term "violence" (Hutter, 1998). Steinmetz and Straus (1974) compiled the bibliography from 400 sources and found almost no material on the most common forms of family violence such as fights and slaps. The reasons for this are speculative, but center on arguments that family violence as an issue is "touchy" or that it was an unfortunate, but expected, aspect of normal families (O'Brien, 1971).

Today, family violence is synonymous with "wife abuse" because women are the most visible victims. According to Koop (1989), domestic violence causes more injuries to women than automobile accidents, muggings and rapes combined. Furthermore, according to the Bureau of Justice Statistics (1995) about 25% of violent acts women experience are from their husbands, ex-husbands or boyfriends – compared to only 4% of violent acts against men. To put this another way, according to Rennison and Welchans (2000) who used the National Crime Victimization Survey, about 85% of victimizations by an intimate partner are against women.

However, some evidence is emerging suggesting that the frequency of husband abuse is higher than expected and that husbands and wives are equally likely to attack one another (Saunders, 1988). This data has not convinced the general public that husband abuse is as serious a problem as wife abuse; however, for a number of reasons. First a wife abusing her husband is contrary to people's concept of gender roles and family power; therefore, many believe that it is less likely. Second, few men speak out about this issue – most likely because they recognize that being abused by a woman does not fit with the stereotypical idea of being masculine. Third, many believe that if women hit men that is it usually in self defense. Finally men generally cause more physical damage than do women; therefore, if husband abuse does occur, it is seen as less personally damaging.

The family environment is not always better for children. In fact, Collins and Coltrane have stated that "for children, the home is often the most dangerous place to be" (Collins and Coltrane, 1995: 476-77). However, even more so than with spousal abuse, people are unsure exactly what constitutes "child abuse". Some definitions are so wide they range from spanking to murder; others are so limited that they only focus on physical violence at the exclusion of neglect and emotional abuse. While, as mentioned previously, laws protecting children from abuse occurred before laws protecting women, it is important to remember that for much of human history, parents were free to "discipline" their children as they saw fit and many behaviors considered abusive today were perfectly acceptable in the past. Keeping this in mind, it is interesting to note that laws existed protecting animals from abuse before there were any laws protecting women or children. In fact, the first legal action to protect children in 1874 was the case of Mary Ellen, a foster child who was neglected and stabbed with scissors by her foster parents. Since no legal defense existed for Mary Ellen, prosecutors argued that, as a member of the animal kingdom, the laws protecting animals should also apply to her (Hutter, 1998). This seemingly misplaced legal effort today stems from both the economic value of animals and the privacy of the family in the not so distant past.

Given the disagreement over what constitutes "child abuse" and since we now have a generally socially protective attitude towards children, committing child abuse is now even more stigmatized than committing spousal abuse. Approximately 2000 children a year die from child abuse (Clinton, 1996); and, according to the National Clearing House on Child Abuse and Neglect Information, in 2000 there were about three million referrals of possible child abuse instances. As Figure 6-2 illustrates, reports of child abuse have increased 2,300% since 1950. Almost one-third of these children were considered maltreated (which includes neglect, physical abuse, psychological maltreatment and sexual abuse) or at risk for maltreatment, with neglect being the most common form of maltreatment (63% of all cases). Contrary to some popular myth that minority children are more likely to be abused, half of all abused children in 2000 were white (51%), 25% were African American and 15% were Hispanic. Horrendous as these statistics may sound, these rates have actually been decreasing over the past 5 years (Children's Bureau Administration on Children, Youth and Families, 2002).

Figure 6-2:   Rates of Reported Incidences of Child Abuse / 100,000 Children 1950-2000

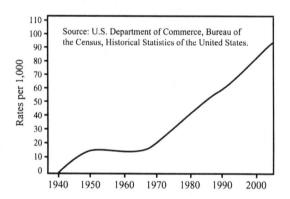

Source: U.S. Department of Health and Human Services and Child Maltreatment: Reports from the States to the United States National Child Abuse and Neglect Data System.

Whether discussing spouse abuse or child abuse, statistics suggest that someone is more likely to be the victim of a violent act by someone they know or a family member than by a stranger (Bureau of Justice Statistics, 1995). This is contrary to the common perception of the family as a warm, loving, safe haven so we need to ask ourselves why this environment that we associate with security can also be the most violent environment we encounter. The reasons for family violence involve the very organization of the family as well as social and individual issues. There are three main factors relating to family organization and structure that are conducive to conflict and violence. The first is the private nature of families. Even in an era of reality TV and sensationalized talk shows, there is still the idea that what goes on behind closed doors is private. Hence neighbors and friends who may suspect abuse may also hesitate to bring it to the attention of the victim, the abuser or the authorities – partly because they do not think that it is "their business." Related to that is their concern that they may be wrong in their impressions.

The second characteristic of family structure that makes it conducive to violence is the hierarchical organization of family roles. Parents have more power and authority than children and, at least traditionally, husbands have more power and authority than wives. Any time hierarchical social relations are present, conflict is possible. Most research suggests that women and children are the most frequent victims. This makes sense given the traditional family roles where women are subordinate to their husbands and children are subordinate to their parents.

Third, the emotions that bind families together can also be sources of conflict. The self-disclosure and vulnerability we typically associate with intimacy can be used against us in two ways. First, those who we love can use the information gained through intimacy against us in fits of anger. Second, because people are emotionally attached, on average, to their spouses, any criticisms or angry barbs from them are likely to hurt us more so than if the same comments came from other people. When some people are hurt, there is the possibility that they will retaliate violently.

Social factors for family violence focus on issues like unemployment, poverty, race, status inconsistency (where either the woman has a higher status than the man or an individual has less status in reality than they feel they should have) and social isolation. Individual factors include alcohol / drug use, the younger a person's age, and whether the abuser comes from a history of family abuse him/herself (Straus, 1993; Gelles, 1995). However, some of these trends have to be interpreted cautiously. For example, while those who are in poverty or racial minorities have higher reported rates of abuse; this does not necessarily mean that people from these social backgrounds are more likely to abuse their partners. Middle class and white family violence is believed to be less visible because 1) middle class individuals (especially women) may be less likely to report an abusive incident for fear that they will not be believed (especially if their partners appear to be pillars of the community); 2) private family physicians are frequently more reluctant to report suspected abuse to social service agencies; and 3) middle class and white families are less likely to live in crowded housing conditions where spousal violence is likely to be, at least indirectly, witnessed by others.

Furthermore socially, while adults who are abused as children generally do *not* become child abusers as adults, those who abuse their children are more likely to be from abusive childhoods than are non-abusers. However, one aspect of child abuse is distinctly unique. While many studies suggest that men are the most frequent perpetrators of spousal abuse, many studies suggest that mothers are just as likely as men to be the perpetrators of child abuse (Breines and Gordon, 1983; Williams, 1980). However, this needs to be interpreted cautiously for a couple of reasons. First, women are more likely to be the caretakers of children; therefore, statistically they spend more time with children and have, statistically, greater opportunity to become vulnerable to the pressures potentially leading to abuse. Second, mothers are more likely than men to be in stressful economic situations – especially if they are single mothers. Finally, because child care is primarily the role of the mother, mothers may feel greater responsibility for failures or misbehavior in their children (Breines and Gordon, 1983).

In response to these changes in family life, local and national organizations formed to improve family conditions. In 1875, the Children's Protective Society (later the Children's Aid Society) was initiated, and the National League for the Protection of the Family was begun in the 1880s. Groups became active in publishing, lobbying, and educating the public about the importance of families. Courses on marriage and the family began to appear in women's colleges. In 1908 the American Sociological Society devoted its entire annual meeting to "the family problem" (Mauss, 1975:500). In the early stages of a Gesellschaft society, the "community" was still involved in regulating behavior – now, however, the community takes on a formal bureaucratic or academic identity. However, even these large groups were not powerful enough to truly minimize the conflict in families. As a result, society began to turn to the Federal Government, the ultimate legal authority, for help in strengthening the family and the transformation to a Geselleschaft society was complete.

In 1909, the First White House Conference on children was held. The major demand of the conference was that a Federal agency be set up to defend and advocate the rights of children. As a result, in 1912 the U.S. Children's Bureau was set up to investigate problems of children with the view of strengthening the American family. After three unsuccessful attempts to outlaw child labor, Congress passed the Fair Labor Standards Act (also known as the Wages and Hours Act) in 1938. It banned employers engaged in interstate commerce from employing any workers under 16, or under 18 in hazardous occupations.

You may have noticed that legal changes in the family focused on the protection of children only. This is because the changing view of children occurred much faster than the changing view of women. Children, unlike women, were seen as defenseless and in need of protection; consequently, it is not surprising that legislation to protect children occurred first. Conflict theorists would argue that children (because they are smaller, not adults, and legally cannot compete in the labor force) are less direct threats to men's power than are women. Therefore, these theorists argue that men are more willing to pass laws protecting children than laws protecting women.

However, even with laws to protect women and children, the privacy of the family still prevails. People are hesitant to report child or wife abuse and many argue that invading the home to prosecute abusive parents and spouses is not an appropriate response due to the inadequacy of other arrangements (Hutter, 1998).

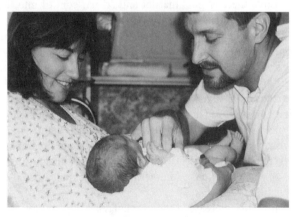

Every child needs two parents

Conflict over Alternate Family Forms

Perhaps one of the most recent changes in the family is the increasing media and societal attention to same-sex families. With Ellen Degeneris' historical "coming out" episode of her television show "Ellen" to Ross Geller's lesbian ex-wife in "Friends" to "Will and Grace", an entire sitcom focused on the interaction between gay and straight characters, homosexuality is becoming increasingly visible in mainstream society. This has led some to erroneously assume that the rate of homosexuality is increasing. Research suggests, however, that the rates of homosexuality have been relatively stable; its visibility is what is changing (Hutter, 1998). Scientific research studies reveal "the percentage of homosexuality in the United States to be around 1% to 3%" (Howe. 1994: 10). How many bisexuals exist has never been calculated scientifically.

This increasing visibility is traditionally attributed to the sexual revolution of the 1970s – an era that encouraged sexual experimentation and visibility. However, recent researchers are beginning to disagree and argue that we need to look at deeper historical changes in the family and society to understand why homosexuality is receiving its current attention. Foucault in his book *The History of Sexuality, Vol. 1* (1978) suggests that the increasing visibility stems from the changing view of marriage we discussed earlier. Foucault argues that in the beginning of the Eighteenth Century, marriage shifted from a means for which extended families used lineage ties to control members to a form where couples married for love. Love thereby puts marital and sexual control into the hands of the individual instead of the family. In fact, Foucault argues that contrary to common beliefs, the Victorian era was not an era of sexual repression, but instead an era of such heightened sexual awareness (due to the new societal focus on love) that strict rules of etiquette were necessary to control sexuality. According to Katz (1995), this increased focus on sexuality led to the formal word "heterosexual" which first appeared in Germany in the 1860s and in America in 1892. Prior to the 1860s there wasn't even a term for "heterosexuality", it was just assumed to be the natural relationship due to the importance of the family for procreation (D'Emilio, 1983). To illustrate the logical opposite of "heterosexual", the term "homosexual" also developed around this time.

Still, this increased homosexual visibility obviously did not occur over night; but, by the 1950s gay urban territories such as sections of San Francisco, California, and Greenwich Village, New York, were firmly established, even if they were marginal. Opposition to same-sex families are voiced from many arenas. Proponents of the Judeo-Christian religion such as the Baptist and Catholic Churches and the American Family Association, who oppose homosexuality do so based on interpretations of Biblical passages and the distinction between sex for procreation (which is favored) and sex for recreation (which is discouraged). (Howe, 1994)   Since homosexuals cannot obviously procreate by natural means, according to those who oppose homosexuality, relations between and among homosexuals should be discouraged. As one recent Christian Sociology textbook put it:

> Despite the psychological, political, legal and moral consequences of homosexual partnerships, gay men and lesbian women will continue to challenge traditional marriage and family values and practices. (Tweedell, 2003: 184)

Others argue that the autonomy and decreased visibility of urban life allowed people who were already homosexually inclined to express their feelings more freely.   This led to a new sexual way of life (D'Emilio, 1983).

Regardless of the view, most agree that the privacy of the family and relative isolation of the family from community control has made it possible for homosexuality to become more visible.   The increased visibility, in turn, has led to increased political and social pressure and conflict to grant same-sex families the same rights as heterosexual families. Like other groups before them, homosexuals are turning to the government to create change. For example, to be legally recognized in all states, marriages have to occur between a man and a woman – which explicitly excludes same-sex couples.   However, same-sex couples have made some changes.   Some cities like San Francisco and New York City allow same-sex couples to register as "domestic partners", thereby granting them limited spousal benefits. Furthermore, in 2000 Vermont became the first state to recognize "civil unions" (which are technically not marriages in the conventional sense) that guarantee same-sex couples in these arrangements the rights and benefits heterosexual married couples receive. But this was only a partial victory for gays. After Vermont voted to recognize 'civil unions', the federal Congress passed the Defense of Marriage Act which stated that the federal government would not recognize same-sex "civil unions" and allowed states to also ignore these unions. Consequently, even if a couple is "married" in Vermont, most states will not recognize that union and, therefore, will not grant the couple the same rights as heterosexually married couples. This situation could

change in the future.   Various religious denominations are now in
serious conflict over this issue of same-sex unions.

Summary and Conclusion

When one puts these seven major family changes and conflicts together, we have a clearer picture of what has happened, and is happening, to the American family historically and socially. Clearly, the defenders of the traditional family would point to each one of the social indicators as evidence of a seriously sick, if not dying American family. They argue that weak community social control resulting from a Gesellschaft society has led to an increasing focus on the fulfillment of individual desires and to flagrant traditional norm violations which have long term personal, social and intergenerational consequences. As people increasingly focus on fulfilling their individual desires, conflict between people inevitably increases, as well as one person's desires may come at the expense of another's. Furthermore, because community and family ties have weakened (according to traditionalists and empirical evidence cited), people increasingly look to government programs (for example alimony in the case of divorce) to enforce what was once a socially understood responsibility of the family. On the other hand, the challengers would use each of the indicators as evidence of how the family is adapting and adjusting itself to our ever-changing culture and society. They argue that many changes and conflicts reflect women's increased freedom and equality and that people are happier now, on average, than in the past.

When viewed from a comparative and historical perspective, present-day American family life as the 21st Century begins presents a great paradox (Kellogg and Mintz, 1993). No other industrialized nation shows a stronger commitment to marriage or invests the family with more responsibility for society's social welfare. At the same time, in no other advanced society are family ties as precarious, or family forms and structures more diverse. The United States has at the same time among the highest marriage and remarriage rates in the West and the highest divorce rate -- roughly twice as high as other advanced societies. In certain respects, the U.S. is staunchly traditionalist reflected in the relatively high proportion of religious weddings, home-ownership and the high value it places on family loyalty and identity. But in other respects, our society appears to have departed farther than others from a life-time commitment to the traditional family. It has the West's highest rate of single parenthood and one of the highest rates of unwed births. Though birthrates have fallen from prior years, the absolute number of births remains about 4 million each year and the overwhelming majority of married couples want children. At the same time, the number of unwanted children has declined and the number of families with 4 or more children has dropped. Though marriage is clearly put off, by waiting or cohabiting, the overwhelming majority of Americans marry at some point in their life. Each person reading this book must judge for her/himself whether the family they know has declined or just changed – for better or for worse.

Critical Thinking Questions

1. Why do you think that an increasing number of adults decide to never marry? How do you think this will affect the family in the long run with regards to issues such as economic well-being or assistance with care when one is old?

2. Reported rates of wife abuse and child abuse have increased in the past 20 years. Why do you think this is the case?

3. Find some articles debating the pros and cons of "spanking", otherwise known as "corporal punishment". What are the main points of each view? Separate the facts from the fallacies. Do you support this practice? Why / why not? Be sure to defend your stance using fact and not fallacy.

4. How do you think the rates of spousal abuse (wife or husband) are affected by our current social changes such as the fewer number of children per family, women's increased labor force participation, the decrease in job opportunities for men, etc.? Why?

5. Do you think that the family as an institution today is healthy? What evidence do you have to support your view? What evidence is there contrary to your view? How do you counter the points raised against your view? (In other words, in the face of opposition, what evidence do you have to defend your stance?)

Bibliography

Arendell, Terry. *Fathers and Divorce*. Thousand Oaks, CA: Sage
      Publications, 1995.
Aries, Philippe. *Centuries of Childhood: A Social History of Family
      Life*. Robert Baldick (trans.) New York: Vintage, 1962.
Amato, Paul and Alan Booth. *A Generation at Risk: Growing up in
      an Era of Family Upheaval*. Cambridge, MA: Harvard
      University Press, 1997.
Amato, Paul and Bruce Keith. "Parental Divorce and Well-Being of
      Children: A Meta-Analysis." *Psychological Bulletin*. 110
      (1991): 26-46.
Aulette, Judy. *Changing American Families*. Boston, MA: Allyn and
      Bacon, 2002.
Baca Zinn, Maxine, and D. Stanley Eitzen. *Diversity in Families*.
      Boston, MA: Allyn and Bacon, 2002.
Bell, Robert. *Premarital Sex in a Changing Society*. Englewood
      Cliffs, N.J.: Prentice-Hall, 1967.
Bennet, Neil, Ann K. Blanc, and David Bloom. "Commitment and the
      Modern Union: Assessing the Link Between Premarital
      Cohabitation and Subsequent Marital Stability." *American
      Sociological Review*. 53 (February, 1988): 997-1008.
Bianchi, Suzanne and Lynn M. Casper. "American Families"
      Population Bulletin 55 (December, 2000): entire issue.
Breines, Wini and Linda Gordon. "The New Scholarship on Family
      Violence." *Signs*. 8 (Spring, 1983): 490-531.
Bumpass, Larry. "What's Happening to the Family? Interactions
      between Demographic and Institutional Change."
      Demography 27 (November, 1990): 483-498.
Bumpass, Larry and Hsein-Hen Lu. "Trends in Cohabitation and
      Implications for Children's Family Contexts in the United
      States." *Population Studies*. 54 (2000): 29-41.
Bureau of Justice Statistics. Victim-Offender Relationship and Sex of
      Victim in Lone-Offender Crimes, 1992-1993. 3 (1995).
Burgess, Ernest W., Harvey J. Locke, and Mary M. Thomes. *The
      Family: From Traditional to Companionship*, 4th ed. New
      York: Van Nostrand Reinhold, 1971.
Center for Disease Control.
      <http://www.cdc.gov/nchs/fastats/unmarry.htm.> (2000a).
——. http://www.cdc.gov/nchs/data/stabab/t991x18.pdf (2000b).

Cherlin, Andrew, ed.. *The Changing American Family and Public Policy*. Washington, D.C.: Urban Institute Press, 1988.

———. *Marriage, Divorce and Remarriage*. Cambridge, Mass: Harvard University Press, 1992.

Children's Bureau Administration on Children, Youth and Families. "National Child Abuse and Neglect Data System : Summary of Key Findings from Calendar Year 2000". <http://www.calib.com/nccanch/pubs/factsheets/canstats.cfm> (April, 2002).

Clinton, Hillary Rodham. *It Takes a Village: and other Life Lessons Children Teach Us*. New York: Simon and Schuster, 1996.

Collins, Randall and Scott Coltrane. *Sociology of Marriage and the Family: Gender, Love and Property*, 3rd ed. New York: Nelson Hall, 1995.

Coontz, Stephanie. *The Way We Never Were: American Families and the Nostalgia Trap*. New York: Basic Books, 1992.

———. *The Way We Really Are: Coming to Terms with America's Changing Families*. New York: Basic Books, 1997.

Current Population Survey, U.S. Bureau of the Census. http://www.census.gove/Press-Release/www/2001/cb01-113.html (March, 2000a).

———. U.S. Bureau of the Census. (March 2000b). <http://www.census.gove/Press-Release/www/2002/>

Darling, Carol, David Kallen and Joyce VanDusen. "Sex in Transition, 1900-1980." Pp. 151-160 in *Family in Transition*, 7th ed., edited by Arlene S. Skolnick and Jerome H. Skolnick. New York: Harper Collins, 1992.

Davidovitch, Andre. "Criminialite et répression en France d epuis un siécle 1851-1952." *Review Française de Sociologie*, 2 (1961):30-49.

D'Emilio, John. *Sexual Politics, Sexual Communities*. Chicago: University of Chicago Press, 1983.

Demos, John. "The American Family of Past Time." Pp. 59-77 in *Family in Transition*, 2nd ed., edited by Arlene S. Skolnick and Jerome H. Skolnick. Boston: Little, Brown, 1977.

Fastats, A to Z. National Center for Health Statistics, Divorce. *Monthly Vital Statistics Report*, 45, 12 (1996):60.

Faust, Kimberly A. and Jerome N. McKibben. Pp. 475-499 in
    Handbook of Marriage and the Family, 2nd ed., edited by
    Marvin Sussman, Suzanne K. Steinmetz, and Gary W.
    Peterson. New York: Plenum Press, 1999.

Foucault, Michel. *The History of Sexuality. Volume 1, An
    Introduction*. New York: Random House, 1978.

Furstenberg, Frank F. Jr. "Divorce and the American Family," *Annual
    Review of Sociology*. 16 (1990):379-403.

Frenkiel, N. "Shape up or Ship Out" *Baltimore Sun*. (May 2, 1990):
    1F, 8F.

Gallagher, M. *The Abolition of Marriage: How We Destroy Lasting
    Love*. Washington, D.C.: Regnery, 1996.

Gelles, Richard J. *Contemporary Families: A Sociological View*.
    Thousand Oaks, CA: Sage, 1995.

Glasco, Lawrence. "The Life Cycles and Household Structure of
    American Ethnic Groups," Pp. 281-285 in *A Heritage of Her
    Own: Toward a New Social History of American Women*,
    edited by Nancy Cott and Elizabeth Peck. New York: Simon
    and Schuster, 1979.

Goldscheider, Frances K. and Linda J. Waite. *New Families, No
    Families? The Transformation of the American Home*.
    Berkeley: University of California Press, 1991.

Goode, William J. *World Revolution and Family Patterns*. New
    York: The Free Press, 1963.

Greenstein, Theordore N. "Marital disruption and the employment of
    married women.: *Journal of Marriage and the Family*. 52, 3
    (1990): 657-676.

Gwartney-Gibbs, Patricia. "The Institutionalization of Premarital
    Cohabitation: Estimates from Marriage License Applications
    1970-1980." *Journal of Marriage and the Family*. 48
    (1986): 423-434.

Henslin, James M. *Sociology: A Down to Earth Approach*, 2nd ed.
    Boston: Allyn and Bacon, 2002.

Hochschild, Arlie. *The Second Shift: Working Patterns and the
    Revolution at Home*. New York: Viking Penguin, 1989.

Howe, Richard G. *Homosexuality in America: Exposing the Myths*.
    American Family Association: Tupelo, Mass., 1994.

Howitz, Allan V., Julie McLaughlin and Helene Raskin White. "How
      the Negative and Positive Aspects of Partner Relationships
      Affect the Mental Health of Young Married People." *Journal
      of Health and Social Behavior*. 39, 2 (June, 1998):124-136.

Hunt, M.M. *The Affair: A Portrait of Extramarital Love in
      Contemporary America*. New York: World, 1969.

Hutter, Mark. *The Changing Family*. 3rd ed. Boston: MA: Allyn
      and Bacon, 1998.

Jacobsen, Paul. *American Marriage and Divorce*. New York:
      Rinehart, 1959.

Jekielek, Susan M. "Parental Conflict, Marital Disruption and
      Children's Emotional Well-Being." *Social Forces*. 76
      (1998):905-935.

Katz, Jonathan Ned. *The Invention of Heterosexuality*. New York:
      Dutton, 1995.

Kellog, Susan and Steven Mintz. "Family History, Family Structures,
      1925-1944." in *Encyclopedia of American Social History*,
      Vol. III. Edited by. Mary K. Cayton, Elliot J. Gorn and Peter
      W. Williams. New York: Charles Scribner's Sons, 1993.

Kirpatrick, Clifford. *The Family as Process and Institution*. 2nd ed.
      New York: Roland Press, 1963.

Klein, Matthew. "Women's Trip to the Top." *American
      Demographics*, (February, 1998): 22.

Koop, C. Everett. "Violence Against Women: A Global Problem."
      Paper presented at the Pan American Health Organization.
      Geneva, Switzerland (May, 1989).

Krishnen, V. "Premarital Cohabitation and Martial Disruption."
      Journal of Divorce and Remarriage. 28 (1998): 157-170.

Kurian, George. *Datapedia of the United States: 1790-2000*. Laham,
      Maryland: Berman Press, 1994.

Laslett, Barbara. "The Family as a Public and Private Institution: An
      Historical Perspective." *Journal of Marriage and the Family*.
      35 (1973): 480-492.

Laumann, Edward, John Gagnon, Robert Michael and Stuart
      Michaels. *The Social Organization of Sexuality: Sexual
      Practices in the United States*. Chicago: University of
      Chicago Press, 1994.

Luker, Kristen. "Dubious Conceptions: The Controversy Over Teen
    Pregnancy." Pp. 160-172 in *Family in Transition*, 7th ed.,
    edited by Arlene S. Skolnick and Jerome H. Skolnick. New
    York: Harper Collins, 1992.

Magnol, Lynn, Terrie E. Moffett, Arshalom Caspi and Phil A. Silva.
    "Hitting Without a License: Testing Explanation for
    Differences in Partner Abuse Between Young Adult Daters
    and Cohabitors." *Journal of Marriage and the Family*. 60, 1
    (February, 1998):141-156.

Mauss, Armand L. *Social Problems and Social Movements*.
    Philadelphia: Lippincott, 1975.

McManus, Michael. "Cohabitation Presents Dilemma." *Morning
    Call Newspaper*. (October 24, 1998): B-25.

Messerschmidet, James W. *Masculinities and Crime: Critique and
    Reconceptualization of Theory*. Lanham, Maryland:
    Rowman and Littlefield, 1993.

Mindel, Charles, H., Robert W. Habentein, and Roosevelt Wright, Jr.
    Ethnic Families in America: Patterns and Variations. Upper
    Saddle River, NJ: Prentice Hall, 1998.

Mooney, Linda A., David Knox, and Caroline Schacht.
    Understanding Social Problems. 2nd ed. Albany, NY:
    Wadsworth Thomson Learning, 2000.

Morin, R. "How to Lie with Statistics: Adultery". *Washington Post*
    (March 6, 1994): C5.

National Vital Statistics Report. Vol. 59, No. 10
    <http://www.cdc/hchs/fastats/birth.htm> (2001).

O'Brien John E. "Violence in divorce-prone families." *Journal of
    Marriage and the Family*. 33 (1971):692-698.

Packard, Vance. *The Sexual Revolution: The Contemporary
    Upheaval in Male-Female Relationships*. Toronto, Canada:
    Musson Book Co., 1970.

Palen, John. J. *The Suburbs*. New York: McGraw Hill, 1995.

Paul, Pamela. *The Starter Marriage and the Future of Matrimony*.
    New York: Villard, 2002.

Phoenix, Ann. *Young Mothers*. Cambridge, MA: Basil Blackwell,
    1991.

Polikoff, Nancy. 1983. "Gender and Child Custody Determinations:
    Exploding the Myths." Pp. 183-202 in *Families, Politics and
    Public Policy: A Feminist Dialogue on Women and the
    State.*, edited by I. Diamond. New York: Longman, 1983.

Popenoe, David. *Life Without Father: Compelling New Evidence that Fatherhood and Marriage are Indispensable for the Good of Children and Society*. New York: Free Press, 1996.

Rennison, Callie Marie and Sarah Welchans. "Intimate Partner ' Violence." *Bureau of Justice Statistics*. NCJ 178247. 2000.

Saunders, D.G. "What do You Know about Abuser Recidivism? A Critique of Recidivism in Abuser Programs." *Victimology: An International Journal*. (1988).

Scanzoni, Letha and John Scanzoni. *Men, Women and Change: A Sociology of Marriage and Family*. New York: McGraw-Hill, 1976.

Schechter, Susan. *Women and Male Violence: The Visions and Struggles of the Battered Women's Movement*. Boston: South End Press, 1982.

Schwartz, Pepper and Virginia Rutter. *The Gender of Sexuality*. Thousand Oaks, California: Pine Forge Press, 1998.

Skolnick, Arlene. *Embattled Paradise: The American Family in an Age of Uncertainty*. New York: Basic Books, 1991.

Shorter, Edward. *The Making of the Modern Family*. New York: Basic Books, 1975.

Solomon, Theodore. "History and demography of child abuse." *Pediatrics* (Part 2) 51, 4 (1973):773-776.

Statistical Abstract of the United States. 115th ed. U.S. Bureau of the Census. Washington, D.C.: U.S. Government Printing Office, 1995.

———. 118th ed. U.S. Bureau of the Census. Washington, D.C.: U.S. Government Printing Office, 1998.

Steinmetz, Suzanne and Murray A. Straus, eds. *Violence in the Family*. New York: Dodd, Mead, 1974.

Straus, Murray. "Identifying Offenders in Criminal Justice Research on Domestic Assault." *American Behavioral Scientist*. 36 (May, 1993): 587-600.

Tweedell, Cynthia Benn, general editor. *Sociology: A Christian Approach for Changing the World*. Marion, Ind.: Triangle Publishing, 2003.

United States Bureau of the Census. QT-P18. Marital Status by Sex, Unmarried Partner Households and Grandparents as Caregivers: 2000. (2000a).

————. Profile of Selected Social Characteristics: 2000. (2000b). United States Bureau of the Census. <http://www.census.gov/PressRelease/www/2003/cb03ff02.html> (2000c)

————. <http://www.census.gov/Press-Release/www/2001/cb01> (2001)

Walker, Lenore E. "The Battered Woman Syndrome Is a Psychological Consequence of Abuse." Pp. 133-153 in *Current Controversy on Family Violence*, edited by Richard J. Gelles and Donileen Loseke. Thousand Oaks, California: Sage Publications, 1993.

Wallerstein, Judith, Julia M. Lewis, and Sandra Blakeslee. *The Unexpected Legacy of Divorce: A 25 Year Landmark Study*. New York: Hyperion, 2000.

Weitzman, Lenore. *The Divorce Revolution: The Unexplored Consequences*. New York. The Free Press, 1985.

Welter, Barbara. "The Cult of True Womanhood: 1820-1860." *American Quarterly*, 18 (Summer, 1966): 151-174.

Weston, Don. *Twenty Good Reasons not to Cohabit before Marriage. A Strategy for Counseling Couples Cohabiting Before Marriage: A Tool Box Monogram*. Kansas City, Mo.: Family Life Ministries, 1998.

Widdison, Harold A. and H. Richard Delaney. "Social Problems: Definitions, Theories, and Analysis." *Annual Editions: Social Problems*. Dushkin Publishing Group, 1993.

Williams, Gertrude. "Toward the Eradication of Child Abuse and Neglect at Home." Pp. 588-605 in *Traumatic Abuse and the Neglect of Children at Home*, edited by Gertrude Williams and John Money. Baltimore, MD: Johns Hopkins University Press, 1980.

Yllo, Kirsti A. "Through a Feminist Lens: Gender, Power, and Violence." Pp. 47-62 in *Current Controversy on Family Violence*, edited by Richard J. Gelles and Donileen Loseke. Thousand Oaks, California: Sage Publications, 1993.

Young, Michael and Peter Willmot. *The Symmetrical Family*. New York: Pantheon Books, 1973.

Chapter 7

Education and Schools as a Social Problem

"If you keep doing the same old thing, he same old way, you'll get the same old results."

Leon Hudnall, Morse Elementary School Principal, Chicago, Ill. (Quoted by Anjetta McQueen of The Associated Press, June 17, 1999)

Public education has played a prominent role in the social history of the United States. In a very diverse nation - - racially, ethnically and socially - - the public schools attempted to socialize young people by offering a common curriculum rooted in Anglo-American culture. This has prompted debates over the purposes, content and control of public schooling. In a country with an egalitarian political tradition, people increasingly came to see education as the key to equal opportunity. In an advanced capitalist economy, they came to see schooling as crucial to individual success and social prosperity. These cultural, political, and economic agendas combined to reinforce the importance of public schooling. They also provided the conflicting purposes and curriculum of public schools (Kaestle, 1993: 2493).

Nowhere does society and the State work together closer than in educating the young. Even grown persons by the millions return to school at night to complete or pursue higher education. Formal education in schools involves millions of citizens, both young and old alike. Both society and the State see education not only as an asset but they also see four major social problems in education and schools:

1. Conflicting purposes and curriculum
2. Unequal access (causing or reflecting inequality)
3. Funding and financing schools
4. Bureaucracy that is dysfunctional

Conflicting Purposes and Curriculum

What are the purposes of education? What is the point of school? And what should be taught in our schools?

Two major answers have been given to these questions. Both involve "hidden ideologies". One is the "liberal" answer; the other answer, "conservative". One emphasizes change; the other stresses stability and the "status quo".

The liberal stance is that the primary purposes of education "must be rooted in the experiences of the child; it must take seriously the interests, purposes, and involvements of each student" (Morshead, 1975: 16). Since the student's interests and concerns are continually changing, John Dewey, famous liberal educator, argued that "the education process has no end beyond itself" (Morshead, 1975: 16).

The liberal view of the purpose of education, then, is to help the student grow and develop as a whole person, not just for intellectual or career achievement. Learning for learning's sake, and knowledge for knowledge's sake, are the ends and goals of a liberal education.

The other answer to the question about the purposes of education is the conservative view. For the conservative, school ought not to be an institution or social system that reforms society or changes things. Instead, the prime purpose of education is to conserve and transmit the values and knowledge that make up the essential intellectual, historical and moral basis of our society. Schooling, according to this view, should be focused on the mind and heart. The mind is shaped through hard, demanding tasks requiring "discipline". The teacher directs and drills the child to master "the discipline" being studied. The scholar-teacher serves as an ideal model of an educated person. Knowledge mastered should be helpful in getting a job later. Mastering the *moral values* should make one an acceptable citizen and employee in the near future.

According to the conservative purposes, the way schools should operate is *like a factor*. There are "inputs" conveyed by the teacher to the student so he can "work on them" and "put out" on a test or exam. This knowledge "output" and "production" are counted and weighted by a system of grades or marks. When the student has produced (or re-produced) the proper output after a given number of years, he "graduates" to a higher level of educational input and output.

This kind of education lends itself well to measurement of effectiveness
- - test scores for reading, math, science or anything else can be
compared and contrasted with other schools and nations.

The debate over the purposes of education is couched in terms
and ideologies beyond merely "liberal" or "conservative". Some see
the problem of purpose as a battle *between intellect* and *emotion* - -
between the *mind* and *heart*. Charles Silberman poses (and resolves)
these two opposing purposes of education. He writes:

> The insistence that systematic and disciplined intellectual
> effort is a waste of time…at its best is sentimental
> foolishness.   More important, both this view and its
> opposite, the emphasis on disembodied intellect, represent
> badly mistaken conceptions of the nature of the mind,
> which encompasses feeling no less than intellect and
> intellect no less than feeling (1970:8).

So the debate over the purposes of education, and what should
be taught, rages on.   The problem over defining the purposes of
education revolves around the *school's role with respect to social
change*. Should and can our schools *promote* social change?   Or is
their role to *preserve and transmit what already exists?*   The early
pioneers of education in America, such as Horace Mann, George
Counts, and John Dewey all saw the school as the catalyst for a better
society. Some of their hopes were realized. Some were not. Many
more are still unfilled in the 21st Century, as most parts of the
educational system pass on and perpetuate our existing economic,
social and political system.

Others, whether liberal or conservative, argue that education's
primary purposes are stratification and socialization of the young. Our
schools feed young people into jobs.   They provide manpower for
industry and reinforce our existing social class system.   The
stratification purpose is like an elevator carrying many people from the
basement to the top floor of a high rise. They all start together in the
kindergarten "basement". A few never get on the elevator, and stay in
the basement the rest of their lives. As the elevator rises, the young
people step off, or are kicked out, at certain levels. *Most* stay on until
the high school floor is reached. But the four levels before those take
their toll. Some get off before they graduate. *Most get off after they
get the high school diploma.*   Others continue the ride to the
community college level. Some go on to even higher educational

levels. A few continue and hold on until they reach the top floor - - professional schools for medicine, law or engineering.

Thus, the *"educational elevator stratifies society, dropping off woman* and *manpower* at *different occupational floors.* Even though education is not often connected with actual job performance, it is *used as a screening sieve into the job market.* We are still very much a "credential" society. So our schools screen out and stratify the work force in our society. Often this system leads to poor and minority students not finishing high school. Working class students move on to vocational schools or community colleges. Middle class and upper class kids surge on to colleges and universities - - if they can afford them. As Colin Greer notes, "the basic function of the schools is as the primary selector of the winners and losers in society" (1969: 84). As the White House Conference on Children put it: "The schools have become great sorting machines, labeling and certifying those who presumably will be winners and losers as adults. The winners are disproportionately white and affluent. The losers, too often, are poor, and brown, or black, or red" (Report to the President, 1970: 76).

The purpose of schooling is not just to stratify society. It also *aims to socialize children for society.* The family starts the job, but the school finishes it. With compulsory education, masses of the young are socialized to prepare themselves for society. The schools aim to form and forge the mind of almost every child in society. They stress obedience, conformity, and adherence to rules. Schools are bureaucratic organizations that socialize the young to accept a bureaucratic society. That is their chief purpose it is argued. Whatever depersonalization, if not alienation, exists in our schools, it stems form the stratification and socialization purposes of education.

The definitions of education's purposes also zero in on curriculum - - what the schools should teach. Should they teach subjects that are connected with "how to live" or "how to make a living?" Should the focus be on practical job-related, career type courses or on more general "liberal-arts" life-enriching ones? During the 1950s and early 1960s there was not much conflict over this issue. No matter what students took in school, they usually ended up in some kind of job. If a guy or girl went on to college and graduated, they usually ended up with a good-paying job. These were the golden years for education in America and for graduates. But the golden years are over and education's image has become tarnished.

So education at all levels faces serious problems today, centering on its purposes and functions in a rapidly changing society. Trying to second-guess what the job demand in any field will be four or five years ahead is hazardous, especially for educators who are not usually well informed about changing market conditions. If Congress appropriates billions for space, or child care, or health care, then job demand zooms. If it does not, it drops. And who can predict the mind of Congress?

The fact is that nobody *really* knows what skills we'll need five years from now. So if education is in doubt about its purposes, aims and curriculum, it is because the outlook of society and the economy is not too clear and precise.

History of Education

Today there may be confusion about the purposes and aims of education, but at one time we did not even agree on the need for formal education at all. The early American colonists brought with them from England their social institutions. This included their school. They were elite and classical, and usually established for religious purposes. The primary purpose for teaching the young to read was so they could learn the Bible. Education in early America was viewed as private rather than public and was designed for the upper classes, not the masses. In Massachusetts in 1664, compulsory schooling was made the law. It required each town to provide schools and schoolmasters (Greer, 1972: 14). A committee of townsmen ran each local school, and these school committees eventually evolved into local school boards. Though established by government, these schools were religiously motivated, and the 3 rs, "reading, 'riting and 'rithmetic", dominated the curriculum.

After the American Revolution, schools began to gradually take on four democratic hallmarks. The schools were to be free, public, non-sectarian and universal (compulsory) (Pounds and Bryner, 1973: 59). The Northwest Ordinance of 1787 required each township to set aside a mile square section for school use. Our tax-supported public schools are so universal in the United States today that it is difficult to grasp the long struggles and battles that took place to get them set up. We first established private, tuition-based schools. But since a democracy required literate people, the private schools were opened to others whose tuition was paid by taxes. Such "free" education from taxes was considered by many in the early Nineteenth Century to be "socialistic" or "communistic". In Pennsylvania, for example, a free public education law barely survived its first passage in 1834. Only an impassioned plea by Thaddeus Stevens, and some political arm-twisting, saved the experiment from being repealed. Even the states that passed such laws left it up to local boards of education to decide whether or not, or how, to provide such education.   This public education also only applied to the "common school" (elementary level).

Horace Mann, Secretary of the Massachusetts Board of Education, led the fight for improvements in education. He fought for better pay for teachers and better training of teachers in State "normal" or teacher-training schools. In 1842, Mann visited schools throughout Europe.   He championed features of European education, like no corporal punishment and a non-sectarian system of schools.   He reported back on "the beautiful relation of harmony and affection" between teachers and pupils in Europe's schools. "I heard no child ridiculed, sneered at, or scolded for making a mistake" (Silberman, 1970: 59). He advocated this approach in our schools, but a group of Boston grammar school masters attacked Mann's suggestions. They rejected any child-centered approach to education, or any reforms making it pleasurable or joyful. Strict punishment, discipline, and obedience were more properly an integral part of the early school's purpose. They wrote that nothing was likely to cause more "mischief" or be more "subversive of real happiness than mistaking what may afford the child present-gratification, for that which secures him lasting good". To place the child's interests or needs first would threaten "...the welfare, both of the individual and society, by sending forth a sickly race, palsied in every limb, through idleness" and determined "to gratify a morbid thirst for pleasure" (Silberman, 59-60).

This expression about the purpose of education was widespread in 1840 America.   Public schooling was designed to "diminish the vice, crime and moral degradation" that came from the New Irish immigrants. The lower classes had to be taught obedience and this could not be instilled in children by coddling them in school. From the very start, public schools never were too effective in meeting the *real* human needs of immigrant or lower-class children (Greer, 1972).   Starting with Massachusetts in 1852, the states in the Nineteenth Century began to pass compulsory school attendance laws (the last passed by Mississippi in 1918).

Very early in their history, the schools took over the curriculum and teaching methods of certain elite European schools. Their system was designed mainly for the European upper classes, and little attention was given to special needs for other social classes. The school was to discipline the immigrant and prepare him for obedience and conformity to the social order.   The Nineteenth Century conservative William T. Harris, speaking to the National Education Association in 1894 when the country was in the "throes of labor disorders," observed that "the school provided the people with training in those habits of regularity, silence, and industry". The schools would "preserve and save our civil order", and students would learn "first of all to respect the rights of organized industry" (Curti, 1959: 330).

Dr. Leonard Covello, the first Italian-American to become a principal in the New York City schools, described what schools meant to him and other Italians at the turn of the century:

> Every day before receiving our bowl of soup we recited the Lord's Prayer. I had no inkling of what the words meant. I knew only that I was expected to bow my head. I looked around to see what was going on. Swift and simple, the teacher's blackboard pointer brought the idea home to me. I never batted an eyelash after that...Silence! Silence! This was the characteristic feature of our existence at the Soup School. You never made an unnecessary noise or said an unnecessary word. Outside in the hall we lined up by size, girls in one line and boys in another without uttering a sound. Eyes front and at attention. Lord help you if you broke the rule of silence (Silberman, 1970: 57-8).

In addition, Dr. Covello goes on to point out the negative image the school gave him of his ethnic heritage and even his parents. He wrote: "We soon got the idea the 'Italian' meant something inferior, and a barrier was erected between children of Italian origin and their parents. This was the accepted process of Americanization. We were becoming Americans by learning how to be ashamed of our parents" (Silberman, 1970: 57-8).

Late 19th Century high schools were vastly different than today's. Half the teacher's didn't have a college degree. All were very poorly paid. "In New York State, the average teacher's salary in 1899 was $700 - - the equivalent of about $15,000 today" (Crossen, 2003: B-1). Many taught more than one subject and also trained the school choir or cut firewood for the school. The students lessons were prescribed by textbooks, such as "McGuffey's New High School Reader" or "The Normal Mental Arithmetic" (Crossen, 2003).

Caroline Ware, writing about the "progressive" schools of Greenwich Village in the 1920s and '30s, points out "the local schools were indifferent" to the Italian children. They did not consider it necessary to be familiar with the background of the children to prepare them for their role in our society. The Lynds in the famous study of "Middletown" in 1926, pointed to the Muncie, Indiana, schools as failing to meet the needs of lower-class children. As W. Lloyd Warner summed it up: "One large group is almost immediately brushed off into a bin labeled "non-readers", "first-grade repeaters", or "opportunity class" where they stay for eight to ten years and are then released through a chute to the outside world to become "hewers of wood and drawers of water" (W. Lloyd Warner et al., 1944: 61). August Hollingshead in his community study *Elmstown's Youth*, observed that the schools were unresponsive to the needs of lower-class students. Conflicts over purposes, relevance, and responsiveness of the school, then are nothing new historically.

The one room elementary school house in 1907 combined all grades

        In elementary schools we have gone from lay examination of teachers by school boards to professional examination and state certification from accredited colleges of teacher education. Elementary school standards have changed in the last 150 years or so. Early "grammar" schools used to huddle all the children together as a group, the famous one-room schoolhouse. Eventually students were separated into grades.   From subjective evaluation of students, we moved historically to objective testing. Eventually, from reading, writing and arithmetic, and reliance on McGuffey's Reader, other standardized courses were established. By 1965, some 35 million children attended elementary schools. Today some 38 million attend and by 2002, 38.7 million (Statistical Abstract of the United States, 1998: 161). As the nation grew, education grew beyond its elementary level.

History of High School
        With the founding of the first private American Academy in Philadelphia in 1751, secondary schools were established to prepare

small groups of students for college. The first public high school began in Boston in 1820. By the middle of the Nineteenth Century there were 40 such schools. By 1865, Wisconsin had 11 high schools; California had only six or seven. Gradually public high schools were seen to be the institution that would replace the old private academy.

In 1874, the famous "Kalamazoo" Michigan, decision approved the use of elementary school money for public high schools. Thus the high school became a vital link in the public school system. It filled the gap between the elementary school and college. By 1890 enrollments had increased to the point where 3 ½ percent of our citizens were high school graduates. In 1860, prior to the 1874 state Supreme Court decision, there were only 40 public high schools in the U.S. but by 1900 there were 6,005 (Crossen, 2003). But compulsory education and mass education at the high school level has only occurred within the past eighty years. As late as 1893, the Report of the "Committee of Ten" on Secondary School Studies saw the chief purpose of free public high school to be "...to prepare for the duties of life that small proportion of all children in the country who show themselves able to profit by an education prolonged to the eighteenth year, and whose parents are able to support them while they remain so long in school" (1893: 56-7). That same committee backed the teaching of traditional subjects.

In 1900, only about 8% of Americans 14 to 17 years old attended high school. Of those, only about 10% expected to attend college. Education beyond the age of 14 wasn't compulsory in most states, and dropout rates were higher than today.

This attitude confirmed the chief function of high school to be a college-prep school. Yet the majority of students were not going to college. By 1918 the Commission on Reorganization of Secondary Education developed a different concept - - the need to educate students as future citizens to take their part in a democracy. By that same year, all 48 states had compulsory school attendance laws. The floodgates were now open. Enrollment in high school doubled each decade between 1890 and 1930. Enrollments increased by 750%, while national population grew a little over 60%. Programs and purposes expanded to meet the crunch. The age of mass education was upon us. The historical results are familiar. In 1920 only about 35% of seventeen-year-olds were in school. Today more than 90% of such youngsters go to school (U.S. Department of Education, 1998: 52). In 1997, 82% of American adults (25 and older) had graduated from high school, while 18% had dropped out of high school (Mooney et al., 2000: 312).

Yet even in the 1920's test scores on state exams were a problem and concern, as it is today. Test scores of students who made it to the 12th grade were as discouraging to educators then as they are now. "In 1924, 19% of high school students who took the New York State regents exam in English failed; 30% failed the math exam and 31% failed Latin" (Crossen, 2003: B-1).

In 1965, 13 million students were enrolled in high schools (both public and private). By 1980, 14 ½ million were enrolled and almost 15 million by 2000 (U.S. National Center for Education Statistics, 1998: 161). By 2008 it is projected that over 16 million students will be in high school.

But something else happened to high schools (and elementary schools) in 1900. That was the year that Ellen Key, the Swedish Feminist and educator, published her book *The Century of the Child.* Translated into many languages, it inspired "progressive" educators in many countries. Progressive education was a system of teaching based on the needs and potential of the child, rather than on the needs of adults or society. Similarly, the influence of John Dewey, historically, still affects education today. He stressed learning through varied concrete activities rather than formal abstract curricula. He opposed authoritarian methods in the classroom, as such methods did not prepare students to participate in a democratic society. High school was destined to be a mix or compromise between the elite academic approach and the pragmatic vocationally oriented one. Tracking systems within each school, and different programs according to ability and desire, became the rule in American high schools as it is today.

Community Colleges

The third level of education historically is "Higher Education". For two centuries or so, this level consisted of four-year colleges or universities.

During the late 1940s and 1950s, however, a revolutionary change took place in America's system of higher education. To accommodate masses of younger and older students beyond high school, a new tier was added to education. Junior colleges, today called community colleges, began to spring up all over the United States. The idea behind such schools was to train persons in the community from all social classes in a wide variety of technical, semi-vocational, and academic subjects. Some community colleges serve as "feeder schools" for four-year colleges and universities. They serve as a testing or proving ground for some students before they decide to go on to college. For others, the community college acts as a springboard to a good-paying technical job for high school graduates. For still others, it trains them more thoroughly in their jobs or careers. By 1975, more than 3 ½ million students (or 18% of recent high school graduates) were attending one of our 1,200 community colleges (Yarrington, 1975: 15). By 1996, 23% of all recent high school grads started Community College (U.S. Department of Education, 1998: 54). About 45% of all first-time college undergrads started in a community college (U.S. Department of Education, 1994: 62). As the two-year college has evolved from a junior college into a community-oriented institution, its primary purposes and the processes of education have changed. The community college has spearheaded innovation and change in education. Its major thrust is learning through *actual* experience in the community. Such experiential education is not new. What is new is the incorporation of work experience into the curricula so that it is a formal part of the course of study. Academic credit is given for such experience. This experience might involve placement in a day-care center; or in schools for the mentally retarded; or in police stations; or any other agency or organization in the community (Gleazer, 1975: 12).

The development of this progressive, innovative tier of higher education historically should affect what is offered at higher levels and how it is presented.

College and Universities

The pioneers of higher education in the U.S. were residential liberal arts colleges starting with Harvard in 1636 and William and Mary in 1693 (Koblik, 1999: 13). Colleges began as religious training schools or seminaries for the clergy. Harvard, Yale, and William and Mary all started with religious aims and purposes. Nevertheless, the first colleges all saw a connection between sacred and secular learning. As Richard Hofstadter and Wilson Smith note: "They believed that the collegiate education proper for a minister should be the same as for an educated layman. They expected that the early colleges would produce not only ministers but Christian gentlemen who would be civic leaders" (1961: I: 2).

The Charter for Harvard "College" referred to its purposes as "the advancement of all good literature, arts and sciences" and "the education of the English and Indian youth of this country in knowledge and godliness" (Hofstadter & Smith, 1961: I: 2). So from the very beginning of high education in the United States, colleges were committed to a combination of religion, "liberal arts" and science. Also from the start there was at least token mention of the need to educate minority-group people.

Though the church became disestablished in the various states early in our history, many colleges clung to a religious sectarian point of view. Change came slowly. When King's College (Columbia) and the College of Philadelphia (University of Pennsylvania) opened in the Eighteenth Century, they stressed that "there is no intention to impose on the scholars, the peculiar tenets of any particular sect of Christians" (Hofstadter & Smith, 1961: 97). Other colleges like the College of Rhode Island (Brown), Queens College (Rutgers) and Dartmouth followed in their footsteps. The idea of religious tolerance and respect for different ideas made headway in our early colleges.

After the American Revolution, we were torn over how higher education should be handled. By church or government? By individual states? A national university? Or should local units of government establish them? In the South, since private religious colleges had made little inroad, Georgia, Tennessee, North Caroline and South Carolina set up state universities. Jefferson planned for an ambitious state institution, the University of Virginia. The idea of state universities spread West. In 1817, 20 years *before* Michigan got statehood, the legal groundwork was laid for a State University there. President Washington more than once proposed a national university to Congress. He argued, "the more homogeneous our citizens can be made in [principles, opinions, and matter], the greater will be our prospect of permanent union" (Hofstadter & Smith, 1961: 148). James Madison backed the idea. Robert Finley, President of the University of Georgia, went one step further. He proposed all colleges use the same textbooks. It would make the nation's higher education more systematic and uniform.

The famous Dartmouth College case in 1819 established the nature of colleges as private rather than public corporations. It meant that colleges and universities, once chartered, would be immune from state interference in their operation. Nevertheless, a college with influence in the state legislature could get not just a charter, but supporting grants often in the form of land (Hawkins, 1999: 2). This gave a firm legal base for small church-related colleges, and they began to mushroom throughout the country.

During the Nineteenth Century, colleges were severely criticized for being too traditional and classical (Greek and Roman classics). The Yale Report of 1828 defended its intent to discipline and develop the mind. In 1830, however, critics of the colleges met in New York City to found a "serious center of higher studies", to open up admissions to students who have not mastered the "dead" languages, Greek and Latin. The next year New York University was founded.

College presidents like Philip Lindsley of the University of Nashville, in 1828, bemoaned the fact that the colleges were doing the work of the high schools.   In 1837, Jasper Adams, President of Charleston College, South Carolina, blamed the trustees for the shortcomings of colleges and universities.   In 1842, Francis Wayland, President of Brown University, called for an entire re-examination of the structure of higher education in America.   Wayland questioned everything: the trustee system; the faculty; the cost of education; the low salaries of teachers; the inadequate curriculum.   Edward Everett of New England pointed out in 1848 that colleges, especially Harvard, were not receiving enough state funding for scientific research.   In 1856, Frederick Barnard, then President of the University of Mississippi, argued with trustees that the faculty and administrators should be given more power to run the university without interference from the Board of Trustees.

The issue of academic freedom was very much an issue in the Eighteenth and Nineteenth Century colleges and universities. Professors, such as Francis Lieber at South Carolina College, and Reverend D.D. Whedon, at the University of Michigan, were summarily dismissed in the 1850s for their anti-slavery views.   In 1854, conservative trustees of Columbia rejected liberal nomination to a professorship of Dr. Oliver Gibbs, a distinguished chemist and M.D. Gibbs was rejected because his religious beliefs and church membership were more important than knowledge and research in the physical sciences.   G.T. Strong, a trustee who voted for Gibbs, recorded in his diary in January 24, 1854, that "Columbia College is destined to be a sleepy, third-rate high school for one or two generations more". Two historians noted that: "As for Gibbs, he moved to Harvard to take the Rumford chair in chemistry and went on to many years of distinguished scientific work" (Hofstadter & Smith, 1961: 44).

The point here is that the concerns and problems of colleges in the 21st Century are *nothing new* historically.   Purposes, power, costs, and curriculum have been major problems for colleges and universities since they were founded.

Many people think that violence on college campuses was something that happened only during the 1960s.   Historically, this too is not the case.

During the Eighteenth and Nineteenth Centuries, violence and bloodshed were fairly common on some college campuses.   Frederick Rudolph, in *The American College and University,* notes: "Among the victims of the collegiate way were the boy who died in a duel at Dickinson, the students who were shot at Miami in Ohio, the professor who was killed at the University of Virginia, the president of Oakland College in Mississippi who was stabbed to death by a student, the president and professor who were stoned at the University of Georgia, the student who was stabbed at Illinois College, the students who were stabbed and killed at the University of Missouri and the University of North Carolina" (1962: 24).   Violence on college campuses was not just a peculiar "happening" that occurred during the 1960s.

But all students in all Nineteenth Century colleges were not violent. Many demanded "critical social relevance" as part of their education. Since the formal system did not always provide it, the students at many colleges formed their own literary or debating societies and clubs. One author calls these clubs "...the most vital element in American education through the first third of the Nineteenth Century. Their purpose was to study and debate the issues of the day..." (Roszak, 1967: 6).   The clubs also brought controversial speakers onto the campus, such as Ralph Waldo Emerson, who was frequently denied the use of college buildings on campus when he spoke. These literary societies also assembled the best libraries of then-current magazines and literature available. While tolerated, these clubs were never "well accepted" by college administrators or faculty.

With the coming of the Civil War, and the question of slavery, it was felt that the Federal Government should do more to help colleges and not just rely on society to support private colleges and universities. In 1862 the Morrill Land Grant Act was passed. It declared that American public universities should be an integral part of the community and serve the needs of the people and society. This was the beginning of the famous "land-grant" colleges established by the Federal government in each state. The law required these colleges to teach such branches of learning as are related to agriculture and the mechanic arts but without excluding other scientific and classical studies (Hawkins, 1999: 3).   These colleges were to be more democratic and "service-oriented" than the elite aristocratic colleges had been historically. They were "to promote the liberal and practical education of the industrial classes in the several pursuits and professions in life" (Morse and Hendelson, 1973: 34). Amendments to the Act in 1890 and 1907 gave more federal government money to each state to develop land-grant colleges.

State universities of California, Illinois, Maine, Minnesota, Nebraska, Ohio, Pennsylvania, West Virginia, Wisconsin and Wyoming, as well as Iowa State University of Science and Technology, and Purdue University are land-grant colleges. Today there are about 72 land-grant colleges and universities. They receive about $230 million a year in federal funds. Though they make up only 3% of all colleges and universities, they enroll more than 20% of four-year college students and award about 30% of the doctorates in the country. Historically, the Morrill Act was a turning point in higher education, as it made possible a "mass" higher educational system financed by the Federal and State governments. It also emphasized more professional and practical pursuits than the academic pursuits of private colleges.

Historically, large and great American universities oriented toward scientific research took time to develop. After the granting of the first American Ph.D.'s - - by Yale in 1861 and Harvard in 1873 - - came the opening in 1876 of John Hopkins University with research and graduate study as its central purpose (Hawkins, 1999). Just 75 short years ago, any student of science seriously pursuing scientific research had to go to Europe for his higher degree. The Nobel winner for physics, I. Rabi, tells the story of how bad U.S. universities were in the 1920s. When he studied at the university in Germany then, he recalls "so little of consequence was happening in United States research...German universities used to arrange to get an entire year's set of the *Physical Review* from the United States at one time, in order to save postage" (Silberman, 1970: 17). So our universities were "written-off".

One of the most successful critics of higher education was Abraham Flexner. A graduate of Harvard and the University of Berlin, his first book, *The American College: A Criticism* stirred controversy in academic circles, but little reform. His next two works, *Medical Education in the United States and Canada* (1910) and *Medical Education in Europe* (1912), led to meaningful changes in the way U.S. medical schools educate and train our doctors. In 1930, in Flexner's work *Universities: American, English, German*, he called on universities here to stop coddling undergrads and get on with the job of training scientific scholars and researchers to add to our store of knowledge. He argued that the massification and democratization of higher education - - as seen in university schools of business, social work, journalism, and library service - - had started American universities on a "disastrous downward course". In contrast, he pointed to German universities where pure scientific research was carried on. We had no great university "...neither Columbia, nor Harvard, nor John Hopkins, nor Chicago, nor Wisconsin". In 1930, Flexner wrote: "Fifty years ago, the degree of Ph.D. had a meaning in the United States; today it has practically no significance. The same is true of research" (Silberman, 1970: 17). That was in 1930, when only 5% of Nobel Prizes were held by Americans. Today it is about 40%.

Higher education, more and more, has become open to the people. After the Morrill Act in 1862, and the Industrial Revolution, the number of students enrolled in college rose five times to nearly a quarter of a million by the turn of the century. But this only represented about 4% of the youngsters of college age (McGrath, 1975: 9). From these 250,000 students, by the end of World War I (1918) that figure had more than doubled; it doubled again by 1929 and doubled once more by the end of World War II (1945). Immediately after WWII (1945) private colleges and universities educated about half of all U.S. students. The other half was in government-funded ones. Starting with WWII and Korean War (1950-54) G.I. Bills for education, and continuing through the baby-boom years of the 1960s, the notion took hold that a college education was the right and goal of every middle-class family. College enrollments began to surge - - from 2.3 million in 1950 to over 8 ½ million by 1970 (McPherson & Shapiro, 1999: 48). Today some 14 million people are enrolled in college, representing nearly 65% of U.S. students who graduated from high school the prior year (McQueen, 1999: A-33).

Today about l4 million students attend one of the some 2,700 schools of higher learning. These schools enroll nearly two-thirds of the population of college age. Never in the history of the world have so many young people continued their education beyond high school as in America today.

Millions of students attend college today

The question is, can we continue to provide higher education for all, at a reasonable cost, without affecting the quality of education? Recent history suggests that trying to educate masses of young people on massive campuses can cause problems. During the 1950s and 1960s, universities boomed. Intellectuals, from Daniel Moynihan to George Schultz to Henry Kissinger, became part of the power structure. Their ideas on campus became part of the knowledge explosion and "brain industry".

James Ridgeway has documented the ways in which higher education does the work and bidding of big business, big Government, and the Military. The Boards of Regents, as well as local boards of education, are often packed with spokesmen for the rich and big business. Many researchers in education follow the government's green path of dollars, no matter where it leads them academically. The Pentagon remains a pot of gold for some universities. If the government wants an educator to study germ warfare, or how to prevent revolution in underdeveloped countries, a school and its scholars will analyze it - - it the grant is large enough. For years the connection between cigarette smoking and lung cancer was denied by some scholars. Why? "Because the tobacco companies were paying for the research work in some of the universities. Columbia University even became involved in promoting a filter-tip cigarette", according to Ridgeway (Steward, 1976: 89).

Or look at the way land-grant agricultural colleges have hurt the small farmer and helped the corporate giants. These schools have consistently followed curricula and research that make the big farms bigger and benefit the large food processors, but ignore the plight of the small family farm. So higher education generally supports and helps the powerful and rich, while ignoring the needs of others who also could use educational help.

During the 50s and 60s, administration and bureaucratic structures bloomed overnight. On top of thousands of clerks, advisers, deans and staff assistants, the university took on more specialized staffers, from counselors to advisors, to affirmative-action people and research project directors. Federal, state and foundation money flowed onto campus, and grant-getting faculty members built empires and reputations.

The growth in size, prestige and influence had a different effect on college students. Many became a computer number; a cog in the giant education machine of lecture courses for 2,000 students or more. Students at large "multi-versities" met their professors once a year - - if that. Many colleges were now too big for personal relations between professors and students. Alienation, isolation, and anomie were the logical results. Was it any wonder that flocks of such students turned in desperation to protest, demonstrations, and violence? No one would listen, so they tried to get the attention of those in power. Feelings of "community", "humanity", or "commitment" bound together small enclaves and large social movements of college students. They could not find these feelings by relating to research-oriented faculties or bureaucratic administrators, so they turned to one another.

Current Problems and Changes in Education

The problems in education (at all levels) reflect its past problems:

1. Conflicting purposes and curriculum
2. Unequal access (causing or reflecting inequality)
3. Funding and Finances
4. Bureaucracy

Today the conflicts over purposes and curriculum are evident in battles over educational standards, as well as performance and testing outcomes.   Unequal access, due to racial or social class inequality, mirrors itself in battles over funding and financing, and vouchers.   Bureaucracy continues, as in the past, and is reflected in debates over teacher training, large unions and charter schools.

The Battle Over Educational Standards

To resolve the historical conflict over purposes and curriculum a movement is growing in the U.S. for standards and performance outcomes. These standards, both content and performance, are being used by states, school districts and schools to work toward systemic reforms. They would revamp testing, textbooks, teacher training and methods for measuring success or failure in education. Standards are desperately needed since "nearly everyone agrees that the modern [educational] system is in deep trouble" (Clark, 1994: 219).   The average fourth grader in Japan and Russia is said to be two years ahead of the average U.S. fourth grader.   Albert Shanker, a noted former President of the American Federation of Teachers, told the story about having dinner with a couple who had just emigrated to New York City from economically devastated Russia. "They said that even though they had their eighth-grade daughter in a very good private school, she was learning what she had learned in the third grade" in Russia (1991: 6).

Bigler and Lockard in their book, *Failing Grades: A Teacher's Report Card on Education in America* noted that "colleges and universities complain bitterly that professors are now forced to add remedial courses to teach incoming students how to write simple sentences and to compute basic mathematical formulas" (1991: 14).

The National Assessment of Education Performance (NAEP) showed that 75 percent of students in 1992 scored below proficiency levels in math, while two-thirds scored below par in reading. In a 1991 international assessment of physical science and math, five countries (France, Taiwan, Korea, Switzerland and Hungary) all out-performed 13-year-olds in America (National Education Goals Report, 1993). Across the country, concerned parents and politicians point to "soft and fuzzy" curricula and the widespread practice of "social promotion" to the next grade (as Washington, D.C schools do for first and second graders). Though efforts are being made in Chicago, Los Angeles, New York City and Boston schools to keep back students who don't achieve grade-level, it is often a costly and losing battle (McQueen, 1999(b)). Hence, the need for national education standards, it is argued, the reason no *national* educational standards were established officially before 1994 (when Title V of the Goals 2000: Educate America Act became law) was the tradition of local independence (within state guidelines) for society's 16,000 school districts. The closest our society came to creating a national curriculum was in 1893. A committee of college presidents headed by Harvard University President Charles Eliot issued the "Report of the Committee of Ten on Secondary School Studies". It recommended a traditional array of courses in Greek, Latin, math, chemistry, natural history, government and geography. Studying Greek and Latin "trains the mind" and geography "enhances the powers of observation and reasoning" (Hirsch, 1985: 117-18). The rise of discipline in child development and the social sciences, plus a war (WWI) "to make the world free for democracy", led to a new and different report in 1918. "The Cardinal Principles of Secondary Education", was written not by elite university presidents but by education specialists, public officials and high school principals. Greatly influenced by the "progressive philosophy" of John Dewey, it stressed "health, command of fundamental processes, worthy home membership, vocation, citizenship, worthy use of leisure and ethical character" (Ravitch, 1983: 48).

The same year a historic book *The Curriculum*, by Franklin Bobbit, a University of Chicago education professor, emphasized psychology and real-world applications of knowledge in elementary and high schools. He argued that human life "consists in the performance of specific activities. Education that prepares for life is one that prepares definitely and adequately for those specific activities"

(Ravitch, 1983: 49). It was this basic approach that would be followed by many school districts for much of the 20th Century.

The turning point for setting up educational standards came in 1983. The National Commission on Excellence in Education issued a report, *A Nation at Risk: The Imperative for Educational Reform* (Billitteri, 1997; Clark, 1994; Graubard, 1995; Louis, 1998). It stated that "...the educational foundation of our society is presently being eroded by a rising tide of mediocrity that threatens our very future as a nation and a people. What was unimaginable a generation ago has begun to occur - - others are matching and surpassing our educational attainments" (Graubard, 1995: v). The most famous and most-quoted part of the report read: "If an unfriendly foreign power had attempted to impose on America the mediocre educational performance that exists today, we might well have viewed it as an act of war" (Billitteri, 1997: 927). It called for a longer school day and school year and for standards in content and performance. "It clearly affected all schools and brought pressure on them", Arthur Gosling, Superintendent of Schools for Arlington, Va., said recently (Clark, 1994: 231). The report's impact is still felt today. In California a statewide history curriculum with standards was started and nationally, math teachers started on their standards project.

By 1986 it was clear the states needed more direction and guidance from the Federal Government to help establish standards. A task force of governors released an influential report *Time for Results* in 1986. It called for "a horse trade" agreement between government and school districts exchanging flexibility and economic incentives for local accountability by initiating performance standards, with more input from parents and students (Koch, 1999).

The present standards movement was launched in earnest by the Federal Government in 1989 by then President George Bush. He called an education summit meeting in Charlottesville, Va. There, he bucked former conservative president's reluctance to actively involve Washington in education (Koch, 1999). At the conference six national education goals were agreed to:

1. By the year 2000, all children in America will start
   school ready to learn.
2. The high school graduation rate will increase to at least
   90 percent.
3. American students will leave grades 4, 8 and 12 having
   demonstrated competency in challenging subject matter,
   including *English, mathematics, science, history and*

geography, and every school in America will ensure that
all students learn to use their minds well, so they may be
prepared for responsible citizenship, further learning and
productive employment in our modern economy.
4. U.S. students will be first in the world in science and
mathematics achievement.
5. Every adult American will be literate and will possess
the knowledge and skills necessary to compete in global
economy and exercise the rights and responsibilities of
citizenship.
6. Every school in America will be free of drugs and
violence and will offer a disciplined environment
conducive to learning. (Clark, 1994: 232)

In 1994 these six items were made law in Title V of the Goals 2000:
Educate America Act. Once again the Federal Government had moved
into an area once handled locally by society itself. Now the Federal
Government mandates what a state must do in education to receive
federal funds.

Once this happened a great national debate began over the
whole issue of establishing a national curriculum and standards. Three
major questions are raised about national standards: 1). Will national
standards threaten local control of education? 2). Should the
effectiveness of standards be measured by nationwide or statewide
testing? 3). Will standards be unfair to minorities and disadvantaged
students?

Local or National Control of Education?

Under the Goals 2000 law a National Education Standards and
Improvement Council was set up to oversee the creation of standards
by panels of educators in each subject area. Conservatives argued that
the bill in effect creates a "national school board" that undermines local
control of the schools (Clark, 1994: 221). William J. Bennett, former
U.S. Education Secretary, who heads a group called Empower America
wrote: "Over the last 20 years, federal involvement has increased
dramatically and educational achievement has gone down" (Clark,
1994: 221). A newsletter for Citizens for Excellence in Education
reported that Goals 2000 will create a national outcome-based system
which would require attitude and belief changes. That is what
happened at the state level in California when it established standards
in its schools. On top of that, "we do not believe the system will be
voluntary, since students who don't attend certified schools will suffer

limited employment and college opportunities" (1993: 1). One possible solution to this fear of federal control of education came in 1994. The Goals 2000 law gave states money to let the states and business community set the standards in each state. In 1996, a non-profit consortium of governors and corporate officials was set up to act as a clearinghouse for information on all state standards. Forty states now have standards in all four core subjects - - English, math, science and social studies (Koch, 1999) consequently, "for the first time in American history, states are moving to state-wide curriculums" and will hold students and teachers accountable for reaching those curriculums. That's what this whole movement is all about" (Koch, 1999: 404).

Is National Testing Really Necessary?
        The next big question has to do with national testing. Is it really necessary? The President proposed both national standards and national tests. The U.S. Education Department's Mike Cohen stated: "The idea has always been to have some kind of national consensus on testing so parents can know whether their kids are really measuring up" to the standards (Koch, 1999: 405). Once again conservatives fear this is another attempt to mandate Federal standards and tests developed by the U.S. Department of Education. The National Alliance of Business, in favor of educational reform, stated, "We've got a constitutional tradition in this country regarding state responsibility for education. Plus we have 15,000 local school districts that always had control over curriculum" (Koch, 1999: 405) Randy Tate of the Christian Coalition, that opposes national tests administered by the federal government, says "There are many types of measurements for schools". He also argues that the kind of cross-district comparative information the Federal Government says a national test would provide is already available from real estate agents. "If you've ever gone house-hunting you know which are the good schools, which are safe, which excel", he says (Koch, 1999: 406).
        The National Assessment of Educational Progress (NAEP) was authorized by Congress since 1996 as part of its Goals 2000 Program. It tests children in grades 4, 8 and 12. It is given to a statistical sampling of 31,000 youngsters across the U.S. In 1998, the school children boosted their scores as compared with 1994. Since 1994 scores were so low, the latest test results only brought student reading performance to about where it was in 1992. Despite the small progress, the results in 1998 showed "that 38% of fourth-graders, 26% of eighth-graders and 23% of 12th graders still read at *below minimum*

achievement levels (Kronholz, 1999: 14-16). Yet, for the first time, all three grades showed improvement from 1994, an average of 3 or 4 points.

Nine states were initially reported as significantly improving their reading scores from 1994 to 1998. Connecticut, Louisiana and South Carolina had the largest score gains, as did Maryland and Kentucky. Two months later, the U.S. Education Department reported that these states had excluded a higher percentage of special education students than they had in 1994. The states with the largest score gains - - Connecticut, Louisiana and South Carolina - - all would have had lower average scores had special education students been included in the test as in 1994. "At least 18 of the 36 participating states (50%) left out more special education pupils from the 1998 testing sample than from the 1994 group" (McQueen, 1999(2)).

In addition, some states have shown failure and success. For example, in 1995 Virginia adopted "Standards of Learning" in English, math, history and science. In the first round of testing in Spring, 1998, more than 97 percent of Virginia flunked their standards. "A mere 39 of about 1,800 scored high enough to dodge the threat of eventually losing state accreditation" (Anderson, 1999). By 2004, high school students who fail the test will not get a diploma. "By 2007, schools must have 70 percent of their students achieve a passing grade, in most cases, to avoid losing state accreditation", Anderson reported (1999: A-9).

On the other hand, North Carolina and Texas were among the first states to try standards-based reform in the early 1990s. From 1990 to 1997, they posted the largest average gains in the country on seven key National Assessment of Education Progress (NAEP) tests - - a national standardized test that is considered "the nation's report card" (Grissmer and Flanagan, 1998). A National Education Goals Panel (NEGP) study of how the two states achieved their results, pointed to: "strong, long-term support from the business community, consistent bipartisan political support and a willingness to stick with systemic reform on a long-term basis rather than switching to the 'reform du jour'" (Grissmer and Flanagan, 1998: 408).

As more states move to standardized achievement tests to judge the success of schools, a growing chorus of students, parents and teachers complain that "the tests hurt the curriculum and school accreditation" (Bayles, 1999: 10A).

1. Parents and educators are venting their anger and
    opposition over the months spent in school largely
    preparing for a 2-week long series of tests in
    Massachusetts.
2. In Wisconsin a committee of legislators voted to end
    funding for a statewide high school graduation test, after
    a lobbying campaign by parents.
3. New York City's Board of Education cancelled a
    citywide reading test for second graders, after parents and
    principals complained that the children were tested too
    much.
4. A boycott against the Michigan Educational Assessment
    Program has reached 90% in some school districts,
    despite the promise of college tuition assistance for
    students who pass the state exam.
5. Chicago area students and parents angered over the time
    spent preparing for three assessment tests have begun
    campaigning against testing. One group staged a
    demonstration outside the Board of Education offices
    (Bayles, 1999: 10A)

Will Standards Be Unfair to Poor and Minority Students?: American
and Latino Congressional caucuses fear that poor results on national
standards tests would be used to cut funding to children in already
under-funded, low-performance schools. They feel that national tests
would be unfair to disabled and non-English speaking students.

Advocates say that states farthest along in standards and test
efforts are seeing some of the fastest-rising test scores in the country.
Both North Carolina and Texas, with large, poor minority group
students, as well as Chicago and Philadelphia, have shown
improvements in their test scores. "There's definitely momentum in
some very high poverty cities", says Kate Haycock, President of the
Education Trust, a non-profit organization promoting high academic
achievement among poor minority students (Koch, 1999: 405). But
there's another side, including many in the civil rights community, who
say that until you can guarantee poor kids have exactly the same
supports that rich kids have, you cannot put these standards into place"
(Koch, 1999: 407). A resource guide by the U.S. Department of
Education, stated: a test "which has significant disparate impact on
members of any particular race, national origin or sex is
discriminatory" unless an institution can show that the test is
educationally necessary and that there is no "practicable alternative"
(Marklin, 1999: 5-D).

Yet a report by the Council of Great City Schools (CGCS), a first-ever study of the impact on urban schools of the $8 million Title I part of the Elementary and Secondary Education Act, revealed reading and math scores were improving steadily and substantially, though they still aren't up to the suburban school level (Lewis, 1999). Of the 24 urban school districts reporting, 88% showed increased reading scores among disadvantaged students. Some 83% showed higher math scores over both 2 and 3-year periods, especially fourth grade reading.

Unequal Access Due to Re-Segregation and Funding

Another major problem of education today is unequal access of minorities to an equal education. This is reflected in the current issue over racial segregation or re-segregation, funding and financing, as well as the debate over school vouchers and school choice.

A majority of the nation's African American children attend schools that are more than 90% African American. This "has caused many to wonder which side actually won in Brown vs. Board of Education (the Supreme Court decision in 1954 that ruled separate, segregated schools were inherently unequal)   (Mooney et al, 2000: 210).

A Harvard University study ("Resegregation in American Schools") in 1999 found that both African-American and Hispanic students are cut off from white students (as cited in Bronner, 1999: 40). The Harvard report notes that nearly 75% of Hispanic students and 69% of African American students attend schools with predominately non-white students. The typical white student's school is more than 80% white (Hendrie, 1999: 6).

In the South, the authors decry a "process of Resegregation" that is eroding the gains in racial integration made between the mid-1960s and late 1980s. For example, in 1954, when segregated schools were declared unconstitutional, virtually no Southern African Americans attended white schools. By 1988, about 43 ½ % of African American students attended white schools; but by 1996, the report says, less than 35% did (Hendrie, 1999: 6). This pattern appears nationwide. Most states increased integration in the 1970s but had a rise in segregation from the mid-1980's to 1996. "The largest increases were in Rhode Island, Wisconsin, Florida, Oklahoma, Maryland, Delaware and Massachusetts" (Bronner, 1999: 40). Even in suburbs, the typical African-American or Hispanic student attends a school where at least six in ten students are non-white.

Three pending federal court cases – one in Boston, one in San Francisco, the third in Louisville – are trying to eliminate race as a factor in assigning students to their local schools. As one report noted: "Both cases underscore the uncertainty and historic role reversals…as the drive to desegregate American schools, that began half a century ago, winds down" (Hendrie, 1999(b): 1). In San Francisco, the lawyer for three Chinese-American families said: "We believe the use of racial classification is a violation of the 14th Amendment" ("Lawsuit Could Decide the Future of Desegregation", 1999: A-14).

Socio-economic status interacts with race and ethnicity and often determines school success or failure. Minorities my be hindered educationally by speaking a different language (some 2.3 million students), by being from a different cultural background, and be disadvantaged by unequal access by overt racism and discrimination. Consequently, with the exception of Asian-Americans, racial minorities achieve lower levels of education than non-minority whites. Minorities are often segregated in inner-city schools that are poorly funded. The institutional racism in education results in inner-city students receiving a much poorer quality education than middle and upper class students in suburbs.

For years, schools have been financed by local property taxes (about 45%). Local school funding often leads to inequality of access to a decent school. The local tax system has been challenged in 35 states and been declared illegal in 18. On April 1, 1999, a State Supreme Court order in New Hampshire "bans the use of local property taxes to finance schools. The court ruled in late 1997 that the system created education gaps between rich and poor communities" (Bayles, 1999: 2-A). The controversy centers on a basic question: Is it fair for children of a tax-rich town to reap the educational benefits of smaller classes and well-equipped facilities while children in a nearby tax-poor town take their lessons in crowded, aging and ill-equipped classrooms?

The amount of money available in each school district varies by the socio-economic and racial status of the district. For example, public school expenditures per pupil (in 1997 constant dollars) for instruction and services vary by median household-income in the district. Those with annual incomes less than $20,000 receive only $3,052 for instruction and $1,745 in services while districts with $35,000 or more receive $3,806 for instruction and $2,174 for services (U.S. Department of Education, 1998: 314).

This system of local financing of education has several adverse effects on minorities and the poor:

1. In the inner city, houses are generally older and more
   run-down, less desirable. African American or poor
   neighborhoods
   are hurt by "white flight" to the suburbs. The result is a
   very low tax base for schools in that area.
2. Low SES school districts are less likely than others to
   have business or retail stores where tax revenues are
   generated. Such businesses have closed or moved away.
3. Schools in the downtown areas are more likely to
   include hospitals, museums and art galleries, which are
   all tax-free properties. They do not generate taxes for the
   schools.
4. Poor and racially segregated neighborhoods are often in
   need of the greatest share of city services – fire, police,
   sanitation and public housing consume available taxes.
   Little is left for schools in such areas.
5. In low SES districts, most tax money available needs to
   be spent on repairing old schools, so little is available for
   teaching children (Mooney, et al, 2000: 318).

The Arizona State Superintendent of Public Instruction
observed: "We used to finance education based on property taxes, like
most of America. Wealthier neighborhoods naturally got more money
than lower-income neighborhoods...It cannot be overstated how
inherently unequal those systems are" (Koch 1999(b): 295). As
Jonathan Kozol put it: "All the kids I know in the South Bronx are
wonderful. If you could just plunk them down in Great Neck outside of
New York City, instead of spending $6,000 a year each on their
education, we'd be spending $16,000" (Raney, 1998: 12).

To overcome such unequal funding and access for poor and
minority students, both the states and Federal Government have
supported the concept of "Ed-Flex" (Ed-Flex Reflex, 1999). This gives
local school districts more say in how Federal and state funds will be
used. The Education Act passed by Congress in 1999, adopted "Ed-
Flex" and some $10 billion (about half of Federal spending on
elementary and secondary schools) was earmarked for programs to
benefit poor school children (Koch, 1999: 1-A). Also the bill included
about $11 billion to fund the administration's long-term plan to hire
100,000 new teachers so schools can reduce class sizes (Koch, 1999:
1A).

The Voucher Controversy

Another controversial way to better fund education is the use
of vouchers or school-choice plans. One national magazine called the
use of vouchers "the decade's most divisive education issue" (Toch and
Cohen, 1998: 25). Vouchers are public tax money given to parents of
students who want to send their child to a private school, or a better
public school. The amount of a voucher varies from $2,250 in
Cleveland to $3,400 a year in Florida (Archer, 1999: 20; Sandham,
1999: 23).

In 1999 alone, five State Supreme courts and one Federal
appeals court have ruled on vouchers and tax credits for religious
school students. Little clear consensus has emerged from conflicting
rulings. Perhaps one of the most important decisions came from the
U.S. Supreme Court in November, 1998. It was asked to review a
pioneering voucher program in Milwaukee, Wisconsin that allowed
low-income children to transfer to private schools, even religious
schools, at state expense. Both sides of the issue hoped the Supremes
would resolve a basic question: Can publicly-funded vouchers include
religious schools without violating the First Amendment – forbidding
government establishment of religion? It refused to review the case.
This let stand the Wisconsin State Supreme Court's ruling that said the
school-voucher program in Milwaukee did not violate the First
Amendment (Koch, 1999: 283).

Meanwhile, Arizona, Florida, Maine, Ohio and Vermont are
involved in the voucher controversy in court over essentially the same
issue (Walsh, 1999: 14-15). Yet historically this is not a new issue.
Maine's tuitioning programs have existed since the 18th Century,
Vermont's since 1869. They are similar to using vouchers. Small
towns with no public high school pay the tuition for residents who
attend public or private high schools outside the town. In Vermont,
students could attend religious schools until 1961 when the state
Supreme Court outlawed using tax money to pay tuition in such
schools.

In 1994 the same court reversed itself and allowed tuition
refunds to parents sending their children to private schools but the
state's education commission refused to reimburse Catholic school
parents. So the school board of tiny Chittendas, Vt. sued the state. The
Vermont Supreme Court ruled in June, 1999, that such payments
"would violate the state constitution's prohibition against compelled
support for religion" (Walsh, 1999: 14).

In spite of the early history of "tuitioning programs" in New
England, most scholars trace the roots of the modern voucher

movement to a 1955 essay by economist Milton Friedman (1955: 127-34).   He said vouchers would give parents greater flexibility in choosing their child's school.   They also would eventually improve public schools by injecting competition into the system.   Vouchers would especially benefit the poor, he argued, because they often are forced to send their children to inferior local ghetto schools.   When vouchers began in 1990 in Milwaukee, the program issued vouchers worth $2,446 a piece for up to 1,110 low-income students to attend non-religious schools.   The first year, only 337 students benefited because not enough private school spaces were available.   In 1998 enrollments reached 5,830, mainly because inner-city Catholic schools are now eligible to accept voucher students.   Enrollments are still no where near the 15,000 students authorized by the state legislature in 1995 (Koch, 1999: 293).   The amount of each voucher has increased each year, reaching $4,894 in 1998-99.   Voucher opponents fear it will drain tax money away from the public school system to private, religious schools.   In Milwaukee, the total amount used for vouchers was $733,000 when begun in 1990-91; in 1997-98, $7 million was used.   The money lost by public schools rose sharply in 1998-99 to $28 million after religious schools began participating in the voucher program (Koch, 1999: 293).   Furthermore, opponents argue student performance is no different in districts with vouchers than those without such programs.   Nevertheless, public support for vouchers (and other school-choice programs) appears to be growing, especially among racial minorities (Koch, 1999: 281).   The future of vouchers will ultimately be determined by the U.S. Supreme Court and the parents of children in public schools.

Bureaucracy, Teacher-Training, Unions and Charter Schools

Because of excessive bureaucracy, some parents are taking matters into their own hands.   For about a million parents, home schooling is the answer (Hayes, 1999; Lahrson-Fisher, 1998).   For others they are insisting on more adequate teacher training.   In 36 states, parents are turning to "charter schools".   All are attempts to circumvent and overcome the perennial bureaucracy that, more and more, administers and controls the education system in America.

In 1996, Linda Darling-Hammond was the primary author of "What Matters Most: Teaching for America's Future".   She presented a blistering indictment of American public education – especially teacher training (Billitteri, 1997: 915).   He noted: "Although no state will allow a person to write wills, practice medicine, fix plumbing or style hair without completing training and passing an examination, more than 40 states allow school districts to hire teachers who have not met these basic requirements" (Billitteri, 1997: 915). More than a quarter of new public school teachers in 1990 were not fully licensed. Almost one-fourth of secondary teachers, and more than 30% of math teachers, lack even a minor in their main teaching field, according to the National Commission on Teaching and America's Future (1996). More than half of the high school students taking the physical sciences are taught by teachers without minor or major in the subject, as are 27% of math students. In fact, the report notes that only 500 of the nation's 1,300 Schools of Education are accredited. Even Columbia University's Teachers' College in New York City is not accredited.

To make matters worse, over the next decade, more than 2 million *new* teachers will be needed. They will account for more than half of the nation's teaching force in 2006 (Billitteri, 1997: 916). Hence, steps are being taken to upgrade teacher education and certification. Certification is part of a constellation of reforms aimed at improving and professionalizing the nation's 2.7 million public school teachers. Innovations include rigorous proficiency tests for new teachers, peer review of veteran teachers and new approaches to teacher training. Linda Darling-Hammond comments that: "What distinguishes the era we're in now is that there are really dramatic, radical reforms of the teaching profession going on" (Billitteri, 1997: 915).

What makes the reforms so revolutionary is that the existing bureaucratic teachers unions – the National Education Association. (NEA) and the American Federation of Teachers (AFT) – have vowed to cooperate with, rather than oppose, these changes.

For example, for the first time, the 2.3 million members of NEA in 1997 endorsed peer review of teachers. Many see this change as a challenge to the long time tradition of tenure, which virtually guaranteed a teacher a job for life. The AFT also vows to increase its support of peer review.

Teacher organizations, the NEA and AFT, have been viewed as opponents of most educational reform, including, but not limited to vouchers and charter schools. While they have transformed the teaching professions from a timid, exploited group their formation is one of the "top 10 educational events of the 20th Century" (Brodinsky, 1999: 4). To the dismay of some teacher unionists, NEA President, Bob Chase, has advocated a "new unionism" in which teachers would play a more cooperative role with school administrators to reduce bureaucracy and improve public education. "It was all inputs", contends a former president of the Pa. State NEA. "He (the NEA

President) says a lot of the right things, but I don't think much is really changing" (Bradley, 1999: 44). President Sandra Feldman of the AFT also called on her union "to get out front in closing down failing schools" (Billitteri, 1997: 915). Some people question the motives of the unions, saying they are more concerned with survival than improvement.

Charter Schools

Besides home-schooling, improved teacher education and cooperative unions is the recent appearance of charter schools. Starting in 1991, charter schools have tripled in the last two years (1996-97 to 1998-99) and 36 states now have such laws. Charter schools are publicly-funded schools designed to operate free from certain state rules and bureaucracy "in exchange for being held accountable for student results" (Schnailberg, 1999: 13). These small, innovative schools are generally freed from some curriculum requirements and such constraints as local union teacher contracts. They are free to hire their own teachers and experiment with new teaching techniques. "The idea is to relieve schools of bureaucratic burdens so they can focus on students educational needs", Kathy Koch writes (1999: 292). Advocates for charter schools believe they will stimulate public schools to be less bureaucratic and more responsive to parents concerns. U.S. Senator Joseph Lieberman notes that, "Competition from charter schools is the best way to motivate the ossified bureaucracies governing too many public schools" (1999: 31). Many charter schools target students at risk of failing, dropping out or "falling through the cracks" in traditional public schools.

Charter schools draw some opposition from the NEA and other traditional public school supporters. They oppose "permissive" state laws that grant charter status to individuals and for-profit corporations with no experience in education. They also claim the charter schools are being used by private schools to get "back-door" funding by re-labeling them "charter" schools (Koch, 1999: 292).

Conclusion

So both society and the state continue to grapple with the persistent problems of conflicting purposes and curriculum, unequal access to quality education due to segregation and discrimination, funding, and bureaucracy. New approaches to address these problems began to emerge about 1983. It was then that the National Commission on Excellence in Education issued a wake-up call for America in its report *A Nation at Risk*. This led to intervention by the Federal

Government to give states and local schools an impetus to set educational standards and measure performance and testing outcomes.

Questions still remain over local or national control of education, as well as over standards and national testing. To remedy problems of unequal access and racial discrimination in the schools, legal challenges were made over the funding and financing of education in many states. One innovative and controversial program was the use of vouchers to give parents a choice as to the best school, private or public, they could send their children. The issue is still unresolved and will eventually have to be settled by the U.S. Supreme Court. The Federal Government's use of "Educ-Flex" funds have given local school districts more flexibility in how they spend Federal money (Ed-Flex Reflex, 1999: A-22).

Bureaucracy, as in the past, in some ways still impedes the learning process by rigid control of the system. Debates over teacher education, reform of labor unions, NEA and AFT, as well as charter schools aim to loosen or circumvent bureaucracy that harms or hurts the educational system in America. Violence in the schools after 1999 has been addressed and dealt with effectively at a local level, with State and Federal help.

Critical Thinking Questions

1. One of the Goals 2000: Educate America Act was for U.S. students to be first in the world in science and math. Why hasn't our educational system met this goal? What concrete steps will be needed to make this goal a reality? Will we ever reach this goal? Explain why or why not.

2. Why is the use of vouchers considered "the decade's most divisive education issue? What is your position in respect to the use of vouchers? Why are you for or against the use of vouchers? What are some of the social implications if vouchers are used?

3. What is the social significance of the "Charter School" movement? Is this movement an attempt to "water down" the curriculum in American high schools and drain money from the standard public school system?

4. Discuss and debate the key ideas and philosophy of education of John Dewey. In what ways have some of his ideas been used in high school and college? In what ways have some of his ideas been rejected or ignored?

5. As a student who has gone through national achievement tests in high school, how do you see this attempt to establish national standards in education? What preparation for such tests did you have in high school? Did you go to a private agency to get prepared for taking such tests?

Bibliography

Anderson, Nick. "Va. Raises Education Bar, Misses Grade." *Los Angeles Times* (March 21, 1999): A-9.

Archer, Jeff. "Two Cleveland Voucher Schools Plan Rebirth with Charter Status." *Education Week.* 18 no. 44 (July 14, 1999).

Bacon, John. "Nine States Boost Reading Scores." *U.S.A. Today* (March 5, 1999): A-3.

Bayles, Fred. "School Equality: NH Tradition Come in Conflict." *U.S.A. Today* (March 5, 1999(a)): 2A.

———. "Standardized Exams Coming Under Fire." *U.S.A. Today* (June 11, 1999(b)): 10A.

Bigler Philip and Lockard, Karen. *Failing Grades: A Teachers Report Card on Education in America.* New York: Vandamere Press, 1992.

Billitteri, Thomas J. "Teacher Education." *CQ Researcher,* 7 no. 39 (October 17, 1997): 913-36.

Bradley, Ann. "New Union Boss." *Education Week* 18, no. 41 (June 23, 1999): 40-5.

Brodinsky, Ben. "Top 10 Education Events of the 20th Century." *Education Digest* 64 (April 4-7, 1999): 4-7.

Bronner, Ethan. "Resegregation Is Emerging In Schools, Study Finds." *New York Times* (June 13, 1999): 40.

Clark, Charles S. "Education Standards." *CQ Research,* 4, no. 10 (March 11, 1994): 217-40.

Citizens for Excellence in Education. *Education Newsline* (July-August 1993): 1-4.

Crossen, Cynthia. "In 1860, America Had 40 Public High Schools: Teachers Chopped Wood." *Wall Street Journal* (September 3, 2003): B-1.

Curti, Merle. *The Social Ideas of American Educators.* Totowa, New Jersey: Littlefield, Adams, 1959.

Ed-Flex Reflex. *The Wall Street Journal* (March 23, 1999): A-22.

Flexner, Abraham. *The American College: A Criticism.* New York: The Century Company, 1908.

Freidman, Milton. "The Role of Government in Education." Pp. 127-34, in *Economics and the Public Interest,* edited by Robert A. Solo. Chicago, Ill.: University of Chicago Press, 1955.

Gleazer, Edmund J. "The Emergence of the Community College as a Center for Service Learning." *Synergist* 4, no. 1 (Spring, 1975): 10-14.

Graubard, Stephen R. Preface. "American Education: Still Separate, Still Unequal." *Daedalus,* 124, no. 4 (Fall, 1995): v-xxv.

Greer, Colin. "The Myth of the Melting Pot." *Saturday Review* (November 15, 1969): 84.

Grissmer, David and Flanagan, Ann. "Exploring Rapid Achievement Gains in North Carolina and Texas." *National Education Goals Panel* (November, 1998) 408. Washington D.C.: U.S. Government Printing Office.

Hawkins, Hugh. "The Making of the Liberal Arts Identity." *Daedalus* 128, no. 1 (Winter 1999): 1-26.

Hendrie, Caroline. "Harvard Study Finds Increase in Segregation." *Education Week* 18, no. 39 (June 23, 1999): 6.

————. "Race-Based Assignment Challenged." *Education Week* 18, no. 42 (July 14, 1999): 1 & 14.

Hirsch, E.D. *Cultural Literacy: What Every American Needs to Know.* New York: Houghton Mifflin, 1985.

Hayes, Laurie L. "The Rise of Home-Schooling a Unique Challenge for School Counselors." *Counseling Today* 42, no. 3 (September 1999): 31.

Hofstadter, Richard and Wilson Smith. *American Higher Education: A Documentary History.* 1. Chicago: University of Chicago Press, 1961.

Kaestler, Carl. "Public Education." Pp. 2493-2506 in *Encyclopedia of American Social History,* edited by Cayton, Gorn and Williams. 3, New York: Charles Scribners, 1993.

Koblik, Steven. Preface. "Distinctly American: The Residential Liberal Arts College." *Daedelus* 128, no. 1 (Winter, 1999): 5-12.

Koch, Kathy. "National Education Standards." *CQ Research* 9, no. 18 (May 14, 1999): 401-24.

————. "School Vouchers." *CQ Research* 9, no. 13 (April 9, 1999): 281-304.

Kronholz, June. "Students Improve Reading Scores Amid Sour Notes." *Wall Street Journal* (February 11, 1999): A-16.

"Lawsuit Could Decide the Future of Desegregation." *New York Times* (February 16, 1999): A-14.

Lewis, Sharon. *Reform and Results: An Analysis of Title I in the Great City Schools, 1994-5 to 1997-08* (March, 1999). Washington, D.C.: Council of Great City Schools.

Liberman, Joseph. "Schools Where Kids Succeed." *Readers Digest* (January, 1999): 28-32.

Louis, Karen S. "A Light Feeling of Chaos: Educational Reform and
       Policy in the United States." *Daedalus* 127, no. 4 (Fall, 1998):
       13-18.
Marklin, Mary Beth. "Testing Guidelines Scare Schools Using SAT,
       ACT." *U.S.A. Today* (June 23, 1999): 5-D.
McGrath, Earl J. *Values, Liberal Education, and National Destiny.*
       Indianapolis, Ind.: Lilly Endowment, 1975.
McManus, Michael J. "Vouchers Need to Go Higher: Ethics
       and Religion." *Morning Call* (June 12, 1999): B-24.
McPherson, Michael S. and Shapiro,, Morton O. "Future Economic
       Challenges for the Liberal Arts Colleges. Distinctively
       American: The Residential Liberal Arts Colleges." *Daedalus*
       128, no.1 (Winter, 1999): 47-76.
McQueen, Anjetta. "College Enrollment Dips Slightly." *Associated
       Press* (June 26, 1999): A-33.
———. -"Ending Social Promotion Tough Job for Schools."
       Associated Press (June 16, 1999): A-24.
———. "States' Gains In Reading Scores Weren't Real, Fed
       Officials Say." *Associated Press* (May 15, 1999): A-26.
Mooney, Linda A., Knox, David and Schacht, Caroline.
       Understanding Social Problems, 2nd ed. Belmont, CA:
       Wadsworth, 2000.
Morse, Joseph L. and William Hendelson, eds. "Land Grant Colleges."
       Funk & Wagnalls Encyclopedia. 15. New York: Funk &
       Wagnalls, 1973.
Morshead, Richard W. "The Clash of Hidden Ideologies in
       Contemporary Education." *Education Digest* 41 (November,
       1975): 16-19.
"National Education Goals Report". *National Education Goals Panel.*
       Washington, D.C.: U.S. Government Printing Office, 1993.
Pounds, Ralph L. and James Bryner. *The School in American Society.*
       3rd ed. New York: Macmillan, 1973.
Raney, Mardell. "Jonathan Kozol on Today's Children of Poverty."
       The Education Digest, 64 (December, 1998): 10-18.
Ravitch, Diane. *The Troubled Crusade: American Education 1945-
       1980.* New York: Basic Books, 1983.
"Report to the President." *White House Conference on Children.*
       Washington, D.C.: U.S. Government Printing Office, 1970.
Roszak, Theodore, ed. *The Dissenting Academy.* New York:
       Pantheon, 1967.

————. "Educating Contra Naturam." Pp. 63-81 in *High School,* edited by Ronald Gross and Paul Osterman. New York: Clarion, 1971.

Sandham, Jessica L. "Florida Governor Poised to Sign Statewide Voucher Bill." *Education Week* (May 20, 1999): 1 & 23.

————. "Ohio Lawmakers Reinstate Voucher Program." *Education Week* (July 14, 1999): 17 & 20.

————. "Voucher Plan Struck Down in Florida Court." *Education Week* (March 22, 2000): 1 & 23.

Schnailberg, Lynn. "An Apparent First: Colo. Charter School Gets S&P Rating." *Education Week,* 18, no. 44 (July 14, 1999): 13.

————. "Oklahoma, Oregon Bump Up Charter Law States to 36." *Education Week,* 18, no. 41 (June 23, 1999): 20 & 23.

Shanker, Albert. "Achieving Higher Standards." Address to the AFT Quest Conference, New York, 1991.

Silberman, Charles. *Crisis in the Classroom: The Remaking of American Education.* New York: Vintage, 1970.

Sizer, Theodore. *Horace's School: Redesigning the American High School.* Boston. Houghton & Mifflin, 1992.

Statistical Abstract of the United States. "School Enrollment: 1965-2008." Table 250. U.S. Census Bureau. Washington, D.C.: U.S. Government Printing Office, 1998.

Steward, Elbert. *The Troubled Land.* New York: McGraw-Hill, 1976.

Toch, Thomas and Cohen, Warren. "Public Education: A Monopoly No Longer." *U.S. News and World Report* (November 23, 1998): 25.

U.S. Department of Education. "The Condition of Education: 1998." National Center for Education Statistics. NCES 98-013. Washington, D.C.: U.S. Government Printing Office, 1998.

————. "School District Fiscal Data." National Center for Education Statistics. Washington, D.C.: U.S. Government Printing Office, 1998.

Walsh, Mark. "Spat of Legal Ruling on Vouchers, Choice Yields Little Consensus." *Education Week* (June 23, 1999): 14-15.

Warner, W. Lloyd et al. *Who Shall Be Educated?* Harper & Row, 1944.

Yarrington, Roger. "The Two-Year College Student: An Investor in the Future." *Synergist* 4, no. 1 (Spring, 1975): 15-17.

Chapter 8

Medical and Health Care Problems

The advance of medicine and people's health has been a long uphill battle against superstition, fear, ignorance, cost and availability. As the medical sociologist Renee Fox argues, a number of attitudes and behaviors, like insanity, that we now think of as "illnesses" to be treated by medicine were once considered sinful or criminal rather than sick. She concludes: "There has been a general tendency in our society to move from sin to crime to sickness...to the degree that the concept of the 'medicalization of deviance' has taken place in social science writings" (1977:11).

Today we realize that disease and sickness largely result from physical, emotional and sanitary causes. Therefore, modern science now tries to control the forces causing disease and ill health by physical, psychological, social and technological means. In this chapter we shall see how the perspective and ideas of medicine and have changed since Colonial America. In the process, there were always, and continue to be, crises and conflicts.
These include:

1. Conflicts between medicine as a profession vs. medicine as a practice.
2. Conflicts over the causes and cures of illness and disease.
3. Conflicting schools of thought in opposition to orthodox medicine.
4. Conflicts over women in medicine.
5. Evolution of the hospital and conflicts over access to quality care

    6. Conflicts over the role of government and public
    health in medicine.
    7. Conflicts over cost and payment method
    (insurance, Medicare and Medicaid).
    8. Privilege or Right? The Conflict Over National
    Health Care

Richard Shryock writes: "There have been crises in medicine before; indeed, this has been almost the normal state of things since medical science began to stir from its ancient lethargy some three centuries ago." (1966:xii). This chapter will examine these various conflicts.

Conflicts Between Medicine as a Profession vs. Medicine as a Practice

Most care in early America was based on folk medicine and home remedies, including ideas from the Native Americans. Both men and women pursued medical practice on a free-lance, part-time basis. Most "medical students" had no preliminary education and at the age of 14-18 became an apprentice to some medical practitioner in their community for about 3-7 years. At the completion of this term, the young "physician" was released, free to establish his own practice, with little more than a certificate to verify his apprenticeship. Young physicians relied primarily on their skill and energy to earn a living. Given these dubious beginnings, more traditionally educated physicians overseas and contemporary writers frequently labeled American physicians as "quacks". This does not imply that skilled physicians were unavailable in the Colonies, just that medicine in general, and American physicians in particular, were not well regarded – in America or elsewhere.

To address the conflict between medicine as a profession verses medicine as a mere practice, New York set up the first examination and licensure program around 1760. In 1722, the New Jersey Medical Society persuaded the State legislature to establish an Examining Board and licensure for the entire state, with penalties for violations. Between 1780 and 1810, most states placed granting licenses for practicing medicine in the hands of state-appointed boards or granted that power to the state medical societies founded during that time.

Around the same time a movement to increase educational credentials for medicine gained momentum. In 1765, Dr. John Morgan founded the first American medical school in Philadelphia. This school was initially affiliated with the College of Philadelphia and was later called the University of Pennsylvania (Bordley and Harvey, 1976; Margotta, 1996). However, conflict occurred even within the education institution. Physicians teaching in medical schools believed dissections was the best way to learn about the body. The public and legal system disagreed. At that time, bodies of the dead could not be legally obtained, but each student was required to have a corpse for his sole use in dissection lab. So students, under cover of darkness, stole corpses from "Potter's Field" and the Black burial grounds because these bodies were buried in common graves without coffins and, therefore, could be easily dug up and removed. (Heaps, 1970).

By early 1788 "body snatching" had become common. However, when students took a body from the graveyard of Trinity Church, the oldest one in New York City, public rage increased. The two weekly newspapers blasted the students and doctors for it. This rage was fueled by an unfortunate and tactless incident on April 13, 1788 that led to a two day Anti-Dissection Riot. Several medical students and doctors at New York Hospital were dissecting a corpse. It was sunny that day and the windows were open. Ladders from some painters were on the ground below and a group of small boys climbed up the ladders and looked in the open window. At that moment a doctor-student, John Hicks, waved a dead arm on the windowsill to frighten one of the boys away. He tactlessly shouted, "this is your mother's arm; get off the ladder or I'll hit you with it" (Heaps 1970:21). The boy fled in terror, ran home and told his father. By a one-in-a-million coincidence, the boy's mother had actually died a few weeks before. The outraged father and many of his friends started out toward the hospital and thousands joined them as the story spread as to what the doctor and students had done. They smashed and destroyed the anatomy museum on the lower floor. They then broke into the dissecting labs and waved the legs, arms and other body parts to the mob below. They would have killed four students who were hiding at the hospital had not the sheriff and mayor arrived together with a few prominent citizens just in time to prevent it. The students were placed in the city jail, under the protection of regular guards and a few militiamen. Most of the other students and doctors also sought refuge in the jail. The next day the mob grew in size to over two thousand or more. Governor George Clinton and the mayor realized the seriousness of the situation so they read the Riot Act to them and pleaded with them to leave. They promised an official investigation would be made of all reported grave robbers and the guilty would be punished. Most refused to disperse. The crowd began searching doctors' offices amassing corpses. Finding more they began moving together toward the jail to take vengeance on the doctors and students locked up inside. The crowd threatened to tear down the jail unless the students were turned over to them. Those inside the jail were terrified and barricaded the doors and windows. By this time the crowd and mob had swelled to about five thousand people who were determined to knock down the doors to the jail. The authorities now realized that force was necessary to break up the mad mob. Governor Clinton called out the New York State militia, but only 50 men could be assembled. It then became necessary to round up any available experienced soldiers. Prominent, well-known citizens such as Alexander Hamilton, John Jay, and Baron Von Steuben, who helped organize the Colonial American Army, joined these soldiers. Night had fallen by the time the military unit and citizens moved toward the jail. This group drew near the waiting mob. It took no action until the soldiers were "within ten paces of the jail door" (Heaps, 1970:25). The mob mistakenly believed the militiamen were under orders not to fire at the crowd, so it began throwing bricks, rocks and stones at the soldiers and prominent civilians. When Baron Von Steuben was struck on the head by a brick, he yelled out loud, "Fire!" The commander of the troops gave the order to fire at point blank range. The mob stopped in shock as five rioters fell dead and seven or eight additional wounded fell to the pavement. The crowd remaining in front of the jail broke up and ran in all directions.

Surprisingly, given their little power, physicians won this conflict. As a result of New York City's Anti-Dissection Riot, New York State passed the first U.S. law to aid anatomy study in 1789. This law legally permitted dissection and spelled out specific punishments for grave robbers. Consequently, a limited supply of legal cadavers would now be available for the medical profession. In 1790, the First Congress of the U.S. passed legislation similar to the New York law. This is an example of how conflict sometimes produces positive social changes. Nevertheless, doctors and teachers in individual states still had difficulty in legally obtaining sufficient bodies. Hence, body snatching continued in rural areas well into the 1800's. (Heaps, 1970)

Conflicts Over the Causes and Cures of Illness and Disease

By the eighteenth century, Europe had made some progress in understanding the human body and experiments and quantitative methods were beginning to be applied in physiology. Medicine, including in America, continued to focus on the patients' "systems". Ancient notions (going back to Aristotle and Galen) usually explained "system" as the state of one's body fluids, or "humors" -- blood, bile and phlegm. Hence "cures", such as bleeding, use of leeches, purging or drugs were supposed to rid the body of excess or impure fluids. George Washington was "bled" when he was seriously ill and he died from loss of blood, as did many bled patients. Yet many doctors were firmly convinced that it would work. For instance, Benjamin Rush (1745-1813), one of America's best-known physicians, claimed "fever" was caused from an "irregular action or convulsion" of the blood vessels. He read some manuscripts about a "fever" epidemic in 1741, and was greatly impressed with certain passages that said to purge and bleed the victim. In almost religious fervor, he believed purging and bleeding were the answer to all types of "fevers". He wrote: "Never before did I experience such sublime joy as I now felt in contemplating the success of my remedies. It repaid me for all the toils and studies of my life." (King, 1958: 234). But he was wrong – dead wrong. Yet because he was popular as a writer and teacher, Rush's notion of bleeding spread across the nation and persisted until about 1850. Critical thinkers such as William Cobbett, an English writer who came to America in 1792, attacked Rush's ideas. His satiric articles in conflict with Rush's ideas of bleeding and purging, led to a law suit for libel by Rush. Cobbett studied the mortality rates of Philadelphia's great epidemic of yellow fever (1793) and created the impression that many of Rush's patients died not from yellow fever but from bloodletting. The case was tried before what Cobbett described as "a packed bench and packed jury." (Bordley and Harvey, 1976:36) Rush was awarded $5,000 for libel damages. Cobbett recorded ironically that on the very day in 1799 they ruled in favor of Rush, George Washington died "in precise conformity to the practice of Rush." (Bordley and Harvey 1976:37)

Those of you reading these accounts are likely to find these practices primitive...and dangerous. By today's standards, they were. But it is important to remember that medicine at this time was not a formalized institution. The development and spread of knowledge was slow. Consequently, being a physician was not nearly as prestigious then as it is now. In fact, if a son told his parents he wanted to be a doctor, the parents were likely to be disappointed. The rise of medicine as a respected profession was fraught with conflict.

Why? There are many reasons, but two large ones stand out. The first reason has to do with the relative ease in claiming the title of "physician" that we discussed in the previous section. The second reason involves the general lack of concrete, or *specialized*, medical knowledge to warrant a prestigious profession. Remember that a boy could enter a physician's apprenticeship as early as 14 years old and by the time he was seventeen or eighteen (depending on how long his apprenticeship lasted), he was a full-fledged doctor. There was no extensive formalized education like there is now. In order to try to raise the status of their profession, doctors used highly technical terms (as many are accused of doing even today), purposely unintelligible to laymen. Physicians argued that knowledge of anatomy and natural philosophy was necessary to medicine and those who did not understand anatomy (complete with the technical terms) but instead "understood only how to restore the sick to health, they branded with the ignominious name of empircks." (King, 1958: 36). However many, perhaps correctly, believed that this appearance of complexity was merely a fiction created by doctors to serve their own interests. Lay people felt that medicine should be presented in ways that were understandable to ordinarily intelligent men, much like other aspects of society like law, government and religion (Starr, 1982).

A more formal period of education and training may have justified physicians' tactics or beliefs (depending on your view of the above); however, medical education grew slowly. It was easy to get charters to start a medical school, but medical students of the time were condemned in newspapers and magazines as "crude, coarse and ignorant." So as we see, there was serious conflict between lay people, who thought physicians tried to make the profession too unreachable, European physicians, who thought American medicine was too simplistic, and American physicians, who strongly wanted to change the view of the other two.

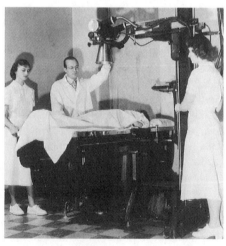

Technology is constantly changing in hospitals (Credit: Sacred Heart Hospital, Allentown, Pennsylvania)

Conflicting Schools of Thought in Opposition to Orthodox Medicine

Also contributing to the conflict over medical school attendance were conflicting schools of thought regarding ideas and practices in opposition to orthodox medicine. Some of them were eventually incorporated into our medical care system or even exist today as accepted alternative "systems of medicine". Four such groups or practices were:

1. Hydropaths
2. Osteopathy
3. Christian Science
4. Homeopathy (Bordley and Harvey, 1976; Porter, 1997)

The Hydropaths

The first group was *the hydropaths*. Their ideas were imported from Vincent Priessnit (1799-1851) of Germany in the 1840's. Contrary to orthodox medicine, the hydropaths advocated avoiding the popular drugs of the time, and to use water, both internally and externally, in the form of therapeutic baths and the drinking of 12 glasses of water a day. They also stressed exercise, good hygiene, a diet of coarse bread, milk and "natural" foods, and profuse sweating followed by cold baths. Millions of Americans today rely on these or similar methods to prevent illness and retain good health. Recently emphasis has been placed on drinking 8 glasses of water a day to be healthy. Health clubs, spas and jacuzzi baths today still practice the hydropathic beliefs.

Osteopathy

Instead of emphasis on pathology, disease and death of orthodox medicine, some 19th century Americans believed that nature was essentially good. If humans only heeded "Mother Nature", their bodies would be naturally healthy and resist diseases. Such was the hopeful message of the *osteopathy* movement headed by Dr. Andrew T. Still (1828-1917) in the 1860's. His experience as a soldier in the Civil War, the death of 3 of his children in a meningitis epidemic in 1864 and the obvious inability of the medical profession of his time to control epidemics of yellow fever, cholera, and typhoid fever convinced him that the strong drugs employed by orthodox physicians were not only useless but also harmful and frequently deadly. Osteopathy stressed the intrinsic unity of all parts of the body. He attributed disease to "structural derangements" or "somatic components of the disease processes", also called osteopathic lesions. While he concentrated on the spine, Still's followers extended physical manipulation to the entire skeletal structure. They also enlarged the range of treatment techniques to include electric and water treatments, massage and eventually surgery. It was not until the 20th century that osteopathic doctors, because they reduced their conflict with orthodox medicine by including it in their medical school education, became recognized as part of our larger medical care system today. They bear the initials D.O. rather than M.D.

A direct descent of osteopathic medicine was chiropractic medicine, established in 1895 by Daniel D. Palmer (1845-1939) after he restored the hearing of a man by adjusting his backbone. Palmer based chiropractic on the hypothesis that energy flow from the brain was the essential life-giving force in the body. He believed any destruction of it caused disease. The spine commonly blocked nerve functions, and manipulation by hand ("chiropractic" in Greek for "doing by hand") was the method for treating the spine. Although orthodox physicians criticized chiropractic practitioners (or "bonecrackers") as unscientific or "quacks" these healers became so widely patronized that even health insurance companies today have begun to cover them.

Christian Science

Christian Science, whose healing approach was much gentler than all the other practices, was founded in 1875 by Mary Baker Eddy (1821-1910). She had spent much of her adolescence ill and bedridden. Regular physicians did her no good, although homeopathy (discussed next), as well as the hypnosis treatments of Phineas Quimby (1802-1866) helped somewhat. After reading the Bible and having a divine revelation, she undertook her own self-healing process. Her success led her to establish her own system, declaring "there is but one creation, and it is wholly spiritual." (Porter, 1997:395) Since she believed that all was spiritual, and matter was an illusion or delusion, bodily disease did not exist; all sickness was in the mind – a creation of our own stress or imagination. She explained all this in her book *Science and Health* in 1875. She wrote that true "mind healing" would dispel the "illusions" of sickness and pain. It was a "patient heal thyself" appeal and thousands believed in it. Setting up the Massachusetts Metaphysical College, Eddy taught soe 4,000 students, most of whom were women excluded from medical education at that time. Today hundreds of Christian Science Reading Rooms exist, especially in the Northeast, to spread her original ideas about disease, illness and cures for them. Their national newspaper, *The Christian Science Monitor* is still published today. However, the fact that Christian Science is not a powerful medical force is illustrated by its losing conflict over several court cases in recent years that have forbidden Christian Science parents to withhold modern orthodox medical treatment from their children.

Homeopathy

One of the greatest conflicts and battles over ideas in the history of medicine in the l9th and 20th centuries was *hom'eopathy*. The inspiration and trailblazer for such medicine was Dr. Samuel Hahnemann (1755-1833). Hahnemann got his medical education at Lepzig, Vienna and the University of Erlangen, where he received his medical degree in 1799. From his early practice in small towns and villages he developed a horror for the blunders of the orthodox medical system, especially its use of deadly, lethal drugs. His first published work, *On Poisoning by Arsenic: Its Treatment and Forensic Detection* pointed out the fears he had about the use of drugs by doctors. He began in his publications to formulate his own system of medicine – starting with fresh air and exercise. He argued there were three possible approaches to healing: prevention, the allopathic method of treatment "by opposites" that dominated orthodox medicine and the homeopathic approach "likes are cured by likes" (Porter, 1997:391). Hahnemann believed his experiments proved that large doses of medicine aggravated illness while small doses supported the "body's vital spirit" to overcome disease. This was the second principle of homeopathy: "the law of infinitesimals". (Bordley and Harvey, 1976:43) The smaller the dose, the more effective the medicine.

His approach was met with skepticism as well as outright conflict and opposition from orthodox physicians. For example, Dr. Oliver Wendell Holmes (later a justice of the U.S. Supreme Court) in 1842 professionally and publicly argued that "...homeopathy had no rational basis; that 'likes are cured by likes' and other principles were no more than delusions and was in fact a dangerous form of quackery".(Bordley and Harvey, 1976:44) The comments on Holmes's lectures by the press and a significant part of the public could not have cared less about the charge of quackery as long as homeopathy provided a way to escape "all the painful and debilitating expedients of our present system" (Bordley and Harvey, 1976: 45).

By the end of the 19th century homeopathy consolidated itself as a worldwide movement. It endured while other theories and movements rose and fell. It established its claims to recognition by licensing authorities and eventually was incorporated into orthodox medicine and pharmacy. Homeopathy's lasting appeal stemmed from its stress on purity of medicine (in small doses) and the attractive idea of the body helping to cure itself. (Porter, 1997)

Today many of these unorthodox practices are incorporated into mainstream medicine and health. Usually the conflict between these alternate medical forms and orthodox medicine were minimized by the unorthodox form adopting some elements of orthodox medicine within it. The greater the degree orthodox medicine was incorporated, the more "acceptable" the less orthodox form of medicine became. The less incorporated orthodox medicine was, the more likely the unorthodox form is present today under what is termed "alternative forms" of medical care.

Conflicts Over Women in Medicine

Given the low prestige and internal conflicts of medicine, perhaps it is not surprising that in early America, women frequently practiced medicine. However, as medicine struggled to gain prestige, women were gradually driven out of general practice as "doctors" or "physicians" after 1700, and even out of being "mid-wives" (assisting a woman in childbirth) after 1800. But women did not just passively leave. Encouraged by the feminist movement of 1848, women began to make some inroads into medicine and medical schools. The first medical college for women was founded in 1850; and thus began a long struggle to gain equal access to medical practice. However, a combination of events channeled women into nursing rather than medical school. Perhaps one of the most influential people inspiring this trend was Florence Nightingale, who was the famous English nurse of the Crimean War (1854-1856) and later headed the first nursing school for women in 1860. This spurred America to do the same. In addition, Catholic and Protestant religious orders of women ministered to the poor in city hospitals and on the battlefield during the Civil War (1861-1865). Consequently, over time, American women were steered away from traditional medical practice as doctors and were directed instead toward nursing.

Encouraging women to be nurses rather than doctors may reflect the conflict over both the lower status of women and the struggles of the medical profession for prestige. Early on, the male members of the medical profession, as they struggled for power, may have realized that being associated as a field that welcomed women, who had little power, may hurt their purposes. Therefore, male physicians may have been encouraged to create a niche for women that recognized women's caregiving skills while at the same time also relegated women to a subordinate status that was more consistent with their wider social standing. Unfortunately, this conflict over power did not disappear as medicine increased in prestige. The lower status of nursing, as compared with doctors, continues today (in spite of a shortage of nurses in some areas) as is evidenced by the struggle of nurses to be recognized as a high-paying profession, their dominance by women, and their relatively low wages given their level of education.

Evolution of the Hospital and Conflict Over Access to Quality Care

Evolution of Hospital Care

In early American history, family or friends cared for most sick people. As we would expect, given what you now know about Gemeinshaft societies, there was a strong sense of family and community obligation during America's early history. One simply did not "turn out" their family relatives and friends to be cared for by a stranger. So how did hospital care, as we now know it, develop?

Colonial almshouses are the predecessors to modern American hospitals. Almshouses provided a substitute home for people who were poor or sick, but were only incidentally associated with caring for the sick. Their primary function was to house the poor. By the seventeenth century, almshouses served a variety of individuals: the aged, the sick, the poor, the physically and mentally disabled and the orphaned. The problem, however, was that almshouses treated all these individuals the same. There was no variation in care provided based on the reason people were in the almshouses. The mentally disabled received the same type of care as the orphaned, the physically ill, etc....

The first hospital exclusively for the care of the sick was Pennsylvania Hospital in Philadelphia that opened in 1752. This hospital was followed by New York Hospital (chartered in 1771) and Massachusetts General Hospital in Boston in 1821. Voluntary donations, not taxes, funded hospitals. However, even with the advent of hospitals to care for the sick, in the Gemeinshaft society that was still very present at this time, the use of hospitals was rare. People much preferred to be cared for in a home setting by relatives or even in almshouses (which were more residential in nature than hospitals). Hospitals were people's last choice and were primarily used by strangers or the homeless.

However, after 1828, states abolished home relief and almshouses became even more squalid than they already were.

Almshouses became a symbol of shame and indignity as they physically deteriorated and offered less and less physical support. After the Civil War, reformers devoted much of their time to breaking up almshouses and sending the aged, the orphaned, and the mentally ill to institutions specifically designed for their needs. Early American charity hospitals emerged to provide a better alternative to almshouses for the more respectable poor who had curable illnesses. By this time, these voluntary hospitals were generally cleaner and had less of a stigma than did the almshouses. In order to ensure that these hospitals did not attract the stigma of the almshouses, their managers and physicians excluded dangerous, contagious or morally reprehensible cases (Starr, 1982). Such exclusions allowed hospitals to keep down their mortality rates and avoid the stigma associated with other forms of institutional care.

These attempts, however, do not imply that people willingly flocked to hospitals when they were sick. The Industrial Revolution was not established enough to fully change the Gemeinschaft society still present in the 19th Century. People continued to prefer care by family and friends within their own homes; and, hospitals were designed to treat individuals (e.g. travelers, soldiers returning from war) who were unable to receive family care. However, the foundations of the Gesellschaft society we know today were evident. Dr. W. Gill Wylie, in an essay awarded a prize by Harvard University in 1876, wrote that to encourage hospital use beyond the cases of strangers, the poor, soldiers and the insane would "weaken the family tie by separating the sick from their homes and their relatives, who are often too ready to relieve themselves of the burden of the sick." (Wylie, 1877:57)

However, hospitals were not a pleasant experience. Most of the patients were homeless or strangers and had no standing in the community. Little or no visiting was allowed, so most citizens knew nothing of what went on inside the hospital. There was also no supervision of the nursing. Nurses were so poorly paid, no one who could get any other work would do nursing. Doctors also sometimes sent feeble old people from the poor house to the hospital to help with patients because they got better food at the hospital. Neglect, ill treatment, and death from infections were hallmarks of many nineteenth century hospitals before professional nurses took over. A patient admitted suffering from one disease might easily get another more serious one.

Even given these conditions, by the 19th Century, hospitals contributed to the prestige of medicine in general, and doctors in particular. Contrary to the English practice of educating solely in hospitals and the traditional American practice of educating solely in medical school or, internship, the new American approach was to blend the two. By this time medical education began in medical school, but continued in the hospital with an internship. Hospitals provided a structure for widespread medical education; therefore, for doctors, being affiliated with an educational institution (verses practicing on one's own or under apprenticeship) was a source of prestige. Furthermore, hospitals gave young medical students more direct and diversified medical experience than they previously received, which further contributed to their skill. The spread of hospitals also made access to medical care more available to the poor than previously.

All over America, hospitals are modernizing and expanding

A number of other factors contributed to the advent of our modern hospital. The professionalization of nursing and the beginning of antiseptic surgery both served to shape hospitals into our modern conception, as did the changing practice of surgery. Before the advent of anesthesia, surgery was brutal, often fatal work. The goal of surgery was to get it done quickly, but this obviously facilitated mistakes and, in many instances, death. However, with anesthesia, surgery became more careful, successful, and popular. In the last quarter of the 19th century, people still preferred to be cared for in the home -- it was more private, cleaner and more nurturing. The increasing success of surgery gave hospitals a means of marketing their services. Anesthesia was not really used in the home, so the use of it for surgery in hospitals gave hospitals a much-needed means of encouraging wealthier, middle class patients to submit to this form of care.

Conflicts Over Access to Quality of Care

After about 1900 the old prejudices about hospitals being a place to die diminished, and the demand for hospital care increased. To address the need, hospitals began limiting care to acute periods of an illness, instead of caring for the individual during the entire course of the illness. Hospitals also focused their efforts on curable patients (Starr, 1982).

Furthermore, as hospitals became more socially accepted, they began to increasingly serve the middle class instead of the poor. This created a new conflict over access to quality care. Distinctions between wards and private rooms illustrated patient distinctions in social class. These distinctions continue today; in fact, some argue that hospital clientele has taken a 180-degree turn. Initially hospitals were places where the poor received care; now, hospitals are places for the middle and upper classes.

Contrary to the initial feeling of disdain that American doctors and medicine experienced, many now argue that America has some of the best medical care in the world. This is probably true if you're white, middle class and employed by a company that offers medical insurance. After all, globally, America is among the top fifteen lowest rates of infant mortality (Population Reference Bureau, 1999). However, when compared with other industrialized nations, America lags behind in medical care. For example, while we are in the top 15 nations for lowest infant mortality rate, we are number 12 with 7.0 infant deaths per 1000 live births, compared to Sweden with 3.6, Japan with 3.7 and Germany with 4.9 (to name a few) (Population Reference Bureau, 1999).

Furthermore, American hospitals – even elite hospitals that serve as national examples – are not without their problems. In 2001 the government shut down John Hopkins University's federally-funded experiments after a woman participating in a trial died when researchers used hexamethonium (a chemical treatment for asthma) which was not tested by the Federal Drug Administration. In 2003, doctors at Duke University put the wrong organs into a teenage Latina woman, leading to her death. This was a mistake that would have been easily avoided with the simple check of her blood type, While these case studies are interesting, they are not the only ones and these examples do not perpetuate the critical thinking error of overgeneralization. According to the Institute of Medicine of the National Academy of Science, in 1999 medical errors killed 44,000-

98,000 people a year. Furthermore, the Institute claims that many of these deaths could have been prevented (Altman, 2003).

If mistakes such as those mentioned in the previous paragraph occur at the elite hospitals, imagine the potential mistakes at hospitals more burdened with a high number of patients relative to few doctors and less sophisticated technology. Consequently, how well one rates the quality of American health care is closely tied to one's income. A little under 50% of Americans with an income of over $35,000 rate American health care as "excellent", while only 26% of those with an income of under $10,000 do so (National Center for Health Statistics, 1995). As we have seen in previous chapters, income in America is closely associated with one's race. Therefore, not surprisingly, African Americans have a higher mortality rate than Whites (about 50% higher), have a higher infant mortality rate than Whites (more than double the rate of Whites), have a higher rate of heart disease, and a greater rate of high blood pressure. Clearly, it is dangerous to one's health to be a racial or ethnic minority in our country!

Why these discrepancies? While some of this is undeniably the result of behavioral differences between African Americans and Whites (for example, African American males are more likely to die from homicide than are Whites), the conflict over access to quality care, and therefore overall health, is exacerbated by the structure of medicine today. Unlike in the past, now when people get sick, they are most likely to go to a primary care physician, such as a family doctor or a general practitioner. However, according to the U.S. Department of Health and Human Services (1997), there are only about 12 primary care physicians for every 10,000 people. Why so few primary care physicians? Because this avenue of medicine does not pay as well as specialized medicine (e.g. surgeons), nor does it provide as much prestige under our current system. Consequently, American medicine is currently suffering from *overspecialization*. We have too many doctors who treat specific parts of the body or have specific skills and not enough doctors with a broad practicing knowledge who are willing to see patients with the typical fever and sore throat. Now, we need to be fair to doctors. Part of the desire of doctors to follow the high salaries of specialized medical fees comes from the incredibly high cost of medical education and the high cost of malpractice insurance once the doctor begins treating patients. Many medical students leave school deeply in debt and have sacrificed many years to be in school; the desire to become debt-free and see rewards for the prolonged education are obvious.

However, this need / desire to make money also hurts access to quality care in another way. Doctors are attracted to affluent metropolitan or suburban areas because that is where the paying patients are. But, as we just saw above, the people who need the health care the most are the poor and minorities – who disproportionately live in rural or inner city areas with few physicians. For example, in May 2001, New York City hospital officials sought to shut down more than two dozen school-based and neighborhood clinics where poor African Americans and Hispanics are treated. (Sengupta, 2001)

Furthermore, tied to the above, there are regional differences in medical care. Many hospitals in the South are still unofficially segregated or "highly selective" based on their unwillingness to treat Medicaid patients. In the West, thousands of Native Americans on reservations are left without doctors or hospitals. Special federal programs on Native American reservations to improve health care delivery have been slashed in recent years. In the North, health facilities are available on a somewhat more equal footing. But nonwhites experience a different kind of medical care. They are often treated at a large hospital or neighborhood clinic rather than at a private doctor's office. Here one finds that "institutional racism" is a "built –in feature of the way medicine is learned and practiced in the United States." (Ehrenreich and Ehrenreich, 1971) Young doctors, interns and residents in large urban areas get their training by practicing on hospital ward and clinic patients – usually non-white. Later they make their money by service-paying clients – usually white. White patients are "customers;" African American patients are "teaching material." White patients pay with money; African American patients "pay" with their dignity and comfort. Clinic patients at the hospital affiliated with Columbia University Medical School found this out in a very painful way in the 1970's. They complained that they were never given novocaine when having a tooth filled or pulled. Facts uncovered revealed this was an official policy: "the patient's pain is a good guide to the dentist-in-training – it teaches him not to drill too deep. Anesthetic would deaden the pain and dull the intern's learning experience" (Ehrenreich and Ehrenreich, 1971: 14-15). Such policies and practices have today been stopped.

Finally, stress and the environment also exacerbate the health discrepancies between African Americans and Whites. One study found that stress contributed as much to elevated blood pressure as did smoking, lack of exercise, and a high fat, high-sodium diet (Kreiger and Sidney, 1996). In other words, the stress that African Americans experience due to the discriminations of a white world, threaten their health. However, some evidence suggests that race and income intersect. Middle and upper middle class Whites and African Americans are about equally likely to get high blood pressure (Kreiger and Sidney, 1996). Most researchers interpret this to mean that middle and upper middle class African Americans are not necessarily shielded from the aforementioned stressors, but instead have the money and resources to help them cope more successfully with their stresses than their lower-income counterparts.

In summary, not only are there not enough primary-care physicians available to people, they are also unevenly distributed in a way that increases the conflict the poor and minorities need to overcome in order to obtain care. Plus, minorities and the poor disproportionately experience unhealthy, stressful and life-threatening environments. All of these factors create conflict over the ability to maintain a healthy lifestyle. As the mortality and disease statistics suggest, these groups are not very successful in overcoming these obstacles.

Conflicts Over the Role of Government and Public Health in Medicine

The federal government took almost no responsibility for public health during the first century of our society. Some of this may stem from the distrust of large, government bodies that still carried over from the American Revolution. But it may also stem from the focus on a Gemeinschaft society that we mentioned was present at this time. As we said, many believed that medicine should be understood by the average person, so many people practiced their own brand of folk medicine, rarely involving physicians. This kept medical costs relatively low (except for the rare occasions when doctors were actually called). If people were providing their own medicine or relying on a few community members to help, there was no need for the involvement of the federal government. It was not until we moved to a Gesellschaft society, where knowledge (especially medical knowledge) become more specialized, that people increasingly began to rely more extensively on others for medical treatment. This drove the cost of medical care up – paying for someone's services is more expensive than providing them yourself or receiving them from a friend. As costs increased, the need for regulation, and the government, did as well.

Another stimulus to public health was the Civil War (1861-1865). As stated previously, medical knowledge was very limited. The Civil War illustrated just how much so. Sanitary conditions in camps were unbelievable, and Union Army deaths from disease were greater than deaths due to bomb or bullet.(Bordley and Harvey, 1976) We still lacked the knowledge about how germs could be spread by not washing one's hands; consequently, germs infected most wounds and amputations and the patients died. One historical medical breakthrough in the War was the use of morphine to kill pain. However, so many soldiers became addicted to it that it was called "the soldiers' disease."

Sanitary conditions in these hospitals were also deplorable, leading Dr. Elisha Harris and architect Frederick Law Olmstead to form a Civilian Sanitary Commission in 1861. They reported an appalling lack of hospitals, fresh food, medical care for the sick and wounded; and, they shamed the U.S. military into cleaning up. Sanitary reform in the Army made an impression on the civilian population when occupying troops imposed new sanitary programs on southern towns and cities. Because of epidemics of yellow fever, the southern states persuaded "tight-fisted" legislators to establish Boards of Health, and Louisiana was the first state to do so in 1855 (Porter, 1997). The second state board of health was in Massachusetts in 1869 and other states followed in the 1870's and 1880's.

This is another example of how conflict, in this case war, can be conducive to change. The conditions of the Civil War led to changes in hospital sanitation practices and the establishment of State Boards of Health. Furthermore, the Civil War also ushered in an era of a new scientific foundation for preventive medicine and public health.

As industry spread and people moved from farms to cities, the concern for public sanitation and health grew. As mentioned in the previous section, doctors debated theories of how disease spread, thereby producing conflict within and among physicians and the health care system. Some were very slow to accept the "germ theory". To most doctors it was just another in the long line of theories that had come and gone over the centuries. In some ways it was even more unbelievable and fanciful than other theories. Slowly but surely the promotion of health and prevention of diseases became functions of government, particularly at local and state levels.

The ancient theory that "airs and waters" caused infections convinced Americans that cleaning up their water supply, streets and sewage would help. And it did – more than all the doctors, hospitals and medicine of the nineteenth century put together. Before that, human and horse excrement were left in the streets. Local departments of health were formed in large cities and states created state health departments. In 1872, the American Public Health Association, a private, non-profit organization was founded; and, it fought for federal control of port quarantine. This led to the passage of the National

Quarantine Act of 1878. In 1879, Congress even created a short-lived (4-year) National Board of Health in response to the 1878 yellow fever epidemic.

In 1887 the Federal Government through the Marine Hospital Service began to set up bacteriological labs for disease analysis and control. In 1888 public health labs were set up in Providence and in 1892 New York City. Here Dr. William H. Park (1863-1939) discovered the diphtheria carrier (1893) and developed the first diphtheria anti-toxin outside Europe. It soon became an important research center for scientific investigations into tuberculosis, dysentery, typhoid fever, scarlet fever and the role milk played in spreading disease. By 1900 diagnostic labs were set up in most states and major cities. (Porter, 1997)

When the Marine Hospital Service became the U.S. Public Health and Marine Hospital Service in 1902, Federal involvement in public health grew. During the Progressive Era (1900-1914), Federal legislation was passed to protect the health of Americans nationally. In 1906, the Federal Pure Food and Drug Act was passed to protect the consumer from contaminated food or medical drugs, which still protects us today. But the old conflict over federal and state power, present since the founding of this country, reared its head again as many state boards of health resisted federal intrusion to protect "state's rights". (Porter, 1997) Rejecting setting up a Department of Health, President Theodore Roosevelt turned it into the U.S. Public Health Service in 1912. Ever since, the role of the federal government in health care diminished. How different would the health care of America be today if that National Board of Health in 1879 had been kept in existence and if the Federal government assumed more responsibility for health in the nineteenth century? We can only imagine. It wasn't until the 1950's that the Federal Government set up a U.S. Dept. of Health, Education and Welfare. (Porter, 1997)

Even so, the conflict between the medical profession's quest for prestige and the public's perception of the medical profession was not over. Even with these changes, by the beginning of the Twentieth Century, many German-trained doctors at the best medical schools (Hopkins, Harvard, Michigan) found the laxness and mediocrity of medical education deplorable. They applied to the American Medical Association (a doctor's professional organization founded in 1847) to reform the schools. The Carnegie Foundation for the Advancement of Teaching heard the call and employed an able and critical layman, Abraham Flexner, to survey all U.S. medical schools. The "Flexner model" for medical schools, which was published in 1910, stressed biological research.   Science was to be at the base of all medical education; and, as a result, between 1910 and 1920 weak medical schools (most of the religious and non-university schools) closed or merged all over the U.S. This model has persisted to the present day – and ignores the larger problems of access to efficient health care delivery, costs and even individual ethics of the doctors (Lewin, 1971).

Yet through this new system of education, modern medicine emerged. Through research miracle drugs, such as penicillin and other antibiotics, are now part of the arsenal of weapons doctors have available. Heart scanners, lapascopes and MRIs to see into the body, are just three of the technical innovations that owe much to the Flexner model of medical research and education. Consequently, with the changes in physician education, scientific discovery and medical advances grew. Medical science increasingly became out of reach to lay men; but, unlike the past, this was more due to honest changes in medical knowledge than a tactic by doctors to create the perception of knowledge. Consequently, the prestige of doctors slowly grew. Yet the conflicts over medicine were not over.

Conflicts Over Cost And Payment Method
(Insurance, Medicare and Medicaid)

Conflicts Over Medical Care Cost
Conflict over the cost of medical care is an old story – but the reasons behind the conflict have changed over time. Even in Colonial times, most families could not afford the cost of physician care (Starr, 1982).   The physician fees were not the problem; the practical or indirect cost of medical care, which includes travel time (either for the doctor or the patient in terms of lost productivity), was higher than the fees. During this time, most families were rural and the travel distance and time between houses was extensive (and therefore costly) – either from the doctor's point of view or from the patients' if the patient chose to travel to the doctor him / herself. A 10 mile trip could result in an entire day of lost wages for the typical farmer (Starr, 1982).

Furthermore, much medical care during this time was done on credit.   Many doctors were never paid; but given the status and precarious position of the profession, there was little they could do about it. Probate records for New England doctors shows that many of them were entrenched in a tangled relationship between debt and credit issues right until their deaths (Starr, 1982).

The high indirect costs of medical care persisted until the early 20th century with the advent of the automobile. Doctors were among the first to purchase cars because they recognized the incredible time savers automobiles could be, as well as the greater geographical market they could now reach. The decrease in travel time corresponded to an increase in physician profit. A 1910 survey in which 324 people responded, 3 out of 5 doctors reported an increased income. The 96 physicians in the survey still using horses for transportation reported that their costs of travel were about 13 cents a mile; whereas, physicians using automobiles estimated their cost per mile to be only 5.6 cents (Starr, 1982).

The automobile also decreased costs for patients in that, unlike our farmer mentioned above, patients could now go to the doctors and not necessarily lose a whole day of work (and consequently money) in the process. Therefore, the automobile was instrumental in making physician care more accessible, affordable and profitable. However, the cost of medical care to the individual was still high.

The shift to hospitals did little to alleviate the burdens associated with medical costs. Contrary to popular thought, physicians had very little financial control in early hospitals…much like today. As mentioned previously, hospitals were funded by donations. A managing system of trustees, governors or commissioners, rather than physicians, had the financial decision-making power in both public and private hospitals. While some of these people undoubtedly contributed money in response to some religious, moral or community sense of obligation, these contributors also gained a certain level of prestige (for their community or civic contributions) and power -- power over admissions, power over the management of the endowment, and power in the patronage of appointments (Starr, 1982). However, donations soon became inadequate to run hospitals effectively or profitably. By the late 1900s many hospitals turned to their patients to help pay for the cost of medicine.

So how come costs are still so high that many families cannot afford medical care today? Under the medical system described above, early American physicians were primarily responsible for setting the costs of medical care. They managed their own patients, estimated travel costs and determined the fee for medical services. This does not imply that doctors never abused this system in order to increase their own profits. Because, as mentioned previously, doctors initially tried to increase the prestige of their profession by (among other tactics) using professional jargon to confuse more functionally illiterate lay people and convince them that doctors had specialized knowledge unavailable to the average person. This was more true in the 19th and early 20th Century than it is today. Also, people were less mobile then than now, so physicians were able to pretty much decide their own fees. Furthermore, fees tended to be rather standardized in a community and region (as they are today).

With the advent of hospitals, however, physicians lost some control over their fees. Boards of trustees now decided the cost of care. As hospitals evolved into highly specialized institutions of medical care, they became the only facilities capable of performing the diverse operations and a gamut of medical tests needed. Hospitals then increased profits by conducting more tests and encouraging patients to stay longer. Today, in most cases, hospitals will not keep a patient very long since insurance will not pay hospitals beyond a certain number of days. This may not be in the best interest of the patient or the doctor. The profit associated with tests fueled the conflict over the cost of medical care and led to many abuses where tests or operations that were not necessary were performed in order to increase the hospital's or doctor's profit.

However, insurance costs for hospital services is not the only way insurance increased the cost of medical care for the average person. Over the past 20 years, the cost of medical malpractice insurance for doctors has also skyrocketed – leading some to declare a "health care crisis." This crisis reflects the conflict between doctors, medical malpractice insurance carriers, trial attorneys, and ultimately, the general public (who essentially ends up paying for this conflict with higher health insurance rates). The cost of medical malpractice insurance has increased so sharply in some states that doctors who practice in these areas are leaving them in favor of areas / states with lower malpractice insurance premiums. Doctors frequently blame medical malpractice insurance carriers for their high rates and lawyers who bring costly (and sometimes "junk") lawsuits to court. The medical malpractice insurers blame the general public for instigating the lawsuits and the attorneys who charge high rates for their legal fees. The attorneys blame the system for allowing frivolous law suits to be filed. The public blames all three of these conflicting sides (doctors, attorneys and medical malpractice insurance carriers) because what they primarily see is their increasing costs of health and insurance – many argue is the result of doctors over-ordering tests to make sure that their decisions are "covered" in the case of a law suit. However, research by the organization "Americans for Insurance Reform," which is a coalition of about 100 consumer groups, found that (as shown in Figure 8-1) insurance premiums had increased at a rate much faster than what insurance companies had to pay out.

**Figure 8-1: Per Doctor Premium and Losses among
Medical Malpractice Insurance Companies**

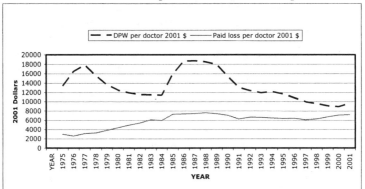

Source: A.M. Best and Co. special data compilation for AIR, reporting data for
as many years as separately available; U.S. Bureau of the Census, 1975 (2001
Estimated); Inflation Index: Bureau of Labor Statistics, 1975 (1985 estimated).
DPW" stands for "Direct Premiums Written" and reflect the amount of money
insurers collected in premiums, while "Paid Losses" is what insurers paid out to
people covered by claims, jury awards and settlements.

Figure 8-1 suggests that medial malpractice insurance rates are not
related to law suits or premiums paid to subscribers, but instead to other
factors such as market forces. However, the conflict has essentially
escalated to the degree that probably all sides have some merit
regarding who they blame. However, blame will not resolve the issue.

Some propose limits or "caps" on jury awards in medical
malpractice cases, as President Bush has done; others propose caps on
medical malpractice insurance rates, and still others propose some type
of filtration system to weed out "junk" lawsuits (after all, they argue,
medicine is a science which still has room for error). Still, others
propose some combination of these three.

Looking to other states that have already addressed this
problem may provide some leads. For example, California was the first
state to seriously address the rising costs of medical malpractice
insurance. In 1975, California passed the Medical Injury
Compensation Reform Act (MICRA), which capped the non-economic
damages a jury could award a victim. The belief behind this was that
high jury awards led to higher malpractice insurance premiums as
insurance companies worked to maintain a profit (after all, they are
businesses). However, under MICRA the malpractice insurance rates

continued to fluctuate and 13 years after the cap (1988) the medical malpractice rates were 450% higher than prior to reform (The Foundation for Taxpayer and Consumer Rights, 2003).

In response to these increasing medical malpractice insurance rates, California instituted Proposition 103 in 1988, which rolled back malpractice insurance rates for most policyholders. Medical malpractice rates in California immediately started to fall and within three years were 20% less than the all-time high in 1988 (The Foundation for Taxpayer and Consumer Rights, 2003). However, this did not alleviate the trial lawyers or the general public from any responsibility. Data suggests that California medical malpractice insurers spent more money fighting malpractice claims (e.g. the costs of lawyers, costs of expert witnesses, etc.) than actually paying claims. So how does this affect the individual? As mentioned previously, doctors who pay higher medical malpractice claims pass the cost on to their patients by charging higher fees.

Third party payment, which is a system of insurance or government medical programs (e.g. Medicaid or Medicare) designed to pay for medical care, also was instrumental in contributing to the cost conflict. Generally, consumers pay about one-third of their physician fees and about one- tenth of their hospital fees. However, under third party payment, which paid the remainder of the costs, the amount of money paid was capped at a certain amount. Consequently, in order to increase profits, physicians and hospitals made sure to charge to that cap....even if the extra services employed to help reach the cap were not necessary. As a result, the cost of medical care grew about twice as fast as the cost of inflation.

However, aside from the advent of hospital care and third party payment, more recent social changes are further causing conflicts. The elderly population is growing rapidly as the baby boomers enter their retirement years. By the year 2023, there will be more people over age 65 than there will be teenagers. Furthermore, increasing proportions of these elderly are going to be the "old-old", those over age 85. Since older people generally require more medical care, this has resulted in a greater use of medical services. Furthermore, the cost of drugs has increased greatly over the last 20 years as has the level of advanced medical technology. New technology is usually costly in its own right, but it also is attached to the indirect (and eventually somewhere direct) costs of hiring / or training technicians or physicians to operate the technology.

Let's take a closer look at the three main forms of payment today: Insurance, Medicaid and Medicare.

Insurance

With the changing face of medicine, private health plans (insurance) began to grow in the 1930s. The issue with insurance was always how to balance services, financial liability and profit. Insurance is founded on the necessity for insured hazards and the costs associated with them beyond the control of the insured. Otherwise, insurance companies would not be able to estimate the costs and would end up taking a loss. A fuller discussion of the differences behind various plans and how they evolved can be found in Paul Starr's *The History of Modern American Medicine* (1982), but is beyond the scope of this chapter.

Suffice it to say that due to high expenses, the only private insurance really available prior to the 1930s was employer-based programs. Even as early as the 1930s, however, insurance carriers recognized the difficulty in monitoring abuse in physician or hospital costs and the purchase of insurance by those most likely to be sick. Still, insurance was rare in the early Twentieth Century. In 1940, only 9% of the population was covered by any kind of health insurance. But by 1950, the number grew to 51% and by the 1990s this was about 71% (Starr, 1982). Yet nearly 40 million people, mostly adults and children in wage-earning families, lack any health insurance. In today's tight economy employers are forcing employees to pay more of the cost for the insurance, and "eliminating coverage entirely". (Epstein, 2002: 521) In 2003, "over 95,000 retired workers and their dependents lost health and life insurance" at Bethlehem Steel when it declared bankruptcy. (Carlson, 2003: 2)

This increase is related to the advent of perhaps one of the best-known insurance providers today, Blue Cross / Blue Shield. Blue Cross, the initial component of what is now referred to as "The Blues", originated in Dallas in late 1929 when the Baylor University Hospital agreed to provide 1,500 school teachers up to twenty-one days of hospital care a year for $6.00 a person. Several other hospitals in Dallas soon adopted this arrangement and expanded the pool of eligible clients beyond just teachers (Starr, 1982).

Insurance plans were facilitated by the Depression. One year after the crash, in 1929, average hospital receipts per person fell from $236.12 to $59.26. Furthermore, the average hospital deficit rose from 15.2 to 20.6 percent of disbursements. (Bulletin of the American Hospital Association, 1930). The effects of the Depression made hospitals realize that they needed a more consistent and guaranteed funding source. While, as Starr (1982) notes, individual hospital plans may have brought more instability to the hospital structure by introducing more competition (thereby reducing service costs – which was problematic since hospitals looked to insurance to *raise* profits by guaranteeing a base income), community hospitals in other areas began to jointly offer service contracts to employed people. The joining of hospitals and the hospital-based "insurance" program that developed in Dallas jointly served as the foundation for the Blue Cross insurance philosophy. Blue Shield is the younger sister organization of Blue Cross, which evolved to help pay for physician fees. In 2003, they split into two separate organizations.

But insurance like "The Blues" is expensive...even for employers. In the 1970's, Health Maintenance Organizations (HMOs) were one proposed remedy for the high insurance costs. HMOs are a flat-fee system to compensate doctors and hospitals. Part of the insurance costs are assumed by the employer and the rest by the employee. In recent years more of the cost has been shifted from the employers to the employees. The HMO then contracts with select providers (physicians and hospitals) that provide services to members. The flat-fee system creates an incentive for the HMO organizations to control costs. Savings are then passed back to the employers. HMOs were at one time the fastest growing means of insuring employees. Today fewer employees and their dependents are insured by their employers through some type of managed care system. Furthermore, HMOs have saved employers *and* employees money while at the same time making billions in profits.   Individuals have found that HMOs save them, on average, about $1,000-$2,000 a year compared to traditional health insurance plans. Furthermore, HMOs tend to be future-oriented and put heavy emphasis on preventive medicine in the belief that a little expenditure on preventive medicine now will diminish the costly expenditures associated with some preventable diseases in the future.

However, this does not imply that the profit motive has disappeared. Quite the opposite. The profit motive is still alive and strong; it just manifests itself in a different way.   One of the key complaints about HMO providers is that patients have little time with the doctor. To increase profits, there is a strong incentive for doctors to see as many patients as they possibly can in a given day. The pressure to "process" patients, results in less individualized doctor-patient attention. Furthermore, HMOs reward doctors who prescribe remedies that cost less than the norm and penalize them for prescribing remedies (including hospital tests) that cost more than the norm.

The remedies HMOs encourage doctors to use may not necessarily be the most appropriate or effective for that patient. For example, hospital stays have been shortened. Some HMOs send new mothers home the day after birth and do mastectomies without any hospitalization. Furthermore, HMO clients often need to have preapproval by their physician in order to go to specialists or the emergency room, otherwise the visit will not be paid. Think about the definition of the word "emergency". Obviously, taking time to obtain doctor approval to receive these services can waste precious time. In fact, each of these issues can hinder the quality of care physicians can provide. This is one of the built-in conflicts among hospitals, doctors and patients. Sometimes physicians are no longer making the medical decisions based on their expertise. Instead, bureaucratic staff members of the HMO are indirectly making medical decisions based on non-individual issues, such as service and product cost. This is why Congress recently passed a "patients bill of rights" to let patients sue their HMO's for inadequate medical care or mistakes. Worst of all, if the HMO's are not reimbursed enough from Medicare they can (and do) cancel their policies. In 1998, "96 HMO's either withdrew from Medicare completely or reduced their service". (Squires, 1999:20) In 2000, 711,000 Medicare HMO patients had to scramble to get new insurance when 18 insurers dropped out. (Appleby, 2000) In 2002, they did the same thing in the whole state of Pennsylvania, leaving thousands of elderly without supplemental insurance, or having to pay much higher premiums for other insurance.

Medicare and Medicaid

Not all Americans were callous to the conflict the poor experienced in trying to obtain affordable quality health care. Various proposals have been raised in Congress to provide a more communitarian focus for medicine. This will be discussed more deeply in the next section; but, one of the results from this push for communitarian health care was Medicare, a government form of insurance for the aged.

By the late 1950s, it was evident to many that the aged especially felt problems of medical and hospital costs. In a given year, one in six people over age 65 entered a hospital and stayed, on average, twice as long as patients who were younger (Starr, 1982). In response to this, in 1958 Aime Forand, a congressman from Rhode Island, proposed a plan to cover the hospital costs for the aged on Social Security (which made this insurance seem less of a "hand out", since the elderly had paid into Social Security when they had worked).

Initially the AMA opposed this proposal, claiming that it posed a threat to doctor-patient relationship, but liberals managed to deflect this claim by focusing on the needs of the aged (Starr, 1982). In 1960, Congress responded to this pressure by passing a substitute measure proposed by Senator Robert Kerr of Oklahoma and Representative Wilbur Mills, chairman of the House Ways and Means Committee. The Kerr-Mills plan, as it was called, stipulated that the federal government would provide between 50-80 percent of the funds going to states for welfare medical programs. However, this plan was limited to the aged poor; and, liberals protested that the focus on the poor would stigmatize the program and cause humiliation for the aged.

Initially, this program was short of votes and it didn't get passed until 1964 under a somewhat revised framework, which Mills was also instrumental in designing. President Johnson signed the new program, called Medicare, into law in 1965. It had three components. The first component, now known as Part A of Medicare, was similar to the initial Kerr-Mills proposal and is a compulsory hospital insurance program which is a part of Social Security. The second layer, Part B of Medicare, is a government-subsidized voluntary insurance plan to cover physician's bills. Under Part B of Medicare, now called Supplementary Medical Insurance (SMI), people over age sixty-five can pay a monthly premium (but one that is smaller than private insurance) and receive help paying hospital and doctor bills. Unlike the initial Kerr-Mills plan, Medicare is not based on a person's income. Anyone over age 65 is eligible. The concern for the poor aged was expanded to include the poor of *any* age under the third part of the plan, now called Medicaid, which is administered by the states.

As the initial designers feared, the program for the poor, Medicaid, does carry a stigma. Its initial objective was to "allow the poor to buy into the 'mainstream' of medicine, but neither the federal government nor the states were willing to spend the money that would have been required." (Starr, 1982: 370) As a result, while Medicaid does ensure the poor some level of medical care, the quality of care is frequently believed to be much lower than the quality of care people receive under private insurance, or even Medicare.

While Medicare escaped the stigma of Medicaid, it still does not provide adequate health coverage. In fact, it only covers about half of the elderly's medical costs. Key medical expenses such as prescription drugs and nursing home costs are not usually covered at all. (Holahan and Palmer, 1988; Pear, 1984) This is significant when one considers that the average cost of nursing home care is almost $40,000 per year.

Summary

It is obvious that these three systems do not work too well for patients. The conflict between available and affordable health care is getting worse. Insurance and managed care are still so profit-driven that costs continue to escalate. Plus, while over 70% of Americans are insured, 30% are not; and, the number of uninsured is still about three million higher than in the early 1990s. (Ho, 2000) Furthermore, many of the uninsured are people who are "playing by the rules". They have jobs, but earn too much for Medicaid and not enough to pay for their insurance premiums. While the government has proposed small supplemental programs like the Children's Health Insurance Program (CHIPs) to provide health insurance for the children of the uninsured, lack of accurate information makes many of these programs under-utilized. (Ho, 2000)

With regards to our two main government programs, Medicare still leaves the elderly paying about a quarter of their incomes for services – incomes that are fixed due to retirement. Medicare also doesn't cover important components of care such as prescription drugs or nursing home care. Medicaid doesn't quite cover 50% of the poor and does not even apply to the near poor – those who are "playing" by society's rules and working, but do not work for employers who offer private insurance. Even so, Medicare currently consumes about 11% of the federal budget (and is growing at a rate of 10% a year). (Tonnen, 1995) And while Medicare is not clearly associated with a lack of quality care, Medicaid is. So what we currently have is a piecemeal approach to medical care that creates many cracks through which large groups of people fall.

Privilege or Right? The Conflict Over National Health Care

Most people feel that good medical care should be available to all people (especially themselves) as a matter of right.   After all, Congress itself benefits from free government-paid medical and health care. The right to life assumes the right to access to medical care for all. But others, for example, some doctors and the American Medical Association, traditionally have defined health care as a privilege, not a right.   It is a privilege that people must pay for from a "private" physician or hospital. The doctor, of course, can elect to render his services as a charity. Such a definition of medical care protects the freedom of independent professionals and insures a private "doctor-patient" relationship. To some scholars it is this "privilege," "private" and fee-for service definition of medicine that is at the bottom of the current health crisis. Those who hold the "privilege" health care definition view it as a private commodity to be bought by individuals on the open market like their appliances or cars.

On the other hand, those who define medical care as a "right" rather than a "privilege" define medical care as a social good, not a private commodity. According to Daniel Bell, social goods are not "divisible into individual items of possession (such as one's own private doctor) but are a community service. (1976: 224) For example, schools, police and fire protection, parks, highways and waterways are all social goods, not private. Social goods benefit the whole society, not just individuals who can afford to pay for them. They are subject to community and societal control not the wishes of private professionals or organizations supplying the service.

This conflict over "right" or "privilege" is at the heart of the national health care debates in our country. Though Germany instituted its national health insurance in 1883, serious lobbying for health care in the U.S. did not start until the early decades of the twentieth century. A group called the American Association for Labor Legislation (AALL) made up of academics, lawyers, labor leaders, business men and social workers, pushed for health care insurance laws in 1913. Two years earlier, in England, sick workers who earned less than a certain amount of money were entitled to services from a doctor. The purpose of the English program was to get the worker back on the job and to reduce the cost to industry of time lost through worker sickness. The AALL called for the payment of regular sums of money by the workers in return for specified medical care when they were sick. Under their leadership, and with the cooperation of the American Medical Association, investigation into state health insurance was started in eight states between 1915 and 1918. The AALL's bill, like its European predecessors, restricted participation to the working class – focusing particularly on workers who earned less than $1,200 a year (remember, this is the early 1900s!). Under the AALL's plan, there were four benefits: 1) medical aid (including all physician, nurses and hospital services); 2) sick pay at 2/3 of wages up to 26 weeks and 1/3 of wages during hospitalization; 3) maternity benefits for the wives of insured men (or for insured working women themselves); and 4) a $50 death benefit to cover funeral expenses. (Starr, 1982). Members of the AALL felt that a program such as this would be most beneficial, by addressing the social problems of illness itself, poverty, and industrial discontent (Fisher, 1917).

The American Medical Association (AMA) initially supported the idea. Later, it bitterly fought and opposed any government system of compulsory health insurance. But in 1916, its Committee on Social Insurance "...expressed a generally favorable attitude toward compulsory health insurance as it existed in Britain". (Bordley and Harvey, 1976: 370)

During the 1930's, four important studies about American medicine and our health care system appeared. The Report of the Commission on Medical Education (1932) and the Report of the Committee on the Costs of Medical Care (1932) both directed attention to the Federal Government and public about inadequacies in the existing system. The committee on costs made four recommendations to improve the system: 1) That group practice centered on hospitals be developed; 2) That the cost of medical care be covered by insurance and/or taxation; 3) That each state and community set up a specific organization to study, evaluate and coordinate its health services; and, 4) That three new types of medical workers be trained---nursing attendants; nurse mid-wives; and, hospital and clinic administrators.

President Franklin D. Roosevelt and some members of Congress responded to these suggestions. The U.S. Public Health Service conducted a National Health Survey in 1935 and 1936. The survey confirmed earlier studies. Those receiving the most inadequate care lived either in the poor sections of a city or in rural areas.

Shortly after this, in 1937, a two-volume report of the American Foundation Studies in Government appeared. It was called *American Medicine Expert Testimony out of Court*. It revealed that many people in the U.S. lacked the medical care they needed. It also presented evidence about the relative merits of state medicine and voluntary health insurance to provide comprehensive medical care for all. (Bordley and Harvey, 1976) The fourth report, a few months later was *Principles and Proposals* headed by a prominent New York doctor by the name of Russell L. Cecil. About 700 doctors signed this report, and it stated the following:

Principles

1. That the health of the people is a direct concern of the government.
2. That a national public health policy directed toward all groups of the population should be formulated.
3. That the problem of economic need and the problem of providing adequate medical care are not identical and may require different approaches for their solution.
4. That in the provision of adequate medical care for

the population four agencies are concerned:
voluntary agencies, local, state, and Federal
governments.

Nine specific proposals called for the use of public funds to prevent illness and disease and improve our medical care system. (Bordley and Harvey, 1976: 118-119).

The publication of the *Principles and Proposals*, which today seem logical and certainly less extreme than some current proposals, gave rise to another conflict and controversy within the medical profession. An editorial in *The Journal of the American Medical Association* accused the signers of being virtual traitors to their fellow physicians. The controversy and the reports which preceded it served to direct public attention to deficiencies in medical care. They also made the public aware of the fact that the AMA did not speak for all physicians and that there was a large group of distinguished medical educators, researchers, and practitioners who believed that American medicine was in need of improvement.

In 1938, President Roosevelt concluded that there was a need for a National Health Program to achieve a fairer distribution of high quality medical care. He suggested, among other items, that the program should include some form of social insurance to reimburse workers for the loss of earnings during an illness. This was not a new idea – between 1911 and 1935 all except four states had adopted workmen's compensation laws. But, the suggestion that a redistribution of medical services be combined with a national social insurance plan led organized medicine to mobilize all its artillery to shoot down what it stigmatized as a plan to introduce "socialized medicine" on a national scale. The battle to prevent the "socialization" of medicine was joined in earnest. In 1939, Senator Robert Wagner introduced a bill to provide a National Health Program through grants-in-aid to states that agreed to meet standards prescribed by the federal government. The Wagner bill was defeated, but this was only one of the early skirmishes in a long and bitterly fought "war" which continues to the present day.(Bordley and Harvey, 1976)

After the Wagner bill was defeated, President Roosevelt then took the view that "the public (and the medical profession) was not yet ready for a major federal incursion into medical care." (Stevens and Stevens, 1974; 14). But historically the need was there. By the end of the 1930's it was evident that the "policy of leaving to localities and states the entire responsibility for providing even nominal public health facilities and services had failed in large measure" (Stevens and

Stevens, 1974:16). A report of the Social Security Board for 1943 noted that about one-third of the children getting Aid to Dependent Children (ADC) were in need because of the physical or mental incapacity of the parent. Furthermore, an estimated one-fourth of the blind could profit by medical care to improve or conserve their vision. By the 1940s, it was clear that modern medicine was imposing acute financial problems on people. Better facilities, equipment and drugs meant more costs. Americans came to live in dread of getting sick. They literally could not afford it.

The debate never went much further than this until the late 1950s to early 1960s. While organizations and Congress became increasingly aware of the gaps in affordability and quality of health care, the AMA vigorously and successfully fought against any form of national health insurance. While many people did not give up on the idea of national health care, many saw the primary need to be the poor and the aged. Since the climate was not favorable for national health care for everyone, some members of Congress at least pushed for the advent of Medicare and Medicaid (discussed previously) to help these two groups.

The debate for national health care briefly re-surfaced in the early 1970s with Senator Edward Kennedy and Representative Martha W. Griffiths' (of Michigan) Health Security Plan. They called for the abolishment of all public and private health care plans, as we know them, into a single, federally operated health insurance system. The Health Security Plan would have called for a national budget, allocated funds to regions, created incentives for prepaid group practice and obliged private hospitals and physicians to operate within budget constraints. There would be no co-payments by consumers (Starr, 1982). However, in response to Kennedy and Griffiths' proposal, President Nixon started this own investigation into the health care crisis that soon led to the establishment of the Health Maintenance Organizations (or HMOs) mentioned previously.

So a national health insurance program was still on hold. The most recent attempt at national health care was President William Clinton's plan proposed in the early 1990s. He proposed a national health care plan that combined competition with a budget cap on health spending. Under Clinton's plan, employers and individuals would each pay a share of the insurance premium – with employer premiums capped at a percentage of payroll and employee premiums capped at a percentage of earnings. This approach was believed to take away much of the stigma associated with a public program, at the same time providing accessible health care to more people. One of people's concerns over previously proposed national health care programs involved the lack of people's choice of doctors and plans. American culture is firmly tied to the concept of choice...choice of higher education, choice of political figures, choice of medical care. Many other country's form of national health insurance seriously restricts citizen choice, but Americans are not supportive of that. President Clinton's plan, however, provided Americans the opportunity to choose between different plans, which would compete with one another based on quality and price (Starr, 1994). Under President Clinton's plan, "health alliances" would be responsible for organizing the market and making a variety of health plans available to consumers. Employers would have paid a minimum of 80% of whatever plan employees chose, and then employees would pay the difference. Employees could, to some degree, regulate their actual medical expenses by the type of plan they chose. If they chose a more expensive plan, they paid more and vice versa. This was designed to give people choice over the options they wanted, while at the same time ensuring people the same level of basic care (Starr, 1994).

Premiums would only vary by family size. Existing health conditions would not be relevant. Under the current system of private insurance, insurers essentially pick and choose their patients to make sure they have a healthy pool. They charge higher prices to individuals or smaller employers, and in specific regions (e.g. regions which have a high proportion of elderly). Under President Clinton's proposed plan, this variation would not exist, thereby helping more people receive better care.

However, as with previous attempts at nationalized health care, the AMA was influential in ensuring that the plan fizzled. A recent article reveals, however, that the AMA is losing power and only represents 32% of all doctors. (Catanzaro, 2001) Additionally, Clinton made the mistake of appointing his wife, Hillary, to head up the Presidential Health Insurance Study Commission. According to Seelye (1994), when Clinton tried to reform health care, more than 650 groups spent more than $100 million over a 15-month period to minimize or block health care reform.

So as it stands, America is one of the few industrialized countries in the world without a national health care policy or plan. And we pay for it in a number of ways. We pay more than the Canadians and Germans, and more than double what the Japanese, Swedes and Britons spend, even though all of these countries have a longer life span and lower infant mortality than we do.

Critical Thinking Questions

1. Review the current federal proposal and two other proposals aimed at decreasing medical malpractice rates. What proposal do you find the strongest? Why?

2. Would you be willing to pay more out of pocket medical expenses if it meant more interaction (e.g. one-on-one) time with your health care provider? Why? If so, how much? How would this option vary for people in different social groups (e.g. elderly, racial minorities, etc.)

3. What are the pros and cons for national health insurance? Do you support a national health insurance policy? Why or why not? Can you provide some thoughts for an alternate plan to maximize adequate health care for all individuals? Be conscious of the critical thinking fallacies discussed in Chapter 1 when you are defending your position.

4. Do you agree with the deinstitutionalization of the mentally ill? Why or why not? What can be done *feasibly* (meaning "realistically" given financial, social, tax, etc. restraints) to facilitate deinstitutionalization?

Bibliography

Appleby, Julie. "Insurers Drop Medicare HMOs Serving 711,000
     Patients." *U.S.A. Today.* (July 12, 2000): 1-A

Bell, Daniel. *The Cultural Contradictions of Capitalism.* New York:
     Basic Books Inc, 1976.

Bordley, James III and A. McGehee Harvey. *Two Centuries of
     American Medicine:* Philadelphia: W.B. Saunders Co., 1976.

Bulletin of the American Hospital Association. "A Statistical Analysis
     of 2, 717 Hospitals". 4 (July, 1930): 68.

Carlson, Elliot, ed. "About 95,000 Retired Workers." *AARP Bulletin.*
     44,3 (March, 2003): 2.

Catanzaro, Michael. "What's Up Docs? The Democratization of the
     AMA." *National Review* (May 14, 2001): 28-30.

Ehrenreich, Barbara and John Ehrenreich. *The American Health
     Empire: Power and Politics.* New York: Vintage, 1971.

Epstein, Keith. "Covering the Uninsured." *CQ Researcher.* 12, 23
     (June 14, 2002): 521-544.

Fisher, Irving. "The Need for Health Insurance," *American Labor
     Legislation Review.* 7 (March, 1917) 23.

Fox, Renee C. "The Medicalization and Demedicalization of American
     Society." *Daedalus* 106,1 (Winter, 1977): 9-22.

Heaps, Willard A. *Riots, U.S.A.: 1765-1970.* New York: The Seabury
     Press, 1970.

Ho, David. "Many Eligible Children Not Getting Low-Cost Health
     Insurance." *Philadelphia Inquirer.* (August 10, 2000): A-5.

Holahan I. and Palmer J., "Medicare's Fiscal Problems: An Imperative
     for Reform." *Journal of Health, Politics, Policy and Law.* 13
     (1988): 53-82.

King, Lester S. *The Medical World of the Eighteenth Century.*
     Chicago, Il: University of Chicago Press, 1958.

Kreiger N. and Sidney S. "Racial Discrimination and Blood Pressure:
     The CARDIA Study of Black and White Adults." *American
     Journal of Public Health.* 86 (1996): 1370-1378.

Lewin, Stephen. "Revamping our Medical Schools." Pp. 24-25 in *The
     Nation's Health.*, edited by Stephen Lewin. New York:
     Wilson (1971).

Margotta, Roberto. *The History of Medicine.* N.Y.: Smith Mark
     Publishers, 1996.

National Center for Health Statistics. *Current Estimates from the National Health Interview Survey, 1994.* Series 10, no. 193. Government Printing Office: Washington, D.C. 1995.

Pear, Robert. 1984. "Linking Medicare and Ability to Pay." *New York Times* (February 20, 1984): A-11.

Population Reference Bureau. *1999 World Population Data Sheet.* Washington, D.C., 1999.

Porter, Roy. *The Greatest Benefit to Mankind: A Medical History of Humanity.* New York: W.W. Morton & Co., 1997.

Seelye, Katherine Q. "Lobbyists are the Loudest in the Health Care Debate." *New York Times* (August 16, 1994): A1 & A10.

Sengupta, Somini. "Health Agency Seeks to Close 27 Clinics." *New York Times.* (May 15, 2001): B 1-2.

Shryock, Richard H. *Medicine in America: Historical Essays.* Baltimore: Johns Hopkins Press, 1966.

Squires, Pamela. "HMO Disaster Sinks In." *Secure Retirement* 8,1 (January and February, 1999): 20-24.

Starr, Paul. *The Logic of Health Care Reform: Why and How the President's Plan Will Work.* New York: Whittle Books, 1994.

Starr, Paul. T*he Social Transformation of American Medicine.* New York: Basic Books, 1982.

Statistical Abstract of the United States. 120th Edition, "Summary Characteristics: 1980-1998. Table 194 Hospitals." Pp. 127. U.S. Census Bureau, U.S. Dept. of Commerce. Washington, D.C.: U.S. Government Printing Office, 2000.

Stevens, Robert and Rosemary Stevens. *Welfare Medicine in America.* N.Y.: Free Press, 1974.

Tonner, Robin. 1995. "No Free Rides: Generational Push Has Not Come to Shove". *New York Times* (December 31,1995): E-1.

U.S. Bureau of the Census, *Historical Statistics of the United States: Colonial Times to 1970.* Department of Commerce. Washington, D.C.: U.S. Government Printing Office, 1975.

U.S. Department of Health and Human Services. "Health United States." Washington, D.C.: U.S. Government Printing Office, 1997.

Wylie, W. Gill. *Hospitals: Their History, Organization, and Construction.* New York: Appleton, 1877.

Chapter 9

Economic Institution: Poverty, Wealth and Unemployment

> "A decent provision for the poor is the test of any civilization" Samuel Johnson, 18th Century British writer, quoted in *The Wall Street Journal,* December 30, 1999: A-12.

> "The poor you have always with you, so you may help them whenever you will..." The Bible, Mark 14:7-8.

> "I see one-third of a nation ill-housed, ill-clad, ill-nourished". President Franklin D. Roosevelt, Second Inaugural Address, January 20, 1937 *(Poverty in the Affluent Society,* ed. Hanna Meissner, 32).

Our economy is the entire social institution that produces and distributes goods and services. It involves technology, jobs, money and social classes - - some rich, some poor. Within that institution, power and conflict effect the distribution of wealth, and produces unemployment and poverty.

Poverty is as old as human beings. From a world perspective, poverty and hunger are still the lot of most people. Half the world's population lives on only 8% of the world's income, while the rest of that income, 92%, goes to the other half. About a fifth of the world's people consume four-fifths of the world's total output. That one-fifth eats 20 times as much food per person as the poorer majority (Cornell, 1974:2). People throughout most of history have been poor. Conflicts and attempts to solve the problem also have a long history as suggested by Daniel Moynihan in these *imaginary* newspaper headlines:

> "Great Debate" Begun: Is Man His Brother's Keeper? (Bible Lands, n.d.)

> Amos Attacks Privileged Classes for "Oppressing the Poor" (Bible Lands Circa 750 B.C.)

> Subsidies for Poor Instituted to Thwart Social Reform: Plato and Aristotle Disagree on Issues – Plato Advocates "Prevention"; Aristotle Higher Relief Standards (Athens, fourth century B.C.)

> Increase of Relief Giving by Monasteries Seen Threat to Parish Relief (Europe, circa A.D. 600)

> Begging Prohibited to Relieve Labor Shortage Resulting from Black Plague: Employers Chalk Up Notable Victory (England, 1349)   (Shostak, 1974: 4-5)

In 1349 the Statutes of Laborers was an attempt by English landowners to assure themselves a willing workforce by outlawing begging. Due to the Black Plague of that year, there was a crucial labor shortage, so the law insured everyone would work or not eat. This was the beginning of Anglo-Saxon government efforts to attack poverty (De Schweinitz, 1943: 1) Prior to that the feudal system serfs were supposed to be cared for by their lords or master.

During the Middle Ages, the Catholic Church was active in dealing with poverty through medieval monasteries and hospitals. They not only provided medical care, but housed weary travelers and cared for orphans, the aged, and the destitute. They provided a variety of services for all those in need (Trattner, 1974: 5). Giving alms to the poor, however, was basically more concerned about the soul of the rich than the life conditions of the poor – a kind of premium on an after-life insurance policy. Good works, especially to help the poor, was thought to be a major road to eternal salvation (Coser, 1965: 107).

By the "high" Middle Ages, a well-developed system of poor relief in Europe had been set up. The Catholic Church was a public institution and the tithe (10% of income) a compulsory tax for all.

With the Protestant Reformation in 1523 came new conflicts and ideas about charitable works and the poor. In 1536, Henry VIII in England took over the monasteries and other Church property. More importantly, the situation of the poor changed to a low status that is still with us today, one that reflects attitudes of the well-off toward those less fortunate.

In Puritan England (from which many of our attitudes, traditions, and laws are derived) the poor were given the position of the "eternally damned". To the Puritan the poor had no "calling", no vocation, nor useful function for society. They were not considered a part of society. William Perkins, a leading Sixteenth Century preacher, wrote:

> Rogues, beggars, vagabonds...commoners are of no civil society or corporation, nor of any particular Church; and are as rotten legges, and armes, that droppe from the body...to wander up and downe from yeare to yeare....they are plagues and banes...and are to bee taken as main enemies of this ordinance of God.   (Coser, 1965: 107)

The poor, by this philosophy, did not belong to society and are not worthy of help or treatment. They were to be shunned and avoided.

After much conflict and wars, the State emerged over the church in Sixteenth Century England and it took over the function of "poor relief". The famous Elizabethan Poor Laws of 1601 were the culmination of years of efforts to do this.   They contained punitive work provisions and a harsh "means test" to determine who was "worthy" of aid. In 1662, the State made each community responsible for its own poor and forbade movement of the poor from one town to another under the Law of Settlement (Crouse, 1993: 2143).

The wandering poor of that period were victimized by vagrancy laws that defined them as criminals deserving harsh, public punishments. These included: whipping, branding, ear cropping, and being "tied to the end of a cart naked and...beaten with whips throughout...town...till his body be bloody" (de Schweinitz, 1943: 21).

The emphasis was put on work, on the Protestant Ethic; the laws were designed to give as little as possible to the poor. The poor were viewed as lazy and irresponsible, attitudes that still prevail today in America. The oppressed poor, however, in the new World, fought the rich to obtain some power and justice for themselves. It was a matter of survival.

In 1676 in colonial Virginia there was a rebellion of white frontiersmen, slaves, and servants against the rich and those in power. It was called Bacon's Rebellion. Times were hard in 1676, according to Wilcomb Washburn who, using British colonial records, did an exhaustive study of Bacon's Rebellion. He wrote, "there was genuine distress, genuine poverty...All contemporary sources speak of the great mass of people as living in severe economic straits" (Zinn, 1980: 40). In July, 1676, Bacon's "Declaration of the People" showed a mixture of popular resentment against the rich and frontier hatred of Indians. It blamed the government for unjust taxes, putting favorites in positions of power and monopolizing the beaver trade. Bacon died of natural causes and after that the rebellion was crushed (Zinn 1980: 41). It was a desperate move on the part of the poor to share in or equalize the wealth through "hopes of leveling". According to Zinn, "leveling" was behind countless (and fruitless) "actions of poor whites against the rich in all the English colonies, in the century and a half *before* the Revolution" (1980: 42).

As in England, the system of indentureship was established in the early United States as a way of controlling labor, wages and the poor. The English workhouse and almshouse that Charles Dickens wrote about in *Oliver Twist* were transplanted to the colonies. In Philadelphia, right after the Revolution, the poor were seen as two types: The "industrious" or "deserving" poor, and the "indigent" or "vicious" poor. The latter's chief characteristics were described as: "Worthless and vagabond types;...drunken, rioting, sulking, lazy fellows" (Davis and Haller, 1973: 16). The "industrious" poor were the people for whom charity drives were held each year, especially to help them during the winter when they could not work. These were the poor who were struck by yellow fever in the great epidemic of 1793 because they could not afford to leave the city or find work. Massive relief funds were needed to save them from starving. Prosperous Philadelphians were told to help the "industrious" poor but not the "indigent" or "vicious" poor. But when the wealthy wrote about the dangers of society from the poor, "the distinctions between the industrious and the worthless poor tended to melt away" (Davis and Haller, 1973: 16).

The major conflicts and struggles were between the rich, who held positions of power, and the poor and working class who fought for economic justice. Between 1794 and 1845, farmers in Pennsylvania, poor tenant farmers in upstate New York and working class poor in New York City and Rhode Island all rebelled against oppressive taxes, rents, the price of flour for bread and voting requirements (Zinn, 1980). Historically these uprisings of the poor were known respectively as: The Whiskey Rebellion (1794); the Flour Riot of 1837 in New York City; the Anti-Renter Movement in the Hudson Valley (1839); and, Dorr's Rebellion in Rhode Island (1841-1845).

In Philadelphia, working class families lived 55 to a tenement house, usually one room per family, with no toilets, no garbage removal, no fresh air or water. There was some fresh water pumped from the Schuykill River, but it went to the homes of the rich.

Howard Zinn wrote about conditions of the poor in New York City during the 1830's and 1840's:

> You could see the poor lying in the streets with the garbage. There were no sewers in the slums, and filthy water drained into yards and alleys, into the cellars where the poorest of the poor lived, bringing with it a typhoid epidemic in 1837, typhus in 1842. In the cholera epidemic of 1832, the rich fled the city; the poor stayed and died. (1980: 213)

In the "Panic" or economic Depression of 1837, prices rose in many cities. Working poor people, already hard-pressed to buy food, found that flour that had sold at $5.62 a barrel was now $12 a barrel. In New York City, several thousand poor people rallied in front of City Hall and then moved on to a flour store in the area. They broke in and "…barrels of flour, by dozens, fifties and hundreds were tumbled into the street from the doors, and thrown in rapid succession from the windows. About one thousand bushels of wheat, and four or five hundred barrels of flour (in all) were destroyed…Amidst the falling and bursting of the barrels and sacks of wheat, numbers of women were engaged…filling the boxes and baskets…and their aprons with flour, and making off with it…" (Zinn, 1980: 220) This was the Flour Riot of 1837.

During the economic crisis of that year, 50,000 persons (one-third of the working class) were without work in New York City alone, and 200,000 (of a population of 500,000) were living, as one observer put it, "in utter and hopeless distress".

Most help to the poor came from private contributions of the rich and middle class. Local private charity groups developed, like Philadelphia's Western Association of Ladies for the Relief and Employment of the Poor, founded in 1846 by a group of Quaker women. They did whatever they could to help the "worthy" poor or "paupers". This group provided a workshop where poor women could come and bring their children. They would be given a hot meal at noon and a supper, as well as a little (very little) money. For this they worked by making clothes that were sold by the Association at a low cost (Geldart, 1966), This was somewhat like the "thrift stores" that exist in poor areas today.

In the 1850's large numbers of charity relief societies, called Associations for Improving the Condition of the Poor, sprung up in cities in the northeast as they grew in size and as the poor increased.

The Federal government at this time played a very insignificant role in helping the poor, leaving this matter up to local government and especially to local private charities. When President Pierce in 1854 vetoed a bill to grant land to states to help the insane, he made it clear that poverty was none of the federal government's business. He pointed out that the Federal government did not have the constitutional right to provide "for the care and support of all those among the people of the United States, who, by any form of calamity, become fit objects of public philanthropy". Caring for the poor belongs "exclusively to the states" (Zietz, 1969: 58). This position of the Federal Government led to the establishment of State Boards of Charity to coordinate state spending in institutions for the poor. These were the organizational forerunners of State Board's of Public Assistance and Welfare in the Twentieth Century.

Once again the poor were hit with an economic crisis in 1857, since Capitalism goes through economic cycles. The rich had begun to expand manufacturing and railroads and speculate in stocks and bonds. This led to a wild expansion and then an economic crash. By October 1857, 200,000 working poor were unemployed and thousands of recent poor immigrants tried to work their way back on ships to Europe. In New York City, 15,000 poor people marched to Wall Street and paraded around the stock exchange, shouting: "We want work." That summer, riots occurred in the slum areas there. A mob of 500 attacked police with pistols and bricks. The poor were desperate. Parades of unemployed formed, demanding bread and work. In desperation they looted shops. In November, 1857, a crowd occupied City Hall but U.S. Marines were brought in to drive them out (Zinn, 1980).

In 1861 Civil War began and the poor were soon forgotten; but as prices for food and bare necessities of life increased, the poor began to form more unions and strike. Prices of milk, eggs, and cheese were up 60 to 100 percent for poor families who had not been able to pay the old prices. Historian Emerson Fite, described the war-time plight of the working poor: "Employers were wont to appropriate to themselves all or nearly all of the profits accruing from the high prices, without being willing to grant to the employees a fair share of these profits through the granting of higher wages" (1910: 37).

Resentment against the war and high prices paid by poor working people was sparked by the Conscription Act of 1863. It provided that the rich could avoid military service by paying $300, or buying a substitute. Poor Irish immigrants and other poor then called the Civil War, "A Rich Man's War but a Poor Man's Fight". When drafting of men for the army began in New York City in July, 1863, they wrecked the main recruiting station. For three days and nights, crowds of poor workers swept through the city, destroying buildings, factories, street cars and homes. On the fourth day, Union troops, just returning from the Battle of Gettysburg, came into the city and stopped the riot (Stephenson, 1918). Though no exact figures were given, an estimated 400 people were killed. The lives lost were greater in number than any other riot or rebellion in American history. There were anti-draft riots by the working poor in other northern and mid-western cities: Newark, Troy, Boston, Toledo and Evansville all experienced them, though not as long or bloody as in New York City (Zinn, 1980; Fite, 1910; Stephenson, 1918).

In the year 1873, the country was again in the depth of a great Economic Depression. It had a greater impact on the poor than either the "Panic" of 1837 or 1857. Unemployment in an urban industrial society was far more serious for the poor man than in a rural society in the 1830's or 1850's when people could grow their own food. The old story repeated itself - - wage cuts, unemployment, misery. Some three million working-poor were thrown out of work. The number of national unions for workers declined from 30 in 1873 to only 9 in 1877. Reported union membership dropped from 300,000 to 50,000 (Dulles, 1960). There was little recourse for the poor working people except protests, demonstrations and mass strikes, leading to violence by both the poor and the establishment. Unemployment riots and violence in the anthracite cola mines, led by the Molly Maguires in eastern Pennsylvania, were the beginning of a series of national railroad strikes in 1877. So severe was the plight of the poor and the violence on both sides (rich and poor) the period was called "the Great Upheaval" (Dulles, 1960: 114-22). Only the presence of Federal troops finally ended the bloodshed. Over 100 people were dead, a thousand poor people went to jail, 100,000 workers had gone out on strike but the plight of the poor continued in America.

In 1877 in Buffalo, N.Y., the first Charity Organization Society (COS) was formed. Patterned after the COS of London, it made strict investigations of the poor through "friendly home visitors". These were forerunners of modern social workers. The COS coordinated all charity work in the city and gave relief from its own resources only in emergencies. Costs and "worthiness" of their clients were the main concerns. The COS movement spread quickly to other large cities that were just beginning to experience the "urban crisis", spawned by the industrial revolution and new waves of impoverished immigrants (Gillin, 1937: 511)

In the 1880's in England, as well as the U.S., new problems and programs developed. Huge numbers of poor immigrants clustered in large cities. "Social awakening" and "social unrest" grew up together there. One politician said that never before had "the misery of the poor been more intense or the daily life more hopeless and degraded" (Gillin, 1937: 27). The English Socialist organizations were formed; the social settlement movement to help the poor began and spread to America; the Salvation Army under "General" William Booth opened its first food and shelter depot; government investigations also explored the social unrest stemming from poverty.

The first large-scale scientific survey of poverty was undertaken by a retired London merchant, Mr. Charles Booth. His classic study began in 1891 and finished in 1902. It was published as *Life and Labour of the People in London* (London: 1964). He was one of the first social scientists to classify people in a city by socio-economic class. Booth found that out of the eight classes – four below and four above "the line of poverty" – 30.7% of the entire population were poor. B.S. Rountree, in his 1901 survey of York, England, found 33.4% of the "wage-earning" class and 27.84% of that city's population were poverty-stricken (Gillin, 1937: 28; Rountree, 1091, 1922).

It was not until the last third of the Nineteenth Century that social theorists like Edward Bellamy wrote a book *Looking Backwards* (1888; 1960) and began to speculate about a world without poverty, a world in which masses of people need not live their lives in "quiet desperation". But in America this was to remain for many years a radical, utopian concept. The conventional wisdom at that time was that a prosperous economy needed a large supply of unskilled labor. So poverty persisted. Modeled after the English system, eventually we developed in our states and local communities in the 19th Century an institution called the almshouse, or poorhouse, where children, the mentally ill, sick, elderly and able-bodied all were placed to do menial work for a bare subsistence.

It was in the cities in America in the late Nineteenth Century that the seeds of conflict and concern over the poor were sown. Men and women such as Jacob Riis, Jane Adams, Lincoln Steffens, Upton Sinclair, Stephen Crane, and Theodore Dreiser called society's attention to the plight of the poor.

Jacob Riis best described slum life in 1890 New York City in his book *How the Other Half Lives*. He depicted and deplored the horrible conditions he found in the tenements and the human misery and misfortune there. He focused attention on the plight of neglected and abandoned children. In 1890 he wrote about the poor in New York City:

> The Foundling Asylum...stands at the very outset of the waste of life that goes on in a population of nearly two millions of people; powerless to prevent it though it gather in the outcasts by night and by day. In a score of years, an army of 25,000 of these forlorn little waifs have cried out from the streets of New York in arraignment of a Christian civilization under the blessings of which the instinct of motherhood even was smothered by poverty and want.

> Only the poor abandon their children...They come in rags, a newspaper often the only wrap, semi-occasionally one in a clean slip with some evidence of loving care; a little slip of paper pinned on, perhaps with some such message as this I once read, in a woman's trembling hand: 'Take care of Johnny, for God's sake. I cannot.' ...The city divides with the Sisters of Charity the task of gathering them in. The real foundlings, the children of the gutter that are picked up by the police, are the city's ward...Few outcast babies survive their desertion long. Of 508 babies received at the Randall's Island Hospital last year, 333 died, 65.55 percent. Of the 508 only 170 were picked up in the streets, and among these the mortality was much greater, probably nearer ninety percent, if the truth were told. The rest were born in the hospitals. The high mortality among the foundlings is not to be marveled at ...The wonder is, rather, that any survive (Riis, 1890: 60-1).

In New York City in 1890 nearly a half million people (in a population of a million and a half) were begging for food, and one person of every ten who died was buried a pauper in Potter's Field. Today we can't even imagine what poverty was like then.

Wages were so low a family barely had enough food to eat, or clothes on its back, or a roof over its head. A cost of living report by the U.S. Commissioner of Labor in 1903 showed that the breadwinner in most families could not earn enough to survive. His income had to be added to by the wages of his children (McVeigh, 1962: 30).

Robert Hunter, in his classic book *Poverty*, wrote about the life of children in 1904:

> The girls go to the mills, the boys to the (coal) breakers...There is hardly an employment more demoralizing and physically injurious than this work in the breakers. For ten or eleven hours a day these children of ten and eleven years stoop over the chute and pick out the slate and other impurities from the coal as it moves past them. The air is black with coal dust, and the roar of the crushers, screens, and rushing millrace of coal is deafening. Sometimes one of the children falls into the machinery and is terribly mangled, or slips into the chute and is smothered to death. Many children are killed in this way. Many others, after a time, contract coal-miner's asthma and consumption...Breathing continually day after day the clouds of coal dust, their lungs become black and choked with small particles of anthracite. There are in the United States about 24,000 children employed in and about the mines and quarries (Hunter, 1904: 238).

Not only young boys worked from dawn to dusk. Young girls were employed in the mills. If you were alive in 1911 and listened closely you could have heard 8-year-old Helen Sisscak answer a judge's questions about her job in a textile mill in Pennsylvania:

> Judge: Helen! What time do you go to work?
> Helen: Half after six evenin's.
> Judge: When do you go home from the mill?
> Helen: Half after six mornin's.
> Judge: What's your pay, Helen?
> Helen: I get 3 cents an hour, sir.
> Judge: If my arithmetic is good that's about 36 cents for a night's work.
> (McVeigh, 1962: 30)

And so it was. There were thousands of Helen Sisscaks working in mills and factories, instead of going to school or playing. This situation inspired on writer to note:

> The golf links lie so near the mill
> That almost every day
> The laboring children can look out
> And see the men at play. (Cleghorn, 1919)

And the children of the poor suffered the most. In Chicago, in 1908, 5,000 children who attended school were "habitually hungry"; 10,000 more, while not such extreme cases, did not have "sufficient nourishing food". Many children lacked shoes and clothing. Many had no beds to sleep in and were homeless and lived in the street.

The Commission on Industrial Relations, set up by Congress in 1912, reported:

> It is evident both from the investigations of this commission and from the reports of all recent governmental bodies that a large part of our industrial population are…living in a condition of actual poverty…It is certain that at least one-third and possible one-half of the families of wage earners…earn in the course of a year less than enough to support themselves. (McVeigh, 1962: 31)

Poverty Policies and Programs in the 20th Century

It was in response to such conditions in America, and to avoid further conflict in the streets, that the "Progressive Era" (1900-1914) emerged prior to World War I. Social reformers and journalistic "muckrakers" abounded. New social policies and programs (private and public) were launched. The field of social work emerged. The concept of the "living wage" and State Mothers and Widows Pensions, and the Federal Children's Bureau (1912) all began to try to come to grips with poverty (Dumenil, 1993). As always happened in time of war, with World War I (1914-1918), poverty was forgotten as industry geared for war; millions of poor men left the work force to bear arms, and jobs became more plentiful at reasonable wages for older men and young women.

After the war, talk of prosperity dominated the 1920's with the promise of "a chicken in every pot". But poverty did not go away. It was real and it persisted because of an exploitive capitalism. States began to help the poor when society's private charitable efforts failed. In 1923, about 130,000 children were receiving meager aid through Mother's Pensions laws in 42 states. The Federal Children's Bureau (founded in 1912) estimated that 400,000 children needed such help. Some 85,000 poor persons still lived in 2,200 almshouses throughout America around 1925. It cost some $29 million to maintain them. Yet they were a very small group in the ranks of the poor. Relief was extended each year "…to hundreds of thousands of the indigent; and food, shelter, and clothing are extended through governments, state and local, to at least 276, 617 insane, to more than 42, 952 of the feebleminded in special institutions and to a large number of blind, crippled or otherwise handicapped citizens" (Kelso, 1929: 37). Yet poverty persisted even in the "prosperous" 1920's.

Then came the stock market crash in 1929, followed by "The Great Depression" of the 1930's. Millions (over 30% of the work force) were unemployed. Men stood on street corners selling apples for a nickel. Most stood in long soup lines waiting to get something to eat. Some were angry and there was talk of revolution in the air. In 1932, thousands of World War I veterans marched on Washington, D.C. to demand veteran's bonus or jobs. They came by rail, car or walked. They were the unemployed, the starving, the homeless, the desperate. The Federal Government responded to their pleas by calling out the Army to burn down their "shanty town" houses (called "Hooverville"), named after then-President Hoover, and drive them out of the city by force.

The state or local "poor laws" from early America remained virtually intact well into the 20th Century. By 1931, residency requirements to obtain help (private or public) were in effect. For example, residency was increased from one year (in most states) to five years in Maine, Massachusetts and New Jersey; seven years in New Hampshire and ten years in Rhode Island. Many states required dual residency - - both in the state and county for the destitute to receive any aid. It wasn't until 1969 in the *Shapiro vs. Thompson* case that the U.S. Supreme Court "struck down residency requirements as an arbitrary device that could be used to discriminate against given individuals" (Crouse, 1993: 2144). It ruled that such practices denied the poor equal protection of the law and interfered with their fundamental right of interstate travel.

For the first time in the history of the U.S., society began to realize that private charity and state agencies were simply unable to help the poor on the scope and scale needed. Therefore, intervention by the Federal Government was absolutely necessary to save the whole society from economic collapse. This was a turning point in our history in the conflict between the rich and the poor, to have the Federal Government help the poor and strengthen our economy and business.

During the 1930's, President Franklin Roosevelt promised the American people, especially the poor, a "New Deal". It started with the National Industrial Recovery Act in 1933. It regulated prices and wages and recognized the legal right of workers to form and join unions. It was declared unconstitutional in 1935 by a 5 to 4 vote of the Supreme Court. But new laws spawned new agencies such as the National Labor Relations Board (NLRB), the Works Progress

Administration (WPA), the Civilian Conservation Corps (CCC), the Agricultural Adjustment Administration (AAA), and the Public Works Administration (PWA). They were all designed to get poor Americans back to work and bolster the sagging economy. Most of all the "New Deal" gave hope that things could change. The WPA provided jobs for thousands of poor unemployed men and women. The CCC took thousands of poor young men out of the cities and put them in rural areas to conserve and restore the land (and avoided having hungry young mobs clustered in cities). The Social Security Act was passed in 1935. It not only provided retirement benefits for the elderly (starting in 1940) but established guidelines for state welfare programs of Aid to Families of Dependent Children, as well as other key welfare programs like Aid to the Blind. The Wagner Act in 1935 gave workers the legal right to unionize, through elections held by the NLRB. Unemployment compensation was set up to help laid-off workers and Workers Compensation was established by states to help workers injured or killed at work, and in 1938 a minimum wage law (Fair Labor Standards Act) became law. It also finally outlawed child labor in interstate commerce.

Then, as a new war engulfed us, our concern for the poor receded. During World War II (1941-1945), work was plentiful and reasonable wages prevailed, though frozen during most of the war. In 1946, the Federal Government committed itself, at least on paper, to provide jobs if need be to returning veterans and others. But the Employment Act of 1946 was not needed then. After the war, pent-up consumer demand had to be met and a baby boom, starting in the late Forties, propelled the U.S. into a period of prosperity never before experienced in history. These were the affluent 1950's, when John Kenneth Galbraith in his book *The Affluent Society*, (1958) asserted that poverty was pretty much a thing of the past in America. He was wrong.

In 1962, Michael Harrington shocked us by forcing us to look at *The Other America*. In that America dwelt "somewhere between 40 million and 50 million citizens of this land. They were poor. They still are" (1962: 9). Great masses of people were "invisible". It took too much effort by the mind and heart of Americans to see them. Yet society and the Federal government began to see them and do something about their plight. First, Congress passed a medical assistance plan (Medicaid) to help poor people and in 1965 (30 years after Social Security) established Medicare, a social insurance medical plan for people 65 and older. Also in 1965, the Federal Government launched a so-called "War on Poverty" under the command of the

Office of Economic Opportunity (OEO). Billions of dollars were poured into the programs yet it was not quite clear who the enemy was in this war (or skirmish). At any rate, programs were started such as the Neighborhood Youth Corps, the Job Corps, Head Start for children, and Community Action Programs. Much of the money never quite got down to the poor masses but it did give some temporary jobs to middle-class and a few poor people.

During the '60's, the official poverty rate fell sharply, from 22.2% of the population in 1960 to 12.8% in 1968 (Sklar, 2000: D-5). Today (2000 figures) the poverty percentage rate (11.3%) is a bit lower than in 1968, but is far worse in the number of people affected (31 million) (Statistical Abstract of the United States: 2002, 2001: 441). Eventually in the late '60's, our society got bogged down in the mire of an unpopular war in Vietnam, in Asia, costing us about $30 billion a year and thousands of lives. Once again, a war diverted our attention away from the poor. The war in Vietnam killed the "War on Poverty". Most of its programs and promises came to an end in the early 1970's as a new Administration, Richard Nixon's, came into power in Washington, D.C.

In January, 1973, House resolution #50 called for national policies to guarantee a job to anyone who needed one. In 1975, the Federal Government started funding public jobs under the Comprehensive Employment and Training Act (CETA). It spent billions of dollars to do so, without too much success for the poor. It often trained them for jobs that were not available.

In the mid-1970's our society became immersed in a new economic situation, as we entered our third century as a nation. Inflation, an increase in the cost of living, was rampant and reached 8 to 12% a year. The price of gasoline, for example, increased from about 30 cents a gallon in 1970 to over $ 1.30 a gallon by 1974 when Middle Eastern countries began to control the production, and set the price, for imported oil into the U.S. Unemployment was still high, and living standards of some middle-class Americans began to slip downward. Under such circumstances, most working people were not too worried about poor families, except for the added taxes that may have cost them. As middle-class families and elderly struggled to make ends meet, they did not have too much time to think about social issues such as poverty. They had their own personal "poverty" problems to handle. To maintain or retain their standard of living, millions of middle-class women joined the work force in larger numbers than ever before in our history. A new era was being born.

During the 1980's, the Regan Administration cut public welfare and assistance programs for the poor that had been set up in 1935. Military spending increased three-fold. Much less attention was given to our domestic poor while more and more attention was given to the "Cold War" with Russia and China and to "brush-fire" wars in the world. It was estimated that one-half of the increase in poverty in the 1980's was due to the Regan budget cuts (Rosenbaum, 1984). This reluctance for government, Federal or State, to adequately support the poor continues to the present time. For example, only 50% of the children living in poverty receive any welfare, down from 80% in the early 1970's (DeParle, 1992). Today it's even less than half.

In 1988, the Family Support Act was passed. It was an attempt to transform welfare from an income-maintenance system to one stressing education, training and job assistance. It was called "work-fare" and represented a societal change from viewing and receiving welfare as a "right" to a "privilege". It was an attempt to break the cycle of long-term welfare dependence. The law provided for extending welfare to *both* parents who were unemployed, so that fathers wouldn't leave their families so they would be eligible for welfare, as in the past. Greater enforcement of child-support payments took place so that some families wouldn't have to go on welfare (Sullivan and Thompson, 1994: 187).

Although "workfare" was met with severe criticism as "a way of throwing the poor into the streets" its initial results were to reduce the welfare rolls. Many states reduced their welfare members by more than 50%; Wisconsin by 75%. Overall in just five years our society's welfare rolls dropped 44% to their lowest level in 30 years (Associated Press, 1999; DeParle, 1999). This reduction occurred during the longest boom period in the U.S. economic history. So we don't know how many people will return to welfare when the next "bust" hits our economy (Henslin, 2000).

In spite of the public's attitudes toward the "unworthy" poor and the "freeloaders" on welfare, Federal, State and local welfare programs have reduced potential poverty significantly. For example, in 1996, 57.5 million people (12.5 % of our population) *would have been poor* if government benefits (i.e. "transfer payments") were not a part of their income. With them, poverty figures dropped by nearly a half, to 30.5 million people (or 11.5 % of Americans). This means government benefits lifted 27 million people out of *potential poverty*. This is particularly true of the elderly(Center on Budget and Policy Priorities, 1998).

In 1996, the most momentous change in the 60 year program of Aid to Families of Dependent Children took place. It was replaced by Temporary Aid to Needy Families (TANF), with the emphasis on "temporary". This was because of a new Federal law, "The Personal Responsibility and Work Opportunity Act (PRWOA). President Clinton, when first elected in 1992, promised to change welfare as we know it" (Kornblum and Julian, 1998: 252). No longer would being destitute, homeless or hungry guarantee anyone a welfare check. It turned the entire welfare program over to the states, along with "block grants" to the states, who, (within federal guidelines) could experiment with harsher rules. This new law affected numerous public assistance programs.

Under the new law in 1996, after two consecutive years of receiving cash aid, recipients are required to work at least 20 hours per week or participate in a state-approved work program. Going to school to earn a degree doesn't count. A lifetime limit of five years is set for families receiving benefits. Able-bodied recipients, ages 18 to 50, and without dependents have a two-year limit. States are allowed to exempt 20% of their caseloads from these limits (Mooney, Knox and Schacht, 2000). To qualify for TANF benefits, unwed mothers under the age of 18 are required to live in an adult-supervised environment (usually with their parents) and to receive education and job training. Immigrants (with few exceptions) are not eligible to receive benefits.

Figure 9-1 Number of Families on Welfare Cut in Half (1996-2000).

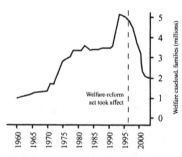

Source: Statistical Abstract of the of the U.S. : 2001.

Welfare "reform" in 1996 resulted in cutbacks in federal food assistance programs, especially the food stamp program. Families with children lost an average of 13 percent of their food stamp benefits by 2002. William Julius Wilson, a prominent urban sociologist asked: "Where are the jobs coming from? With a dozen or more applicants for each low-skilled job during a period of *low* employment, what is the welfare person to do when his or her time limit is up? For this "reform" to succeed it will need large expenditures of money for child care, training and creation of private and public service jobs. Those expecting such welfare reform to reduce welfare costs are in for a big surprise" (Wilson, 1996) Yet, though costs might not have gone down much the number of families on welfare have been almost cut in half, as Figure 9-1 shows.

As we enter the 21st Century such a regressive reform only suggests that in the richest nation in the world, the rich and middle-class still resent having to pay taxes to help their brothers and sisters and children in desperate need. Many people still feel that most of the poor are unworthy of help and besides "they are not their brothers (or sisters) keepers."

The Economic Social Institution and 20th Century Poverty

The U.S. since its beginning always had social classes - - groups of people who occupy basically different rungs on the economic and social status ladder. Where people are born on this ladder effects their "life chances" in respect to life expectancy, education, occupation, health, wealth and power. The economy involves not only money, jobs and social status; it is the entire social institution that produces and distributes goods and services. How this social institution operates, impacts upon every individual, group and community in the U.S., especially the poor.

Historically our economy always has gone through periods of "boom" or "bust", prosperity or scarcity, rise or decline (Henslin, 2000). These cycles are inherent in any economy, especially capitalistic ones like ours. For example, during periods of prosperity we have experienced the last nine or ten years (1991-2001), college students find it easier to get the job they want than during periods of decline or recession, as in the 1980's. Obviously, during "busts", poverty often becomes worse; in periods of prosperity jobs are easier for the poor to get. They often don't get out of poverty, or do as well as the rich or upper middle class. Even during economic prosperity, poverty persists (Sklar, 2000: D-1).

The poor have always been with us, but we have not always welcomed them with open arms or hearts. For many years in America, poverty was so common we just assumed not much could be done to help - - and not much was done. Besides, society was not responsible for an individual's tough luck or laziness; but as attitudes changed both society and government got more involved in fighting poverty. Our national interest and concern in the issue have gone up and down like a yo-yo. As noted earlier, in the 19th Century meager local help was given, via almshouses and private charity groups. Groups to improve the condition of the poor and Charity Organization Societies were formed in our large eastern and mid-western cities. During the Progressive Era (1900-1914) of the early 20th Century, we worried about the poor and tried to help them. During World War I (1914-1918) the economy picked up and many poor men were in the Army. In the 1920's there would be a "chicken in every pot" and "the beginning of the end of poverty", according to the then-President of the U.S. In the 1930's when the Great Depression hit, most people worried about poverty in a very personal way. The 1940's found us at war again or at work. In the 1950's we achieved our "affluent society" but in the 1960's we rediscovered poverty, thanks to Michael Harrington's book *The Other America* (1962). In 1964 we launched a War on Poverty (or was it a skirmish?). In the 1970's we had no time to worry about the poor - - we were too busy trying to make ends meet in our inflated, job-scarce economy (McVeigh and Shostak, 1978: 237). In the 1980's, the Federal Government began to cut the welfare budget. In the 1990's government insisted that poor people (especially women with children) get off welfare and begin to work, no matter what. By 2003, we still had about 11% of our population living in poverty and 15.5 % (ll million) of our children (Statistical Abstract of U.S.: 2002; 2001: 441). We still haven't solved the poverty problem because income and wealth in America is not distributed evenly.

Maldistribution of Income and Wealth in the U.S.

Wealth or poverty produces social inequality. We know that all Americans, since the start of our society to today, are not equal economically or socially. For example, the life chances of a janitor's daughter differ immensely from those of a son born to a rich corporate executive. Structural inequality is built into our economy and other social institutions. This is seen most sharply in the inequality of income and wealth in America. It has always existed historically in the U.S. and in the world. There is no reason to think that such inequality will not continue and persist in the future. Let's look at what has happened over time in the U.S. to see the gap between the rich and the poor - - between prosperity and poverty overall.

The first attempt to estimate (roughly) the distribution of income and wealth in the U.S. was made by Charles B. Spahr in 1896 (based on 1890 data) (Spahr: 1896). Spahr's final conclusion about the distribution of property in the U.S. is as follows:

> Less than half the families in America are propertyless, nevertheless, seven-eighths of the families hold but one-eighth of the national wealth, while one percent of the families hold more than the remaining ninety-nine (69, as quoted in Parmelle, 1916: 63).

As for the distribution of income alone, Spahr writes:

> One percent of our families receive nearly one-fourth of the national income, while fifty percent receive barely one-fifth. One-eighth of the families in America receive more than half of the aggregate income, and the richest one percent receive a larger income than the poorest fifty percent. (87-92: 120 as quoted in Parmelee, 1916: 64).

In 1904, the year Robert Hunter published his classic book *Poverty*, the U.S. Bureau of Labor published its annual report for 1903, dealing with the cost of living and retail prices for food (U.S. Commission of Labor for the Year, 1903). The report was based on a survey of 25,440 families in 33 states of workers earning less than $1,200 in 1901. The report concluded: "...the total income per family was $749.50...and the total expenditure per family was $699.24" (1903: 157). This study excluded the unemployed and unemployable, so the figures were conservatively high (Parmelle, 1916: 66).

Another study (by F.H. Streightoff) reported income for 1904. On the basis of data from a variety of sources, he estimated the distribution of incomes in the U.S. primarily from labor. Of the 19.6 million males employed in 1904, 12.7 million earned under $600 yearly (i.e. under $12 a week); 5.3 million from $600 to under $1,000 ($12 to under $20 weekly) and 1.6 million earned $1,000 or more yearly. Hence, 65% of working people in 1904 earned under $600 a year. Based on these figures, the overwhelming majority of working people were poor or near poor (Streightoff, 1912).

In 1905, the U.S. Census Bureau's Census of Manufacturers had data on wages of workers in manufacturing. Over 3 million workers were covered (80% were men, the rest women and children). It found that overall *weekly* earnings in 1904 were $10.06; men earned $11.16, women $6.17 and children $3.46 (U.S. Census Bureau, 1905: 643).

A later study of wages in the Northeast from 1908-1910, by Scott Nearing (1911) concluded that "...average wages in all industries and for employees, range from $500 to $600. In short, the range is from an average *daily* wage for the year of $1.50 to $2" (1911: 72-3).

In the U.S. Census reports of 1910 some general statistics (for 1909) were used by Maurice Parmelle to make a rough estimate of wages paid to workers in manufacturing in 1910. The average weekly wage was not quite $10. The 1905 Census of Manufacturers found that the average weekly wage (in 1904) was $10.06. Parmelle observed that "...this seems to indicate that wages were decreasing between 1904 and 1909" (1916: 71).

Because of seasonal employment, the Census Bureau didn't compute numbers employed or wages paid in agriculture. The U.S. Department of Agriculture issued a bulletin in 1912 showing that wages in agriculture were much lower than in mining or manufacturing (U.S. Bureau of Statistics, 1912). It revealed that "...outdoor farm labor by the day, in harvest work averaged $ 1.71 in 1909, outdoor farm labor with board averaged $1.43 a day, while the average wage rate per month for outdoor farm labor, hired by the *year*, without board, was $25.46 in 1909" (Parmelee, 1916: 71). These men were the poorest of the poor in the working class at that time.

Data in the 1910 Census indicated that the "...very large class of workers receive perhaps sixty percent of the national income, while a very small class of property owners receive perhaps as much as forty percent (Parmelee, 1916: 74). Of greater importance, according to Parmelee, were figures by G.P. Watkins that revealed the fact that wealth in the U.S. was rapidly becoming more and more concentrated in a few hands (Watkins, 1907). This trend was shown by Census data. They indicated:

> During the six decades from 1849 to 1909 the amount paid in wages in manufacturing increased 14 fold while the value added by manufacturing increased by 18 times. The amount of capital invested in these industries during these six decades increased by about 34 times (Parmelee, 1916: 75)

This was a further indicator of the trend toward concentration of wealth.

The Annual Report of the U.S. Commission of Internal Revenue in 1914 reported the Federal Tax returns for 1913 (the *first* year Federal Income taxes were collected). It revealed that 5,214 individuals reported incomes of over $50,000 a year (1914). These people would have been considered near-millionaires in 1913. A book in England, *Riches and Poverty* revealed that in 1908 "...one-half of the entire income of the United Kingdom is enjoyed by about 12 percent of its population" and "more than one-third of the entire income of the United Kingdom is enjoyed by less than one-thirtieth (1/30th) of its people" (Chiozza Money, 1911: 47-8). The maldistribution of income was probably just as unequal in America about that time in history. W.I. King in 1915 showed that over half of all income in the U.S. came from ownership of property in the form of profits, rent and interest collected (1915: 158-60).

Different family budgets for the poor, starting with Booth and Rountree in 19th Century England have been constructed. Using 60 such budgets for working families in the U.S., computed by government or private agencies, Oscar Ornati at the New School for Social Research showed three different amounts of income needed from 1905 to 1960 to be defined as poor. These three levels of poverty were: "Minimal Subsistence", "Minimum Adequacy" and "Minimum Comfort" (1966: 12). For "minimum comfort"

"...a poor family would have needed (in constant 1960 dollars) about $3,200 in 1915, the same in 1923, $3,700 in 1935, $4,000 by 1940, $4,700 by 1945 and $5,700 by 1960. Due to maldistribution of wealth and income during these years (and even today) the poor need more and more money over time to obtain a "minimum comfort" of living. An index of unskilled male labor wages since the early 1900's have been equal to the "minimum subsistence" level of poverty from 1900 to 1935. By 1960, men's low wages exceeded the "minimum subsistence: level but did not equal the "minimum adequacy" level of poverty (Ornati, 1966: 15).

By the late 1940's more accurate calculations of national income by fifths (quintiles) shed new light on maldistribution of income in the U.S. In 1935-36 the poorest fifth (20%) of families and unattached individuals, had 4.1% of all income while the richest fifth had 51.7%. In 1953, the lowest fifth had 4.9% of all income and the highest fifth had 44.7%. In Table 9-1 appears Ornati's chart showing the distribution of income from 1935-1959, with percent changes involved between selected years.

Table 9-1
Distribution of Family Personal Income, 1935-59
(Families and Unattached Individuals)

Per Cent of Income								Per Cent Changes		
1935/36	1941	1947	1950	1953	1955	1958	1959	1935-53	1953-59	1935/36-59
Total										
100.0	100.0	100.0	100.0	100.0	100.0	100.00	100.0	-- --	-- --	-- --
Lowest Fifth										
4.1	4.1	5.0	4.8	4.9	4.8	4.6	4.5	+19	-8	+9.7
Second Fifth										
9.2	9.5	11.0	10.9	11.3	11.3	10.9	10.9	+23	-3.25	+18
Third Fifth										
14.1	15.3	6.0	16.1	6.6	16.4	16.2	16.2	+18	-2.4	+14.9
Fourth Fifth										
20.9	22.3	22.0	22.1	22.5	22.3	22.7	22.7	+7.6	+2.2	+8.6
Highest Fifth										
51.7	48.8	46.0	46.1	44.7	45.2	45.6	45.7	-13.5	+2.2	-11.6
Top 5 per cent										
26.5	24.0	20.9	21.4	19.9	20.3	19.9	19.9	-25	no change	-25

Source: Statistical Abstract of the United States, 1961; Ornati, 1966: 155.

Looking at the maldistribution of income by fifths in more recent years, the situation has gotten worse for the poor. Income distribution today is much worse than it was during the 1940's and 1950's. As you can see from Ornati's chart, in 1947 the lowest fifth had obtained 5% of all national income (its highest level ever reached) and the richest fifth had 46% in that year and 44.7% by 1953 (Ornati, 1966: 155; Statistical Abstract of U.S., 1961). Recently, James Henslin reports that "...despite numerous anti-poverty programs, income inequality today is greater than it was in the 1940's" (2002: 220).

From 1977 to 1988, according to the Congressional Budget Office, the income of the richest one percent in America increased by 120% while the incomes of the poorest fifth decreased by 10%. This was a time of tax breaks for the rich and against the poor (De Parle, 1991: E-2). The working class also got poorer as jobs in manufacturing declined and jobs in lower-paying services increased. The middle class stayed about the same, so it also lost ground to the rich (Phillips, 1990).

During the 1980's, the U.S. Census revealed that child poverty grew by more than 20%. Racial minority children suffered the most. Among the smallest children, under 6, the proportion living in poverty rose 12% from 1979 to 1996, based on a study by the Columbia University School of Public Health (The Millenium Breach, 1998:2).

The New York Times reported that the child poverty rate in the U.S. is *four times* the average of Western European countries (Bradsher, 1995: A-1).

In 1979, average family income among the richest 5% was more than 10 times that in the poorest fifth. A decade later (1989), that ratio had increased to nearly 16 to 1; by 1999 it stood at 19 to 1 (almost *double* that of the 1979 average). This is the biggest gap between the rich and the poor since the Census Bureau began keeping track of them in 1947 (Lardner, 2000: 40). In the 1940's the lowest fifth got 5.4% of all income; today it is down to 3.6% (Henslin, 2000: 220; Lardner, 2000: 43). In the 1940's, the richest fifth got about 41%; today it is up to 49.2%. In just the last 20 years, the ratio of chief executive officers (CEO's) pay at the 365 largest U.S. corporations, compared with the average non-management workers pay, has jumped over 16 fold. In 1980 the ratio of CEO's to workers pay was 42 to 1; today it is projected to be 691 to 1 (Lardner, 2000: 42). In Europe and Japan the ratio is much less.

Our society, via government programs and policies, made more progress in the 1960's in reducing the poverty rate than during the prosperous 1990's. During the 1960's the poverty rate fell sharply, from 22.2 percent of our population in 1960 to 12.8 % in 1968. During the 1990's it fell only slightly, from 13 ½ % in 1990 to 12.7 in 1998, about where it was in 1968 (Sklar, 2000: D-1) By 2000, about 11.3% of the population lived below the poverty line (Holmes, 2000: A-12). Yet racially, only 9 ½% of whites were poor, whereas 22% of the Blacks and Hispanics were poor, twice as high as whites (Statistical Abstract of U.S.: 2002, 2001: 441).

We still have a long way to go in the 21st Century to reduce the maldistribution of income and wealth, and at the same time reduce significantly our poverty rate in the U.S.

Conflicts Due to Unemployment and Underemployment

The early industrial revolution added to all the labor-management conflict in the workplace by spawning persistent unemployment and underemployment as a social issue. This fact led one economic historian, Harold Falkner, to refer to unemployment under Capitalism as "technological unemployment". More money or capital is put back into the business for new technology, so fewer workers are needed. He goes on to observe that "technological unemployment" has been more or less continuous since the Industrial Revolution" (1954: 142). The early skilled trade unions that were formed in the 1790's were effectively destroyed by a serious economic depression in 1819. In 1837, a national depression (or "Panic") hit, leading to widespread unemployment among workers. "Trade and commerce dried up, manufacturing sharply declined, and business stagnated in the formerly prosperous towns and cities of both the Atlantic seaboard and the west", one labor historian wrote. (Dulles, 1960: 71). In the 1840's and 1850's (especially 1857), there were periods of depression and high unemployment. But with the Westward Expansion and the Civil War (1861-1865) unemployed workers could find work (for a time).

But the "panic" of 1873 made it clear that unemployment/underemployment were crucial social problems that could no longer be ignored. There were disorders and riots of workers who wanted steady work. In New York, Chicago, Boston, Cincinnati, and Omaha, crowds of unemployed workers gathered in mass demonstrations to protest their lack of work. Unemployment riots and violence broke out in the coal fields of eastern Pennsylvania, led by the miners union and the "Molly Maguires". Unemployment in a Gesellschaft industrialized factory system was far more critical than it had been in a less complex, smaller Gemeinschaft farming society of the first half of the Nineteenth Century and before. In a Gesellschaft society you couldn't grow crops on a paved road or sidewalk in the middle of a large city.

In 1877, the dangers of unemployment became clear. As business slumped, employers laid off workers and cut wages of those employed. This led to a whole rash of strikes by unions, especially by the Knights of Labor in the railroad industry. Federal troops and State militia had to be sent into Baltimore, Pittsburgh, Martinsburg, West Virginia, and other cities to quell the riots. Many other protests and riots against unemployment, hours of work, and low wages continued in the 1880's. So many strikes, protests and demonstrations by workers occurred during the 1870's and 1880's that the period was called "The Great Upheaval" (Dulles, 1960: 114). As never before, the nation and the rich started to realize the explosive force in the great masses of industrial workers who didn't benefit from changing technology, as did the corporate giants. Workers began to sense that more extensive and larger union organizations were needed to insure decent employment, wages, hours, and working conditions. They worked in a technological system that treated the worker as a replaceable part who could be thrown on the scrap heap when no longer needed. So workers tried to unionize - - with not too much success at first. Bloody conflicts and clashes between workers and company police took place at Homestead, Pennsylvania (steel industry); Pullman,

Illinois (railroad); Coer d'Alene, Idaho (metal miners); and Ludlow, Colorado (copper miners) when they tried to unionize and strike. The "army of unemployed" in the early 1890's swelled to some three million, about 20% of the workforce at that time. Almost three-quarters of a million workers were out on strike (Dulles, 1960: 171).

What was true of Nineteenth Century unemployment and worker unionization proved to be true also for the Twentieth Century. As before, a war helped to improve the employment situation. Just as the Civil War in the early 1860's drained millions of men from the workforce and required war production, so did the First World War (1914-1918). Wages increased and more women and Blacks appeared in industry in larger numbers. But after the War was over, another economic depression hit the society in 1920 and 1921. In 1921, over five million workers were without jobs. Because of the war, technological changes affected industry. New machinery and labor-saving devices in road construction, textiles, the tire industry, and electrical equipment cut the labor needed anywhere from 25% to 60% (Dulles, 1960: 244). There was persistent unemployment throughout the 1920's - - ranging from 10 to 13% of all workers. At least two million workers were out of work in prosperous 1928. But then the "Great Depression" of the 1930's struck. Over fifteen million workers found themselves on the streets - - selling apples at corner stands, lining up for free soup and bread. About 1/3rd of the workforce was unemployed. Though the entire country suffered, the workers (as usual) felt the most pain and were hurt by unemployment. Through a series of new Federal programs and agencies, our society began to make our way out of the Great Depression. But by the end of the 1930's, millions were still out or work. It took another war (World War II – 1939-1945) to rescue our economic system from chronic unemployment.

Since mass unemployment was expected after World War II, Congress considered a bill called "The Full Employment Act of 1945". It committed the Federal government to "...provide such volume of Federal investment and expenditures as may be needed...to assure continuing full employment" (Press Associates, 1976: 5). Labor unions, liberals, church and civic groups backed the bill. Big business was against it, with one spokesman arguing that "...depressions are inevitable under the free enterprise system" (Press Associates, 1976: 5). Before it was passed in 1946, the word "full" employment was dropped. The Employment Act of 1946 called for a Federal policy and responsibility "to promote maximum employment, production and purchasing power." This law has been the rationale for the Federal

Government job-creating bills today, and has led to the concept that Government should be "the employer of last resort" when the private sector cannot provide jobs for people. Yet unemployment persists. In mid-2003 nearly 9 million people were out of work, or about 6% of the civilian work force (Altman, 2003: A1 & C14).

Figure 9-2: The Unemployment Picture in Mid-2003

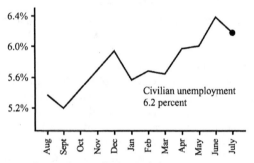

Source: Bureau of Labor Statistics.

Figure 9-3: The Employment Picture in Mid-2003

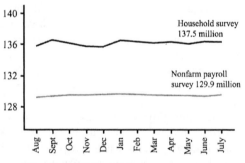

Source: Bureau of Labor Statistics.

Source (Both Figures): U.S. Bureau of Labor Statistics. July, 2, 2003

Yet anywhere from 130 to 137 million people were working in the U.S. From July, 2000, to July, 2003 manufacturing jobs fell "…from 17.3 million to 14.5 million - - a loss of almost one job in six" or almost 3 million jobs (Broder, 2003: A-17). And these were for the most part good paying jobs, averaging $54,000 a year. Many blame the loss of U.S. jobs on "free trade" agreements we have signed with Mexico and other foreign countries. Today the Federal government rather than creating jobs uses tax cuts, especially for the rich, to try to "jump-start" the economy. This is what it did in 2002 and 2003. So unemployment remains a social problem today.

Safety and Health Conditions: The Last Hundred Years

Besides unemployment, job dissatisfaction, alienation, anger and violence at work, the last major social issue today, faced by workers and their families, are the dangerous physical and health conditions under which many workers must labor everyday. Dangerous health and safety conditions are, and were always, a way of life (and death) for far too many workers in the U.S. To employers it costs money to make work safe. To employees it is often a matter of life and death - - theirs. Corporations have learned it is cheaper to have a dangerous work environment than a safe one.

As pointed out earlier, in this chapter, the workplace was always "hazardous to your health", as well as life and limb. The situation was so critical that states at the turn of the 20th Century began to pass workers' compensation laws to give killed or seriously injured workers, or their families, some monetary compensation. The first such law was passed in Maryland in 1902, but the U.S. Supreme Court promptly declared it unconstitutional. It did not reverse its decision until 1917. Once legal, by 1934, all but four southern states had adopted worker compensation laws. The intensity of the accident and injury problem in industry in the 1930's can be seen "by the annual number of work-related accidents estimated by Dr. I..M. Rubeniow: 30,000 men were killed; 74,777 suffered dismemberments of one or more parts of the body; 3,540 were permanently disabled; 78,608 suffered partial permanent disability; 6,888 were disabled for over six months"; and three million more were disabled for less than six months (Minton and Stuart, 1937: 65). Moreover, workers received hardly any protection against occupational diseases. In addition, safety legislation, varying widely from state to state, failed because of few safety inspections and improper or corrupt methods of enforcement. Compensation laws gave meager payments to injured workers and excluded many categories of workers.

Environmental pollution is real to workers. Many work and live in a polluted workplace every day. Pittsburgh Corning Corporation shut down its asbestos insulation plant in Tyler, Texas. A government survey showed ventilation was poor and asbestos fibers were being inhaled by the workers. Nearly half of the long-time workers had symptoms of asbestosis (scarring of the lungs from inhaling asbestos fibers). It is "a significant illness by almost any standard, in that it is irreversible, untreatable, often disabling, and frequently fatal" (Brodeur, 1974: 5). No medical follow-up had been done on the 832 men who worked at the plant over the years. A class action law suit for $100 million was brought against the company for exposing employees to asbestos fibers "in extremely dangerous concentrations" causing them to suffer from asbestosis and/or lung cancer and other diseases. The workers won the case.

Workers face pollution daily (Credit: Joseph Elliott)

Dr. Nicholas Ashford of MIT, after a two-year study of industries, reported that "...a significant proportion of heart disease, cancer and respiratory disease may stem from the industrial process" (Dembart, 1976: 23). This includes white-collar workers, and not just blue-collar workers. Job-related diseases have only recently become a social issue and begun to receive public attention in the 1970's. But workers have known about their adverse effects for years, and so have the companies.

Workers have risked their lives in coal mining for years. In 1993, ten miners died in a methane gas explosion at a coal mine in Kentucky. The company pleaded guilty to "a pattern of safety misconduct" that included "falsifying reports of methane levels and requiring miners to work under unsupported roofs" (Reiman, 2003: 288). The U.S. Mining Enforcement and Safety Administration had cited the mine many times for safety violations. The charge by the government against the company said that it "...repeatedly exposed the mine's work crews to danger and that such conditions were frequently concealed from Federal inspectors responsible for enforcing the mine safety act" (Reiman, 2003: 289). "Why do ten dead miners amount to a 'disaster' and six dead suburbanites killed the same day a 'mass murder'," one sociologist asks (Reiman, 1994: 294). Some work-related injuries and deaths could be prevented if Federal and State governments criminally prosecuted corporations when workers die because of inadequate safety measures. Instead the mine company only paid a fine of $3.75 million to the government. Clearly, profits take priority over the health and safety of workers, with the tacit approval or apathy of the government (Lauer, 1998).

We now know, because of the deaths of three workers at the B.F. Goodrich Company plant in Louisville, Kentucky, that vinyl chloride (used in the plastics and chemicals industries) is dangerous to workers' health. It causes liver cancer. We learned that toxic chemicals used in making Kepone , an ingredient in ant poison, can poison workers, too. After worker complaints, state health officials shut down the Kepone plant at Hopewell, Virginia, when it was evident that workers' lives were at stake. The real danger here, however, is often hidden. It may take ten or twenty years for a chemical to cause the death of a worker. It is less dramatic than a worker losing his arm or leg. But the danger is still quite real for millions of workers and their families in America. The Annual Report of the President's Council on Environmental Quality emphasized that exposure to cancer-causing substances at work was one of the "biggest environmental threats" ("Environment Blamed for 60% of Cancer", 1976: 7).

Studies revealed that chemicals, lead, x-ray exposure, and other work-related materials are especially harmful to pregnant women. Women who work in beauty parlors, factories, and hospitals run a special risk of losing their babies or having babies with birth defects. Not only that, but women and their babies may be contaminated by the materials a man works with on his job. For example, a continuing study of the families of 354 asbestos workers in Patterson, New Jersey, revealed that 35 percent of the wives and children showed up with lung problems similar to those of the men who worked with asbestos. Four people died from it (Sullivan, 1976: D-8).

Another study by five government scientists of a Pottstown, Pennsylvania,plant showed that the wives of workers who came in contact with vinyl chloride had twice as many miscarriages and still births as wives of workers who didn't work around the material (Burnham, 1976: 42).

Workers run hidden health hazards, even in an office. Researchers at Mt. Sinai School of Medicine in New York, found high levels of asbestos fibers (from fireproofing materials) in office buildings in New York, Boston, San Francisco, Berkeley, and Chicago. Dr. William Nicholson, who directed the research study, said the levels of asbestos are "dangerously high" in some cases (Sullivan, 1976: D-8).

Not just chemicals, but noise and other unsafe physical work conditions affect the health of millions of workers. Many Americans work in places noisy enough to impair their hearing. For protection of public health and people's hearing, the Environmental Protection Agency's "Levels Document" of goals in industry calls for a daily average sound level of 70 decibels. Yet many people work every day in noise well above that level (Weaver, 1976: 160). One Federal law that has been relatively effective is the Occupational Safety and Health Act of 1970. The Occupational Safety and Health Administration (OSHA) was created by Congress "to ensure safe and healthful workplaces for all Americans giving OSHA the power to set safety and health guidelines, inspect workplaces and help employers" (Herzog and Pflieger, 1996: A-1 & A-4). Around 2,100 inspectors work with investigators, labor unions, engineers and doctors to set up and enforce safety standards (OSHA, 1996). Overall, the workplace death rate has been cut three-fold since 1970. In 1970, 13,800 workers lost their lives on the job compared with 4,800 in 1996 (Statistical Abstract of U.S.: 1998: 441) but rose to 5, 915 in 2000 (Statistical Abstract of U.S. 2002, 2001: 80). The death rate was 18 per 100,000 workers in 1970, but fell to four per 100,000 in 1996 and 2.4 in 2000. The occupational injury and illness rates (per 100 full-time workers) fell from 11.0 in 1973 to 7.4 in 1996 (Conway and Swenson, 1998: 37). Nevertheless, almost 4 million workers suffered disabling injuries in 1996 and 2000 (Statistical Abstract of U.S.: 2002, 2001: 408-09).

Yet, politically, OSHA has been attacked by both labor and management. Organized labor says OSHA needs more staffing, money and enforcement power to improve safety and health of workers. Management, business lobbying groups and foes in Congress want less regulation and control of business by OSHA. So OSHA is caught in the middle with their staff and budget being cut in recent years. This has affected the number of inspections OSHA is able to make out of the millions of businesses in the U.S. For example, in 1994, OSHA made 42, 542 inspections nationally. In 1995, it made less than 29,000 (Herzog and Pflieger, 1996: A-4). Today, with more cutbacks in its budget, it is even less.

So you can see that although the results of OSHA are impressive in spite of limited resources, accidents and deaths at the workplace persist. As long as the issue remains a civil rather than a criminal offense, work hazards will continue to put many workers at an unnecessary high risk of death and serious injury.

So the capitalistic economic institution, by its very structure and organization, produces excessive wealth for a few, poverty for many and consistent technological change, causing continual unemployment and unsafe, dangerous working conditions. Yet, the standard of living in America is better for the majority of people compared with most other societies in the world.

Critical Thinking Questions

1. Have you ever held a job (full or part-time) where you became to angry you felt like punching someone out, as described in Chapter 9? What did you eventually do about your anger on that job? What did you learn about work life from that work experience?

2. Did you ever work a job (full or part-time) where you were concerned about your safety or health on the job? What, if anything, did you do about the situation?

3. Since poverty has been in our society since its founding in 1776, do you believe or think we will ever solve poverty as a social problem? Why or why not? Give reasons for your position.

44. It's obvious historically that most people are better off financially than at the turn of the 20th Century (1900). What kind of progress, if any, do you envision in the U.S. distribution of wealth by 2020? What in your opinion would cause a fairer, or less fair, distribution of wealth than it is today?

5. Have you ever been laid-off or fired from a job? Did you have your family of origin bale you out? If you didn't have your family's help, how did you feel when you were unemployed? What did it teach you about our economic system in the U.S.?

Bibliography

Altman, Daniel. "Job Losses in July Add to Mixed Signs on the Economy". *New York Times.* (August 2, 2003): A-1 & C-14.

Associated Press. "Clinton Will Announce Welfare Rolls are at Their Lowest Level in 30 Years". *Wall Street Journal* (January 25, 1999): 1.

Bellamy, Edward. *Looking Backward*: 2000-1887. New York: Signet Classic. The American Library, 1888; 1960.

Booth, Charles. *Life and Labour of the People in London*: 1891-1903. London: Macmillan & Company, 1969.

Bradsher, Keith. "Gap in Wealth in U.S. Called Widest in West". *New York Times* (April 7, 1995): A-1.

Broder, David S. "Loss of Jobs Due to Free Trade Can't Be Ignored". *Morning Call.* (August 31, 2003): A-17.

Brodeur, Paul. *Expendable Americans.* New York: Viking, 1974.

Burnham, David. "Rise in Birth Defects Laid to Job Hazards". *New York Times* (March 14, 1976): 42.

Cayton, Mary K., Elliot J. Gorn and Peter W. Williams, eds. *Encyclopedia of Social History, 1-3.* New York: Charles Scribners Sons, 1993.

Center on Budget and Policy Priorities. Strengths of the Safety Net: How the EITC, Social Security, and other Government Programs Affect Poverty. http//www.cbpp.org/snd98-rep.htm (September 28, 1998).

Chiozza Money, L.G. Riches and Poverty (10th ed.), London: Griffin Bohn and Company, 1911.

Cleghorn, Sarah N. The Conning Tower. New York: New York Tribune, 1919.

Conway, Hugh and Jens Swenson. "Occupational Injury and Illness Rates, 1992-96: Why They Fell". *Monthly Labor Review*, 121 (November, 1998): 36-42.

Cornell, George. "Partner of Poor: Yule Joy Clouded by Mass Starvation". *Allentown Evening Call-Chronicle* (December 17, 1974): 1-2.

Coser, Lewis. *Men of Ideas: A Sociologist's View.* New York: *Free Press,* 1965.

Crouse, Joan M. "Transients, Migrants and the Homeless". Pp. 2134-56 in *Encyclopedia of American Social History, III*, edited by Mary Cayton, Elliott Gorn and Peter Williams. New York: Charles Scribners Sons, 1993.

David, Allan and Mark Haller. *The Peoples of Philadelphia: A History of Ethnic Groups and Lower-Class Life, 1790-1940.* Philadelphia: Temple University Press, 1973.

Dembart, Lee. "Health Problems Traced to Jobs". *New York Times* (March 17, 1976): 23.

DeParle, Jason. "Richer Rich, Poorer Poor, and the Lather Green Book." *New York Times* (May 26, 1992): E-2.

———. "Wisconsin's Welfare Plan Justifies Hopes and Some Fear." *New York Times* (January 15, 1999): 3.

De Schweinitz, Karl. *England's Road to Social Security.* New York: A.S. Barnes, 1943.

Dulles, Foster Rhea. *Labor in America.* New York: Thomas Y. Crowell Company, 1960.

Dumenil, Lynn. "The Progressive Era Through the 1920's". Pp. 173-82 in the *Encyclopedia of American Social History,* edited by Mary Cayton, Elliott Gorn and Peter Williams. New York: Charles Scribners Sons, 1993.

"Environment Blamed for 60% of Cancer". *Philadelphia Evening Bulletin.* (February 27, 1976): 7.

Falkner, Harold U. *American Economic History.* 7th ed. New York: Harper & Brothers, 1954.

Fite, Emerson. *Social and Industrial Conditions in the North During the Civil War.* New York: Macmillan, 1910.

Galbraith, John Kenneth. *The Affluent Society.* Boston: Houghton Mifflin, 1958.

Geldart, C.B. Personal Correspondence about the History of the Western Association of Ladies for the Relief and Employment of the Poor (December 7) Philadelphia, Pa., 1966.

Gillin, John L. *Poverty and Dependency: Their Relief and Prevention.* 3d ed. New York: D. Appleton-Century, 1937.

Harrington, Michael. The Other America. New York: Macmillan, 1962.

Henslin, James M. *Social Problems.* 5th ed. Upper Saddle River, New Jersey: Prentice Hall, 2000.

Herzog, David and Martin Pflieger. "OSHA Races to Reform Itself, Or Else." *Morning Call* (June 25, 1996): A-1 & 4.

Holmes, Steven. "Incomes Up and Poverty Is Down, Data Show". *New York Times.* (September 27, 2000): A-12.

"How Many Live in Real Want? Profile of America's Poor." *U.S. News & World Report* 81 (November 8, 1976): 55-8.

Hunter, Robert. *Poverty.* New York: Macmillan. 1904.

Kelso, Robert W. *Poverty.* New York: Longmanns, Green and Company, 1929.

King, W.I. *The Wealth and Income of the People of the United States.* New York: The Macmillan Company, 1915.

Kornblum, William and Joseph Julian. *Social Problems*, 9th ed. Upper Saddle River, New Jersey: Prentice Hall. 1998.

Lardner, James. "The Rich Get Richer." *U.S. News & World Report* (February 21, 2000): 39-43.

Mayhew, Henry. *London Labour and the London Poor.* 1. New York: Dover Publications, Inc., 1861, 1968.

McVeigh, Frank J. "The Good Old Days." *Voice of Cement, Lime & Gypsum Workers International Union 25*, no. 10 (October 1962): 29-31.

McVeigh, Frank J. and Arthur Shostak. *Modern Social Problems.* New York: Holt, Rinehart and Winston, 1978.

The Millenium Breach: *The American Dilemma, Richer and Poorer. Executive Summary*, 2d ed. New York: The Milton S. Eisenhower Foundation and the Corporation for What Works, 1998.

Minton, Bruce and John Stuart. *Men Who Lead Labor.* New York: Modern Age Books, Inc. 1937.

Mooney, Linda A., David Knox and Caroline Schacht. *Understanding Social Problems,* 2d ed. New York: Wadsworth, 2000.

Nearing, Scott. *Wages in the United States, 1908-1910: A Study of State and Federal Wage Statistics*, New York: Hoffat, Yard & Company, 1911.

Ornati, Oscar. *Poverty Amid Affluence.* New York: 20th Century Fund, 1966.

OSHA. *Occupational Safety and Health Administration. Information about OSHA.* Internet: http://www.osha.gov/. 1996.

Parmelee, Maurice. *Poverty and Social Progress.* New York: The Macmillan Company, 1916.

Phillips, Levin. *The Politics of Rich and Poor.* New York: Random House, 1990.

Press Associates, Inc. "Washington Window." *AFL-CIO News 21*, no. 10 (March 6, 1976): 5.

Reich, Robert. *The Work of Nations.* New York: Vintage, 1992.

Reiman, Jeffrey. "A Crime by Any Other Name." Pp. 294-302 in *Taking Sides: Clashing Views on Controversial Issues*, 8th ed., edited by Kurt Finsterbusch and George McKenna. Guilford, Conn.: Dushkin Publishing Group, 1994.

————. "The Rich Get Richer and the Poor Get Prison: Ideology,
    Class and Criminal Justice." Pp. 288-96 in *Taking Sides:
    Clashing Views on Controversial Issues*. 12th ed. edited by
    Kurt Finsterbusch. Guilford, Conn.: McGraw-Hill/Dushkin,
    2003.
Riis, Jacob. "How the Other Half Lives: Studies Among the
    Tenements of New York." in *Jacob Riis Revisited,* edited by
    Francesco Cordaso. NewYork: Anchor, 1968. [1890]
Rosenbaum, David. "In Four Years, Regan Changed Bases of Debate
    on Domestic Programs." *New York Times* (October 25,
    1984): 15.
Rountree, B. Seebohm. *Poverty: A Study of Town Life.* London:
    Longman's Green & Company. 1901, 1922.
Shostak, Arthur. *Modern Social Reforms: Solving Today's Social
    Problems.* New York: Macmillan, 1974.
Sklar, Holly. "Poor Left Out of Record-Breaking Growth.   *KRT
    News Wire*(February 6, 2000): D-1.
Spahr, Charles. *An Essay on the Present Distribution of Wealth in the
    United States.* New York: The Macmillan Company, 1896.
Statistical Abstract of the U.S. "Distribution of Family Personal
    Income 1935-62 (Families And Unattached Individuals)."
    Table 467, 341. 86th ed. U.S.
    Census Bureau. Washington, D.C.: U.S. Government Printing
    Office, 1965.
————. National Safety Council "Workers Killed and Disabled on
    the Job: 1960-1996. Table 705, 441. 118th ed. U.S. Census
    Bureau. Washington, D.C.: U.S. Government Printing Office,
    1998.
————. "Persons Below Poverty Level...1960 –1997." Table 760,
    483. 119th ed. U.S. Census Bureau. Washington, D.C.: U.S.
    Government Printing Office, 1999.
————. "Deaths, Death Rates by Selected Causes: 1999-2000."
    Table 101, U.S. Census Bureau. Washington, D.C.: U.S.
    Government Printing Office, 2001.
————. "Persons Below Poverty Level...Race and Hispanic Origin:
    1970 to 2000." Table 668, 441. 122d ed. U.S. Census
    Bureau. Washington, D.C.: U.S. Government Printing Office,
    2001.
————. "Workers Killed or Disabled on the Job: 1970-2000". Table
    621, 122d ed. U.S. Census Bureau. Washington, D.C.: U.S.
    Government Printing Office. 2001.

Stephenson, Nathanial,, *Abraham Lincoln and the Union*. 29. New Haven: Yale University Press, 1918.

Streightoff, Frank H. "The Distribution of Income in the United States in the Columbia University Studies" in *History, Economics and Public Law*, 52, No. 2. New York: Columbia University Press, 1912.

Sullivan, Brian. "Science Finds Technical Advances Often Bring Concealed Hazards." *Allentown Sunday Call-Chronicle* (January 25, 1976): D-8.

Sullivan, Thomas and Kendrick S. Thompson. *Introduction to Social Problems*. 3rd ed. New York: MacMillon Publishing Company, 1994.

Trattner, Walter. *From Poor Law to Welfare State*. New York: Free Press, 1974

U.S. Bureau of Statistics. *Wages Paid in Agriculture: U.S. Department of Agriculture.* Bulletin 99. Washington, D.C.: U.S. Government Printing Office, 1912.

U.S. Census Bureau. *Census of Manufacturers. Part 4. 643-48.* Washington, D.C.: U.S. Government Printing Office, 1905.

U.S. Commission of Labor. *18th Annual Report for the Year 1903.* Washington, D.C.: U.S. Government Printing Office, 1904.

U.S. Commissioner of Internal Revenue. *First Annual Report of Federal Income Tax Returns*. Washington, D.C.: U.S. Government Printing Office, 1914.

U.S. Department of Labor. Bureau of Labor Statistics. *Unemployment Rates by Occupation, Industry, Employment and Earnings.* Table A-11 (September) 16. Washington, D.C.: U.S. Government Printing Office, 1999.

Watkins, G.P. "The Growth of Large Fortunes" in the *Publication of the American Economic Assn.* 8, no. 4 (November 1907).

Wilson, William Julius. *When Work Disappears: The World of the New Urban Poor.* Chicago: University Of Chicago Press, 1996.

Zietz, Dorothy. *Child Welfare: Services and Perspectives.* 2d ed. New York: Wiley, 1969.

Zinn, Howard. *A People's History of the United States.* New York: Harper & Row, 1980.

Chapter 10

Population and the Environment as an Issue

For the overwhelming amount of human history, the *total* population of the earth hovered around 500 million. That ended about 250 years ago. Now the world's population increases by 77 million people- about the size of a small country- *each year alone*! But should this concern us? After all, you may recall hearing somewhere that the less developed countries are primarily responsible for the increases in population. So what does population growth have to do with the United States? Do industrialized societies have a population problem too? The answer is that we should care because we *do* have population problems; however, they are of a different nature than those experienced by the less industrialized societies.

Consider this: the United States generates 1 billion pounds of solid waste *each day*? Furthermore while the industrialized world only contains about 1/4 of the world's population, it generates over 3/4 of its' waste (Shaw, 1989). Industrialized nations usually have fairly high living standards, and these living standards require a lot of energy to obtain and, in turn, produce a lot of waste. Furthermore, in the industrialized world, over 70% of the population lives in urban settings whereas in the non-industrialized world, the majority of its population is rural (Lowe and Bowlby, 1992). As we will see, while overpopulation threatens underdeveloped countries, the dense population of urban areas in industrial countries also has important ramifications for population issues and the environment.

Herodotus, an ancient Greek historian, perhaps said it best when he said "Man stalks across the landscape, and deserts follow in his footsteps." There is some truth to this quote. The Sahara Desert was once the breadbasket of the Roman Empire – a land rich in agricultural resources. Now it is a dry, barren desert (as the name implies) that is as large as the United States.

It is now undeniable that changes in the population are linked to environmental issues. Furthermore, population growth affects virtually every social institution –the family, the school, the economy, and even religion. Therefore, in order to understand the historical relationship between population changes, environmental changes and their related social problems, we need to first examine the issues around our changing population.

Defining the Problem of Population Growth

Population changes stem from three major social processes: fertility (births), mortality (deaths), and migration (movement in or out of an area). The relationship between these three demographic variables determines what happens to a society's population growth. For most of human history, population growth was relatively slow and based primarily on high birth and equally high death rates. Families during these times were large because their economic survival depended on human labor. The more children, the more potential workers and the greater potential productivity. However, as we covered in the chapter on the development of medicine, infectious disease was difficult to treat so mortality was also high during this time. Therefore, high fertility was offset by high mortality, creating a relatively stable population size.

All of this began to change about 250 years ago. In the United States, the number of children per family has been declining since 1800, when women bore an average of seven children to our current levels where women bear, on average, 1 to 2 children (Thomlinson, 1965). So, if our birth rate is decreasing, why isn't our population growth decreasing? The answer lies in the mortality rate. Remember, the relatively stable or slow-growing populations of the past were due to a balance between the birth and mortality rates. Since the mid-1700s, however, mortality rates have been declining as medical and sanitation advances improved people's health and curbed the spread of infectious diseases. But birth rates were slower to change.

Researchers call this process *demographic transition*. Demographic transition occurs when the equilibrium established by high birth and death rates is replaced by a decline in death rates even though the birth rates stay high. This is common among countries that are beginning to industrialize and was first noticed in Europe during the eighteen and nineteenth centuries (Figure 10 – 1).

Figure 10 – 1: The Demographic Transition Theory

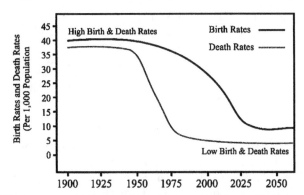

This widening spread between high birth rates (about 40-45 per 1000 population) and lower death rates (about 10-15 per 1000 population) produced a "demographic gap." This gap today is causing a population explosion in developing countries. A long period of transition occurs before low birth and death rates finally balance population. In Western nations, it took well over 100 years to close the gap (Stockwell, 1968)

This led to a sharp increase in population. Even a sharp, relatively sudden increase in population can plant the seeds for continued population growth in the future. For example, what had been a billion people in the world in 1800 became 1.6 billion in 1900, 2.5 billion by 1950 and then 6.1 billion by 2000. (Engelman et al., 2002) The addition of even one more child per family can spell the difference between population stability and increase. And the United States isn't alone. In fact, the United States' rate of population growth from fertility / mortality has slowed, as has the world population growth rate. Even so, the world's population did not double in any century before this point, and in the Twentieth Century, it increased *fourfold*, with 96% of that growth in least developed countries (LDC). We will examine what to make of these changes later in the chapter. Philip Hauser, a leading demographer from the University of Chicago, puts the matter this way:

> The revolutionary changes in population size, composition and distribution during the modern era, and especially during the course of this century, have precipitated problems which are among the most serious confronting the world...Revolutionary population change is still underway. It is not an event which has already occurred, to which

adjustment can be made in leisurely fashion. The 'population explosion' is unlike the ordinary explosion, [it is] a chain reaction which began several centuries ago and is still going on. Fortunately, man has the ability to observe the process even while being a party to it. And in analyzing the facts and assaying their implications man, also fortunately has the capacity to devise policies and programs to control the process, and thereby to ameliorate or prevent its undesirable consequences." (1970: 1-2)

The basic cause behind population growth in developing countries is that most of them are still going through their period of transitional growth. Less than half of the world's people have completed this transition. To make matters worse, the "base" population in developing nations is much larger than it was when Western countries started their transition. On top of that, the developing countries, with our help, make use of modern medicine, insecticides, and sanitation immediately. It took Western nations many years before the widespread application of these techniques made a substantial dent in the death rate. But in developing nations, with modern means available, the death rate is cut in half in a short period. However, many of these countries are not fully industrialized; therefore, their growing populations are more likely to experience hunger, malnutrition and other obstacles to life that Americans often do not experience.

But remember, fertility and mortality are only two-thirds of the equation. Especially for the United States, migration heavily influences population size and composition – but more notably immigration, or migration *into* the United States. The United States has a long history of immigration with its reputation as the "Land of Plenty" and its promotion of the "American Dream". The mid-1800s to about the 1920s saw a huge immigration of European Americans – so much so that the American government imposed quotas to slow immigration growth. Even back in this early time, there was conflict about the types of immigrants coming to America. Politicians designed quotas to ensure that immigrants resembled the "Americans" who were already here, namely White, Anglo-Saxons, – ignoring that, aside from Native Americans and Latinos on the west coast, the majority of Americans themselves were immigrants! In other words, at least temporarily, those in power wanted, and were able, to control who had access to the American Dream. Moreover, they made sure that these people closely resembled themselves as much as possible.

The Immigration Act amendments of 1965 removed these quotas and encouraged a new wave of immigrants, largely from Asia and Latin America. Consequently, there was a demographic shift in the face of America. At the beginning of the last century (1900), 90% of immigrants were from European countries; at the beginning of this century (2000), 90% of immigrants were from non-European countries. These immigration changes are instrumental in the racial and ethnic changes and conflicts occurring in the United States that we discussed in earlier chapters.

So what does this all mean? We are unsure how to define these changing numbers. One could argue that the problems of population growth to be more critical for less-developed countries. These supporters argue that the main criterion for overpopulation is a nation's inability to produce or obtain enough food to feed its population. Thus, what is needed to ensure survival and subsistence is lacking. This is overpopulation in an "absolute" sense, in that it involves questions of life and death. India is a classic example of this situation; its food production has not increased at the same rate as its population.

However, in ignoring the role of the wealthy industrialized countries when discussing the problems of population, one risks the fallacy of overgeneralization. Consequently, another way to view overpopulation is from the criteria of the comforts and conveniences of life. In contrast to absolute overpopulation, this involves relative overpopulation, some degree of deprivation felt by a people as compared with that enjoyed by other people or classes in the same country. Another view is that the most developed countries are bigger problems because they have higher standards of living where people continually compete to possess the most material goods. People in these societies consume more resources than their counterparts in less developed countries. Industrialized societies have also become more disposable societies, in that the time devoted to obtaining material wealth takes away time from other pursuits like cooking, making clothes, fixing items in disrepair, etc. Therefore, now people grab food on the go (which creates trash as we toss the food wrappers), dispose of clothes as soon as they need repair or are a bit worn, and throw-away items like CD players, television sets, and the like instead of trying to repair them when they break. We even save time by purchasing disposable goods like razors, pens, and diapers. All of these goods produce waste, but are designed for our convenience. Furthermore, many of these goods are made of materials like plastic which do not easily (if ever) biologically degrade. Consequently, people in industrial societies produce more waste that is hurting our environment (and therefore other factors such as food sources) and threatening life on this planet due to pollution. Perhaps more importantly from a sociological point of view is that in a Gesellschaft society, having these personal conveniences is more important than worrying about greater environmental good. Consequently, as we will see, enacting changes in population and environmental practices is challenging.

Tied to this latter argument is the recognition that industrialized societies are frequently dominated by big businesses that support their large economies – these businesses are also accused of threatening the environment and state of the earth in a multitude of ways that we will discuss soon. Consequently, large societies mean more people using land and more people using goods, which means more factories, even more land use (to build factories), more pollution (from the production of those factories), more waste (both in the factories and from used up personal consumer items), and the situation snowballs from there.

Therefore absolute overpopulation usually stems not from the absolute numbers of people per se, but the inability (or unwillingness) of a nation to develop its potential natural resources and the maldistribution of wealth in the world. Conversely, the relative overpopulation stems from people's perception of what they think they should have in relation to others, which creates competition for material goods. The latter is the situation in the U.S. and other developed countries.

Regardless of which side of the debate you fall (and likely, the answer is a little of both sides), some undeniable conflicts have arisen. This chapter is going to focus on five conflicts, which are:

1. Conflict stemming from the changing population demographics and urbanization
2. Conflict between the population growth and the environment
3. Conflict over the control over food production and distribution
4. Conflict between industrialization and the environment
5. Conflict over the solutions for population control and environmental issues

Conflict from the Changing Population Demographics and Urbanization

As we mentioned earlier in this chapter, the United States is a nation built on immigration. The vast majority of its current residents came from other countries, usually in distinct waves.   In Colonial America, there were about 750,000 Native Americans and only about 50,000 colonists, the majority of whom came from Great Britain.   By the mid-1800s there were large influxes of people from northern Europe, especially Germany and Ireland.   Consequently, disease introduced by the Europeans and war caused the Native American population to decrease to about 250,000, while the European population increased to 23 million.   However, by the late 1800s to almost mid-1900s there was a large influx of people, especially Italians, Poles, Hungarians, Greeks and Jews, from southern Europe to the eastern United States.   At the same time there was a large number of Mexicans immigrating to the western United States.

To control the high rate of immigration, the United States imposed quotas through the Immigration Act of 1921; however, these were loosened in 1945 to accommodate refugees from World War II, and in 1965 Congress completely ended the quota system.   However, a huge influx of Mexicans, Latin Americans, and Asians resulted, especially in areas like California.   Furthermore, there was a concern that many new immigrants were in the United States illegally (a point we will discuss in more detail shortly), which led Congress to enact the Immigrant Control and Reform Act in 1986.   This Act gave amnesty to illegal immigrants already in the United States, but outlawed hiring undocumented immigrants to prevent future illegal immigration.   States, like California, who had the largest minority population, further restricted the benefits of illegal immigrants.   Even so, the rate of immigration has accelerated in the 1990s creating interesting changes in our population's demographics, as well as some new social conflicts, leading Congress to once again limit immigration – this time to 675,000 annually.

One of the problems of American immigration stems from the urban concentration of immigrants.   Immigrants tend to settle in very specific areas, such as New York, Los Angeles, Miami and Chicago, because large cities are frequently racially and ethnically diverse.   Therefore, in these areas, new immigrants are more likely to find people like themselves.   Furthermore, immigrants tend to follow a process called "chain migration," which means that they settle where there may be friends and relatives who came before them.   Since previous immigrants settled in large metropolitan areas, newer immigrants, following the pattern of chain migration, do so as well – which increases the concentration of immigrants in the cities.

You may be wondering, so what?   So people want to settle where there are friendly faces from their home country, where the subculture reminds them of "home" even while they can take advantage of the economic opportunities in America. If everything was as simple as that, this practice wouldn't be a problem. But life isn't as simple as that. First, ethnic enclaves such as we are describing here can quickly become overpopulated, making jobs and economic opportunity scarce. As people compete for economic opportunity, those who are already established think of an area as "theirs" and expect certain rights (like to work) to follow. Therefore, "old" immigrants become tense with the newcomers, who the "old" immigrants perceive as competing for "their" jobs, housing, etc. This leaves little room for the newcomers as those who are established forget that they too were once "new." Consequently, economic tension can potentially translate into ethnic or racial tension, which in turn can lead to anti-immigration feelings, ethnocentrism or even attacks on immigrants. Even if there are economic opportunities in nearby towns, immigrants may not move there because the people who share their culture, language, etc. are not there as well.

Second, education in these resulting ethnic enclaves may be difficult, especially when language barriers are present. Consequently, children may have trouble in school, drop out, and / or develop behavioral problems. Furthermore, the lack of education hurts people's access to other social institutions such as medical care. If people do not know the services available to them or cannot afford them, they tend to postpone seeking medical aid until it is an emergency. This leads to the third problem which is that immigrants are unlikely to have health insurance or understand their way around our medical institution; therefore, their health care is paid by taxes…which need to keep increasing in order to address the increasing demand as urban areas swell. This contributes to the conflict and concern over medical access that we discussed in the medicine chapter.

Furthermore, people in these areas are vulnerable to exploitation known as environmental racism. Toxic waste plants and other industry which create environmentally hazardous conditions are more concentrated in low income areas. These areas frequently have high concentrations of minorities (hence the "racism" in "environmental racism") and immigrants – both of whom are disproportionately represented among the poor. This occurs for many reasons. One is that these people are so desperate for jobs that they are less critical of *any* income producing industry that moves into their area. Second, these people are frequently less aware of or less able to organize to protect their rights; therefore, they are less likely to successfully protest the entrance of such industry into their areas even if they are so inclined. Both of these conditions create a path of least resistant for big corporations or toxic waste plants, making these overcrowded areas economically attractive. Hence we are more likely to find environmentally unfriendly industry among in overcrowded areas than we are in spacious middle class suburbs.

Lastly, as we mentioned, some immigrants continue to enter the United States illegally. While the exact number of illegal immigrants is obviously impossible to tell, some estimates put it at as high as 7 million as of 2000, with 5 million being the average (U.S. Immigration and Naturalization Services, 2003). These people pose a whole new host of problems. Employers may exploit illegal immigrants by working them long hours for little money that is given "under the table"; or those who brought them to this country may force the immigrants to work in illegal operations such as gambling. While exploitation of newcomers by those sponsoring them has occurred since the indentured servants of the Colonial era, unlike the Colonial indentured servants, since these modern immigrants are here illegally, there are no laws or personal rights to protect them. Furthermore, many take extreme risks to enter this country. For example, in 2003, about 19 immigrants suffocated to death in a truck in Texas trying to enter the U.S. illegally (Romero and Barbozz, 2003).

Conflict Between Population Growth and the Environment

It should be clear from the beginning of this chapter that the problems of population growth are relatively new – at least for the last 200 years or so. Prior to the coming of the industrial revolution in the Eighteenth and Nineteenth Centuries, the brutally harsh condition of life kept the population in balance. With the advent of industry and large cities, the first real burst of population growth started. With industry emerged modern science. Modern society broke the pattern of high death rates which had been man's lot for over a million years, and which had successfully kept the population from growing too much. Vaccination, as well as improved sanitation and medicine, improved people's chances of surviving, especially babies and young children. Combined with better technology for raising food and better transportation for distributing it, socioeconomic forces were set in motion to dramatically lower death rates in the U.S.

Population and Environmental Pollution

The practices of people in non-industrialized societies that we discussed are aimed at short-term survival; however, they have deleterious long term consequences. Even so, non-industrial countries are not the only culprits. The United States alone has added almost 100 million people to its population in the last 50 years. And it adds about one million more each year. Furthermore, keep in mind, that these numbers are for population *stability*. In industrial countries, although there is little or no population growth, there is still the threat to the environment due to the rapid consumption of goods and services. The problems of pollution have been most severe (thought not exclusively) in the city. The worldwide trend is toward large congested urban centers. This concentration of the population in one geographical area puts ecological pressure and overload on the system – causing environmental stress. Traffic, crowding, and noise pollution just add to the problems of air, water and land pollution.

Furthermore, how do we feed, clothe, house and provide material goods for all these people? And what do we do with all the trash and human waste these people produce? The answer: we take resources from the environment to support all of these people and we give the environment back these people's trash – usually in environmentally damaging and degrading forms.

For example, in the 1960s each U.S. citizen generated 2.7 pounds of garbage on any day; by 1996 this figure jumped to 4.3 pounds which amounts to almost 160 *million* tons of waste a year (Statistical Abstract of the United States, 1995; National Solid Wastes Management Association, 1991). And those figures are just for the "friendly" wastes. In addition to the waste each person generates, in 1997 there were 1, 231 hazardous waste sites in the United States (Statistical Abstract of the United States, 1998).

Our waters aren't much better off. Although almost two-thirds of the globe is covered with water, 97.5% of that is saltwater and another 2.5% of the earth's water is in the form of glaciers or ice caps. Only 0.7% of the earth's water is in lakes, rivers, swamps and the like. Even so, every day, city sewers discharge into our rivers, lakes, streams and oceans some 40 billion gallons of sewage – after various degrees of "treatment," or none at all. But that is not all. In urban areas, rain and dew pick up so much pollution from the air, as well as from garbage dumps, gasoline stations, parking lots and yards; it could be classified as sewage.

In addition, our pollutants are harming ocean life. Most ocean fish (and all shellfish) are found on an ocean shelf that extends from the coastlines. However, given the shelf's closeness to the coast, and therefore to people, when people dump waste into the ocean, they are essentially dumping it onto this life-supporting ocean shelf. Human waste often contains bacteria or viruses that are unfamiliar to ocean life; and, like any new "bug" introduced to an organism; human "bugs" are killing ocean life. According to some scientists, 10% of our coral reefs (which are essential environments for ocean life) are already dead and another 30% are threatened (New York Times, 1999).

Now stop and think about this for a minute. The obvious problem is that these practices contaminate our drinking water and kill ocean fish that we may eat. But is that all? Of course not. The contaminated water in these streams, rivers, lakes, etc. feed fish and plants. Other animals eat these fish and plants, and humans, in turn, eat either the animals which ate the animals that fed off contaminated water (and are, therefore, contaminated themselves) or the plants (which too are contaminated). So, essentially, water pollution potentially affects every branch of the food chain - beginning (in terms of pollution) and ending with humans (by us eating food and animals contaminated within the waters).

And let's not forget air pollution. Our reliance on fossil fuel from everything to running our factories (to produce all of those material goods Americans feel they need) to making sure we can quickly get to the supermarket 2 miles away (and just think about the increasing car market as the population continues to increase!) create huge amounts of toxic emissions like hydrogen fluoride, sulfuric acid and hydrochloric acid. While one-fifth of these emissions go directly into the soil, four-fifths of it goes into the air...ready for you to breathe or absorb from acid rain. In the United States alone about 80 million people are exposed to air that causes health problems (Kemps, 1998).

But unpleasant as breathing hydrochloric acid sounds, there is more possible air damage in the form of chlorofluorocarbons (or CFCs), which are frequently found in refrigerators, aerosol sprays, dry cleaning solvents and other solvents. CFCs are believed to hurt the earth's atmosphere, which is responsible for filtering out dangerous ultraviolet rays from the sun. Ultraviolet rays increase the earth's temperature, which hurts food crops and causes sea levels to rise (which throws off the delicate ecosystem of the ocean, independently of the other trouble man is causing these bodies of water); and even damage human skin, thereby causing skin cancer.

Finally, in wondering how we will provide enough clothing, cars, shelter, etc. for America, and the world's increasing population, we have to realize that we are in jeopardy of exhausting our existing resources. Barry Commoner points to the logic behind resource exhaustion. In a finite world, "mineral resources, if used, can only move in one direction – downward in amount. Unlike the constituents of the ecosphere, mineral resources are nonrenewable." (1971: 121)

University of California Geologist, Ian D. Macgregor (1975), points to the historical example of the depletion of iron reserves on a national level. In Western Europe, peak production was reached between 1880 and 1910. As the resources became exhausted in a nation, imports increased. Today this is beginning to happen with some metals in short supply in the world.

Many expect that resources will become further exhausted as presently developing countries begin to industrialize. These countries will need and demand the same scarce mineral resources that industrial countries use so freely today. This will only exacerbate the problem in the future.

So as you can see, we have a whole host of environmental issues to contend with – polluted water, polluted food, ultraviolet rays causing cancer and damaging crops, declining resources, etc. Perhaps, these individual issues would be less problematic if they occurred in an isolated bubble. Unfortunately, (as you probably expect) that is not the case. Four factors are at work that increase the incidence and prevalence of environmental degradation. These four factors, according to Ehrlich and Holdren (1971: 616) are: 1) Synergism; 2) Threshold effects; 3) Trigger effects; 4) Time lag effects.

Synergism is the interaction of two or more factors that yield a total effect greater than what would happen if they acted alone. An example of synergism would be the interaction of sulfur dioxide (from fossil burning fuels) and asbestos particles (from car brake linings), which together could induce lung cancer.

The threshold effect, on the other hand, refers to the ability of the environment to withstand pollution. The environment can naturally absorb many kinds of pollution without adverse effects if those levels are below a certain threshold. But when the threshold is exceeded, nature's system can become overloaded. Rivers in the early Nineteenth Century could easily absorb the sewage and industrial wastes. Today their thresholds have been exceeded, so nature can no longer accommodate man's pollutants in a mass, technological society.

The third factor, the "trigger effect," is a situation in which an environmental balance is upset by a relatively small man-made input. For example, man's filling of the reservoirs behind large dams may trigger earthquakes. Or jet plane exhaust may weaken the ozone layer in the atmosphere that screens the earth against ultraviolet radiation from the sun.

Lastly, "time delay" refers to situations in which cause may precede effect by years or even decades. We are just now discovering that people who once worked in or lived near factories making polyvinyl chloride contracted liver cancer, many years later. Exposure to radiation today may produce cancer 20 years later (Ehrlich and Holdren, 1971)

The Effects of Population Growth

What is the end result of all of this? The conventional wisdom that population growth is the principal cause of environmental pollution is being seriously questioned today. Population is a contributing factor, but not as much as we may have assumed in the past.

**Population growth occurs when women have three or four children
(Credit: Sacred Heart Hospital, Allentown, Pennsylvania)**

According to the U.S. Commission on Population Growth and the American Future, "Population growth is clearly not the sole culprit in ecological damage. To believe that it is, is to confuse how things are done with how many people are doing them….The way things are done can, to a significant degree, be changed regardless of how many people are doing them." (1972: 71-72)   The Commission goes on to assert that pollutants can be eliminated by enforcing EPA standards for pollution emissions, no matter how much population growth occurs between now and later in the Twenty-first Century.

Then how important is population growth relative to the other causes of pollution? Ronald Ridfer analyses that question in terms of the time dimension involved and the kind of pollution involved. He concludes that "although still important, population growth appears to be somewhat less responsible than other causes for pollution and resource shortages." (1973: 113)

But the concerns of pollution do not address the next environmental concern – the availability of resources, most notably the conflict over food.

Conflict Over the Control of Food Production and Distribution

According to Pimentel and colleagues (1998), in 1950, 500 million people (about 20 percent of the world's population) were considered malnourished; by the late 1990s that number grew to more than 3 billion people...or about *one half* of the *world's* population. The most obvious concern about all these people is how to feed them. When we remember that most of the yearly population growth occurs in poorer developing countries, the shocking numbers of malnourishment become more obvious.

However, concern over resources and population growth isn't new. All the way back at the turn of the Nineteenth Century, Thomas R. Malthus theorized on the problems arising from unchecked population growth. In his *Essay on the Principle of Population* (1798), Malthus argued that populations grow exponentially or geometrically (e.g. $2 + 4 + 8...$) food supply and other resources to sustain population grow linearly or arithmetically ($1 + 2 + 3 + 4...$). Furthermore, distress causes people to limit the number of children (and therefore potential people to feed). If we find a utopian society, it would eventually be self-defeating because people would have more children and we will outstrip our food sources faster (Hardin, 1993).

So obviously the concern over population size and food availability is not new; however, it is especially a concern now in poorer developing countries. President John F. Kennedy urged the United States and developed world countries to combine increasing amounts of fertilizer with higher yield crops to help address world hunger. In a famous quote, President Kennedy said "We have the means – we need only the will." Unfortunately, will wasn't enough.

Today we realize that, contrary to Malthus' ideas, food production really isn't the issue. Food production is increasing (thanks to the use of chemicals that create a higher yield) as is availability, regardless of season. Consequently, studies reveal that the world's farmers produce enough food to feed the world's 6 billion or so people...yet, as we said, about 3 billion people are still malnourished. How so? As you should be expecting by now, given the theme of this book, the reason there is such a high rate of malnourishment even given our food supply result from conflicts in distribution. The majority of malnourished people live in those poorer countries that we have mentioned. These people, and countries, lack the political power or the financial resources to produce food or to bring food in from other countries. Yet, at the same time countries like the United States enjoy a wide selection and availability of food any time of year (even though this is at a cost to Americans, which we will address later). Why this conflict? Because if the people in power weren't so profit driven, they would work with these poorer countries to bring in resources and / or food even if it resulted in less or no profit. But obviously that isn't happening any time soon.

Conflict Between Industrialization and the Environment

With the spread of industrialization and affluence, the environment and nature were seriously hurt. The number of urbanites doubled and per capita real incomes quadrupled every 40 years. Rising income results in an increased demand for environmental amenities. The problem of supplying conveniences and amenities, however, as we mentioned previously, is that they become a drag on the environment. With increasing industrialization and affluence, people demanded air-conditioned living and workspaces, central heating, paved superhighways, etc. Cars became even more popular – and bigger, as today's ever-increasingly-large sport utility vehicles (SUVs) illustrate. As man attempts to meet the consumers' demands for comfort and convenience, it led to environmental deterioration. So as we have become more prosperous and rich, our environment has become more polluted and poor.

One of the main causes in the technology – environment conflict is the revolutionary and rapid changes in our product technology. For example, farmers now use more pesticides and chemical fertilizers and generally no longer grow food organically (except in some specialty instances). Detroit also now turns out millions of cars that are big, powerful gas-guzzlers that wreck the environment and deplete our oil reserves. If cars got 30 miles to a gallon, instead of 20, we could seriously cut our consumption of oil down. We also fill our homes with an endless supply of electrical gadgets from computers to toothbrushes. In short, most of our environmental disasters stem from changes in our product technology. The environmentalist Barry Commoner argued 30 years ago, but it still holds today:

> The overall evidence seems clear. The chief reason for the environmental crisis that has engulfed the United States in recent years is the sweeping transformation of productive technology since World War II. The economy has grown

> enough to give the United States population about the same
> amount of basic goods, per capita, as it did in 1946.
> However, productive technology with increasing impacts
> on the environment have displaced less destructive ones.
> The environmental crisis is the inevitable result of this
> counter ecological pattern of growth (1971: 177)

What do we mean by this? Computers do not just make themselves, nor do cars, or video games, or that electric toothbrush. As we mentioned previously, they have to be made, which requires factories....which requires land....which requires plastics and other materials that are made from still other resources...which produces waste and pollutants...well, you probably get the picture by now. Moreover, some of these amenities impose costs that cannot be directly observed. Think of the disappearance of grassy knolls and of mountainous areas teaming with the sounds of birds and forest creatures. Whatever land decisions humans make affect not only them, but also the habitats of countless animals and plants.

We may also be hurting ourselves in more direct means as well. Air pollution that results from factories, automobile exhaust, the processing of waste disposal, power generating processes in homes, and a number of other sources releases chemicals into the atmosphere that contribute to problems such as smog and global warming. To put this another way, each ton of carbon emitted into the atmosphere produces 3.7 tons of carbon dioxide and because, globally, we produce about 5.6 billion tons of carbon a year, that results in almost 21 *billion tons* of carbon dioxide released into the atmosphere *a year!* The United States alone is responsible for about one –fifth of this production (Read, 1994). Growing populations and increasing demand for material goods may easily lead this figure to escalate.

So why don't we change our behavior? Part of the reason stems from the conflict between our cultural symbols of success (big houses, big cars, many appliances and "toys") and the manufacturing issues mentioned previously that create these material symbols. But part of the reason also stems from the conflict over how to interpret the consequences of these issues. Perhaps one of the biggest controversies is that which surrounds the issue of the "greenhouse effect" or global warming. According to scientists, the greenhouse effect occurs when carbon dioxide and water vapor combine and, while allowing the sun's light to reach the earth, traps heat. This leads to warming temperatures, stronger ultraviolet rays (associated with skin cancers), and an overall warming of the atmosphere (global warming). This in turn, may cause ocean temperatures to increase (which can hurt the sensitive ecosystems of aquatic life), lead to increased risk of ailments like skin cancer, lead to warmer summers (which will in turn increase demand for air conditioning – and consequently electricity which may further exacerbate the problem), increase the risk of forest fires, droughts and insects, and increase the risk for certain diseases such as malaria and cholera. As evidence of this concern, the National Oceanic and Atmospheric Administration claims that the winter of 2000 was the warmest in U.S. history and that 9 of the 11 years prior to that have been the hottest in the 119 years since records were first kept (CBS News, 2000; McDonald, 1999).

However, others disagree. Some scientists argue that in the last 3,000 years alone, the earth has experienced a number of extended periods that were warmer than today (and warmer than the trends noticed by the National Oceanic and Atmospheric Administration). These individuals agree that the temperatures have been rising; but, they argue that they have been rising over the past 300 years - long before the advent of industrialization and our current population issues – and are still below the 3,000 year average temperature (Singer, 1997; Stevens, 1998).

When experts disagree over the ramifications of a social phenomenon, making a convincing argument for people to change widely held and enduring social values (such as the materialism present in capitalistic Gesellschaft societies) is very difficult. Hence, the conflict over global warming and our individual culpability in the matter is not likely to be resolved soon. Which may lead to another related problem – that of capital flight and the environmental consequences of it?

The United States, and the world, is in conflict over what to do with environmental issues. On the one hand, there has not been strong cultural pressure for people to re-evaluate their materialistic ways. As we mentioned, over the past 20 years, houses and cars are getting bigger, we have become a more disposal society and we continue to consume finite resources at alarming rates. On the other hand, the United States recognizes, on some level, the potentially harmful consequences of how we produce and consume goods. Hence it created the Environmental Protection Agency (which we will discuss in the next section) and tries to legislate more environmentally friendly ways of running factories and using automobiles, for example. Furthermore, many of us do not even think twice about recycling now – a practice that was virtually unheard of 20 years ago.

However, some companies argue that the restrictions the government places upon them for worker wages, product regulation, and safety and environmental concerns (to name a few of many) cut into their profits – making production in the United States cost-prohibitive.

Industry often pollutes the local community

Consequently, it is cheaper for them to move production to other, less developed countries, where they do not have stringent government regulations and where they can pay much lower wages with fewer benefits than in the United States. Now, to be fair, it is unreasonable to argue that any company would move production to another country simply because of environmental guidelines. However, environmental restrictions are frequently more lenient (if present at all) in other, less developed countries – further enticing companies to relocate there. This hurts the nation in a number of ways. Obviously, it results in the loss of work for United States citizens and some question how much these companies benefit the workers and areas in which they settle. However, more relevant to the discussion of this chapter, is the concern about environmental consequences. As we mentioned previously, the environmental practices of one country has global ramifications. Consequently, even if industrialized countries enact and enforce environmental standards, if companies operating in other countries do not practice the same (or better) environmental precautions, then the effectiveness of the existing policies are weakened. Capital flight, therefore, not only directly hurts United States workers by the loss of jobs, but it can also further exacerbate environmental concerns if these companies are not required to follow similar environmental standards in their new countries of operation.

Conflict Over the Solutions for Population Control and the Environment

Population and the environment are classic cases in which, once a situation was defined as a serious social problem; "collective action" was taken to solve the problem. However, people still disagree as to which solutions are the most viable.

Environmental Legislation

The year 1970 was a big one for the environment. First, President Richard Nixon established the Environmental Protection Agency (EPA) in recognition of developing environmental concerns. The EPA was originally responsible for identifying pollutants, tracing their behavior through the ecological chain, determining pollutants' effects on man, and seeing how different forms of pollution interacted. The EPA would then use this information to determine where in the ecological chain pollution interventions would be most appropriate.

Before the EPA, various individual agencies, such as the Federal Water Quality Administration, the National Air Pollution Control Administration and the Bureau of Solid Waste Management, addressed singular and specific aspects of the previously mentioned goals. The formation of the EPA, however, allowed *one* agency to focus on these issues which gave that agency more power to set and enforce standards, allowed the creation of more consistent standards, and facilitated the ability to amass information and see its interconnectedness. Since its inception, the EPA has been responsible for creating the Safe Drinking Water Act of 1973, making car manufacturers post car emission ratings on their automobiles (and they even regulated emissions in certain areas), banning the use of chlorofluorocarbons in aerosols and banning the dumping of sludge and sewage into the oceans.

The government's recognition of environmental issues stems, in part, from growing public pressure, as well. Around the time the EPA was formed, the public was becoming more vocal about their environmental concerns. The first Earth Day celebration, which also occurred in 1970, symbolized this increased attention. The first Earth Day was organized by Gaylord Nelson and Dennis Hayes in order to spread environmental awareness. Since 1970 it has expanded into an entire network which includes over 5,000 organizations and involves

184 countries that sponsor yearly activities meant to educate and stimulate environmental conservation.

While the EPA itself is not directly linked to the Earth Day celebrations (although the formation of the EPA can be said to be related to increased public pressure regarding the environment that started prior to Earth Day itself), some argue that the Clean Air Act of 1970 (and its amendments in 1977) are. The Clean Air Act, which stems from the Air Quality Act of 1967, is primarily concerned with air pollution and is most noted for establishing national standards for air pollution control. Before the Clean Air Act, pollution was believed to be a necessary, but unfortunate, byproduct of economic growth, and its control was only regional. Regional control, however, failed miserably and not all were convinced that killing the environmental was unavoidable in economic expansion. The Clean Air Act changed both of these ideas. It placed all control under the national government, which created national standards for air purity and deadlines for compliance. The effects of the Clean Air Act also illustrated that economic growth and environmental protection can actually go hand in hand.

However, the success of the Clean Air Act is mixed. According to the EPA, our nation's air is undeniably cleaner than it was 30 years ago. First, air pollution declined 25% between 1970 and 2003 even though the nation's population, economy and number of vehicles have grown. Second, there has been a 48% decrease in the toxic chemicals released by industry since 1988 (Seelye and Lee, 2003).

However, this change took longer than expected and our nation's waters are still in trouble. According to the same EPA report just discussed, there are warnings about fish consumption in 14% of the river miles, 28% of lake areas and 100% of the Great Lakes waters (Seeley and Lee, 2003). Furthermore, we now are dealing with air quality concerns that originate in other countries, but are flowing into ours. Consequently, enforcement is still a major conflict. In 1991 the EPA scored the largest criminal damage settlement in history, $25 million in fines, $100 million in immediate payment to the Alaskan and U.S. government for restoration and a $900 million remediation fund, against the Exxon Corporation and Exxon Shipping for their role in the Alaskan oil spill. However, victories such as this are rare; and environmental threats such as the oil spills that occurred in 2002 off the coast of Spain, still occur.

Population Control Vs. Reproductive Freedom

While we have discussed that population is not the sole reason for environmental problems, many argue that controlling population growth can contribute to a healthier environment. In 1968 the organization Zero Population Growth (ZPG) formed to encourage world countries (including the United States) to lower their population growth. The main tactic of this organization was education about the dangers of population growth and supporting policies aimed at reducing population growth. However, critics argue that by limiting population growth, inadvertently countries will unbalance their dependency ratios. Fewer births mean fewer workers (who, aside from aiding production, also pay taxes) and fewer people available to pay and care for the larger aging populations.

The premise behind the goal of programs like zero population growth is family planning. Family planning is not a new concept; however, the rather highly reliable methods we associate with family planning today are. For much of history, people relied on a combination of continual breast-feeding and folk medicine / lore to prevent pregnancy. These methods, however, were not necessarily reliable.

While the birth control movement gained support during the Twentieth Century, people felt that the term "birth control, coined in 1914 by Margaret Sanger, was obscene and favored the euphemism "planned parenthood" instead. However, this wasn't a smooth transition. Ms. Sanger opened the first birth control clinic, named "Planned Parenthood" in 1916 and was jailed for doing so (Ehrlich, Ehrlich and Holdren, 1977). It wasn't until even later that courts permitted physicians to prescribe birth control for health reasons. Eventually, more Planned Parenthood clinics opened, but the movement only gained support when they balanced their message of family planning with treatment for infertility. In doing so, Planned Parenthood developed "credibility...[since] they were in the business of *helping women to have the children they wanted when they wanted them* [sic]" (Hardin, 1993, p. 255). However, as Harden indicates, whether the initial goals of Planned Parenthood were to slow population growth or simply help women avoid unwanted babies was always unclear.

Could voluntary birth control really make a dent in population control? Some, including Charles Galton Darwin, a grandson of Charles Darwin who proposed the concept of "survival of the fittest," argued that this would not work because if you accept the Darwinian concept that the genetically strongest will survive, then there is something genetically different in people who want large families and / or are unwilling to practice birth control compared to those who are not. Because those practicing birth control will have fewer children than those not practicing family planning, the proportion of family planners will continually decline until they will be a small part of the population, thereby having no effect on population control (Hardin, 1993)

Now whether anyone paid any attention to Mr. Darwin's grandson is unclear; however, the idea that population control cannot be merely left to individual choice has taken root, for better or for worse. Perhaps the most well known government effort to control population is China's "One Child Only" policy. Chinese citizens who have only one child are rewarded with monthly financial bonuses, free education for their child, free medical care, release time from work and other pro-planning incentives. However, this has produced conflict. China has a strong cultural tradition favoring male children. Because daughters become the property of their husband's family when they marry, biological sons are the ones who work the field and take care of elderly parents. Although the Chinese government has tried propaganda that favorably shows parents with female children, the high infanticide rate of females shows that this hasn't worked. To discourage female infanticide, parents who have a daughter are allowed a second chance at having a son if the parents and daughter meet strict conditions.

Furthermore, culturally, there is conflict over reproductive issues which exacerbate population problems. For example, in countries like Kenya (which has one of the fastest growing populations in the world), people *desire* large families. As mentioned earlier in this chapter, many of the non-industrialized countries, like Kenya, mostly have a rural population where children are economic investments. Young children work the land, thereby contributing to the family's resources. When the parents are old, older children are expected to care for the parents since less-developed countries generally do not have social welfare programs. Furthermore, women in these societies culturally have very little power because they are economically dependent on their husbands. Therefore, the women have little say in how large the family will be. Ottaway (1990) cites an example of where women of the Nyeri district received funding from the Kenyan Family Planning Association to start their own pig rearing cooperative, the women had an independent income for the first time in their lives. The association also provided education on the economic advantages of small families, contraception use and family planning. Consequently, the birth rate began to fall in this area and married women's acceptance of contraceptives rose 43%.

However, keep in mind that not all countries are experiencing population booms. Some countries like the European countries have the problem of too *few* births and only maintain population stability through immigration. And again, this is not new. During World War II, in order to promote what Hitler referred to as the "pure race," he awarded crosses to mothers of large families based on the number of children they had. An iron cross was given to mothers of 4 children, silver to mothers of six, gold to mothers of eight and gold and diamond to mothers of 10. German youth were expected to salute women who wore the motherhood cross because it was a sign of prestige and support for the German cause.

So in many industrialized countries, policy is aimed at *increasing* births. For these countries, they face concerns over a shrinking workforce, an increasing elderly population and an increasing dependency ratio. Today countries do not hand out motherhood crosses or other momentoes; they generally encourage births indirectly through tax cuts to families, help paying medical or education costs, etc. The only people who benefit from these programs and tax cuts are those with children. In the United States., the child dependent tax break was raised by $400 in 2003 to $1,000 per child.

However, not all population policies are welcomed. Westerners for example, often find China's One Child Policy to have unintended consequences (e.g. female abortions or infanticides) that are too high to justify. The United States proposed population control for certain groups in the early 1990s with the norplant – welfare debate. Norplant is a contraceptive which consists of six matchstick-size silicone capsules that, when inserted into a woman's upper arm, release small amounts of protein that inhibit pregnancy over a 5 year period. Norplant works automatically, is easily monitored and requires medical assistance for removal; therefore, it was believed to lack the problem of human error present in other forms of birth control. The concerns over poor women, especially those on welfare, having large families which they could not financially support, made (for some) Norplant a tempting requirement for receiving welfare. However, this lead to a conflict over the basic legal right in our country to control one's body over the expectation that people who cannot afford a family should not keep reproducing. While conflict theorists would predict the tax-paying population to win because they are in power, here they did not. The First Amendment protects poor women in this instance and therefore, it is illegal for the government to condition welfare receipt on whether a mother chooses not to procreate. However, as we said, women in other countries do not necessarily enjoy the same personal rights as women do in America.

But even tamer policies like family planning programs in least-industrialized countries and tax incentives to encourage / discourage birth are frequently fraught with conflict. Also, there is the concern that such policies are racist for a few reasons. First, Black Africans and Asian generally populate most of the countries that would need such control. Secondly, some believe such programs are class biased in that they are only aimed at the poorer least industrialized countries or the poor within industrialized countries. This creates a conflict over whose rights are important...the poor? the rich? society at large?

Economic Issues

When you shop, how many of you "price shop" for the "best buy"? While not wanting to be overcharged for items we purchase is understandable in a capitalistic society, our quest for the "best bargain" financially does impede change in some of these environmental issues.

For example, the desire to keep prices low in order to attract customers, but not too low to hinder profits, is part of the reason behind capital flight that we discussed earlier. The cheaper a company can manufacture an item, the more likely they are to pass some of those savings on to the consumer as a means to attract his / her business. However, as we covered, cheaper manufacturing sometimes involves moving production outside of the United States to a country that, among other perks, has fewer environmental standards. This weakens the effectiveness of U.S. environmental regulations.

Our quest for "bargains" also influences our food purchases and quality. Food companies frequently rely on artificial additives to create artificial flavor in food or prevent spoiling. As a result, produce is now available almost any time of year – even if it is not in season. Animals are bigger with less fat, more meat to sell. Interestingly, this helps keep the price of food down because farmers can produce more goods, thereby reducing costs. However, this increased productivity comes at a price. Meat processing frequently occurs at such rapid speeds that there is an *increased* risk of contamination. For example, Intersoll (1990) found that in one poultry plant, over half (57%)the chickens arrived at the plant with bacteria such as salmonella, but over three quarters (76%) were infected with it when they were done being processed. Furthermore, fruits and vegetables are frequently coated with chemicals to prevent insect damage or fertilized with powerful drugs to produce bigger results. These chemicals can leech into the food itself and then be ingested by us when we eat it. Again, however, these steps are not necessary. Organic farmers raise animals and grow fruit and vegetables without all of these added chemicals or unsanitary processing practices. However, as a result, they produce fewer goods which means that they have to charge more to generate enough profit to continue their practices. While people are increasingly willing to pay more for less adulterated food, these people are clearly the minority nation-wide. Consequently, it is ironic that one has to pay more to get food with less added to it; and, this conflict over price makes a viable solution, less popular.

<u>Societal Changes</u>

This is a broad category that encompasses everything from religious beliefs, to changing women's position in society, to changing the values that associate masculinity with family size. Historically, many religions oppose family planning; however, today the Roman Catholic Church, and perhaps some Muslims, are really the only groups who still actively advocate against birth control. Yet, some argue that religion isn't a very strong argument today because even though a religious doctrine may discourage family planning, many individuals still chose to practice it. For example, in the United States, Catholics are just as likely as non-Catholics to practice birth control and frequently have small families as well.

Many argue instead that our current population and environmental concerns have more to do with the role of women in the least industrialized countries and the value of materialism in the most industrialized countries. As we mentioned previously, in many poorer countries, women have little if any rights or power. This affects population in a number of ways. First, for many of these women, their only source of status is in their ability to have children. The more children they have the more respect (but rarely power) in the community. Secondly, in some countries women have to ask their husband's permission in order to even receive contraceptives. Even if a woman *wants* to practice family planning, if her husband does not, there is little she can do. She has no power over her body; her husband does.

Many agree that education is key to changing women's experiences. Studies consistently show that in poorer countries, the more education women receive, the more likely they are to delay their first birth, use birth control and limit or space their children (United Nations Population Fund, 1997). However, remember that education is only part of the story. If greater movement for social equality isn't also followed, these women's husbands are not likely to support their wives' education or men will not look for educated wives when choosing spouses, which means that little will change.

Lastly, we need to change our values – especially our values about material wealth. One hundred years ago, we didn't have the concept of trash that we do today. Everything had its value…and when that value diminished, people found a new use and value for the item. So, for example, the grandmother of one of the authors *still* saves wrapping paper and ribbon to use for another package, saves the cotton wads at the top of aspirin containers to use as cotton balls, recycles old socks into dust rags and uses nylons with runs in them to tie together newspaper that goes into the recycling. Some of these habits are a direct result from being part of the Depression generation who suffered that historical collapse of the economy; but, some of this also stems from the lessons she learned from her own mother who came over from Europe at the turn of the century. And she is not alone. Many in her cohort still practice the same behaviors as she does. So what changed?

Well, through the Twentieth Century, the United States and other industrialized countries began to enjoy unprecedented levels of wealth.   Plus, as women entered the workforce, family income increased and "time saving" products became highly desired. Hence, we now have entire lines of products whose sole purpose is to be disposable – from disposable pens, to disposable diapers to disposable razors…to be used and thrown out when their usefulness is exhausted. Previously we discussed the difficulty in actually disposing of all of this "disposable" stuff. In a Gesellschaft society we are more focused on our individual ease of living without much consideration to the wider community impact of our disposable society. Moreover, the only way to change this is to change our attitudes about disposable goods. Disposable diapers, for example, do not readily decompose and will be sitting in landfills possibly for centuries. Cloth diapers are a little less convenient (one actually has to take the time and wash those or pay for a service to do so), but will not be filling a landfill for longer than the child who soiled those diapers will even be walking the earth.

Recycling is another means of changing our attitudes about a disposable society, and the recycling movement has met with some success. Recycling is now very common in the United States as many communities accept various forms of paper, glass, plastic and aluminum for transformation into other usable goods. This is a move in the right direction; but it still doesn't address our incredibly high consumption of non-recyclable but disposable goods.

Unless changes in our value system occur, lakes such as this will be unusable

Summary

During the last 200 years, the industrial world has changed rapidly, and with it, new concerns over population demographics and the environment have evolved. Some see the industrial countries as the main culprit due to their population concentration in urban areas, their material society, their large factories and their disposable attitudes. Others see the developing non-industrial societies as the culprit because they are the ones responsible for the most rapid population growth worldwide.

Regardless of where the majority of the responsibility lies, the conflict over available resources like food, land and material goods is undeniable. Those who are in the more powerful industrial countries are in the position to direct these resources for their own purposes (e.g. the manufacturing of more goods). Those who are in the less developed countries are left clamoring for scraps. Their political powerlessness helps exacerbate the problems their growing populations produce.

While change has begun, such as in the area of recycling, conflict also exists over other viable solutions. Many proposed solutions are problematic because they have an ethnocentric focus that sees the industrialized middle class behavior as the normative behavior. Others are problematic because their approaches violate our sense of individual freedom (such as China's "one-child" policy) or are economically costly.

Regardless, it is clear to many that more needs to be done soon. At the heart of any change will be a change in attitude that is more Gemeinschaft- focused from our current individualistic Gesellschaft ways. Until we have some sort of change in social ideology, there is little hope for serious change in our current population and environmental behavior.

Critical Thinking

1. Do you think the United States encourages people to have children? If so, how and do we encourage this for all people or simply certain groups?

2. The issue of the "greenhouse effect" and the related "hole in the ozone" are hotly debated issues. Find information for *both* sides of the debate and use your critical thinking skills from Chapter 1 to evaluate which side is more scientifically compelling.

3. What can be done to control global environmental issues? The chapter discusses that environmental problems in one country are not contained in that area alone, but instead spreads. Furthermore, the chapter also discusses that companies have moved production to countries with less restrictive environmental safeguards. How can we balance the individual desire for material wealth, companies search for profits and environmental responsibility?

4. What does your school cafeteria do with its extra food? Why? Is this feasible from a distribution perspective? What conflict does it address?

5. Ehrlich and Holdren (1971) argue that synergism, threshold effects, trigger effects and time lag effects increase the prevalence of environmental degradation. Which do you think is the *most* detrimental? List as many examples of each that you can. Which is the most easily corrected? Why?

Bibliography

CBS News. "Winter of 2000 Warmest in History of U.S." March 9, 2000.

Commoner, Barry. *The Closing Circle: Nature, Man and Technology.* New York: Knopf, 1971.

Ehrlich, P.R. A.H. Ehrlich. and J.P Holdren. *Eco-science: Population, Resources, Environment.* San Francisco, CA: Freeman, 1977.

Ehrlich, Paul R. and John Holdren. "Population and Environment." Pp. 21-30 in *The Population Debate,* edited by Daniel Callahan. Garden City, N.Y.: Anchor, 1971.

Engelman, Robert, Brian Halweil and Danielle Nierenberg. "Rethinking Population, Improving Lives." Pp. 127-148 in *State of the World*, edited by Linda Starke, New York: W.W. Norton, 2002.

Hardin, Garrett. *Living within Limit: Ecology, Economics, and Population Taboos.* New York: Oxford University Press, 1993.

Hauser, Philip. *Population Perspective.* New Brunswick, NJ: Rutgers University Press, 1970.

Ingersoll, Bruce. "Fatter Slaughter Lines are Contaminating Much U.S. Poultry." *Wall Street Journal*, Pp. A1, A6 (November 16, 1990).

Kemps, Dominic. "Deaths, Diseases Traced to Environment." *Popline*, 20(May-June, 1998): 3.

Lowe, M.S. and S.R. Bowlby. "Population and Environment" in *Environmental Issues in the 1990s.* edited by A.M. Mannion and S.R. Bowlby. New York. John Wiley and Sons Ltd., 1992.

MacGregor, Ian. "Natural Distribution of Metals and Some Economic Effects." *Annals of the American Academy of Political and Social Science.* 420 (1975): 31-45.

Malthus, Thomas Robert. *First Essay on Population 1798.* London: Macmillian, 1798.

McDonald, Kim. A. "Debate over Global Warming Heats up Meeting of Climatologists." *Chronicle of Higher Education* (February 5, 1999): A17.

National Solid Wastes Management Association. "New Landfills Can Solve the Garbage Crisis." Pp. 122-127 in *The Environmental Crisis*, edited by David L. Bender and Bruno Leone. San Diego, CA: Greenhaven Press, 1991.

New York Times (Author Unknown) "As Oceans Warm, Problems from Viruses and Bacteria Mount." *New York Times*. Pp. 15 (January, 24, 1999).

Ottaway, R. *Less People, Less Pollution: An Answer to Environmental Decline Caused by the World's Population Explosion*. London: Bow Group, 1990.

Pimentel, David, Maria Tort, Linda D'Anna, Anne Krawic, Joshua Berger, Jessica Rossman, Fridah Mugo, Nancy Doon, Michael Shriberg, Erica Howard, Susan Lee, and Jonathan Talbot. "Ecology of Increasing Disease: Population Growth and Environmental Degradation." *BioScience*. 48 (1998): 817-7.

Read, P. *Responding to Global Warming: The Technology, Economics and Politics of Sustainable Energy*. Atlantic Highlands, NJ: Zed Books, 1994.

Ridfer, Ronald. "The Impact of Population Growth on Resources and Environment." Pp. 109-119. in *Toward The End of Growth*, edited by Charles F. Westoff. Englewood Cliffs, N.J.: Prentice-Hall, 1973.

Romero, Simon and David Barbozz. "Trapped in Heat in Texas Truck: 18 People Die" *New York Times*. Pp. A-1 (May 15, 2003).

Seeley, Katharine Q. and Jennifer Lee. "E.P.A. Calls U.S. Cleaner and Greener than 30 Years Ago." *New York Times*. Pp. A28 (June 24, 2003).

Shaw, R. P. "Rapid Population Growth and Environmental Degradation: Ultimate versus Proximate Factors." *Environmental Conservation*. 16:3 (1989): 199-208.

Singer, Fred S. "The Sky Isn't Falling and the Ocean Isn't Rising." *Wall Street Journal*. Pp. A22 (November 10, 1997).

Statistical Abstract of the United States, 115th ed., Table 402. U.S. Bureau of the Census. Washington, D.C.: U.S. Government Printing Office, 1995.

———. 118th ed, Table 407. U.S. Bureau of the Census. Washington, D.C.: U.S. Government Printing Office, 1998.

Stevens, William K. Science Academy Disputes Attack on Global Warming." *New York Times* (April 22, 1998).

Stockwell, Edward G. *Population and People*. Chicago: Quadrangle, 1968.

Thomlinson, Ralph. *Population Dynamics: Causes and Consequences of World Demographic Change*. New York: Random House, 1965.

United Nations Population Fund. *1997 State of the World Population*. New York: United Nations, 1997.

U.S. Commission on Population Growth. *Population Growth and the American Future*. New York: Signet, 1972.
U.S. Immigration and Naturalization Services, U.S. Department of Justice. "INS Releases Updated Estimates of U.S. Undocumented Resident Population". (January 31, 2003) http://www.immigration.gov/graphics/publicaffairs/summaries

Chapter 11

International Social Problems – Globalization, War and Terrorism

Every social problem discussed in this book has an international dimension. After World War II ended in 1945, a movie about the destructive power of the first atomic bomb was shown in our schools. The film was called "One World or None". Its message? Nation states and societies must cooperate to form a united world so nuclear war would not destroy us all. In 1946 we helped form the United Nations. Soon we all knew the world had gotten smaller in many ways. We all now lived in what some scholars called "a global village". Changes in transportation and communication ushered us into the electronic-atomic age. Supersonic jets, satellite TV transmissions and instant phone calls or faxes made the world one in a way it had never been before. As sociologists Perucci and Pilisuk pointed out over 30 years ago: "...the growing international involvement of most countries would seem to demand that domestic problems be placed within an international perspective..." (1971: xvii).

Contacts and connections for drugs and crime occur daily. International agencies, such as Interpol, are at work also to police and control such social problems. Alcoholism is not just a U.S. problem but effects nations like France and Russia, just to mention two societies.

As everyone knows, the battle for gender equality is a never-ending battle both at home and abroad. Women in underdeveloped countries, from Afghanistan to Zambia, are fighting today to get basic and secondary education for all girls and women. The conflict over education for women often meets stiff opposition from male-dominated societies around the globe.

The racial problem, of course, is not restricted to the U.S. Bias, discrimination and racial segregation dominate both developed and underdeveloped nations from England to Zanzibar. Even gradations of one's color determine life chances and job opportunities in Brazil and Hawaii. Racial differences continue to be a constant problem in most societies throughout the world.

The aged and elderly as a group are coming to dominate some European countries and Japan. The U.N. projects that Europe's population will decline to 632 million in 2050 from 728 million today (Kauffman, 2003: 259). The number of people over 65 will triple and the number of people over 80 will increase fivefold. Enormous expenditures on private and governmental pensions are driving some nations to the brink of financial disaster. Just how long a declining work force can support a growing elderly population is problematic. Just how much longer a younger population will pay for medical and health care bills for an aging population remains to be seen. Could some nations begin to turn to euthanasia as a solution? The recent heat wave in France took its heaviest toll on elderly people. The French government was severely criticized for not responding sooner to the crisis. Is this a preview of coming events as the elderly population continues to grow in France?

The family as a basic institution is beginning to change throughout the world, especially as industrialization continues to spread to underdeveloped countries. More and more young people leave their families of origin in rural areas and flee to the cities in search of work in modern factories and offices. This often weakens and undermines the traditional extended and nuclear families in rural areas. Such a situation opens up, for the first time in underdeveloped countries, a "Pandora's box" of troubles and problems, and opportunities for change, explored in Chapter 7 on the family.

Education affects all societies. Many underdeveloped societies send their smartest and best students to study abroad. The social problem is that many of these students decide to stay in the U.S. where jobs and the way of life is freer and more beneficial financially. This causes a serious "brain-drain" from underdeveloped countries. For example, doctors and teachers leave India every year to come to the U.S. to pursue their careers, while the desperate education and health needs in India suffer as a result. Mental health problems exist in many different forms in all countries of the world. Mental hospitals have historically been used by totalitarian nations as a way of confining and controlling political protesters and dissidents. In the old Soviet Union until 1989, people were sent to mental hospitals and Gulogs as punishment for opposing the state. North Korea and other totalitarian states still do that today.

Poverty and unemployment are of epidemic proportions throughout the world. In hundreds of underdeveloped countries, "the rich are getting richer and the poor poorer." Facts will be provided under the "Globalization" section in this chapter. Our prosperity, technology and wealth, via multi-national corporations, sometimes make poverty and unemployment worse in underdeveloped countries – worse than it might otherwise be.

Every nation has some kind of population and environment problem. As pointed out earlier, Europe and Japan are now confronted with a growing aged population while its young working-age population is not growing as fast as it did in the past. Many underdeveloped countries, though making some progress on controlling its overall population, are still growing too fast to provide decent, steady employment for its youth. Consequently, youth gangs roam large cities in their society to somehow eke out a living. Some turn to crime or drugs (like sniffing glue) to alleviate their poverty and despair.

In Brazil the rain forest is slowly being depleted as multi-national corporations from the U.S. and elsewhere exploit its natural resources. In the Sudan, a civil war broke out when oil was discovered in southern Sudan, and the Moslem-led government began pushing out and persecuting the Christian minority in that area. Thus, paving the way for foreign development and investment in the oil fields there.

And so it goes. Every social problem we have discussed and analyzed has some kind of international connection and dimension to it. In this chapter we will examine and explore three major conflict processes that literally have changed the world and will continue to do so: Globalization, War and Terrorism.

Globalization

If anyone had any doubt that we live in a global society today, the events of September 11, 2001, proved it. In addition to the many American lives lost, nearly 500 foreigners from 91 different countries all over the world were killed that day – accounting for more than 17% of all casualties (Kugler, 2002). Globalization's role in the terror attacks is clear since most terrorists come from the Moslem middle-East.

In 1973, Anthony J. Wiener, Chairman of the Research Management Council of the Hudson Institute wrote: "Changing international relations - - as they are affected by varying growth rates -

- new patterns of trade and the growing role of the multi-national corporation will be important in the immediate future" (1973: 48).

In 1974 Paddy Chayevsky wrote a screenplay and a book, *Network*. In the movie, the Chairman of the Board of the television network explained to Howard Beale, a very popular TV commentator, the kind of global system we have developed today.

> You are an old man who thinks in terms of nations and peoples. There are no nations. There are no peoples. There are no Russians, no east, no west, no Communists, no Third Worlds. There is only one holistic system of systems. One vast and immane, interwoven, interactive, multi-variant, multi-national dominion of dollars: Petrol-dollars, elctro-dollars, Yens, Pounds, Rubles and sheckles. It is the international system of currency which determines the totality of life on this planet. That is the structure of the world today. That is the atomic, and sub-atomic, and galactic structure of things today. And you have meddled with the primal forces of nature, Mr. Beale and you will atone...

Then the Chairman of the Board continues:

> You get up on your twenty-one inch screen and howl about America and democracy. There is no America. There is no democracy. There is only I.B.M. and I.T.T. and A.T. & T, and Dupont, Dow, Union Carbide and Exxon. Those are the nations of the world today. We no longer live in a world of nations and ideologies Mr. Beale. The world is a college of corporations, all inexorably determined by the immutable by-laws of business. The world is a business, Mr. Beale, and it has been ever since Man crawled out of the slime.

> (*http://www.bridgeboymusic.com/billyboy/network.htm* January 5, 2003)

In the opening of his 1992 book, *The Work of Nations*, Robert Reich declared:

> We are living through a transformation that will rearrange the politics and economics of the coming century. There will be no *national* products or technologies, no national corporations, no national industries. There will no longer

> be national economics, at least as we have come to
> understand the concept (1992: 3).

The same can be said for our national society, as we have known it
historically.

In 1999, Thomas Friedman in his best-seller book: *The Lexus
and the Olive Tree: Understanding Globalization* put it this way:

> What is new today is the degree and intensity with which
> the world is being tied together in a single globalized
> marketplace. Daily foreign exchange trading in 1900 was
> measured in millions of dollars. In 1992, it was $820
> billion a day...and by April, 1998, it was up to $1 ½ trillion
> a day, and still rising (xv).

Anthony Giddens shares this same view in his book, *Runaway
World: How Globalization is Reshaping Our Lives* (2000). In 2001,
the Society for the Study of Social Problems recognized Globalization
as a crucial social issue by devoting the whole *Social Problems*,
November issue, edited by David Smith, to that topic.

But today's globalization is not only different in degree from
the past it is also different in kind. The previous era of globalization
(pre-WWII) was built on falling transportation costs (via railroad,
steamship, trucks and autos). Today's era is built on falling
telecommunications costs - - thanks to microchips, satellites, fiber
optics and, what has been called "the Eighth Continent", the Internet
(DePalma, 2002: vii).

Leslie Sklair offers a new way of looking at our global system
- - one based on "transnational practices'. They operate in three
spheres: economic, political and cultural ideology (1991: 6-7). A
major conflict has emerged within and outside these three systems
between Corporate International Power and Police vs. the Global Social
Justice Movement (GSJM) to retain freedom and autonomy of the U.S.
and defend rights of women, labor and the environment worldwide.

In exploring this major conflict between the power of
globalization and the GSJM, in this section we will: 1) Look at the
various meanings and definitions of globalization; 2) Describe the
growing size, power, and wealth of multinational corporations while
world poverty increases; 3) Present a brief history about how the
World Bank, International Monetary Fund and the World Trade
Organization - - the Big 3 social institutions - - are establishing the
foundaton and "constitution of a single global economy" (Clarke,

2002: 44); 4) Examine and analyze from a conflict perspective the mobilization, actions and tactics of the Global Social Justice Movement (GSJM) opposed to globalization; 5)   Last, some ideas will be presented as to the actions some scholars feel need to be taken by our society and government to contain and control the power of multi-national corporations.

Definitions of Globalization
Let's look at a few definitions and meanings of globalization. Kurt Finsterbusch in his book, *Taking Sides* (2003: 352) notes that:

> ...Globalization stands for worldwide processes, activities and institutions. It involves world markets, world finance, world communications, world media, world religions, world popular culture, world rights movements, world drug trade, etc. The focus of most commentators is on the world economy, which many believe promotes strong growth in world wealth.

Herman   Daly   contrasts   "internationalization"   with "globalization".

> Internationalization refers to the increasing importance of relations among nations. Although the basic unit of community and policy remains the nation, increasingly trade, treaties, alliances, protocols and other formal agreements and communications are necessary elements for nations to thrive....Globalization, on the other hand, refers to global economic integration of many formerly national economies   into   one   global   economy....Economic integration is made possible by free trade - - especially by free capital mobility - - and by easy or uncontrolled migration.   In contrast to 'internationalization', which simply recognizes that nations increasingly rely on understandings among one another, 'globalization' is the effective erasure of national boundaries for economic purposes (2003: 362).

The German "Research Group World Society" and Dirk Messner see an evolution from an "international system" to an "international society" to eventually a "world society", as shown in Table 11-1 (1996; 2002).

Table 11-1
Evolution Toward a World Society

International system	*Interrelation* of and *interaction* states.
International society	*In addition: institutionalization processes.* Institutionalized rules of conduct for states, based on common interests. Intensificaiton of systematic insternational relations with the common goal of developing norms and institutions (international organizations, regimes). Stabilization of expectations by Rules governing international relations.
World society	*In addition: diversification and diffusion of actors, further differentiation of action levels, stabilization of universal guiding principles,* Apart from states, economic and social actors are becoming global players in world politics. Transnational spaces are emerging. Local, national, regional and global levels of action are more and more densely interwoven. Universal guiding principles are in the Process of being established.

Source: *Forschungsgruppe Weltgesellschaft* 1996: 18(modified). Messner, 2002: 27.

Such an evolution involves a "higher degree of organization" and "increasing involvement of non-state actors in transboundary interactions and a multiplication and networking of political, economic and social levels of action" (Messner, 2002: 27).

Manfred Steger distinguishes "Globalism" – a market ideology based on free-market capitalistic meanings going back to Adam Smith – and "Globalization" – a social process defined and described in different, often contradictory, ways (2002: 13). He argues that "Globalism" is a new-liberal ideology endowing any definition of "Globalization" with certain norms, values and beliefs that assume capitalism can only benefit the world.

Others argue that so-called "Globalization" is really just so much "Glo-baloney", or a myth, for three reasons:

1. It is not a sufficiently precise or exact term, transcending many different academic disciplines (Strange, 1996; Weiss, 1998).
2. The process is limited to essentially developed countries in Europe, America and East Asia (Hirst and Thompson, 1999).
3. International trade and agreements are not recent processes but began about five centuries ago (Frank, 1990; Gilpin, 2000; Wallerstein, 1979).

So sociologists and other scholars differ on what precisely globalization is or means.

Growth of Power and Wealth of Multi-National Corporations
      What sociologists all agree on is that multi-national (or transnational) corporations have much power today. Large corporations exploring new worlds is not new. The East India and Hudson Bay Companies did so in the 16th Century. What is new today, however, is that multi-national corporations now wield more economic and political power than most nation states.
      Most recently, Tony Clarke, Chair of the Committee on Corporations of the International Forum on Globalization, observed:

> In the last decade or so, the transnational corporation has virtually supplanted the nation state as the central institution dominating the lives of people in most parts of the world. By creating a global market system that now spans the four corners of the planet, the transnational corporation has moved into the very center of our history as a dynamic colonial force reshaping the destiny of people and nations...These corporations now hold the reins of power more firmly than do many of the world's governments (2002: 41).

      By creating a global market system, huge corporations have moved into the very center of history as a dynamic and dominant new-colonial force, reshaping the future of peoples and nations. But this does not occur without conflict and harmful effects on millions of people.

Conflict over globalization centers around opinions whether it is helpful or harmful to underdeveloped nations. Some argue it is helpful since it encourages free trade that creates more jobs and money for poor people. For example, Brian Gallagher, on the editorial page of *U.S.A. Today*, in 1999, commenting on the WTO Seattle meeting cites the following statistics: "Average incomes worldwide have tripled in 50 years. About 66% of humanity enjoys what the United Nations calls a "medium" level of development, compared with 55% in 1975. Ten percent of mankind is "very poor", by the U.N.'s global measure compared with 20% in 1975." (1999: 14A).

Most sociologists argue that multi-nationals are harmful as they exercise power over the governments, societies and environments of underdeveloped countries in such a way that they actually function as colonial machines of exploitation. For example, foreign-based corporations are no longer obligated by law to create a certain quota of local jobs, or have restrictive quotas on using natural resources of a country. Former domestic corporations who have gone global have largely abandoned their local or national responsibilities in favor of larger markets and lower production costs overseas. For example, there are over 800 so-called "free-trade zones" around the world where no requirements to meet labor, social and environmental standards even exist. Deregulation, privatization, and huge political contributions to both political parties in the U.S. make multi-nationals a powerful political and economic force in the U.S. and abroad.

U.S. jobs are lost due to globalization (Credit: Joseph Elliott)

The fact is that these companies can move their operations from one country to another at a moment's notice for more profitable investments, or to avoid an increasingly unfavorable business climate (for example, as Congress and the SEC recently have enacted some legal accounting changes). Also this freedom for companies has taken its toll over time on lowering real wages, neglecting environmental safeguards, and ignoring local development priorities. Under worldwide free trade expansion, multinational corporations have acquired unprecedented and unregulated control over resources, people, cultures, government, food and water supplies - - virtually every conceivable aspect of public life in developing nations. The result? Increased concentration of wealth and increased poverty in the world.

For example, the richest 225 individuals on earth are mostly CEO's of multinational corporations. They have a combined wealth equal to *half* of all the people on earth. In comparing the nation of Zambia with the multinational Goldman Sacks, *The Guardian Newspaper* noted: "One is an African country that makes $2.2 billion a year and shares it among 25 million people. The other is an investment bank that makes $2.7 billion a year and shares it among 161 people" (Clarke, 2002: 42). This is not only true in respect to underdeveloped countries but among industrialized states as well. He also points out that:

> In less than 20 years, the number of globe-spanning corporations has jumped from seven to over 45,000, a 650 percent increase. Today, 52 of the top 100 economies around the world are trans-national corporations rather than nation states. Mitsubishi is bigger than either Denmark or Norway; Daimler-Chrysler now outstrips South Africa and Saudi Arabia; and, Siemen's yearly income is greater than Ireland's or Chile's (2002: 41).

What is most striking about global corporations today is not only their vast economic power but also the way they penetrate and dominate the social, political, and cultural lives of nation states and its people. International Action Center (IAC) co-founder, Sarah Flounders asserts that, "...The World Bank and IMF policies have impoverished the entire developing world" (Brundage, 2001: 21). In the last five to 10 years, poverty on a global scale has more than doubled. At the same time, the wealth of the top *half of one percent* has doubled.

A 1998 U.N. Human Development Report noted the income disparity between the top 20 percent and the bottom 20 percent of the world's population is now 150 to 1, double what it was 30 years ago. Sociologist Anthony Giddens pointed out that "the share of the poorest fifth of the world's population in global income has dropped from 2.3

percent to 1.4 percent between 1989 and 1998. The proportion taken by the richest fifth, on the other hand, has risen" (2002: 33).

A recent World Bank study found 2.78 billion people, nearly half the world's population, living on less than $2.00 a day, or less than $370 a year (Toedtman, 2002: 10). So the rich are getting richer and the poor poorer. Let's now look briefly at the history of three international organizations that have aided and abetted the power of multinational corporations in the world.

Brief History of "The Big 3" Bretton Woods Organizations

The three "Bretton Woods" international organizations - - the International Monetary Fund (IMF), the World Bank (WB), and, the General Agreement on Tariffs and Trade (GATT) [and later the World Trade Organization] - - were formed in 1944.

These three major social organizations were started at a New Hampshire resort area, Bretton Woods, where representatives of 33 nations met to design the world's post-WWII economic order. America laid the foundation then for global capitalism modeled after U.S. corporate capitalism. In the early post-war years, the U.S. wanted a system of fixed exchange rates to control currency fluctuations; an International Monetary Fund to ensure a quick flow of money in the world; a World Bank to gather together and direct development finance; and, a General Agreement on Tariffs and Trade to ensure an open global trading system that would benefit the U.S. The World Trade Organization (WTO) evolved later in the 1990's, but functions as a third sister to the World Bank and I.M.F. (Daly, 2003: 363; Reich, 1992: 63).

With this international foundation, in 1975 David Rockefeller, through the Trilateral Commission, brought together 325 CEO's, presidents, prime ministers and senior government officials from Europe, Asia and North America. A strategy was put in place it was alleged, to dismantle and replace the public sector of government and give business more power via privatization and de-regulation, and for-profit corporations to replace government services and non-profits, especially in health care. As a result, big business coalitions like the European Round Table of Industrialists, The Club of Rome, and the U.S. Business Round Table were formed.   They aimed to reorganize the role and functions of governments throughout the world to accommodate the interests of multinationals' marketing and investment and make it easier for them to expand abroad
(Clarke, 2002: 43).

In the early 1980's, the U.N. Center for Transnational Corporations, which had been established to monitor the operations of transnational corporations and develop an international code of conduct, was effectively dismantled due to mounting pressure by corporate elites in the U.S. During this period, the so-called "Washington Consensus" under the Reagan Administration called for the liberalization of trade, investment and finance and was vigorously promoted through the Bretton Woods institutions.

In 1989, with the collapse of the U.S.S.R. and eastern Europe, new untapped markets began to open up for large multinational corporations and investments in that area of the world.

The crucial turning point came with the creation of the World Trade Organization (WTO) [to replace GATT] in 1994, followed by regional trade agreements such as the North American Free Trade Agreement (NAFTA), which some claimed threatened the export of many U.S. jobs to Mexico. The WTO's "economic constitution" was written behind closed doors by trade bureaucrats and corporate lobbyists. They had little if any input from any sector other than big business. It isn't surprising then that under the WTO only large corporations are the beneficiaries of the rights it creates. The interests of consumers, citizens and others in society and in the world are nowhere to be found (Shrybman, 2002: 43). This is undemocratic and violates the core values of a free, democratic society. It borders on arbitrary and dictatorial use of economic power.

The WTO was designed to become a global governing institution about trade, investment and finance. To carry out this purpose the WTO was given not only judicial powers to settle trade disputes but also legislative powers. Under the WTO, a group of unelected trade officials would, in effect, have the power to override economic, social and environmental policy decisions of nation states and democratic legislatures around the world.

For example, if any country decides to ban the export of raw logs as a way of conserving its forests, or ban the use of cancer-causing pesticides, it can be charged under the WTO by member states on behalf of their corporations for "obstructing the free flow of trade and investment". A secret tribunal of trade officials would then decide whether these national laws were " trade restrictive" under the WTO's rules and regulations. Once the secret tribunal issues its ruling, no outside appeal is possible. Nations have agreed to this since they apparently benefit economically from other WTO rules and regulations. The country convicted is obligated to change its national law or face perpetual trade sanctions (Clarke, 2002: 43-44). It's no wonder the Global Social Justice Movement has held public demonstrations at meetings of the WTO and the Bretton Woods or U.N. organizations about trade and finance since the people or the environment often are harmed by WTO rulings, while multinationals benefit.

<u>Conflict Theory and the Global Social Movement</u>
        We are all familiar with various theories of conflict - - Marx, Lenin, Dahrendorf, Coser, Wallerstein (1979). Some accept the inevitability of globalization with all its centralized powers, ultimately held by multinational corporations. Others, however, want such globalization to be more democratic and include more people and groups that are concerned about women's status, labor conditions, and the environment. This causes conflict. Groups and organizations have for many years argued whether colonialism was basically good or bad. Colonialism occurred when developing nations completely controlled underdeveloped countries in the 19th Century just as England dominated the early U.S. colonies. So it is with globalization - - as previously mentioned, some groups maintain it is good for everyone, including the poor in underdeveloped countries (Weidenbaum, 2003: 354-63). Others assert it only benefits the rich and wealthy, and hardly anyone else (Daly, 2003: 362-67).

<u>Three Major Tactics of the Global Social Justice Movement</u>
        The Global Social Justice Movement (GSJM) employs three different tactics to obtain its goals: 1). Protests and demonstrations; 2). Negotiations through non-governmental organizations (NGOs), and, 3). Direct pressure and lobbying its own government. What the mass media called the 'anti-globalization movement', (the Global Social Justice Movement) started in Europe in the early 1990's and as its primary tactic, has demonstrated and protested at international meetings throughout the world. It mobilized internationally and was present at international meetings in Seattle, Quebec City, Genoa, New York City, France, and other places, most recently in Cancun in 2003 (Roth, 2002: A-10). Their principal targets were the World Bank, the International Monetary Fund and the WTO - - "The Big 3".
The GSJM involves more than 700 groups. The International Action Center, Direct Action Network, the U.S. Green Party and other environmental groups, Partnership for Civil Justice, Fifty Years is Enough, the Ruckus Society, International Forum on Globalization, Global Exchange, Focus on the Global South, Third World Network, the Rainforest Action Network, and smaller college and activist groups

around the world   (Steger, 2002: 119).   One group, Project South: Institute for the Elimination of Poverty & Genocide, is a community-based membership organization that conducts popular economic and political education with action research. It organizes local communities and helps to overcome injustice anywhere in the world. It creates change that will solve the problems of "...those who are most oppressed, exploited and marginalized" (Project South Leaflet, 2003). It also is critical of and critiques the capitalistic system and its global corporate agenda for the continuing and deepening inequality and injustice in society. The Project South timeline of today's globalization summarizes a hundred years of economic history, government policy, and popular movement history.

Various groups originally were planning to picket the IMF and World Bank meeting on September 28-29, 2001. Due to the terrorist attacks on 9/11/01 that meeting was cancelled. The GSJM instead planned a demonstration in Washington, D.C. for peace at the nation's Capitol on September 29th. The attorney for Partnership for Civil Justice met with park police, local police and U.S. government representatives to secure permits for that day. This time, they assured their members, there would be no problem with the police. The fact that it was a permitted demonstration was very important to people after 9/11, since they fear terrorist acts wherever large groups of people gather. Just days before the planned demonstration the GSJM received its first taste of political opposition. The Secret Service revoked the permits, banning large demonstrations in Lafayette Park for 30 days with an unlimited extension.   This government power to protect "national security" passed without a hitch, forcing demonstrators to move their protest to the smaller Freedom Plaza.   Hence, the government and police blunted the effectiveness of the GSJM.

The GSJM engages in legal protests and demonstrations. They are not terrorists. All the group wants to do is to end the predatory lending practices of these multinationals throughout the world as well as curb the arbitrary, undemocratic free trade practices and arbitrary power of WTO, as explained earlier. The WTO's practices have created staggering worldwide poverty, environmental devastation, slave labor and sweatshop working conditions, mass starvation and medical deprivation (Brundage, 2001: 17). Nike, for

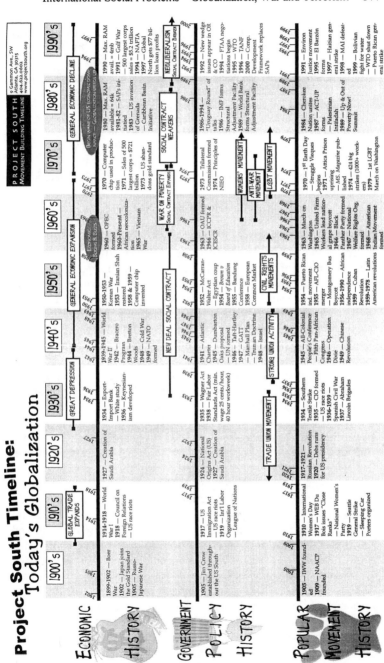

instance, "subcontracts production to 75,000 workers in China, South Korea, Malaysia, Taiwan and Thailand" (Steger, 2002: 28).

> Children really are toiling at menial labor in Bangladesh and elsewhere. Dangerous working conditions are pervasive in Mexico and other parts of Latin America. Abusive Chinese officials do deprive workers of their right to defend their interests. More factories really do mean more smokestacks and pollution (Gallagher, 1999: 14A).

So the concerns of the GSJM are real and their protest tactics are aimed at bringing about meaningful social change.

At the World Economic Forum in New York City in February, 2002, "...the protestors were driven by such causes as lowering the cost of AIDS drugs, improving treatment of workers in poor countries and protecting the environment" (Ibarguen, 2002: A-10). So the conflict over the power of multinationals and international organizations and the democratic power of the people goes on. It is a struggle for rights of women, labor and the environment on the international stage.

Given our nation's newfound obsession with terrorism and the passage of the Anti-Terrorism Act of 1995 and the Patriot Act of 2001 many within the movement feel that they will be unfairly targeted by the U.S. Government. The Government is "going to take action against political dissenters, against immigrants under the guise of security when these actions are not security related; they are an expansion of police powers and government powers to monitor political discussion", one GSJM leader stated (Brundage, 2001: 19). Another leader, Sarah Watts, spoke with gravity about the level of unchecked police violence. "The use of force really opened my eyes to what we were up against. The use of tear-gas indiscriminately, even if protestors were just holding a sign - - 99% of these protestors just want to get their message across" (Brundage, 2001: 19). Another leader of the Partnership for Civil Justice, Mara Berheyden-Hilliard, said that during the IMF march on Washington, D.C. in April, 2001, she witnessed a rise in unchecked, illegal police tactics as the social justice movement has grown against globalization. There was extreme conduct by police such as "...illegal mass arrests, detention of hundreds of demonstrators who were lawfully demonstrating. They kicked people out (of the area), containing them, hog-tied them wrist to ankle, kept them on buses, denied them food, water and bathrooms" (Brundage, 2001: 19).

"In the ensuing days, folks were beaten who weren't demonstrating at all. There was a raid by police on the meeting hall, convergence center and offices of the demonstrators where they confiscated thousands...of pages of First Amendment-protected literature because it contained political statements. They confiscated banners, signs, and medical supplies" (Brundage, 2001: 21).

Subversive police tactics, rarely the subject of media scrutiny, involve police operating under cover to incite a riot. The mass media give attention to the Black Bloc, a small group of anarchist youth who practice acts of vandalism against corporate buildings. The media paints the entire GSJM as violent. "They tend to call us all terrorists or stigmatize the Black Bloc when a lot of the so-called Black Bloc are government agents. ...Unfortunately, the focus of much mainstream media coverage of social movements is what goes wrong, not what goes right," as Bill Moyer recently noted (Kanaracts, 2001: 25).

American protestors share their struggle with a worldwide network of activists who together are no match for the power of the "Big 3" Bretton Woods organizations or multi-nationals. But at the core of the GSJM's conflict with corporate power is the generally accepted democratic idea that governing bodies must be held accountable for their actions. Thanks to increasing globalization is it any wonder the GSJM struggles against such overwhelming wealth and power?

Negotiations Through NGOs

Besides protests and demonstrations, a second tactic used by the GSJM is to negotiate with the "Big 3" directly or through existing or newly formed Non-Governmental Organizations (NGOs). Robert O'Brien et al. researched the Big 3 (what they called Multilateral Economic Institutions – (MEIs) and their relations to the Global Social Movements – GSM (2000). They pointed out: "Since the MEIs and the GSM surveyed in this study are often engaged in a hostile relationship, the question becomes why do MEIs, which occupy positions of power in comparison to the social movement, bother to interact with the GSM?" (O'Brien et al., 2000: 35) MEIs find the GSJM useful in two areas – policy implementation and influencing key government actors, who finance and control the fate of the MEIs. In policy implementation, the GSJM might assist or resist MEI policies or rules. The GSJM often has specialized local knowledge and influence that is unavailable to staff of the MEIs. MEIs are often unfamiliar with vulnerable sectors of society, such as the poor or women. Parallel to this is the MEIs desire to use the GSJM as tools to implement their favorite policies to restructure the economy. In the case of the World Bank, NGOs can assist in the delivery of development services. In respect to the IMF, it is hoped that organized labor will exert pressures on states to limit corruption and maintain good oversight of MEIs economic restructuring programs.

The other side to these negotiations is that the GSJM may be able to resist "Big 3" programs locally. For example, social mobilization in India may result in canceling a World Bank dam-building prospect. Another example would be a social movement lobbying against trade liberalization measures, or for environmental concerns. In 1989, riots against plans of the IMF in Venezuela left over 300 dead and made it extremely difficult to implement structural adjustment policies (O'Brien et al., 2000: 19).

Not all negotiations with NGOs or the GSJM center around conflict. Particular NGOs cooperate with MEIs to benefit directly. For example, the World Bank may contract selected NGOs to assist in policy implementation. This allows some NGOs to push their agenda and obtain privileges over other NGOs. In some cases, NGOs may feel international organizations will give them a better hearing than their own nation states. The attempt by some NGOs and the GSJM to influence MEIs may be a recognition that government is now a multi-layered matter requiring participation at the local, national, international and global levels.

No one knows exactly how many NGOs exist. But Jessica Matthews, a Senior Fellow at the Council on Foreign Relations, is certain it is "...in the millions, from the tiniest village association to influential modestly-funded international groups like Amnesty International to larger global activist organizations like Green Peace and giant service providers like CARE, which has an annual budget of nearly $400 million" (1997: 53).

The roles and influence in the U.N. for NGOs have grown in the 1990's. Their expertise approximates and sometimes exceeds those of small government and international organizations, such as the U.N. Center for Human Rights. Today NGOs deliver more official development assistance than the entire U.N. system (except the World Bank and International Money Fund). In many countries, NGOs are delivering the services, in urban and rural community development, education and health care, that faltering governments can no longer manage. Increasingly, NGOs are able to push around even the largest governments. When the U.S., Canada, and Mexico set out to reach a trade agreement in secret behind closed doors, NGOs stepped in. They demanded to see provisions in the NAFTA on health and safety, pollution, consumer protection, immigration, child labor, and debt relief. NGO coalitions, via computer networks, were formed in each country and across borders. The opposition they generated in early 1991 endangered Congressional approval of the "fast track" negotiating authority for the U.S. government. After months of resistance by both Presidents Clinton and Bush, the agreement was open to environmental and labor concerns. The tightly closed world of trade negotiations has been changed forever (Matthews, 1997: 54).

Technology plays a key role in the new clout of NGOs. The non-profit Association for Progressive Communications provides 50,000 NGOs in 133 countries access to tens of millions of Internet users for the price of a local phone call. At the same time, cross-border NGO computer networks offer citizens groups new channels of influence. Women's and human rights groups in many developing countries have linked up electronically with more experienced, better funded, global media and lobby their own governments to pressure leaders in developing countries, creating a circle of influence that is accelerating change worldwide.

According to Matthews, NGOs have worked their way into the heart of international negotiations and into the day-to-day operations of international organizations. They bring new priorities, demands for democratic procedures and justice that give voice to groups outside of government, such as the GSJM and NGOs (1997: 56).

In broader political terms, not only influence and negotiations take place with the "Big 3" by NGOs and parts of the GSJM, but a third tactic is used to successfully lobby their own governments. The key example would be the success of the U.S. environmental movement and Germany's Green Party in lobbying their legislative branches to put conditions upon funding from the International Monetary Fund (IMF). Environmentalists threatened to derail the "Uruguay Round" of trade agreements in the early 1990's. The present WTO leaders hope that opening relations with NGOs and the GSJM will secure future public support for rounds of liberal trade agreements (O'Brien et al., 2000: 19-20). O'Brien et al. notes the Women's Eyes on the Bank Campaign, by U.S. and Latin American women's groups, succeeded in lobbying the World Bank directly and to "leap frog" over the opposition or indifference of their own nation states (2000: 61-2).

Policy Changes & Actions Needed to Control Multi-Nationals

Since protests and demonstrations have, for the most part, been ineffective to bring about significant democratic change in the world globalization system, what actions or policy changes can be taken to curb the power of multinational corporations? Some scholars say nothing can be done – globalization is not only the wave of the present but also the future. More globalization is inevitable (James, 2001: 1). It is an idea whose time has come (Weidenbaum, 2003: 360). Just recently Ireland voted to join and include 10 more nations into the European Common Market, bringing together Western and Eastern nations, an historic event. They will soon be integrated into, or locked into, a common European global market system ("Europe, Bigger and Better", 2002: A14). James, on the other hand, used the examples of the Renaissance being destroyed by the Reformation and the collapse of early 20th Century international commerce by the Great Depression of the 1930's that globalization is *not* inevitable or all-powerful (2001).

Clarke, after documenting the overwhelming growth in size and power of multinationals, concludes his article by asserting, "...the time has come for citizen movements to focus their energies on this new corporate colonialism" (2002: 455). This, however, is easier said than done as we have already seen in the case of the GSJM. Stanley Hoffman, Harvard University, in his article "Why Don't They Like Us?" makes five concrete suggestions so that the world may begin to like us for doing the right thing rather than the profitable economic thing (2002: 193). Some of these ideas for action apply to our role in the global market system. In addition, Manfred Steger notes:

The 2000 Summit of the World Social Forum in Brazil showed that there already exists a plethora of specific policy changes to transform the current shape of globalization with regard to global governance, social and economic equality, and human rights. Concrete policy proposals include, but are not limited to, the following items:

1. Blanket forgiveness of all Third World debt.
2. Levying of a tax on international financial transactions.
3. Abolition of offshore financial centers that offer tax havens for wealthy individuals and corporations.
4. Implementation of stringent global environmental agreements.
5. Implementation of a more equitable global-development agenda.
6. Establishment of a new world-development institution financed largely by the global North, through such measures as a financial transaction tax, but administered largely by the global South. Establishment of international labor-protection standards, perhaps as clauses of a profoundly reformed WTO.
7. Greater transparency and accountability provided to citizens by national governments and international

institutions.
8. Making all governance of globalization explicitly
gender-sensitive. (2002: 146)

These are all positive steps away from the steps the U.S. has taken in the past and present. Just how these proposed changes will actually come about is hard to envision. But, meaningful social change rarely occurs without conflicts over power.

The Ultimate Conflict – War and Terrorism

The most obvious and oldest form of conflict is war. War is often violence
on an international level. The "Cold War" between Communist Soviet Union and Capitalistic United States lasted from 1945 until 1989. It included a "Hot War" in Korea in the early 1950's, a near-nuclear war in Cuba in 1962, and a war between Communist North Vietnam and democratic South Vietnam from 1961-1973. Though the U.S. and Russia became friends, the threat of war in the world never ended. Ronald Glossop notes that:

> As the weapons of war have become more devastating and
> as the proportion of people affected has increased, it has
> become clear that war is more than just one of many social
> problems. The war problem has become the most urgent
> problem facing the human race. Either the war problem
> gets solved or humanity becomes extinct (1983: vii).

This is why the Carnegie Commission on Preventing Conflict invited five world leaders to write about the kind of leadership needed to prevent future wars. Qualities of leadership needed to prevent war involve: vision, eloquence, cooperative spirit, courage and political intuition (Ghali, 1998: 1-6). In addition, "conflict prevention is not just a one-time act, but a broad orientation, a pervasive way of thinking and relating to other leaders" (1998: vii). Since these qualities are missing among most world leaders, a war structure and system are in place in the world today.

As Michael Renner put it:

> The war system is alive and well. The war making
> institutions remain in place, the permanent war economy
> continues to command large-scale resources and, perhaps

most importantly, the view that military rivalry among
states is both rational and inevitable....still enjoys wide
allegiance (1993:140).

Every generation trains for war

Yet the truth is, as former President Jimmy Carter said in receiving his
Nobel Peace Prize in 2002: "War only breeds more war...War may
sometimes be a necessary evil, but no matter how necessary, it is
always an evil, never a good. We will not learn to live together in
peace by killing each others children" (Mellgren, 2002: A-11).
Perhaps war will always be hanging over our heads during your
lifetime. War always has been a major concern for most people in the
U.S. Gallop polls, taken since 1935 about "America's most important
problem", have included war more often than any other social problem
(Lauer, 1998: 530).

In this section we shall look at major global conflicts in the world by examining: 1). The extent of the problem of war historically; 2). The loss of human life, especially children and civilians; 3). Terrorism, a new kind of war, and the Homeland Security Department to fight terrorism worldwide; and, 4). The present and future wars between Western and Non-Western civilizations, especially the Moslem Middle East, according to Sam Huntington (1993; 1996; 2001).

Extent of War Problem

The question here is: "Is war becoming more frequent with more deaths than in the past historically?" Pitirim Sorokin estimated that about 35 million soldiers were killed in some 862 wars in Europe between 1100 AD and 1925 (1937). Quincy Wright, a scholar at the University of Chicago, recorded "...311 hostilities of sufficient magnitude to be called war in the material sense from 1480 to 1970" (1970: 52). In another study of wars that took place between 1816 and 1965 (about 150 years), Small and Singer (1970) counted 93 international wars, with 29 million deaths of military personnel. Among their findings were:

1. An international war was fought in 126 out of the 150 years from 1816 to 1965.
2. On an average, an interstate war broke out every three years.
3. The beginning of World War I and World War II (1914 and 1939) were the bloodiest for military deaths, with more than 8 million in 1914 and more than 15 million in 1939.
4. When population growth and the number of nations are considered, there is no increase in the number of wars during the 150-year period.
5. The most frightening fact from this study is: There seems to be no level of losses that causes a nation to concede defeat. Nor does the victorious side necessarily have a smaller ratio of battle deaths. In about one-third of the wars, the victors lost as many or more than the losers (Lauer, 1998: 531).

The good news was that the U.S. was not the most war-prone nation in the Singer and Small study. France and England each had nineteen wars during this period. In our first 200 years (1776-1976) we were directly involved in nine official wars (in the sense that we sent troops and publicly acknowledged our involvement). Other types of violent conflict, however, persisted within our own country during this period. For example, constant battles with Indian tribes occurred without formal declarations of war as white settlers and the U.S. Army moved west (McVeigh, 2002).   Also, violence and bloodshed erupted in the South after the Civil War by whites and the Ku Klux Klan against freed blacks to "keep them in their place".

When the U.S. is not directly involved in war we tend to think that the era is one of peace. Yet we should never forget the large number of wars that plague the world at any given time. For example, between 1946 and 1999, 151 armed conflicts in the world were reported (Cinent, 1999).   In the early 1990's, 35 nations – most of them in Asia or Africa – were involved in major armed conflicts (Renner, 1993). It is always possible, of course, that the U.S. could be drawn into these wars. That is exactly what happened during the first U.S. – Iraqi conflict in 1991; the Bosnian-Serbian war from 1992-1995, Mogodisu in Somalia, Africa, in 2000, and the second U.S. – Iraqi war in 2003 - - in spite of opposition from the U.N. and millions of people all over the world. Although these wars were brief, the damage done was massive due to modern weapons of war. In fact, there were a number of events that occurred in the 1990's and early 21st Century that could easily produce future wars. For example, Middle-Eastern and Asian Nations are involved in a modern arms race to acquire ballistic missiles and nuclear weapons, like Pakistan, India and North Korea. India and Pakistan fought over Kasmir, located between the two nations. North Korea started producing nuclear weapons in 2003, after stopping in 1994 (Sanger and Schmitt, 2003). The United States is the world's leading arms supplier to other nations, $842 billion worth in 1997 (Statistical Abstract of U.S., 2001). We live in a world today that is never free of the threat of war.

Loss of Human Life in War: From Military to Civilian Lives
More people have died from war in the 20th Century than in any other century in history. With improved technology for killing, 20th Century wars led to greater casualties. Some 10.5 million people died in World War I and another 52 million in World War II (Kornblum and Julian, 1998). When the atomic bomb was dropped on the Japanese cities of Hiroshima and Nagasaki to end WW II in 1945, 250,000 people were killed (Mooney et al; 2000). What is often forgotten or unspoken is that dropping the atomic bomb saved millions of American and Japanese lives had the war continued. Since 1945 (the

end of WW II), 135 wars have killed over 22 million people. The figures for American military deaths and wounded (non-fatal) in various wars since the 1860's are listed in Table 11-2.

Table 11-2
War Deaths and Wounded of U.S. Armed Forces
(In Thousands)

	Battle Deaths	Wounded (Non-Fatal)
Civil War (1861-1865)	215	282
Spanish American (1898)	<500 only	2
World War I (1917-1918)	53	204
World War II (1941-1945)	292	671
Korean War (1950-1954)	34	103
Vietnam War (1961-1973)	47	153
Gulf Iraq War (1991)	<100 only e	<300 only e
Iraq War (2003)	<150e	<300e

e = estimated

Source: Adopted from Statistical Abstract of the United States, 2001 (121st ed.) U.S. Bureau of the Census. Washington, D.C.: Government Printing Office. 2001. Table 506, 332.

As you can see from the table, from the Civil War to the present at least 700,000 American military persons have died in battle, and about 1.5 million have been wounded. But that is only the tip of the iceberg of the deaths and wounded in war. Civilians made up a higher percentage of war casualties and war-induced disease and starvation every year. For example, in 1950, civilians were half of all war-related deaths; by the 1980's, 75% of all war deaths and 90% in 1990 (Renner, 1993: 9).

Another way to show the shift toward civilian deaths is to look at the reversed ratios of military to civilian deaths in the 20th Century. In the early part of the 20th Century (particularly WW I), about 9 times as many soldiers compared with civilians died in war, while in recent wars in the 1980's and 1990's, 9 times more civilians than soldiers have died in deadly conflicts (Mollica et al., 1994).

Most civilians who died from war are children (Crossette, 1995). A UNICEF report found that some 2 million children have been killed in wars over the past 10 years. Some 4 to 5 million are disabled

388   Brief History of Social Problems

and another 12 million are homeless. After the first Iraq-U.S. war, about 80% of those who died from war-related injuries, disease or starvation were children (Burleigh, 1991). To make matters worse, Olara Otumma, a U.N. spokesman, reports nearly 300,000 children in 40 countries are fighting as soldiers in wars   (Lehrer, News Hour, 2002).

Destruction and death from war come in many ways. Obviously bombs and bullets kill many. But bombs or guided missiles, even "smart" bombs, sometimes hit hospitals and power plants. Without electricity hospitals cannot operate basic equipment like incubators, refrigerators or operating rooms.

Many other civilian deaths or permanent injuries come from land mines. Over a million people have been killed by land mines since 1975, 80% of them civilians (Renner, 1994: 20) Mines are buried in great numbers and they kill people long after the war is over. Up to 110 million land mines are estimated to still be buried in some 64 countries. They kill or maim more than 20,000 civilians each year (Wren, 1995). In countries with the highest concentration there is a mine in the earth for every three to five people.

All the wars in the last century have not just taken a great toll of human lives (mostly civilians), but have made millions of people in the world homeless refugees.

Terrorism – A New Kind of War
Prior to September 11, 2001, few Americans were concerned about terrorism.   That always happened in other countries – not the United States. Yet social scientists had always been concerned about terrorism. They defined it, analyzed different types and came up with various ways of dealing with it or preventing it. The U.S. government finally established a Department of Homeland Security in 2002 to fight terrorism.

Such conflicts, viewed by many as a new kind of war now, is defined as "…the premeditated use, or threatened use, of violence by an individual or group to gain a political or social objective" (Interpol, 1998 in Mooney et al., 2000: 442). It is a type of violence or force that inflicts damage or harm on people and property. Three elements are usually involved: "The creation of terror, the random use of violence and the targeting of the innocent or of non-combatants" (Frey and Morris, 1991).   Terrorists, such as al Qaeda members, who crashed two airliners into the World Trade Center and another into the Pentagon "…constitute a radical break with reality. They operate outside the basic rules of civilization, while holding contempt for the legal and moral norms of all societies. These outlaws glorify violent deeds for the sake of their own sanctified cause" (Tavin and Alexander, 1986: vii).

The advance of science and technology are slowly turning everyone throughout the world into a potential victim of terrorism. There is no immunity for the noncombatants of the world or nations or peoples who have no direct connection to particular conflicts or to specific grievances that motivate acts of violence. The difference between a state of war and a state of peace is becoming more and more blurred. Hence, George Orwell's famous slogan in his novel, *1984*, that, "peace is war" is today part of our global reality (Tavin and Alexander, 1986: xi). As President George Bush said the day after 9/11, "It is the beginning of a global war against terrorism" (Page, 2001: 9A). Terrorism is now a tactic and strategy in the struggle for power within and among nations. It is an established international mode of conflict.

What has changed for the U.S. with the advent of terrorism? The two great oceans that protected the U.S. for centuries from international attack no longer can protect us today. It is true that less powerful countries cannot afford vast armies, or the latest expensive rockets or technological weapons to wage war against us. Yet, a handful of dedicated terrorists know they can harm us through modern, sophisticated techniques. These include: bio-chemical weapons such as small amounts of anthrax or ricin in our water supply; computer hacking to disrupt or destroy our computer information; or knocking out our centralized electrical system, on which we are all dependent. And, of course, they can use the ultimate weapon – suicide bombers who are willing to blow themselves up (used so effectively against people in Israel) in the middle of crowded American cities.

The basic question Americans asked, and attempted to answer, after the Twin Towers and Pentagon were destroyed on September 11th, 2001, was why? The reasons for terrorism against the U.S. are many:

1. The arbitrary use of the U.S.'s power – militarily and economically throughout the world such as in Iraq.
2. Lack of respect for the cultures and religions of other nations.
3. Historically, an implied white racial superiority over non-white races.
4. Exploitation for U.S. profit by multi national

corporations of underdeveloped countries natural resources and environments.

Types of Terrorism

Five different types of terrorism exist, according to Henslin (2000: 541-46): Political, Repressive, Criminal, Narco and Nuclear-Biological.

Political terrorism includes: revolutionary, repressive and state-sponsored. In revolutionary terrorism, enemies of the state use terrorism to try to overthrow the political system, as the Chechens tried recently in Russia. Repressive terrorism is waged by a government against its own people, as in Cambodia and Argentina in the 1980's.

A third type of political terrorism is state-sponsored. It is when a group or government finances, trains and arms terrorists. Osama bin Laden, the terrorist who master-minded the September 11th attacks on the U.S., is the prime example of such "political terrorism". He is a millionaire, exiled from Saudi Arabia, who finances and trains al Qaeda "cells" all over the world.

Such political terrorism had a brief history to it even prior to September 11, 2001. You might say we didn't sense or see what was coming though some social scientists did write about it and warn the U.S. about it (Finsterbusch, 2001).

Recent History of Terrorism

The United States had many brushes with political terrorism even prior to September 11th, 2001. The first major terrorist act on U.S. soil occurred at the World Trade Center on February 26, 1993, when a truck bomb exploded, killing six Americans and injuring more than 1,000 people. It was in retaliation for attacking Iraq, a Moslem nation, in the first U.S.-Iraq War. Many Moslems felt American troops in the Middle East would upset the political balance of power there and had gone too far in staying in Arabia and other Moslem countries, such as Kuwait, after the war was over in 1991. Bin Laden provided support to the six terrorists arrested for the bombing and they were convicted for life. On October 3, 1993, Army Rangers raided a suspected meeting place of a Somalian warlord in Africa. In a 15-hour battle between U.S. forces and bin Laden followers, 18 Americans were killed and 80 wounded. The U.S. immediately pulled out of Somalia, an essentially Moslem nation.

The greatest domestic terrorist act, also an example of political terrorism, occurred on April 19, 1995, when two American citizens bombed the 19-story Federal Office Building in Oklahoma City, Oklahoma, killing 168 people (including 19 children in a day care center) and wounding over 1,500. Later that year, on November 13, 1995, a bomb exploded in a van at the U.S. military headquarters in Riyadh, Saudi Arabia, killing seven people, mostly Americans. The Saudis arrested four Muslim militants who confessed. They were beheaded in 1996.

On June 25, 1996, another truck bomb at a U.S. military barracks in Saudi Arabia killed 19 Americans. Later a federal grand jury found 13 Saudis and a Lebanese guilty of taking part in the attack. Unfortunately, none were in U.S. custody and they were never transferred to U.S. custody. The U.S. suspects that a middle-Eastern government was involved.

A simultaneous, coordinated attack on U.S. embassies in Nairobi, Kenya, and Dar es Salaam, Tanzania, took place on August 7, 1998. Two truck bombs killed 224 people, including 12 Americans. More than 5000 were injured. In retaliation, the U.S. launched a brief missile attack on a bin Laden training camp in Afghanistan. Though bin Laden was found guilty for the attacks, he remains at large.

On October 12, 2000, a small boat filled with explosives blew up alongside a U.S. destroyer, USS Cole, in Aden, Yemen, another Moslem country (just south of Saudi Arabia). It almost sunk the ship and killed 17 sailors on board. Yemen officials refused to cooperate with the U.S., though eight terrorist suspects were arrested. In 2002, three American Christian missionaries were killed in Yemen by Moslem terrorists, again showing how resentful Moslems are to the U.S. presence in sacred Moslem territory. According to one news report: "Anti-American sentiments are running high in the Middle-East because of U.S. support for Israel and Washington's showdown with Iraq. Many in the region's predominantly Moslem population also believe the U.S. war on terrorism is a campaign against Islam" (Kelley, 2002: 1-A).

So between 1993 and 2001, five outstanding terrorist bombings occurred that were directed at the U.S. (Page, 2001). Yet it wasn't until September 11th, 2001, that the U.S. woke up to the immediate danger of such terrorism. Nearly 5,000 people, who were at the World Trade Center and Pentagon, or on the planes used by the terrorists, were killed. On October 7, 2001, backed by an international coalition of nations, the U.S. began its successful war in Afghanistan, another Moslem country. They overthrew the Taliban government and established a democratic society.

But that wasn't the end of terrorists or terrorism in the world. In 2002, the full global power of al Qaeda became apparent. On October 12th, two bombs exploded in a nightclub in Bali, a Pacific tourist island, and just 250 yards from the U.S. consulate near there. The bombs killed about 180 people, mostly Australians, and wounded over 120 (Bumiller, 2002). President Bush connected the Bali bombing to an attack on American troops in Kuwait (near Iraq) that killed one Marine on October 8th as well as to the bombing of a French oil tanker off Yemen on October 6th.

U.S. embassies abroad are often terrorist targets (Credit: Joseph Elliott)

About a month and a half later, in the Kenyan city of Mombassa, three terrorists drove up to the doors of a hotel full of Israelis and detonated their explosives. The bombers killed themselves and at least 12 others (Bennett, 2002). At the same time, two terrorists fired shoulder-launched missiles at a crowded Israeli passenger jet as it took off from Mombassa. It just missed the plane.

In 2003, shortly after the war in Iraq officially ended, a bomb was set off in a residential neighborhood of Riyadh, Saudi Arabia, killing 37 people, including nine Americans. It was a wake-up call for the Saudi government to realize terrorism was an international problem, not just one for America.

From all these terrorist attacks, the U.S. realized the necessity to come up with various ways to prevent such attacks and deal with them more effectively. In the process, however, the U.S. Government failed to see its role in antagonizing Moslem countries in the Middle East by having our troops there. The U.S. also ignored its European allies advice to give Iraq more time to disarm.   By launching an arbitrary war against the Moslem nation of Iraq (and against world public opinion) America can expect future acts of terrorism against it both at home and abroad.

Preventing and Dealing with Terrorism
        Scholars have begun to look at ways to effectively prevent and deal with terrorism. Governments worldwide, especially the U.S., have adopted new social policies to cope with terrorists.
        One scholar said, "You cannot permit terrorism to become a profitable tactic unless you want more of it" (Bremer, 1998). To give in to terrorism is to encourage terrorists. According to Henslin (2000: 546-48), legal and government experts suggest the following as effective social policies against terrorists and terrorism:

1. Promise anything during negotiations. Promises made under threat are not valid.
2. Make no distinction between terrorists and their state sponsors. States that sponsor terrorists are not neutral and should not be treated as neutrals. This principle allows both retaliatory and preemptive acts.
3. Use economic and political sanctions to break the connection between terrorists and the states that provide them weapons, financing, safe houses, training areas, and identity documents in return for terrorism done on their behalf.
4. Treat terrorists as criminals. Track them, arrest them, and punish them. Make certain customs agents watch for known terrorists.
5. Discourage media coverage because publicity is a prime terrorist goal. It should be illegal for the media to pay terrorists for interviews.
6. Establish an international extradition or prosecution agreement: If terrorists are caught anywhere, they should be extradited or tried.
7. Develop an international organization solely to combat terrorism. Such a group would coordinate worldwide intelligence and advise nations. It would also direct international teams to respond to specific events – such as freeing hostages or locating evidence that pinpoints the sponsoring group.

8. Offer large rewards for information leading to the disabling of known terrorists. Just as in the old West, rewards can be paid on a "dead-or-alive" basis. With rewards of $50,000, or $1 million, or $5 million, terrorists will never know if associates can be trusted. Informants should also be offered new identities.

Though the U.S. has done much of this, it still ignores the basic value conflicts, ideas and ideals between Western and Eastern cultures. Huntington's analysis deals with these vital issues later in this chapter. Until these conflicts are taken into account, no program, or policies will successfully deal with terrorism from abroad.

Homeland Security Department Against Terrorism

Shortly after the September 11th, 2001 attack, President Bush appointed Tom Ridge (former governor of Pennsylvania) Director of the White House Office of Homeland Security. On June 6, 2002, President Bush proposed combining and reorganizing 22 federal agencies, with just under 170,000 employees and a total budget of $ 37 ½ billion, into Homeland Security. It became the second largest Cabinet Department, after the U.S. Defense Department. It is the most far-reaching reorganization of Federal agencies since President Harry Truman's reorganization of defense and intelligence agencies in 1949, to successfully fight the Cold War against Russia (Bettelheim and Barshay, 2002).

President Bush made it clear why the U.S. had to do this. He stated, "As we have learned more about the plans and capabilities of the terrorist network, we have concluded that our government must be reorganized to deal more effectively with the new threats of the 21st Century" (President to U.S. Citizens, 2002: 1535). He urged members of Congress to pass such legislation before the end of November, 2002. They did.

The Homeland Security Department has four divisions, each managed by an undersecretary. They are: Border and Transportation Security; Emergency Preparedness and Response; Science and Technology; and, Information Analysis and Infrastructure Protection (Kady, 2002).

The Border and Transportation Division would unify all major federal security operations concerned with U.S. borders, territorial waters and transportation systems. The Emergency Preparedness and

Response Division would coordinate all federal assistance in the domestic disaster preparedness training of local first responders. The Federal Emergence Management Agency (FEMA) would bring all its functions under Homeland Security Department. The Science and Technology Division would oversee the nation's response to possible chemical, biological, radiological and nuclear attack. It also would create a system to identify and assess threats to the country. The last division, Information Analysis and Infrastructure Protection would integrate and analyze all intelligence gathering by the CIA, FBI, National Security Agency, Immigration and Naturalization Service, Department of Energy Administration, Customs, Transportation and other organizations. All these existing agencies and more would be absorbed by the Homeland Security Department, though the FBI, CIA and Coast Guard would not be "substantially affected". They will report directly to the Director of Homeland Security (Bettelheim and Barshay, 2002; Kady 2002).

Conflicts persist over establishing this new Cabinet-level department. Some argue it gives the President, rather than the Congress, too much power to reorganize departments of the Federal government (Bettelheim and Barshay, 2002; Dalrymple, 2002). It is producing conflicts between departments that manage their own agencies now. It is also generating conflicts between Congressional committees and sub-committees that oversee former agencies and have oversight over counter-terrorism. The President suggested that Congress should revamp its committee structure, especially the 88 Congressional committees with counter-terrorism oversight. This means some Committee Chairmen will lose jurisdiction and power over agencies absorbed by Homeland Security (Nather and Foerstel, 2002).

A very controversial conflict was the rights of the workers represented by unions vs. the rights of management to write its own personnel rules and policies. This issue kept the Homeland Security bills tied up by Congress for months. With the Republicans winning in the November, 2002, election they regained control of both the Senate and the House. Hence, in the end the new Office was given "managerial flexibility" to control personnel rules. The unions now fear the new Office will use its power to essentially ban unions. Language in the new Department law "…gives unions two months to review new personnel rules and seek mediation. The Homeland Security Department can impose any new rules at the end of the two month period even if unions still disagree" (Dalrymple, 2002: 3002). In addition, management has the power to remove any employees from their collective bargaining contracts on national security grounds, a power many Congressmen wanted to limit to employees who get new jobs directly related to intelligence or terrorism investigations.

Another major conflict about the powers of this new Federal agency centers around freedom of information on the Internet and personal computers. The agency has new wiretap powers and forces Internet service providers (ISP's) to provide the agency with information on "potential" hackers. It aims to protect government computer networks from hackers. The ISP is protected against lawsuits for invasion of privacy if they believed "in good faith" that the user was a dangerous hacker. Prior to the new anti-terrorism law, the government first had to get a warrant, subpoena or court order to obtain such private information. Now the new law would allow the government to conduct "emergency" surveillance of computers without court approval. An "emergency" is now defined as "...an immediate threat to a national security issue" or "an attack against a computer used in interstate commerce" (Cohn, 2002: 3073).

A lawyer for the Electronic Privacy Information Center (EPIC) added that the provisions of the new law "would open the door for the FBI to use its controversial "Carnivore Internet Surveillance" machine. Civil liberties advocates say that "Carnivore" can obtain just about any information about Internet users habits without their knowing it. They see this as a serious threat to our freedoms and liberty in America. "Big Brother" will be watching what we send by e-mail or our access on the Internet (Dalrymple, 2002). The hope is that the Homeland Security Department will be able to prevent or control terrorism. To truly be successful the U.S. must abandon its ethnocentric Western view of reality and come to terms with Middle-Eastern values, norms and beliefs. Critical thinking demands we see our own biases and prejudices about others, and deal with facts not just our own limited opinions of the world.

The Present and Future Conflict in the World

As the earlier section stressed, war has been around for centuries. After the "Cold War" between U.S. and Russia ended (around 1989) the question became: Who would be the foe of the U.S. in future wars? In the early 1990's the answer became evident: Iraq. In 1993, a Harvard professor, Samuel F. Huntington, hypothesized an even greater (but related) conflict and war in the future - - wars between Western and non-Western civilizations. No specific non-Western country was predicted. In Kishore Wahbubani's words, the wars or conflicts would be between "the West and the Rest", as responses of non-Western civilizations to Western power and values and vice-versa. "The dangerous clashes of the future are likely to arise from the interaction of Western arrogance, Islamic intolerance, and Sinic (Asian) assertiveness" (Huntington, 1996: 183).

Huntington argued that the fundamental source of conflict in the new world order would not be primarily ideological or economic, but cultural. Nation states would remain the most powerful actors in world affairs, but the principal conflicts of global politics will occur between nations and groups of different civilizations - - East and West. What he calls the "fault lines", or ancient boundaries, between East and West in Europe and Asia, would be the battle lines of the future. These conflicts between civilizations will be the latest phase in the evolution of conflict in the modern world. Huntington in building his case describes the nature of civilizations, gives his reasons why they will clash, explains the "kin-country syndrome" (ending up in what he calls a "Confucian-Islamic" military connection) and outlines implications for the West. Many scholars disagree with Huntington's hypothesis and prediction (Rourke, 1996).

So social problems persist throughout the world. Added to them today are the social problems of globalization, war, terrorism and fear of future clashes between civilizations, if Huntington's hypothesis is correct. In any event, conflicts over power and prestige will continue in the future.

Critical Thinking Questions

1. Have you ever participated in a demonstration, on or off campus, for some cause? If not, why not? If so, did it do any good or did things remain the same as before the demonstration?

2. On many campuses there are student groups that are opposed to American corporations who run "sweat shops" in underdeveloped countries. Have you ever joined such a campus group? If you did, was something positive achieved? If you never bothered to join such a campus group, what thoughts or fears led you to not bother joining?

3. Have you ever traveled abroad to an underdeveloped country? If so, did you get to see the extreme poverty there or were you housed and "sheltered" in a clean and prosperous "Western" enclave away from poverty slums or areas? Why do you think that often happens when U.S. citizens and students go to underdeveloped countries?

4. What are your thoughts and feelings about the United Nations? Do you think it does more harm than good? Does the U.N. jeopardize the autonomy and freedom of the U.S. Government to do what it wants to do, or does it strengthen and enhance the U.S. Government?

5. War has existed for most of recorded history? How do you explain why wars occur? Do you think the world will ever learn to settle their differences without recourse to war? Why or why not? Give your best logical reasons for or against war.

Globalization Bibliography

Anthony, Ted. "Is Heyday of Global Freedom Finished?" New York: *Associated Press.* (2001): A-3.

Boli, John and George Thomas. "World Culture in the World Polity." *American Sociological Review.* 62 (1997): 171-90.

Brundage, Brita. "A New Era of Activism." *Valley Advocate* (October 4-10, 2001): 17-24.

Chayefsky, Paddy. Network. http://www.bridgehoymusic.com//billyboy/network.htm. 1974.

Clarke, Tony. "Twilight of the Corporation" Pp. 41-5 in *Social Problems*: 02/03. *Annual Editions.* 13th ed. edited by Kurt Finsterbusch. Guilford, Conn.: McGraw-Hill/Dushkin, 2002.

Daly, Herman. "Globalization and Its Discontents." Pp. 362-67 in *Taking Sides: Clashing Views on Controversial Social Issues.* 12th ed. edited by Kurt Finsterbusch, Guilford, Conn.: McGraw-Hill/Dushkin, 2003.

DePalma, Donald A. *Business Without Borders: A Strategic Guide to Global Marketing.* New York: John Wiley & Sons, Inc., 2002.

"Europe Bigger and Better". *Wall Street Journal* (October 21, 2002): A-14.

Finsterbusch, Kurt, ed. *Social Problems 02/03: Annual Editions, 13th ed.* Guilford, Conn.: McGraw-Hill/Dushkin, 2002.

———. *Taking Sides: Clashing Views on Controversial Social Issues. 12th ed.* Guilford, Conn.: McGraw-Hill/Dushkin, 2003.

Frank, Andre Gunder. "A Theoretical Introduction to 5,000 Years of World System History." *Review* 13, no. 2 (1990): 155-248.

Friedman, Thomas L. *Lexus and the Olive Tree.* New York: Farrar, Straus & Giruox., 1999.

Gallagher, Brian, ed. "Smashing Starbuck's Windows Won't Free World's Oppressed." *U.S.A. Today* (December 2, 1999): 14A.

Giddens, Anthony. *Runaway World: How Globalization is Reshaping our Lives.* New York: Routledge, 2000.

Gilpin, Robert. *"Challenge of Global Capitalism: The World Economy in the 21st Century."* Princeton, New Jersey: Princeton University Press, 2000.

Hirst, Paul and Graham Thompson. *Globalization In Question: The International Economy and the Possibilities of Governance.* 2nd ed. Cambridge: Polity Press, 1999.

Ibarguen, Diego. "Police Bothered More by Rain than Protestors." *Associated Press*. New York. (February 2, 2002): A-10.

James, Harold. *End of Globalization: Lessons From the Great Depression*. Cambridge, MA.: Harvard University Press, 2001.

Johanson, Robert C. "Transnational Politics and Non-Governmental Organizations: Drafting a Treaty to Establish a Permanent International Criminal Court". Paper presented at International Studies Assn. Annual Meeting. Chicago, IL, 2001.

Kanaracus, Chris. "Textbook for the Movement". *The Valley Advocate* (October 12, 2002): 25 & 35.

Kauffman, Jill, ed. "Global Population and Growth Update." *Issues and Controversies on File*. 8, no.12 (June 20, 2003): 254-61.

Kennedy, Paul, Dirk Messner and Franz Nuscheler, eds. *Global Trends and Global Governance*. Sterling, Va.: Pluto Press, 2002.

Kentor, Jeffrey. "Long Term Effects of Globalization on Income, Inequality, Population Growth and Economic Development." *Social Problems* 48, no. 4 (November 2001): 435-55.

Kugler, Sara. "Foreigners Account for One in Six Trade Center Victims." New York: *Associated Press* (April 6, 2002): A-23.

Mathews, Jessica T. "Power Shift." *Foreign Affairs*. 76, no. 1 (January-February 1991) 50-66.

Messner, Dirk. "World Society: Structures and Trends." Pp. 22-64 in *Global Trends and Global Governance*, edited by Paul Kennedy, Dirk Messner and Franz Nuscheler. Sterling, VA: Pluto Press, 2002.

O'Brien, Robert. *Contesting Global Governance: Multi-Lateral Economic Institutions and Global Social Movements*. New York: Cambridge University Press, 2000.

Perrucci, Robert and Mare Pilisuk. *The Triple Revolution: Social Problems in Depth*. Boston: Little, Brown, 1971.

Price, Richard. "Reversing the Gun Sights: Transnational Civil Society Targets Land Mines". *International Organization*. 52 (1998) 613-44.

Reich, Robert. *Work of Nations*. New York: Vintage Books, 1992.

Robertson, Roland. *Globalization*. London: Sage, 1992.

Roth, Katherine. "Conference Will Be Costly, But City Likely to Come Out on Top". New York: *Associated Press* (January 31, 2002): A-10.

Sklair, Leslie. *Sociology of the Global System: Social Change in Global Perspective.* Baltimore, Md.: John Hopkins Press, 1991.

Smith, David A. "Editors Introduction: Globalization and Social Problems." *Social Problems.* 48, no. 4 (November, 2001): 429-34.

Smith, Jackie and Hank Johnston, eds. *Globalization and Resistance: Transnational Dimensions of Social Movements.* Lantham, MD: Rowman & Littlefield Publishers, Inc., 2002.

Steger, Manfred B. *Globalism: The New Market Ideology.* Lantham, MD: Rowman & Littlefield Publisher, Inc., 2002.

Strange, Susan. *The Retreat of the State: The Diffusion of Power in the World Economy.* Cambridge, MA: Cambridge University Press, 1996.

Tilly, Charles. "Social Movements and National Politics." Pp. 297-317 in *State, King and Social Movements: Essays in History and Theory*, edited by C. Bright and S. Harding. Ann Arbor: University of Michigan Press, 1984.

Toedtman, James. "Powell Tells World Forum, Poverty Should Be Target." *Morning Call* (February 2, 2002): A-10.

Wallerstein, Immanuel. *The Capitalistic World Economy.* New York: Cambridge University Press, 1979.

Waters, Malcolm. *Globalization:* New York: Routledge, 1995.

Wiener, Anthony J. "The Future of Economic Activity." *Annals of the American Academy of Political and Social Science.* 408 (July 1973): 47-61.

War and Terrorism Bibliography

Ajami, Fouad. "The Summoning." *Foreign Affairs.* 72, no. 4 (September./October, 1993): 2-9.

Bennett, James. "12 Die as Israelis are Attacked in Kenya: Hotel is Bombed and Missile is Fired at Jet." *The New York Times.* 52, no. 317 (November 29, 2002): A-1.

Bettelheim, Adriel and Jill Barshay. "Bush's Swift, Sweeping Plan is Work Order for Congress." *CQ Weekly*, 60, no. 23 (June 8, 2002): 1498-1504.

Borgatta, Edgar and Rhonda J.V. Montgomery. *Encyclopedia of Sociology.* 2nd ed. New York: MacMillan Reference. USA, 2000.

Bremer, L. Paul, III. *"Terrorism: Myths and Reality."* *Department of State Bulletin* (May 1988) 63.

Brown, Lester R. *State of the World*. New York: W.W. Norton, 1993.

Bumiller, Elizabeth. "Bush Ties Bombing at Bali Nightclub to Qaeda Network."
  New York Times (October 15, 2002): A1 & A-15.

Burleigh, Nina. "Watching Children Starve to Death." *Time*. (June 10, 1991) 56-8.

Cinent, James, ed. *Encyclopedia of Conflicts Since World War II*. Armonk, New York: Sharpe Reference, 1999.

Cohn, Peter. "Privacy Concerns." *CQ Weekly Report*, 60, no.45 (November 23, 2002):
  3073.

Crossette, Barbara. "Children Called Big Losers in Small Wars." New York:
  Associated Press. (December 11, 1995): 1-A.

Dalrymple, Mary. "Departments Blueprint Approved, Final Plan Far From Complete." *CQ Weekly Report* 60, no. 45 (November 23, 2002): 3072-77.

Finsterbusch, Kurt, ed. "The New Terrorism: Coming Soon to a City Near You." *The Economist* (August 15, 2001) 17-19.

———. *Social Problems 02/03: Annual Editions,* 13th ed. Guilford, CT.: McGraw-Hill/Dushkin, 2002.

———. *Taking Sides: Clashing Views on* Controversial *Social Issues*. 12th ed. Guilford, CT: McGraw-Hill/Dushkin, 2003.

Fox, William T., ed. "How Wars End". *The Annals of the American Academy of Political & Social Science*. 392 (November 1970): 1-25.

Frey, R. G. and Christopher W. Morris, eds. *Violence, Terrorism and Justice*. New York: Cambridge University Press, 1991.

Ghali, Boutros Boutros. *Essays on Leaderships: Carnegie Commission on Preventing Deadly Conflict*. New York: Carnegie Corporation of New York, 1998.

Glossop, Ronald J. *Confronting War: An Examination of Humanity's Most Pressing Problem*. Jefferson, N.C.: McFarland, 1983

Hassan, Riaz. "Sociology of Islam" in *Encyclopedia of Sociology*. 2nd ed. edited by
  Edgar Borgatta and Rhonda J.V. Montgomery. New York: MacMillan
  Reference. USA, 2000.

Henslin, James M. *Social Problems*. Upper Saddle River, New Jersey: Prentice Hall, 2000.

Hoffman, Stanley. "Why Don't They Like Us?" Pp. 190-93 in *Social Problems: Annual Editions, '02/'03*, 13th ed., edited by Kurt Finsterbusch. Guilford, CT: McGraw-Hill/Dushkin, 2002

Huntington, Samuel P. *The Clash of Civilizations and the Remaking of World Order*. New York: Simon & Schuster, 1996.

Interpol. (http//www.kenpubs.coInterpol.com/English/fag) Frequently Asked Questions About Terrorism." Pp. 442-43 in *Understanding Social Problems*, edited by Mooney et al., 2nd ed., Belmont, CA: Wadsworth, 2000.

Kady, Martin II. "Fielding the Possible Candidates for Homeland Undersecretaries." *C.Q. Weekly* 60, no. 45 (November 23, 2002) 3074-75.

Kelley, Jack. "Suspects Hunted in Yemen Slayings: Three Americans Killed at Mission Hospital." *USA Today*, (December 31, 2002): 1-A.

Kornblum, William and Joseph Julian. *Social Problems*. 9th ed. Uppersaddle River, New Jersey: Prentice Hall, 1998.

Kurth, James. "The Real Clash." Pp. 339-48 in *Taking Sides: Clashing Views on Controversial Issues in World Politics*, 7th ed. edited by John T. Rourke. Guilford, CT: Dushkin Publishing Group/Brown & Benchmark Publishers, 1996.

Lauer, Robert H. *Social Problems and the Quality of Life*. 7th ed. New York: McGraw-Hill, 1998.

Lehrer, Jim. "Children At War". *The News Hour,* Public Broadcasting System TV. (December 2, 2002).

McVeigh, Frank J. "The History of Violence in the U.S." *Sociological Viewpoints.* 18 (Fall 2002): 9-26.

Mellgren, Doug. " Nobel Laureate Carter Warns That War Begets War." New York: *Associated Press*. (December 11, 2002): A-11.

Molicca, R.F. et al. "The Effect of Trauma and Confinement on Functional Health Status of Cambodians Living in Thailand-Cambodia Border Camps". *Journal of The American Medical Association (JAMA)* 270 (August 4, 1995): 581-86.

Mooney, Linda A., Knox, David and Caroline Schacht. *Understanding Social Problems*. 2nd ed. Belmont, CA: Wadsworth, 2000.

Nather, David and Karen Foerstal. "Proposal Presages Turf Wars." *C.Q. Weekly* 60, no.23 (June 8, 2002): 1505.

Page, Susan. "Why Clinton Failed to Stop bin Laden". *USA Today*. (November 12, 2001): 1A, 9A & 10A.

President to U.S. Citizens. "Press Congress for New Department of
    Homeland Security by Year's End." *C.Q. Weekly* 60, no. 23
    (June 8, 2002): 1535.

Renner, Michael. *Budgeting for Disarmament: The Costs of War and
    Peace.* Washington, D.C.: Worldwatch Institute, 1994.

————. "Preparing For Peace." Pp. 139-57 in *State of the World,*
    edited by Lester Brown. New York: W.W. Norton, 1993.

Rourke, John T. *Taking Sides: Clashing Views on Controversial
    Issues in World Politics.* 7th ed., Guilford, CT: Dushkin
    Publishing Group/ Brown & Benchmark Publishers, 1996.

Sanger, David E. and Eric Schmitt. "Satellites Said to See Activity at
    North Korean Nuclear Site." *New York Times* (January 31,
    2003) A-1 and A-8.

Short, James F. and Marvin Wolfgang, eds. "Collective Violence."
    *The Annals of the American Academy of Political and Social
    Science.* 391 (September 1970): 1-256.

Shrybman, Steven. "The World Trade Organization: A Guide for
    Environmentalists." P. 43 in *Social Problems: Annual
    Editions, 02/03,* 13th ed., edited by Kurt Finsterbusch.
    Guilford, CT: McGraw-Hill/Dushkin, 2002.

Small, Melvin and David Singer. "Patterns in International Warfare:
    1865-1965." *Annals of the American Academy of Political
    and Social Science.* 391 (September 1970): 145-55.

Sorokin, Pitirim. *Social and Cultural Dynamics: Fluctuations of
    Social Relationships, War and Revolution.* 3 New York:
    American Book, 1937.

Statistical Abstract of U.S.: 2001. 121st ed. U.S. Census Bureau.
    "Arms Trade in Constant (1997) Dollars-Selected Countries."
    Table 496, 327. Washington, D.C.: U.S. Government
    Printing Office, 2001.

Tavin, Ely and Yonah Alexander, eds. *Terrorists or Freedom Fighters.*
    Fairfax, Va.: Hero Books, 1986.

Wren, Christopher S. "Everywhere, Weapons that Keep on Killing."
    The New York Times (October 8, 1995): A-1.

Wright, Quincy. "How Hostilities Have Ended. Peace Treaties and
    Alternatives." *The Annals of the American Academy of
    Political and Social Science.* 392 (November, 1970): 51-61.

Chapter 12

Summary and Conclusions

After looking at all the major social problems sociologically and historically, we begin to realize and recognize the important role that conflicts play in bringing about meaningful social change. We now see that the degree and extent of poverty in 1900 is not the same in 2002 because new laws and policies were fought for by various groups over the century. But we also know that weapons of mass destruction today are a far cry from what they were in 1900. Technological change best explains the difference but the worldwide spread of all kinds of weapons centers around the many conflicts and wars fought between nations up to the present day. Just how effectively the United Nations has contained and prevented wars remains to be seen, especially as the U.S., and other nations such as North Korea, insist on going their own ways independent of the United Nations.

To review some of the social problems covered we saw conflicts of ideas, values, norms and beliefs centering around power, status and position. For example, in the Crime and Delinquency Chapter (2) we saw how attitudes and values changed over time about capital punishment, treatment of minorities and the poor. In Chapter 3, we came to grips with the conflict over individual rights in pursuing one's own personal pleasure in drugs or alcohol vs. the harm and injury it does to society and others. In Chapter 4, on Changing Gender Roles we saw the long, historic struggle of women to gain equality with men and overcome their controlling power and status, both at home and at work. Yet sexism and discrimination against women still persist throughout the world. In Chapter 5, we saw the many remaining conflicts based on race such as discrimination in education and employment vs. affirmative action, segregation in housing (cities vs. suburbs) vs. integration, conflicts over voting rights, as well as police violence and racial profiling by white police. Though some progress has been made in the U.S., some 230 years of conflicts, especially legislative battles, to recognize the rights of all African-Americans and other racial minorities, continue.

In Chapter 6, we witnessed the long, historic battles between the defenders of the traditional family and the challengers, who push to expand ever-changing boundaries around the family. Seven major conflicts have long absorbed the energy and time of the family in its many different forms:

1. Conflicts over marital roles.
2. Changes in stability of marriage, and divorces.
3. Changes in family size and birth rates.
4. Conflicts involving births to single mothers.
5. Conflicts in respect to pre-marital sex, extra-marital sex and cohabitation.
6. Conflicts between couples leading to family violence.
7. Conflicts over alternate family forms, including same-sex ones.

All these conflicts boil down to changes in norms, values and beliefs about sex, love and marriage in the U.S. in the last 50 years or so. In addition to the sexual revolution, there is the pill and millions of abortions.

In our educational system (Chapter 7) we explored conflicts in a social institution we all know best, education. It has been a consistent and persistent experience in our early lives for many years. Some of you have experienced, in one form or another, the historical conflicts over:

1. Purposes and curriculum in education.
2. Unequal access, causing or reflecting inequality.
3. Funding and financing schools.
4. Bureaucracy that is often dysfunctional.

But the ground rules for every elementary and secondary school in America has changed, due to recent Federal laws that "no child would be left behind". This law standardizes tests in the schools and makes schools responsible for doing their job or turning the local school over to the state or closing it down. This is an unprecedented change in education.

In describing the historical conflicts and changes in the Medical and Health Care Institution (Chapter 8), we explored the conflicts between the practice and profession of medicine and schools of thought in the 17th, 18th, 19th and 20th Centuries and how modern medicine and technology developed over time. Next we examined the public health movement and the role of government in medicine, an issue not fully resolved even today. Then we analyzed the conflict over access to quality medical care, especially for the poor and African-Americans. Then we studied conflicts over the cost of medical care and payment systems, and malpractice insurance costs. Last, we looked at the ideological conflict over whether medical care is a privilege or right for people; whether it is like a "private commodity" that one must purchase or a "public good" (like roads and schools) that is so important that it is pre-paid for by government taxes. Some argue the best solution to the last conflict is to set up a National Health Insurance System, funded by taxes and administered by the Federal government, as in Canada and England. Of course, such a proposal has long been fought, tooth and nail, by the American Medical Association.

In looking at the economic institution in Chapter 9, it became obvious that from the start of our society in 1776 there has been a continuous conflict between the rich, who hold positions of power via corporations and other groups, and the poor and working class, through unions, fought for economic justice. Due to recurring downswings in the capitalistic economy, via "depressions" or "recessions", the poor and workers engaged in riots or organized protests in the 18th and 19th Centuries. In 1877 "The Great Upheaval" accounted for over 100 people dying, a thousand workers going to jail and some 100,000 workers on strike to try to change the economic system, but without much immediate success. That was to come later in the 20th Century, especially during the 1930's and 1940's, when large industrial unions grew in strength and power to partially offset the monopoly power and money of large corporations in America. Laws were passed that protected workers rights to form and join unions and to strike if necessary.

During the 20th Century the public's and governments concern and conflicts over poverty oscillated depending on the health of the business cycle. From 1900-1914, the Progressive Era, both the public and the states became very concerned about poverty and the need for steady employment and a "living wage", as well as state mothers and widows pensions. Once more, when war broke out in 1914-1918 in Europe, our economy expanded and poverty was reduced a little bit. After World War I in the 1920's, the poor were neglected. Then the

"Great Depression" hit in the 1930's. U.S. President Franklin Roosevelt said he saw "One-third of the nation ill-housed, ill-clad and ill-nourished". Also one-third of the workforce became unemployed and couldn't find work. Then a whole series of "New Deal" laws were passed to help those out of work and those who were poor to earn a living. It also was the beginning of Social Security and our Federal welfare system for the blind, disabled and poor families. Then our involvement in World War II (1941-1945) meant more jobs for the unemployed, as well as for women and minorities, as 11 million men enlisted or were drafted into the Armed Forces. After the war, economic prosperity continued to an extent never before experienced in the U.S. It produced a book called *The Affluent Society* by John Kenneth Galbraith. Yet it overlooked a growing population of the poor. It took another book in 1962, called *The Other America* by Michael Harrington, to rediscover the poor and make politicians and others more conscious of the poverty problem. The Federal Government in 1964 passed laws described as "The War on Poverty". Though millions of dollars were spent by the Federal Government in the late 1960's, the problem of poverty persisted. Some $30 billion, instead, was spent on the War in Vietnam. By the early 1970's, when President Nixon took office, the War on Poverty ceased to exist. By the mid 1970's, the price of gas went from $0.29 a gallon to about $1.30 a gallon and inflation (the cost of living) increased over 10% a year. So poverty was quickly forgotten as middle-class families struggled to make ends meet. New welfare laws in 1988 and again in 1996 led to stricter rules for getting any help. They limited the length of time anyone could get help from welfare. After two years, they were on their own. So today the problem of poverty affects 12 million of our children and 12% of our population, nearly 35 million people (Weisman, 2003). We still haven't solved the poverty problem because income and wealth in America are not distributed evenly, and they never have been in our history. The sad truth is that the rich continue to get richer and the poor poorer, both in the U.S. and in the world.

Problems in our economy are still plagued by recurring and persistent unemployment or underemployment, working part-time or in lower-paying jobs rather than full-time, higher-paying positions. Though some 135 million Americans work, today some 6.2% are unemployed, or nearly 9 million people (Altman, 2003). Such unemployment is a normal part of recurring "business cycles", up or down, in our capitalistic economic institution.

Another major feature and conflict in our economic system is our unsafe and unhealthy working places. Capitalists know it is cheaper to run an unsafe and unhealthy work environment than make it safe for all workers. Environmental pollution on the job is a daily reality for millions of U.S. workers. Though the Federal Government's Occupational Safety and Health Administration (OSHA) has made some strides since the 1970's in forcing business to make some work places safer and more healthy, much more remains to be done. Though the death rate in industry has been cut significantly, almost 4 million workers suffer disabling injuries each year in American industry.

In Chapter 10, "Population and the Environment", we recognized and have experienced some of the conflicts involved. These include:

1. Conflict from a growing immigrant population and urbanization vs. preservation and protection of the environment.
2. Conflict between population growth and the environment.
3. Conflict over the control of food production and its distribution in the world.
4. Conflict between industrialization and the environment.
5. Conflict over proposed solutions for population control.

In Chapter 11, we looked at the international aspects and inter-connections among social problems. We will review this aspect of social problems later in this chapter. The three main issues covered in Chapter 11 were: Globalization, War and Terrorism. We reviewed worldwide power and wealth of multi-nationals and the "Big 3" as well as the continuing conflicts and power struggles with the Global Social Justice Movement. The outcome thus far seems to suggest, in spite of many different tactics used by the GSJM, "the rich are getting richer and the poor poorer". To resolve some of these on-going conflicts, the World Social Forum has suggested specific policy changes to transform the current shape of globalization with regard to governance, equality and human rights. These changes range from blanket forgiveness of all third world debt and taxing all international financial transactions, to making all governance of globalization gender-sensitive.

The most obvious and oldest form of conflict is war, especially today on an international basis. The irony of war today is that most human life lost is civilian instead of military. For example, during World War I about nine times as many soldiers died as civilians, while in recent wars in the 1980s and 1990s, nine times more civilians than soldiers have died (Mollica., 1994). A brief history was presented about a new kind of war and conflict: terrorism. Various types of terrorism were described and a brief history was presented of the U.S.

Homeland Security Department to counter any terrorist acts. A brief look was taken at possible future conflicts in the world, especially with Eastern Moslem civilization based on the hypothesis of Harvard professor Samuel F. Huntington (1996).

Besides the numerous conflicts bringing about social change, was a description and analysis of the development of our society from a small, personal Gemeinschaft society to a large, complex impersonal Gesellschaft society. This development led to many new social problems as we grew in size and spread out three thousand miles across the country from coast to coast, from the Atlantic to the Pacific Ocean. National markets and communication gradually made it possible to deal with national social problems. As a result, our society turned more and more to the Federal Government, rather than local communities to help resolve national problems, such as poverty and unemployment.

Historically, it was during the Great Depression of the 1930s that America first realized that the private local or state sector was unable, and often unwilling, to help the poor. This social problem became so overwhelming we realized that only the resources of the Federal Government could effectively deal with the magnitude of the problem. Ever since, society more and more has turned to the Federal Government to pass new laws or appropriate new funds to fight social problems of crime, drugs, race relations, education and unemployment, just to mention a few. Some sociologists argue that over-reliance on the Federal Government to address our social problems weakens society and its local communities to deal with our social problems. It makes more and more of us dependent on the Federal Government for resources to deal effectively with our local or state social problems. Other social institutions such as religion and local communities, in a Gemeinschaft society were strong and effective in resolving conflicts and social problems. Now in a Gesellschaft society such institutions often turn to the national government for help. The new notion and idea of giving Federal aid to faith-based organizations is a reflection of this new tendency for former private-charity groups to depend more and more on the Federal Government for help.

Another development which is affecting the former strength and power of local organizations and social institutions is the Globalization of business. As pointed out in Chapter 11 on Globalization, the world is getting smaller and smaller and we live today in what scholars have called "a global village". Just think how many of you have already traveled abroad or studied abroad, compared with students in the 1940s or 1950s. The world indeed is changing internationally, and with it our social problems, such as drugs, crime, race relations and the economy, have become worldwide.

So where do all these conflicts, changes from Gemeinschaft to Gesellschaft, reliance on the Federal Government and Globalization leave us? It often leads to new conflicts, including war and terrorism, that effect all of us. We learned that lesson on 9/11/01. We no longer have the luxury of isolating ourselves from the rest of the world. Our two mighty oceans on the East and the West coasts no longer can act as a barrier or protective wall from other hostile nations, as they once did. With modern weaponry and satellite electronic controls we are just as vulnerable as though the oceans were no longer there. For in reality the world has indeed shrunk in size. So what does the future hold for coping with our social problems? That depends on us and our dominant values in the future.

As we have seen, conflicts often emerge over a difference in the priority and importance of certain values. Often the social problems we have discussed and analyzed involved conflicts over values. For example, values such as material wealth and success, or pursuit of individual personal pleasure no matter what the social consequences, rather than concern about other people, might explain the persistence of poverty or the drug problem.

Values are crucial and critical for the survival of any people or society. For instance, in 1140 A.D. the little town of Weinsberg, Germany, was conquered by foreign invaders, who were ready to slaughter all the men in the village. The women and children would be exiled. The commander of the enemy forces told the women that they could leave and carry away on their backs their most treasured and valuable possessions. The women looked at but rejected a wide variety of material goods. Then the women began to walk out of their town carrying on their backs their husbands, fathers, or brothers. The women of Weinsberg chose to be more concerned about people than their possessions (Roselle, 1976). A people-oriented value system could remedy some social problems from poverty to race relations. But such a change in our value system must also lead to action.

We conclude, along with other conflict sociologists, that one proven solution to social problems starts with people purposely acting to change the existing social structure and power positions they hold, as we have reviewed in this book. If history teaches us anything, it is that people in power rarely, if ever, voluntarily give it up. They have too much to gain by holding their position and too much to lose if they gave it up. It is only when confronted directly with various forms of "counter-vailing power" that society and its problems begin to change.

Not everyone, of course, will support social change. Those who benefit from the existing social system will have a vested interest in keeping things the way they are. As one scholar noted:

> I do not here suppose that the rich and powerful are incapable or unwilling to re-examine and change the society. But I do assume that their understandable interests in remaining rich and/or powerful prevent them from making as critical an examination of the fundamentals of their society as would be made by those whom the society is not serving so well (Harding, 1979: 218).

The paradox of power is that those at the bottom of the economy and society are often in the best position to see what is wrong, and what is right with the social system (Frankenberg, 1993). Social change therefore, must ultimately be started by people who perceive that their needs and the needs of others like them, are not being met by existing social institutions or policies of those in power. When this happens, a social movement may form. A social movement is an issue-oriented group specially organized to bring about (or, in some cases, prevent) social change through collective social action. Social movements are "issue-oriented" in the sense that their members take a stand on a specific social issue, and work and act to get their view written into official public policy (Manis, 1984). We saw this most clearly in the case of labor unions in the late 19th and early 20th Century. In the 1960s and 1970s we saw it most clearly in the Civil Rights movement for African-Americans and then for women and then for protection of the environment. Today it is most evident in the numerous protests, demonstrations and negotiations by NGOs of the Global Social Justice Movement to offset the power of multi-nationals and the "Big 3".

Sociologist Neil Smelser has pinpointed six conditions that must be present for a social-change movement to occur successfully (1963). If you are critically thinking about making a difference in your world today, it would be helpful to think about these conditions and how one can bring them about or whether they already exist:

> 1. The social structure must be conducive to change. It is virtually impossible to effect social change within a social structure that is extremely rigid and inflexible. The social conditions must be ripe for change (as in the Great Depression of the 1930s) and windows of opportunity must be open for change agents to act.

2. There must be structural strain, or else no one will see a need for change. People have to feel that there is something radically wrong in society. People seldom wish to change things when they appear to be going well for them. Since the majority of people in the U.S. have done so well financially, it is usually a small minority of people who really engage in a social movement to change things. But when pocketbooks shrink and economic opportunities dry up, people will look for someone or something to lead them to change.

3. When the above conditions are present, the time is ripe for the growth and spread of a generalized belief. People look for some explanations for their stress or distress and are ready to act on a possible solution to their plight. It is necessary to work with others to motivate and educate people about social conditions. This is the idea phase. But to really work, we must move on into the action phase.

4. A precipitating event or events is the spark that is necessary to move people from ideas to action. This triggering event may be natural (like an earthquake) or human-made (like a shooting of someone by police). It helps if this event is widely publicized. It inflames the passions of people to action and overcomes apathy or indifference to action.

5. The mobilization of participants. To make a difference in society people must work together. One person can't effect much social change. The participants in any social movement are the hands and feet to bring any ideology to life. The participants must be educated about the reasons for the change and must also be trained to act to change the situation.

6. Finally, any social movement's members must be prepared for mechanisms of social control to be used against them by the existing power structure. For every social change proposed there will be those in power who will do all they can do to oppose change. When their power or position is threatened, the opposition will be intense. Those in power are benefiting from the existing structure, so they see no need for change. Appeals to reason or emotion may persuade part of the power structure to change.

According to Curran and Renzetti (2000), two other related conditions must exist for a social movement to develop. Individuals must recognize that the problems they are experiencing are shared by others like themselves. Also individuals and groups must see the existing social structure as the source of their problems. Both factors are "critical catalysts" for social and political actions because the dominant ideology of our society leads us to believe that "...social problems are the results of personal failures or that they could be solved if some people would just work a little harder" (Curran and Renzetti, 2000: 412).

As Klein pointed out:

> Having a hard life or being a member of an exploited group does not in itself lead to political unrest...Only when [people] see that their problems are shared by other people like them, the group, can they attribute the source of their concerns to social conditions, such as discrimination, and look to political solutions (1984: 2).

When a social movement develops, it typically endures for a significant period of time, like the labor movement, and may have long-lasting and far-reaching effects on society.

In addition to concluding that social changes come essentially from social conflicts, we can also conclude that the social problems we have examined are often not as discrete or separate as chapter headings might lead us to believe. For example, certain insights on school busing for purposes of racial desegregation could have been also analyzed in discussing the problems of education. Or we might have discussed job discrimination against women in the chapter on poverty. Social problems outside textbooks are often interwoven with numerous other issues. For example, like a color-coded wire that runs through the entire complex of an electrical panel, we could trace our *black* color-coded social wire through areas of crime, drugs and alcohol, the family, work and unemployment, education, population, environment, urban and suburban problems, health care, poverty, racism, the economy and its spending, globalization and other national and international problems. So the second conclusion we must draw about social problems overall is that they are all interrelated and interconnected *because* society itself is structured and organized in ways that produce social institutions, groups, and people that are socially interrelated, interconnected and often engage in conflict.

As long as different and competing groups exist in our society, we will always have different and conflicting definitions of all social problems, as we have shown in every chapter. It is equally important to remember that different definitions of the problem inexorably lead to conflicting solutions. As a matter of fact, in attempting to solve one social problem, we might unexpectedly add to or create another. For example, to alleviate hunger at home and abroad, we encouraged our farmers to increase their use of modern technology, such as gas-driven farm vehicles and chemical fertilizers. Although we have made excellent progress in supplying needy nations with food, we have developed an agricultural industry highly dependent on imported oil and large amounts of electricity. Also, our use of fertilizers may have helped us to grow more food per acre, but they are eventually washed into our streams and rivers, thereby adding to the chemical pollution of our water. So, often proposed solutions to existing social problems cause new social problems.

Another conclusion that might not be so self-evident, is that we have created a social structure whose nature and magnitude we do not fully appreciate. The realities of our society and its institutions – especially their size and magnitude - are not quite comprehensible to our limited minds and life experiences. Just a few examples will suffice.

> In 1976 the United States put two unmanned space vehicles on the surface of our "neighboring" planet Mars, about 230 million miles from earth.

> Our national debt is presently over 6.1 trillion dollars. (Statistical Abstracts, 2001)

> One hydrogen bomb has the explosive force of 58 megatons, equal to 20 million tons of TNT.

All of these facts or occurrences have been produced by our technology and social structure; they are hard to experience concretely or even imagine. Social philosopher Gunther Anders has summarized this situation:

> The basic dilemma of our age is that 'We are smaller than ourselves,' incapable of mentally realizing the realities which we ourselves have produced. Therefore we might call ourselves 'inverted Utopians': while ordinary Utopians are unable to actually produce what they are able to visualize, we are unable to visualize what we are actually producing...This inverted Utopianism is not simply one fact among many, but the outstanding one, for it defines the moral situation of man today. The dualism to which we are sentenced is...our capacity to produce as opposed to our power to imagine (1971: 174).

This is not only the *moral* situation of humans today, but also the *social* situation in which we live today. Our ability to conceive of and imagine the scope and scale of our social problems lags behind the reality of our problems.

Such a situation of not being able to fully grasp reality is accompanied by a separation of problem-definers from the problem itself. For example, some urban planner sitting in his comfortable office on the 25th floor of an air-conditioned high rise in the city (and living in a grass-covered suburban community where homes must be built on at least five acres of land) may make grandiose plans to change the face of the city by tearing down the old apartment buildings in neighborhoods the planner defines as blighted. But the black mother with four children living on welfare in a third-floor flat of the urban ghetto may have a different notion of how the city should be changed. While the planner might think in terms of getting rid of those ghetto third-floor flats, she might be thinking of that apartment as an economical, comfortable, and convenient home.

The point here is that neither the urban planner nor the black welfare mother has really any *firsthand* exposure to, or experience of, what the other's life is like. They live literally in separate worlds, and make decisions and form opinions without ever *once* seeing, smelling, feeling, or being in *physical contact* with the social reality of the other. Distance (physical and social) separates us all in our mass society. Our statistical knowledge and theories of how to spot and solve social problems become reified (abstract) instead of becoming acquainted with *the realities* of the social problem.

This example leads us to one further conclusion. Often the "solutions" offered for our problems involve new laws or better enforcement or funding of existing laws. This is not to deny that laws are helpful to a point in addressing social ills. The conclusion here, however, is that laws in and of themselves cannot solve social problems. For example, passage of the open-housing laws in the 1960s has not produced a racially integrated society. Outlawing certain acts as illegal has not remedied the problems of crime or delinquency. If we are to solve a problem, the people themselves, whenever and wherever possible, must prevent or work to alleviate them before they become too big to handle.

Over reliance on the federal government to solve all our social ills is not only unwise, but also unnecessary in some cases. Society, not the state, must dominate the efforts to control and cure our social ills.

Our hope is that sociologists will continue not only to analyze or envision a better future for all societies, but also to play an important role in creating such societies by pointing out the dangers and possibilities that lie ahead. As C. Wright Mills stated:

> 'Man's chief danger' today lies in the unruly forces of contemporary society itself, with its alienating methods of production, its enveloping techniques of political domination, its international anarchy – in a word, its pervasive transformation of the very 'nature' of man and the conditions and aims of his life (1959: 13).

It is sociology's great promise and legacy to continually point out our chief dangers and to seek to understand and overcome them.

Bibliography

Altman, Daniel. "Job Losses in July Add to Mixed Signs on the Economy". *New York Times.* (August 2, 2003): A-1 & C-14.

Anders, Gunther. *"Theses for the Atomic Age."* Pp. 172-81 in Bernard Rosenberg, Israel Gerver, and F. William Howton, eds. *Mass Society in Crisis: Social Problems and Social Pathology.* New York: Macmillan, 1971.

Curran, Daniel J. and Claire M. Renzetti. *Social Problems: Society in Crisis.* 5th ed. Boston, MA: Allyn and Bacon, 2000.

Frankenberg, R. *White Women, Race Matters: The Social Construction of Whiteness.* Minneapolis, MN: University of Minnesota Press, 1993.

Galbraith, John Kenneth. *The Affluent Society.* Boston, MA: Houghton Mifflin, 1958.

Harding, S. G. "Is the Equality of Opportunity Principle Democratic?" *Philosophical Forum.* 10: 206-33. 1979.

Harrington, Michael. *The Other America.* New York: Macmillan, 1962.

Huntington, Samuel P. *The Clash of Civilizations and the Remaking of World Order.* New York: Simon & Schuster, 1996.

Klein, E. *Gender Politics.* Cambridge, MA: Harvard University Press, 1984.

Manis, Jerome. *Analyzing Social Problems.* New York: Praeger, 1984.

Mills, C. Wright. *The Sociological Imagination.* New York: Oxford University Press, 1959.

Mollica, R. L. *"The Effect of Trauma and Confinement on Functional Health Status of Cambodians Living in Thailand – Cambodian Border Camps".* Journal of the American Medical Association (JAMA) 270 (August 4, 1995): 581-86.

President Franklin D. Roosevelt, Second Inaugural Address, January 20, 1937

Roselle, Daniel, ed. *"Wisdom of the Women of Weinsburg: Editorial Reflections".* Social Education. 40, 1 (January 1976): 5.

Smelser, Neil. *Theory of Collective Behavior.* New York: Free Press of Glencoe, 1963.

Statistical Abstracts of the United States: 2002. 122 edition. *Public Debt of the United States.* Table 449: 305. 2001

Weisman, Jonathan. "1.7 Million Join Poor, Lifting Rate to 12.1%." *Morning Call* (September 27, 2003): A-1, C-14.

Name Index

Subject Index